The Cambridge Companion to Sha

This Companion is designed for readers interested ~~ ~~~~ ~~~ ~~~~~~ ~~~~ tions of Shakespeare's plays, both in and beyond Britain. The first six chapters describe aspects of the British performing tradition in chronological sequence, from the early stagings of Shakespeare's own time through to the present day. Each relates Shakespearean developments to broader cultural concerns and adopts an individual approach and focus, be it on textual adaptation, acting, stages, scenery or theatre management. These chapters are followed by three explorations of acting: tragic and comic actors and women performers of Shakespearean roles. A section on international performance includes chapters on interculturalism, on touring companies and on political theatre, with separate accounts of the performing traditions of North America, Asia and Africa. Over forty pictures illustrate performers and productions of Shakespeare from around the world. An amalgamated list of items for further reading completes the book.

CAMBRIDGE COMPANIONS TO LITERATURE

The Cambridge Companion to Greek Tragedy
edited by P. E. Easterling

The Cambridge Companion to Old English Literature
edited by Malcolm Godden and Michael Lapidge

The Cambridge Companion to Medieval Romance
edited by Roberta L. Kreuger

The Cambridge Companion to Medieval English Theatre
edited by Richard Beadle

The Cambridge Companion to English Renaissance Drama
edited by A. R. Braunmuller and Michael Hattaway

The Cambridge Companion to Renaissance Humanism
edited by Jill Kraye

The Cambridge Companion to English Poetry, Donne to Marvell
edited by Thomas N. Corns

The Cambridge Companion to English Literature, 1500–1600
edited by Arthur F. Kinney

The Cambridge Companion to English Literature, 1650–1740
edited by Steven N. Zwicker

The Cambridge Companion to Writing of the English Revolution
edited by N. H. Keeble

The Cambridge Companion to English Restoration Theatre
edited by Deborah C. Payne Fisk

The Cambridge Companion to British Romanticism
edited by Stuart Curran

The Cambridge Companion to Eighteenth-Century Poetry
edited by John Sitter

The Cambridge Companion to the Eighteenth-Century Novel
edited by John Richetti

The Cambridge Companion to Victorian Poetry
edited by Joseph Bristow

The Cambridge Companion to the Victorian Novel
edited by Deirdre David

The Cambridge Companion to American Realism and Naturalism
edited by Donald Pizer

The Cambridge Companion to Nineteenth-Century American Women's Writing
edited by Dale M. Bauer and Philip Gould

The Cambridge Companion to the Classic Russian Novel
edited by Malcolm V. Jones and Robin Feuer Miller

The Cambridge Companion to the French Novel: from 1800 to the present
edited by Timothy Unwin

The Cambridge Companion to Modernism
edited by Michael Levenson

The Cambridge Companion to Australian Literature
edited by Elizabeth Webby

The Cambridge Companion to American Women Playwrights
edited by Brenda Murphy

The Cambridge Companion to Modern British Women Playwrights
edited by Elaine Aston and Janelle Reinelt

The Cambridge Companion to Virgil
edited by Charles Martindale

The Cambridge Companion to Ovid
edited by Philip Hardie

The Cambridge Companion to Dante
edited by Rachel Jacoff

The Cambridge Companion to Goethe
edited by Lesley Sharpe

The Cambridge Companion to Proust
edited by Richard Bales

The Cambridge Companion to Thomas Mann
edited by Ritchie Robertson

The Cambridge Companion to Chekhov
edited by Vera Gottlieb and Paul Allain

The Cambridge Companion to Ibsen
edited by James McFarlane

The Cambridge Companion to Brecht
edited by Peter Thomson and Glendyr Sacks

The Cambridge Chaucer Companion
edited by Piero Boitani and Jill Mann

The Cambridge Companion to Shakespeare
edited by Margareta de Grazia and Stanley Wells

The Cambridge Companion to Shakespeare on Film
edited by Russell Jackson

The Cambridge Companion to Shakespearean Comedy
edited by Alexander Leggatt

The Cambridge Companion to Shakespeare on Stage
edited by Stanley Wells and Sarah Stanton

The Cambridge Companion to Spenser
edited by Andrew Hadfield

The Cambridge Companion to Ben Jonson
edited by Richard Harp and Stanley Stewart

The Cambridge Companion to Milton
edited by Dennis Danielson

The Cambridge Companion to Samuel Johnson
edited by Greg Clingham

The Cambridge Companion to Mary Wollstonecraft
edited by Claudia L. Johnson

The Cambridge Companion to Keats
edited by Susan J. Wolfson

The Cambridge Companion to Jane Austen
edited by Edward Copeland and Juliet McMaster

The Cambridge Companion to Charles Dickens
edited by John O. Jordan

The Cambridge Companion to George Eliot
edited by George Levine

The Cambridge Companion to Thomas Hardy
edited by Dale Kramer

The Cambridge Companion to Oscar Wilde
edited by Peter Raby

The Cambridge Companion to George Bernard Shaw
edited by Christopher Innes

The Cambridge Companion to Joseph Conrad
edited by J. H. Stape

The Cambridge Companion to D. H. Lawrence
edited by Anne Fernihough

The Cambridge Companion to Virginia Woolf
edited by Sue Roe and Susan Sellers

The Cambridge Companion to James Joyce
edited by Derek Attridge

The Cambridge Companion to T. S. Eliot
edited by A. David Moody

The Cambridge Companion to Ezra Pound
edited by Ira B. Nadel

The Cambridge Companion to Beckett
edited by John Pilling

The Cambridge Companion to Harold Pinter
edited by Peter Raby

The Cambridge Companion to Tom Stoppard
edited by Katherine E. Kelly

The Cambridge Companion to Herman Melville
edited by Robert S. Levine

The Cambridge Companion to Edith Wharton
edited by Millicent Bell

The Cambridge Companion to Henry James
edited by Jonathan Freedman

The Cambridge Companion to Walt Whitman
edited by Ezra Greenspan

The Cambridge Companion to Henry David Thoreau
edited by Joel Myerson

The Cambridge Companion to Mark Twain
edited by Forrest G. Robinson

The Cambridge Companion to Edgar Allan Poe
edited by Kevin J. Hayes

The Cambridge Companion to William Faulkner
edited by Philip M. Weinstein

The Cambridge Companion to Ernest Hemingway
edited by Scott Donaldson

The Cambridge Companion to F. Scott Fitzgerald
edited by Ruth Prigozy

The Cambridge Companion to Robert Frost
edited by Robert Faggen

The Cambridge Companion to Eugene O'Neill
edited by Michael Manheim

The Cambridge Companion to Tennessee Williams
edited by Matthew C. Roudané

The Cambridge Companion to Arthur Miller
edited by Christopher Bigsby

CAMBRIDGE COMPANIONS TO CULTURE

The Cambridge Companion to Modern German Culture
edited by Eva Kolinsky and Wilfried van der Will

The Cambridge Companion to Modern Russian Culture
edited by Nicholas Rzhevsky

The Cambridge Companion to Modern Spanish Culture
edited by David T. Gies

The Cambridge Companion to Modern Italian Culture
edited by Zygmunt G. Baranski and Rebecca J. West

THE CAMBRIDGE
COMPANION TO
SHAKESPEARE ON STAGE

EDITED BY

STANLEY WELLS

Chairman, The Shakespeare Birthplace Trust

and

SARAH STANTON

Cambridge University Press

PUBLISHED BY THE PRESS SYNDICATE OF THE UNIVERSITY OF CAMBRIDGE
The Pitt Building, Trumpington Street, Cambridge, United Kingdom

CAMBRIDGE UNIVERSITY PRESS
The Edinburgh Building, Cambridge CB2 2RU, UK
40 West 20th Street, New York, NY 10011-4211, USA
477 Williamstown Road, Port Melbourne, VIC 3207, Australia
Ruiz de Alarcón 13, 28014 Madrid, Spain
Dock House, The Waterfront, Cape Town 8001, South Africa

http://www.cambridge.org

© Cambridge University Press, 2002

First published 2002

Printed in the United Kingdom at the University Press, Cambridge

Typeface Sabon 10/13 pt.   *System* LATEX 2$_\varepsilon$ [TB]

A catalogue record for this book is available from the British Library

Library of Congress Cataloguing in Publication data

The Cambridge companion to Shakespeare on stage / edited by Stanley Wells and
Sarah Stanton.
p.   cm. (Cambridge companions to literature)
Includes bibliographical references and index.
ISBN 0 521 79295 9 (hardback) – ISBN 0 521 79711 X (paperback)
1. Shakespeare, William, 1564–1616 – Stage history.   I. Wells, Stanley W., 1930–
II. Stanton, Sarah.   III. Series.
PR3091.C36   2002
792.9'5 – dc21   2001052447

ISBN 0 521 79295 9 hardback
ISBN 0 521 79711 X paperback

CONTENTS

List of illustrations   *page* ix
List of contributors   xiii
Preface   xv

1   Shakespeare plays on Renaissance stages   1
    GARY TAYLOR

2   Improving Shakespeare: from the Restoration to Garrick   21
    JEAN I. MARSDEN

3   Romantic Shakespeare   37
    JANE MOODY

4   Pictorial Shakespeare   58
    RICHARD W. SCHOCH

5   Reconstructive Shakespeare: reproducing Elizabethan
    and Jacobean stages   76
    MARION O'CONNOR

6   Twentieth-century performance: the Stratford
    and London companies   98
    ROBERT SMALLWOOD

7   The tragic actor and Shakespeare   118
    SIMON WILLIAMS

8   The comic actor and Shakespeare   137
    PETER THOMSON

9 Women and Shakespearean performance   155
   PENNY GAY

10 International Shakespeare   174
   ANTHONY B. DAWSON

11 Touring Shakespeare   194
   PETER HOLLAND

12 Shakespeare on the political stage
   in the twentieth century   212
   WILHELM HORTMANN

13 Shakespeare in North America   230
   MICHAEL A. MORRISON

14 Shakespeare on the stages of Asia   259
   JOHN GILLIES, RYUTA MINAMI,
   RURU LI, POONAM TRIVEDI

15 Shakespeare and Africa   284
   MARTIN BANHAM, ROSHNI MOONEERAM,
   JANE PLASTOW

   Further reading   300
   Index   310

ILLUSTRATIONS

1. A contemporary drawing of *Titus Andronicus*, by Henry Peacham (reproduced by permission of the Marquess of Bath, Longleat House, UK)   *page* 14

2. John Philip Kemble as Coriolanus. Painting by Sir Thomas Lawrence (Guildhall Art Gallery, Corporation of London)   46

3. Edmund Kean as Shylock (Michael A. Morrison Collection)   52

4. Edmund Kean as Othello   53

5. Edmund Kean as Richard III (Michael A. Morrison Collection)   55

6. *Romeo and Juliet*. Artist's impression of the final scene, from Henry Irving's 1882 production at the Lyceum Theatre, London (Illustrated London News Picture Library)   63

7. *Much Ado About Nothing*. The church scene (4.1), from Henry Irving's 1882 production at the Lyceum Theatre, London (Victoria & Albert Picture Library)   66

8. *Henry V*, from Charles Kean's production at the Princess's Theatre, London, 1859 (Victoria & Albert Picture Library)   70

9. *Much Ado About Nothing*. Edward Gordon Craig's preliminary sketch for the church scene in his 1903 production at the Imperial Theatre, London (Gordon Craig Estate and Bibliothèque nationale de France)   73

10. William Poel's 'Fortune fit-up' at its first use, for his production of *Measure for Measure* at the Royalty Theatre in 1893 (Victoria & Albert Picture Library)   79

11. The stage of the Maddermarket Theatre, Norwich, 1926 (Maddermarket Theatre)   85

12. The Oregon Shakespeare Festival, Ashland, 1949
(Oregon Shakespeare Festival)   88

13. A production of *The Tempest* at the Southwark Globe,
2000 (photo: Donald Cooper, reproduced by permission
of Shakespeare's Globe)   91

14. David Garrick as Macbeth, in the dagger scene (Michael
A. Morrison Collection)   125

15. William Charles Macready as Macbeth (Michael A. Morrison
Collection)   128

16. Laurence Olivier as Macbeth, with the witches; photo:
Angus McBean (Michael A. Morrison Collection)   132

17. Ian McKellen as Macbeth, with the witches; The Other Place,
Stratford-upon-Avon, 1976 (Shakespeare Centre Library: Joe
Cocks Studio Collection)   133

18. Henry Irving as Shylock, 1879 (Michael A. Morrison
Collection)   148

19. Ralph Richardson as Falstaff in the Old Vic production
of *Henry IV*, 1945; photo: John Vickers (Michael A. Morrison
Collection)   151

20. Sarah Siddons as Lady Macbeth in the sleepwalking scene
(Bristol Theatre Collection)   160

21. Charlotte Cushman as Romeo, with her sister Susan as Juliet,
1858 (Harvard Theatre Collection)   163

22. Ellen Terry as Beatrice in *Much Ado About Nothing*, Lyceum
Theatre, 1882   165

23. Judi Dench as Cleopatra with Miranda Foster as Charmian,
National Theatre, 1987 (photo: John Haynes)   170

24. Juliet Stevenson as Rosalind and Fiona Shaw as Celia in
As You Like It, Royal Shakespeare Theatre, 1985
(Shakespeare Centre Library)   171

25. *Richard III*, directed by Leopold Jessner at the Staatstheater,
Berlin, 1920 (Theaterwissenschaftliche Sammlung, University
of Cologne)   215

26. Peter Palitzsch's *Der Krieg der Rosen*, Stuttgart, 1967
(photo: Werner Schloske)   218

27. Heiner Müller's *Hamlet*, 1989/90 (photo: Wolfhard Theile)   222

28. Thomas Abthorpe Cooper (Michael A. Morrison Collection)   233

29. Junius Brutus Booth as Richard III (Michael A. Morrison
Collection)   236

30. Edwin Forrest as Coriolanus (Michael A. Morrison Collection)   238

31. Edwin Booth as Hamlet (Michael A. Morrison Collection)   241

32. John Barrymore as Hamlet, New York, 1922 (Michael A.
Morrison Collection)   248

33. Maurice Evans as Richard II, 1937 (Michael A. Morrison
Collection)   250

34. Paul Robeson as Othello, 1943 (Michael A. Morrison
Collection)   252

35. Christopher Plummer as Hamlet at Stratford, Ontario,
1957 (Michael A. Morrison Collection)   254

36. Earle Hyman as John of Gaunt and André Braugher as
Bolingbroke at the New York Shakespeare Festival, 1994
(Michael A. Morrison Collection)   255

37. *Macbeth*, directed by Yukio Ninagawa, Nissei Theatre,
Japan, 1980 (courtesy Toho Company Ltd)   263

38. The trial scene from *Sandaime Richâdo*, directed by Hideki
Noda, 1990 (courtesy NODA MAP)   264

39. Hermia and Lysander, *A Midsummer Night's Dream*, directed
by Hideki Noda, Nissei Theatre, 1992 (courtesy
NODA MAP)   264

40. *Huaju Hamlet*, directed by Lin Zhaohua, Beijing, 1990
(courtesy Lin Zhaohua)   269

41. *Much Ado About Nothing*, directed by Jiang Weiguo
(courtesy Jiang Weiguo)   271

42. *Barnam Vana*, the 1979 production of *Macbeth*, in Hindi,
in *Yakshagana* style, National School of Drama, New Delhi:
(a) the Witches; (b) the banquet scene   277

43. *Stage of Blood*, the 1979 production of *Macbeth*, directed by
    Lokendra Arambam, Ningthem Pukri Reservoir, Imphal, India:
    (a) Macbeth at Dunsinane; (b) Birnam Wood advances   279

44. *Zeneral Makbef* by Dev Virahsawmy, 1982, at Plaza,
    Mauritius: (a) Zeneral and Ledi Makbef; (b) the end of the play   291

45. The original production of *A'are Akogun*, a version of *Macbeth*
    by Wale Ogunyemi, performed in 1968 at the Arts Theatre,
    University of Ibadan, Nigeria   294

CONTRIBUTORS

MARTIN BANHAM, University of Leeds

ANTHONY B. DAWSON, University of British Columbia

PENNY GAY, University of Sydney

JOHN GILLIES, University of Essex

PETER HOLLAND, The Shakespeare Institute, University of Birmingham

WILHELM HORTMANN, University of Duisburg

RURU LI, University of Leeds

JEAN I. MARSDEN, University of Connecticut

RYUTA MINAMI, Kobe City University of Foreign Studies

JANE MOODY, University of York

ROSHNI MOONEERAM, University of Leeds

MICHAEL A. MORRISON, New York

MARION O'CONNOR, University of Kent at Canterbury

JANE PLASTOW, University of Leeds

RICHARD W. SCHOCH, Queen Mary, University of London

ROBERT SMALLWOOD, The Shakespeare Centre, Stratford-upon-Avon

GARY TAYLOR, University of Alabama

PETER THOMSON, University of Exeter

POONAM TRIVEDI, University of Delhi

SIMON WILLIAMS, University of California, Santa Barbara

PREFACE

This *Companion* is designed for readers interested in past and present productions of the plays and to accompany the increasing number of courses
devoted to the history of Shakespeare in performance. It joins other volumes
in the series, developing one key aspect of the *Companion to Shakespeare*
(edited by Margreta De Grazia and Stanley Wells) and complementing the
Companion to Shakespeare on Film (edited by Russell Jackson).

The book addresses both British and international performance. While
coverage cannot hope to be exhaustive, the first six chapters describe aspects of the British performing tradition in chronological sequence, from
the early stagings of Shakespeare's own time, through the Restoration and
eighteenth century, the Romantic and Victorian periods, bringing the reader
up to the present via developments in the twentieth century. But this is by no
means a uniform narrative: authors have been chosen for their expertise in a
particular period; each has related Shakespearean developments to broader
cultural concerns and, where relevant, to developments outside the UK; each
has adopted an individual approach and focus, be it on textual adaptation,
acting, stages, scenery or theatre management.

Following the chronological chapters is a sequence of three which explore
aspects of tragic and comic acting and the subject of women performers of
Shakespearean roles. The latter part of the book considers international performance, beginning with a chapter on the issue of interculturalism, appropriation and the translation of Shakespeare's plays into other languages. This
is followed by an account of the phenomenon of national and international
touring companies from Elizabethan times to the present. Geographical coverage of performance outside Britain is necessarily selective, but focuses on
those countries or regions that have a continuous and/or highly distinctive
history of performing Shakespeare, sometimes developing styles which have
themselves fed back into the English idiom. Productions of Shakespeare in
Germany, Eastern Europe and South Africa offer examples of the adaptation
of Shakespeare plays to political ends; chapters on North American, Asian

and African stagings provide distinct accounts of how Shakespeare has been assimilated into vastly different cultural and national traditions.

Throughout the book we have interpreted 'Shakespeare on stage' to mean spoken performances of the plays rather than operas or musicals, though the distinction becomes blurred at times, especially in the sections on Asian and African performance.

At the end of the book is an amalgamated list of items for further reading. This begins with references to books in the general area of Shakespearean stage history and proceeds to a set of miniature bibliographies arranged according to the chapter titles.

Quotations from Shakespeare's plays are from volumes in the New Cambridge Shakespeare, where published, and from the Oxford *Complete Works* in other cases.

The selection of pictures is intended truly to illustrate and not merely to decorate the points being made in the text. In this respect, our thanks go to the sources listed for their permission to reproduce items from their collections, and especially to Michael Morrison, whose generous provision of prints from his own collection has enabled us to double the quantity we would otherwise have afforded.

Publishing a book, like staging a play, is a team effort and we have been fortunate in our collaborators. The contributors to this volume have been an inspiration. We have also had invaluable help from Hilary Hammond (copyeditor), Juliet Stanton (proofreader) and Kate Welch (indexer). Our Press editor, Vicki Cooper, has supported us throughout with enthusiasm, tact and tolerance. Both of us, in different ways, have been involved with CUP over many years and colleagues there have, as always, been a pleasure to work with.

SS
SW

I

GARY TAYLOR

Shakespeare plays on Renaissance stages

The business of playing

Shakespeare's plays were born on stage. They might have been conceived 'In the quick forge and working-house of thought', but for Shakespeare that house where you should 'Work, work, your thoughts' was itself a playhouse (*Henry V* 5.0.23, 3.0.25). Shakespeare did his thinking in theatres. 'My muse labours', Shakespeare wrote, 'and thus she is delivered', Iago says, enacting thought, the actor delivering his line as the character delivers his rhyme (*Othello* 2.1.126–7). What the muse conceives is not properly born until it cries out, giving voice to what had before been only 'bare imagination' (*Richard II* 1.3.296). So it should not surprise us that Shakespeare imagined being 'born' as an entrance onto 'this great stage' (*Tragedy of King Lear* 4.5.175). That metaphor depended, in part, upon the Latin motto of the Globe Theatre, '*Totus mundus agit histrionem*' (translated in *As You Like It* as 'All the world's a stage'). But it also reflected Shakespeare's own frequent association of the womb that delivers newborn babes with the theatre that delivers newborn plays. He compares the walls of a circular amphitheatre to a 'girdle', encompassing a 'pit' that is also an 'O' (*Henry V* Pro. 19, 11, 13); he imagines a 'concave womb' echoing with words (*Lover's Complaint* 1), and asserts that a 'hollow womb resounds' (*Venus* 268), as though a uterus were a resonating auditorium. Such associations subordinate female anatomy to the emotional and professional experience of a male actor and playwright. That is why, when the Princess of France anticipates the projected show of Nine Worthies, she says that 'great things labouring perish in their birth' (*Love's Labour's Lost* 5.2.517): she equates performance with parturition. So does Shakespeare.

Consequently, we mislead ourselves if we imagine a play moving *from* text *to* stage, as though textuality and theatricality were separate entities, or as though one evolved into the other. For Shakespeare, a play began life in the theatre. Often enough, the stage itself inspired composition of the text.

A character like Pistol, sampling from old plays, literally embodies memories of treasured theatrical performances; at the same time, he probably parodies the vocal and physical style of the first great English actor, Edward Alleyn. *The Merchant of Venice* – which also went by the now less familiar title '*The Jew of Venice*' – remembers and rewrites *The Jew of Malta*, for years one of the most popular plays in the repertory of a rival company, led by Alleyn; Shakespeare's familiarity with Christopher Marlowe's play can only have come from performances, because it was not printed until 1633. Likewise, *The Merry Wives of Windsor* responds to Henry Porter's *The Two Angry Women of Abington*, a recent hit play performed by the same rival company, and not available in print at the time. Many of Shakespeare's histories, not to mention *Hamlet*, rewrite successful plays of the 1580s. His final comedies, from *All's Well That Ends Well* to *The Tempest*, self-consciously reject the innovative genres of city comedy perfected by Thomas Middleton and John Marston in plays for the Jacobean children's companies; Shakespeare and his aging fellow-actors instead mined nostalgia, resurrecting and reshaping Elizabethan dramatic romances.

Shakespeare, as these examples suggest, was writing not only for himself but for a particular acting company, and against their chief commercial rivals. The Chamberlain's Men – in 1603 rechristened the King's Men – was a joint-stock company, co-owned by its chief actors who, like modern stockholders, received proportionate shares of its profits. From 1594 until his retirement in 1613, Shakespeare worked, as actor and playwright, with the company that he part-owned; in 1599 he also became a shareholder in that company's open-air suburban amphitheatre, the Globe; in 1608, he became a shareholder in their indoor theatre at Blackfriars. In writing plays Shakespeare was deeply invested, emotionally and financially, in the success of that company.

Unfortunately, we have no record of that company's day-to-day proce-dures, no financial accounts or personal memoirs. Nevertheless, a lot of circumstantial evidence suggests that its operations resembled those of other companies. For instance, Philip Henslowe, the entrepreneur personally and financially associated with Edward Alleyn and the Admiral's Men, regularly recorded advance payments to playwrights. The playwright presented to the acting company a 'plot', or scene-by-scene scenario of a prospective play; if the company approved, they would offer the playwright a down pay-ment, and might make subsequent part payments as he completed parts of the play. Such a routine gave the acting company a voice in the evolution of each script, almost from its outset. Every play was conceived and exe-cuted as a corporate capital venture. That was as true of Shakespeare's plays for the Chamberlain's Men, as of Thomas Dekker's plays for the Admiral's Men. But every play also depended upon, and reinforced, a network of personal relationships; in Shakespeare's case some of those relationships were mutually rewarding enough to last decades. In choosing which plays to write, or when to write them, or what kinds of roles to put into them, he must have taken some account of the attitudes and aptitudes of his fellow-sharers.

Playwrighting in these circumstances was an intrinsically social process. Considerably more than half of the known plays of the period were written by more than one playwright. The business of playwrighting often resembled the apprentice–master relationship that structured London trades (and the training of boy actors by an adult veteran). Thus, early in his career Shakespeare apparently collaborated with Thomas Nashe and others in writing *The First Part of Henry the Sixth*, and with George Peele in writing *Titus Andronicus*; *Edward the Third* may also be an early collaboration. For a decade after the formation of the Chamberlain's Men, Shakespeare – perhaps stung by Robert Greene's bitter attack on him, in 1592, as a thief of better men's talent – chose not to team up with other playwrights. But in 1605 he began collaborating again, first with Middleton on *Timon of Athens*, then with George Wilkins on *Pericles*, finally with John Fletcher on *Henry VIII* (or *All is True*), *The Two Noble Kinsmen*, and the lost *Cardenio*. In each case the middle-aged Shakespeare teamed up with a young man who had already successfully captured the new public mood. Such partnerships not only paired individuals; they created a dialogue across generations and theatrical fashions.

To say that early modern plays were masterpieces written by committees would be an exaggeration, but the exaggeration came close enough to the truth that Ben Jonson felt the need to insist rebelliously upon individuality and independence. Shakespeare, by contrast, was a company man. The earliest editions of his plays specified the company that performed them, but no author; not until 1598, with the quarto of *Love's Labour's Lost*, did his name reach the title page. After 1598, plays continued to appear with the company's name, but not his (*Romeo and Juliet*, 1599; *Henry V*, 1600), and the 1623 collection of his *Comedies, Histories, and Tragedies* was prefaced and dedicated and probably edited by two of his old colleagues, fellow-shareholders in the Chamberlain's/King's Men. Even when he was not teamed with another author, Shakespeare was always writing for and with a specific company of actors, and what we call 'his' plays were at the time often considered 'theirs', or both 'his' and 'theirs'. After all, Shakespeare was, in the technical terminology of the period, a 'sharer', the part-owner of a collaborative enterprise; 'Property was thus appalled' by a creative corporation of 'Two distincts, division none' (*Phoenix and Turtle* 37, 27).

The earliest texts of his plays are, accordingly, frustrating documents; reading them is like overhearing someone carrying on an argument with himself, half-vocalised, or listening to one half of a telephone conversation, or trying to follow the elliptical dialogue of twins. Unlike Jonson's plays, or some of Middleton's, Shakespeare's were not printed from manuscripts prepared for the convenience of that consortium of readers called 'the general public'; instead, they were written to be read by a particular group of actors, his professional colleagues and personal friends. He could rely on those readers to bring to their reading much specialist knowledge about theatrical conditions and working practices, and the circumstances of the specific company to which they and he belonged. The written text of any such manuscript thus depended upon an unwritten paratext, which always accompanied it; an invisible life-support system of stage directions, which Shakespeare could either expect his first readers to supply, or which those first readers would expect Shakespeare himself to supply orally. For instance, not a single sixteenth- or seventeenth-century printed text of a Shakespeare play indicates every necessary exit; indeed, even the surviving manuscript promptbooks for the King's Men do not indicate every necessary exit, or the costumes worn by most of the characters. Sometimes the texts do not specify who sings a song, or which song they sing.

Actors who enter must exit, every actor must wear (or not wear) something, every word sung on stage must be sung by someone, and every singer must have words to sing. Exits and costumes and speech attributions and song texts are necessary elements of even the most minimal performance script. Shakespeare's texts, nevertheless, uniformly fail to supply such minimal information. Why? Because Shakespeare expected his fellow-actors to fill in those obvious blanks. That is, he expected parts of the minimal performance script to be 'written' by the actors with whom he was collaborating.

Casting and doubling

Because Shakespeare expected his words to be spoken by actors and heard by audiences, each text is a score for lost voices. He composed roles for the tone and range of the particular human instruments who would perform them. Richard Burbage (like Edward Alleyn) had an exceptionally capacious memory, which meant that playwrights could write for him some taxingly long parts, longer than any parts written for any European actor before 1590: Burbage certainly played Richard III, Hamlet, and Othello (as well as Marston's Malevole and Jonson's Mosca), and probably also first embodied Henry V, Duke Vincentio, and Antony (as well as Middleton's Vindice). These parts not only give a single character thousands of words to speak; they also demand, and enable, an exceptional variety of emotional and vocal display. Burbage was the company's leading actor, and stayed with it even after Shakespeare retired; by contrast, the company's first clown, Will Kemp, left in 1598, to be replaced by Robert Armin. Shakespeare's clowning changed to suit the more intellectual and musical gifts of the new resident comedian. Likewise, as Burbage aged, Shakespeare's leading characters got older: much is made of the age gap between the young Desdemona and the aging Othello, grey-haired Antony is contrasted with the young Octavius, Lear is 'fourscore and upward' (*King Lear* 4.6.58). The only long role for a conspicuously young protagonist in Shakespeare's late plays is Coriolanus, but that might have been played by the rising star John Lowin, who is known on other occasions to have played soldiers. Certainly, when Lowin joined the company, the King's Men began to perform plays which contained not one but two long and complex parts, of a kind hitherto limited to Burbage. The combination of Burbage and Lowin made possible a sustained binary opposition of two strong characters, which in turn shaped the structure of Shakespeare's *Othello* (1604), Jonson's *Volpone* (1606), and Jonson's *The Alchemist* (1610).

More generally, Shakespeare and every other professional playwright designed their scripts to suit a certain size and shape of acting company. In the 1580s and early 1590s, when the Queen's Men set a standard their competitors felt they had to match, Shakespeare was not alone in writing plays that – even allowing for doubling – require exceptionally large casts (all three plays on Henry the Sixth, *Titus Andronicus*). But after the break-up and reorganisation of companies caused by the severe outbreak of plague and subsequent long closure of the London theatres in 1592–3, playwrights began composing for leaner troupes: Shakespeare's later history plays consistently require fewer actors than the early ones.

In plotting and writing all his plays, early and late, Shakespeare would have assumed that some actors would play more than one role. As Costard announces in *Love's Labour's Lost*, the traditional 'Nine Worthies' will become, in their performance, 'three Worthies', because 'everyone pursents three' (5.2.486–8): each actor plays three parts. Likewise, in *A Midsummer Night's Dream*, Bottom, having already been given the role of Pyramus, suggests 'let me play Thisbe *too*', and 'Let me play the lion *too*' (1.2.42, 57; my italics): of course this histrionic self-aggrandisement amusingly characterises Bottom, but it also draws upon a widespread sixteenth-century tradition of character-doubling. From the evidence of surviving cast lists and theatrical documents from the 1580s to the 1630s, in the professional London companies actors playing the lead parts in a play did not (normally) double, and those playing young female characters did not (normally) play adult male characters too; most of the doubling (normally) involved adult male or female secondary characters, with relatively few lines. These casting practices probably explain, for instance, why so many of the secondary characters in the first half of *Julius Caesar* do not resurface in the second half, why some characters materialise only in the first scene of a play (Francisco in *Hamlet*, Archidamus in *The Winter's Tale*), and why in *1 Henry IV* Poins consistently and conspicuously appears alongside Prince Hal in 1.2, 2.2, and 2.4 – and never again.

Even when it seems clear that Shakespeare structured a play with doubling requirements in mind, we often cannot tell which specific roles were doubled in early performances, because several different possibilities present themselves. The actor playing Poins could have doubled as the Earl of Douglas or as Sir Richard Vernon, both of whom first appear in 4.1 (thus explaining why Poins has no role in the immediately preceding 3.3, the first tavern scene from which he is absent). Further uncertainty is created by our ignorance about how much time actors needed to switch roles: early documents from the professional theatres seem to allow at least one intervening scene for such changes, but in practice experienced actors have always been able to switch very quickly, and both actors and audiences sometimes enjoy such feats of virtuosity. Indeed, as Bottom's enthusiasm for engrossing extra roles suggests, actors sometimes enjoy playing more than one character, precisely because doing so permits them to display their shape-changing virtuosity. When the King's Men presented *Cymbeline*, if one actor played both the despicably ridiculous Cloten and his rival, the romantic and almost tragic hero Posthumus, both the actor and the audience might have enjoyed the yoking of such incongruities – and recognised a further level of complexity in the already complex moment when a headless corpse (actually, of the despised Cloten) is mistaken for the beloved Posthumus.

But major roles were not normally doubled, and we can be more confident about early doubling when the roles affected are smaller. The actors who impersonated one foursome of small parts (Flute, Snout, Starveling and Snug) almost certainly also impersonated another foursome of small parts (Peaseblossom, Cobweb, Moth and Mustardseed). Likewise, in both versions of *King Lear* the actor playing Cordelia might also have played the Fool. Both are secondary characters, with relatively few lines. The Fool first appears in 1.4, and last appears in 3.6; Cordelia is prominent in the first scene, then disappears until 4.3; the two characters are psychologically conflated in Lear's 'And my poor fool is hanged' (5.3.279).

Acting gender, acting race

Cordelia is female, and the Fool male, but on early modern stages both parts would have been played by the same kind of actor. There were no actresses in Shakespeare's company; instead, female roles were played by boys, young males a few years either side of puberty. Those same talented youngsters also played the many young boy characters who appear in early modern plays. Shakespeare's *dramatis personae* include more boys than any other major body of drama: Sir John's page in *2 Henry IV*, *Merry Wives* and *Henry V*, one 'young Lucius' in *Titus* and another in *Caesar*, young Martius in *Coriolanus*, William Page in *Merry Wives*, and many anonymous pages in other plays. Like modern choirboys, the performing boys of early modern England were often trained to sing; indeed, the acting company associated with St Paul's Cathedral, which flourished in the 1580s and again from 1600 to 1606, originated as an ensemble of choirboys. Consequently, Shakespeare's boy characters are often also expected to sing. Sometimes – like the two anonymous singing pages in *As You Like It*, or the anonymous singing boys in *Measure for Measure*, *Antony and Cleopatra* and *The Two Noble Kinsmen* – singing is the sole excuse for their existence. But John Lyly, in plays written for Paul's Boys in the 1580s, had also demonstrated the theatrical appeal of putting into the mouths of babes incongruously clever worldly-wise speeches, and many of the roles Shakespeare wrote for boys copy that convention. Armado's page in *Love's Labour's Lost* epitomises such roles: Mote's name alludes both to his small size and to the French word *mot* (word), and he is introduced as a 'tender juvenal' (1.2.8–15), both a soft-skinned juvenile and an oxymoronic 'compassionate satirist' (alluding to the Roman poet Juvenal).

The same boy actors who were trained to display extraordinary verbal legerdemain were also able, on other occasions, to be simply innocent: harmless, helpless, naïve and tragically vulnerable. The death of a child is likely to loosen the tear ducts of even the toughest spectator. Shakespeare often used boys as uncomplicated pathetic victims: Rutland in *3 Henry VI*, Prince Edward in *Richard III*, Arthur in *King John*. Sometimes – with the young Duke of York in *Richard III*, or MacDuff's son in *Macbeth*, or Mamillius in *The Winter's Tale* – Shakespeare united in one role the witty page and the pathetic victim: the boy actor first makes spectators laugh with precociously sophisticated wordplay, and then with his premature death makes spectators weep.

The boy actor who played Hermione's young son Mamillius could also have played, in the second half of the play, Hermione's daughter Perdita – thus reuniting, in the harmonies of the play's ending, mother and lost child. Even when combined, the two roles would require a boy actor to memorise only 1,046 words, much less than either Hermione (1,580) or Paulina (2,372). We cannot be absolutely sure that the King's Men doubled Mamillius and Perdita, but we can say that the King's Men expected their young apprentices to play both boys (like Mamillius) and young women (like Perdita), and also that Shakespeare, thinking theatrically, wrote *The Winter's Tale* in a way that allowed, and in some ways seems to encourage, that particular doubling of roles. We can say the same about the doubling of Lear's Fool with Cordelia. Lear's Fool, as the dialogue ten times insists, is a 'boy', and he displays the wit and irreverence characteristic of Shakespeare's many young pages. The vicarious precocious Fool makes us laugh; the innocent dead Cordelia makes us cry. Both roles combine affection for Lear with criticism of him, and both were well within the range of a trained boy actor.

Because Shakespeare expected the same performers to represent boys and women, the roles he created for women resemble the roles he created for boys. Indeed, he routinely regarded the two identities as interchangeable: beginning in what was probably his first play, *The Two Gentlemen of Verona*, he had Julia disguise herself as a young page, and later he scripted similar transformations for Portia, Nerissa, Rosalind, Viola and Innogen (Imogen). Conversely, in the induction to *The Taming of the Shrew*, he has a page disguise himself as a Lady; in casting the amateur performance of Pyramus and Thisbe, Flute is assigned to play the woman's part, presumably because he is so young he does not yet have a beard (*Dream* 1.2.39). Flute's name identifies the central resemblance between women and boys: 'fluting', high-pitched voices.

Both witty pages and witty young women deal in the pretty, precious and precocious; like the child stars of modern film and television, they amuse audiences by displaying an impertinent intelligence, a witty insubordination, even at times a talent for sexual innuendo, not expected from and deliciously incongruous in such mouths. Like boys, women characters also often exist chiefly for musical purposes: Mortimer's wife 'sings a Welsh song' (*1 Henry IV* 3.1.238.1), Marina and her 'companion maid' sing to Pericles (5.1.73), and songs are required of such minor characters as Dorcas and Mopsa in *The Winter's Tale*, Queen Katherine's anonymous 'gentlewoman' in *All Is True*, and the goddess Hecate in Middleton's additions to *Macbeth*. In addition to singing, women and boys also contributed another characteristic sound effect to early modern performances: ululation. 'A cry within of women', signalling the death of Lady Macbeth (5.5.7.1), is a gendered sound effect, like 'Alarum within' (1.2.0.1). Unlike men but like boys, women were allowed – indeed, expected – to weep easily; like the orphaned children of Clarence in *Richard III* (who serve no other purpose), they often added cries and sighs, shrieking and sobbing to the aural texture of a performance. Helena begins *All's Well That Ends Well* weeping; Cassandra makes her first entrance with a 'shriek' (*Troilus* 2.2.96). Because they specialise in unrestrained lamentation, female characters often embody impotent grief:

Constance in *King John*, the Queen in *Richard II*, Lady Percy in *2 Henry IV*, can only 'weep like a young wench that had buried her grandam' (*Two Gentlemen* 2.1.20), or 'weeping die' (*Errors* 2.1.113).

The association of women and grief was not simply aural. Like the boys who played them, Shakespeare's women are physically and socially more vulnerable than men. Hence, like boys, women in Shakespeare make good victims, whether as protagonists (the sleepwalking suicidal Lady Macbeth) or subordinates (Lady Macduff, who exists only to be murdered). Cleopatra, characteristically, does not die alone; Iras precedes her, Charmian follows, giving an audience three dead women in thirty-five lines. 'Under a compelling occasion, let women die', Enobarbus had joked, but it is not just Cleopatra who has 'a celerity in dying' (*Antony* 1.2.134–40). *Othello* ends with two innocent female corpses on stage. The raped and mutilated Lavinia, having been displayed for five scenes, is finally killed by her father near the end of *Titus Andronicus*; Juliet's is the last, climactic death in the Capulet tomb; Gertrude's death, the turning point in the final scene of *Hamlet*, is arguably its least complicated and most poignant moment. Even when women do not die on stage, their reported or apparent or expected deaths produce similar moments of pathos. Queen Anne in *Richard III* knows that her husband 'will, no doubt, shortly be rid of me' (4.1.87); the 'distraught' Portia's 'grief' drives her to suicide (*Caesar* 4.3.153–5); the discarded innocent Queen Katherine of *All Is True* closes act 4 anticipating her burial; the apparent deaths of innocent wronged Hero in *Much Ado* and innocent young Thaisa in *Pericles* may affect an audience as much as any 'real' on-stage death.

Finally, Shakespeare's most demanding female characters, like his most demanding boy characters, combine the different talents that might be expected of the best boy actors. Ophelia sings, weeps and dies. In her first scene, Hermione is as witty as the wittiest page; that wit stokes her husband's jealousy, which gives the boy actor plenty of opportunities for pathos. Cleopatra, too, is witty, bawdy, and finally dead: unlike the 'squeaking Cleopatra' whom she fears to see 'boy [her] greatness/I'th'posture of a whore' (*Antony* 5.2.219–20), the boy who played her must have been able to control his voice (so that it did not, as the voices of adolescent boys often do, unpredictably squeak), and he must have been capable of more than one 'posture'. And although no actress has ever founded a great reputation on playing Desdemona, it gave boy actors the opportunity to display all their virtues. To the dismay of many subsequent critics, Desdemona, like an impertinent boy, engages in witty bawdy banter with Iago (*Othello* 2.1.123–71); later, she is given the opportunity to sing (4.3.38–54) – 'and she can weep, sir, weep', Othello informs us, and then directs her 'Proceed you in your tears' (4.1.245–7). She also dies on stage, a pathetically innocent victim; indeed, the player gets to die not once but twice in the same scene. The emotional effect of the boy actor's performance of her deaths was recorded by an eye-witness in Oxford in September 1610:

> In the last few days the King's players have been here. They acted with enormous applause to full houses . . . They had tragedies (too) which they acted with skill and decorum and in which some things, both speech and action, brought forth tears. – Moreover, that famous Desdemona killed before us by her husband, although she always acted her whole part supremely well, yet when she was killed she was even more moving, for when she fell back upon the bed she implored the pity of the spectators by her very face.[1]

No actress in the role could accomplish more. Indeed, no actress could accomplish so much, because part of the boy actor's admired virtuosity was his very capacity to make spectators regard him as 'she'. In addition to creating opportunities for banter, singing, weeping, and dying, the role of Desdemona gave its first performer the opportunity to enact femaleness. An actress playing Desdemona can be applauded for dying pathetically, but unlike a boy actor she will not be applauded for gender-switching.

Desdemona speaks only 2,760 words, less than 11 percent of the play's text. The male spectator at Oxford found her most compelling when she was dead silent. Although boy actors may have been precociously talented, they did not have the same capabilities as adults, and neither do Shakespeare's female characters. Shakespeare wrote 1,000 words more for Rosalind than for any other female character, but 'she' speaks many of those as a male ('Ganymede'). Like Portia and Viola and Imogen, Rosalind/Ganymede was written to be played by the company's most experienced boy actor – who by definition would have been pushing the chronological and physical limits of his capacity to impersonate the women convincingly. That is why Shakespeare has Rosalind describe herself as 'more than common tall' (*As You Like It* 1.3.105).

The boy–girl compound called Rosalind/Ganymede speaks considerably less than half as much as Hamlet (for whom Shakespeare wrote 11,563 words). No female role approaches the size of the great roles Shakespeare created for Burbage. Even a character like Kate in *The Taming of the Shrew*, notorious for her tongue, speaks far fewer words (1,759) than Petruccio (4,605), or even Tranio (2,256). If the script overtaxed a juvenile memory, then the boy might well – like Mote, introducing the masque of Muscovites in *Love's Labour's Lost* – forget his lines, thereby disgracing himself and his whole company (5.2.160–73). Shakespeare never wrote a female role like Ibsen's Hedda Gabler, or like Middleton and Dekker's Moll Frith in *The Roaring Girl*. Moreover, he always wrote for companies with more adult actors than boys; consequently, few if any of his own scripts require more than four boy actors, and he never wrote anything like the christening scene (3.2) in Middleton's *A Chaste Maid in Cheapside*, which has eleven speaking female characters on stage simultaneously.

Shakespeare's company was not only homogeneously male, it was also homogeneously Anglo-Saxon. That did not prevent Shakespeare from creating ethnic or racial fictions, any more than the absence of real women prevented him from creating fictional females. But Shakespeare knew that 'black Othello' (2.3.27) would be played by white Burbage. Indeed, when Burbage/Othello said that his reputation was 'now begrimed and black/As mine own face' (3.3.388–9), Shakespeare described a black man's complexion as though it were produced by smearing grime (soot, coal dust) on a formerly white surface; every early modern Othello was not just metaphorically but literally 'sooty' (1.2.70). In the same Christmas season that *Othello* was first performed at court, the faces, hands and bare arms of Queen Anne and eleven other ladies were – as scandalised observers reported – 'painted black' for their appearance in Jonson's *Masque of Blackness*. Shakespeare, like Jonson, wrote for white actors painted black; his plays belong to the theatrical genre of blackface (and were widely adopted and adapted by blackface theatre and burlesque in the nineteenth century). Moreover, his blackface roles were apparently written for different actors: Othello for Burbage, Cleopatra for a boy actor, the one-scene comic part of Morocco perhaps for a hired man, the major but not leading role of Aaron for some sharer other than Burbage, the mute 'blackamoors with music' probably for hired musicians (*Love's Labour's Lost* 5.2.156.1). No one, apparently, specialised in black characters. Any actor could play them, because anyone could paint his face black. Likewise, any actor could paint his face 'tawny' to play Spaniards, like Aragon or Armado, or the characters of the 'Black House' in Middleton's (the King's Men's) *A Game at Chess*. Any actor could put on a 'jew's nose' (one of Henslowe's properties) to play Marlowe's Barabas or Shakespeare's Shylock. Shakespeare wrote for stages where racial and ethnic differences were mimicked by Anglo-Saxon actors for Anglo-Saxon audiences.

Worn identities: clothes and accessories

Identities constituted by race or gender were, for Shakespeare and his acting company, prosthetic. They were created by adding something artificial – false breasts, soot – to the 'natural' template of the white male body. Of all such prosthetic devices, the most important were clothes and the accessories that went with clothes. The area directly behind the stage, where actors prepared for their entrances, was called the 'tiring-house', a place for putting on and taking off attire. According to a poem attributed to Sir Walter Raleigh, 'Our mothers' wombs the tiring-houses be / Where we are dressed for life's short comedy'; if a play is born in performance, its gestation takes place in the tiring-house, where each character is fitted with an identity. Shylock enters, wearing a 'Jewish gaberdine' (*Merchant of Venice* 1.3.104); in the next scene *'the Prince of Morocco, a tawny Moor all in white'*, enters (the prescribed whiteness of his clothing emphasising the darkness of his skin), wearing a 'scimitar' (2.1.0.1–2, 2.1.24) – the same kind of sword worn by another 'Moor', Aaron, in *Titus Andronicus* (4.2.91).

We tend to think of the number of characters in a play as a function of the number of available actors; but that was not true on early modern stages. 'One man', Jaques tells us, 'plays many parts' (*As You Like It* 2.7.142). Indeed, the actor who played Jaques might also have played Denis and/or Le Beau and/or William in the same play. But Denis would have been dressed as a serving man; Monsieur Le Beau, as a French courtier; William, as a peasant; Jaques first appears dressed as a forester (2.5.0.1), but he probably wore something more particular than that, reflecting the distinctive 'melancholy of mine own' of which he is so proud (4.1.15). One character is distinguished from another not by the differences between one actor's body and another actor's body, but by the difference between one outfit and another; one actor could have served for Denis, Le Beau, William and Jaques, but one costume could not. Thus, the number of roles in a play was, for playing companies and their playwrights, a function of the number of costumes. Identity was sartorially constructed.

That is one reason why companies paid more for new clothes than for new scripts. Shakespeare wrote only 134 words for the god Hymen to speak (and another thirty-three to be sung, probably chorally) – but unlike Denis, Le Beau or William, the small role of Hymen required an impressive special costume. For the same god, the printed text of Jonson's *Hymenai* (written to be read by people who had not seen the performance) specified 'a saffron-coloured robe, his under-vesture white, his socks yellow, a yellow veil of silk on his left arm'. The impression made by Hymen in performance depended (and still depends) more upon the wardrobe and the music room than on the playwright.

A new play usually cost £6; by contrast, the actor Edward Alleyn owned a single 'black velvet cloak with sleeves, embroidered all with silver and gold' that cost £20 10s 6d. The Earl of Leicester regularly paid more for a doublet or cloak than Shakespeare paid for New Place in Stratford. Since Shakespeare's plays, like those of his contemporaries, regularly brought earls, dukes and even kings on stage, they had to reproduce convincingly the splendour of contemporary aristocratic dress. In a world without synthetic fabrics or cheap mass-produced apparel, such splendour could only be represented by expensive fabrics, in many cases by the actual articles of clothing formerly worn by the nobility. For performances of Middleton's *A Game at Chess*, the King's Men acquired a 'cast suit' – that is, a used and discarded outfit – of the Spanish ambassador. A quarter of a century earlier, Thomas Platter (a Swiss traveller who visited England in 1599 and saw *Julius Caesar* performed by the Chamberlain's Men) reported that

> The actors are most expensively and elaborately costumed; for it is the English usage for eminent lords or knights at their decease to bequeath and leave almost the best of their clothes to their serving men, which it is unseemly for the latter to wear, so that they offer them then for sale ... to the actors.[2]

The circulation of rich apparel was undoubtedly more complex than Platter realised. Indeed, the early modern economy of England depended upon the production and distribution of worked cloth; increasingly, the London cloth trade created and satisfied a demand for sartorial novelty, for the changing fashions satirised in plays like Middleton's *Your Five Gallants* (which begins in a pawnshop). The actors Platter saw were themselves, technically, 'serving men' to 'eminent lords'; Shakespeare's company in 1599 wore the livery of the Lord Chamberlain, and later of the King. Expensive clothes could be given or bought, but they could also be rented or pawned. Henslowe combined the professions of theatrical impresario and pawnbroker, while the royal Office of the Revels not only supplied clothes for performances at court, but rented them to playing companies at other times.

Clothing was so important to the actors because it so quickly and efficiently established recognisable social identities: gender, status, occupation, wealth. As Polonius declares, 'the apparel oft proclaims the man' (*Hamlet* 1.3.72). Of course, we hear this having already heard, in the preceding scene, Hamlet's acid 'I have that within which passeth show' (1.2.85). But theatrically Polonius was right. After all, 'the trappings and the suits of woe' (1.2.86) do accurately communicate Hamlet's inner state to the audience, not only because of their normal social significance, but because theatrically they contrast so strikingly with the celebratory royal wedding clothes of the other characters on stage with him.

Hamlet's apparel proclaims the man, but not the period. Although the plot (like the source story) belongs to an epoch many centuries before, when England paid tribute to Denmark, the characters wear Elizabethan clothes. On early modern stages, the immediate legibility of clothing, an audience's ability to read the social and emotional meaning of sartorial signs,

1 A contemporary drawing of *Titus Andronicus*, by Henry Peacham.

mattered more than archaeological accuracy. Given the importance of Latin
to Elizabethan education, many spectators might be expected to know a
little about the ancient classical world, but in *Julius Caesar* antique Romans
anachronistically wear modern hats, doublets, cloaks, nightgowns, kerchiefs
and braces (and hear clocks strike). A drawing of *Titus Andronicus*, probably
made between 1604 and 1615, shows Titus in laurel crown, tunic, toga, and
sandals, holding a ceremonial spear; but everyone else is in 'modern dress'.
The principle unifying these eclectic vestments is instant intelligibility: a few
signs that say 'ancient Rome', others that say 'queen', 'soldier', 'prisoner',
'Moor'.

The other striking feature of this drawing is a complete absence of background. *Titus* was performed by London actors in the household of Sir John
Harington, at Burley-on-the-Hill in Rutland, on 1 January 1596; an eye-
witness wrote that 'the spectacle has more value than the subject'.[3] But in
Shakespeare and Peele's play 'the spectacle' was provided entirely by actors.
One man's costume illustrates the grandeur that was Rome; one man's skin
colour displays the exoticism of a far-flung empire; 'others as many as can
be' (according to the stage direction at 1.1.69) carry as many halberds and
swords as possible, dozens representing legions. Writing masques for the
royal court, Ben Jonson could summon up dazzling scenes and machines,
but that forced him to collaborate, not once or twice but continually, with
the architect Inigo Jones; eventually the scenewright dominated and displaced the playwright. By contrast, Shakespeare, an actor himself, wrote for
a company of actors.

The centrality of the actor

Actors did not have to compete with scenery; actors *were* scenery. Scenery that moved. In *Othello*, a handkerchief passes from an Egyptian to Othello's mother to Othello to his wife Desdemona to her servant Emilia to her husband Iago to his fellow-soldier Cassio to his mistress Bianca, then back to Cassio; early modern relationships were traced, on stage and off, by movements of cloth. But actors described and executed those movements. They carried the handkerchief. For the final scene a bed must be 'thrust out' on to the stage or 'discovered' behind an arras, but the Folio stage direction reads simply *'Enter Othello, and Desdemona in her bed'* (5.2.0), subordinating the bed to the entrance of Desdemona, as though the furniture were a servant or an accessory. Desdemona enters wearing a bed, just as she wears a nightgown.

Both the bed and the nightgown emphasise Desdemona's vulnerability; they signal the intimacy of a private space where she should be safe, and thereby contribute to the pathos of the actor's performance, described by that eye-witness in Oxford. Actors were not only scenery that physically moved, they were scenery that moved emotionally. Thomas Nashe, in the earliest description of audiences' responses to a play at least partly by Shakespeare, claimed in 1592 that the death of Talbot in *The First Part of Henry the Sixth* elicited 'the tears of ten thousand spectators at least'. Forty years later, an encomiast claimed that a spectator, watching Shakespeare's characters on stage, 'Joys in their joy, and trembles at their rage', crediting Shakespeare with an ability 'To steer th'affections'.[4] The early modern playwright, according to his contemporaries, was an engineer of affect. The King's Men played *Othello*, the Oxford eye-witness tells us, 'with enormous applause to full houses'. Despite the disapproval of preachers and city authorities, despite the risk of physical infection or moral corruption, people flocked to see plays; by one estimate, there were perhaps 50 million individual visits to the commercial theatres between 1580 and 1642. People were willing to pay to have their feelings artificially stimulated by fictions. Plays did that better than other texts, in part because, as Francis Bacon observed, 'the minds of men in company are more open to affections and impressions than when alone'.[5] When full, an amphitheatre like the Globe may have contained as many as 3,000 spectators, each contributing to the emotional feedback loop described by Bacon. For the first time in human history, the early modern theatre capitalised, and routinised, the commodification of emotion.

Consequently, Shakespeare's most often quoted line, in early modern England, was not Hamlet's intellectual meditative 'To be or not to be' but Richard III's passionate, desperate 'A horse, a horse, my kingdom for a horse!' One witness reports that 'Burbage cried' out this line; another writes of the actor/character 'in his heat of passion . . . troubled many ways, crying' out the words. Like the elegy which remembers Burbage's performance of 'kind Lear, the grieved Moor', such testimony confirms the emotional emphasis and power of Burbage's acting style.[6] But it also confirms the centrality of the actor. 'Sit in a full theatre', Sir Thomas Overbury wrote, 'and you will think you see so many lines drawn from the circumference of so many ears, whiles the actor is the centre.'[7] As soon as Shakespeare completed a full draft of the script, it would have been copied and parcelled out as a collection of 'parts' for individual actors to read and memorise; rather than a copy of the whole play, each actor received only a text of his own speeches, and the cues for them. Presumably the longest parts, like Burbage's, were copied first, so that the actors with the most to memorise could begin the soonest.

The centrality of the actor produced a corresponding centrality of character. Shakespeare wrote texts which he expected to circulate, not in the form of printed books, but as parts, minimally linked components organised by role – not acts, scenes, locations, plots or subplots, but roles for individual actors, actors who would focus on their own responsibilities and opportunities, and trust others to take care of the rest. Not surprisingly, Shakespeare was most admired for his creation of characters: he was, primarily, the creator of Falstaff (a.k.a. Oldcastle), rather than the author of something called *The History of Henry the Fourth*. The memory of Burbage was inextricably bound to a set of individual fictional persons: Richard III, Lear, Othello, Hamlet.

> Oft have I seen him leap into the grave –
> Suiting the person (which he seemed to have)
> Of a sad lover with so true an eye
> That there I would have sworn he meant to die . . .

By about 1600, acting was no longer considered a mere subcategory of oratory, but an art of 'personation'; Thomas Heywood's *Apology for Actors* demanded that a good actor should 'qualify everything according to the nature of the person personated'.[8]

Burbage was emotionally moving, but he was also constantly in motion. Performances were regulated backstage by a 'plat', which reduced each play to its spine, a series of necessary entrances. Actors had to get on to the stage at the right moment, from the right direction; once on stage, an actor might remain still, but to get off stage he had to move again, and any intervening stillness stood out partly by contrast with the fundamental law of flow. Props therefore had to be portable, carried on and off the stage in the same movements that brought actors on and off.

Laws of perpetual motion governed more than the structure of performance. For Shakespeare's working life, every day the acting company would
perform a different play; even the most popular plays would normally be
performed only once a week; the first recorded 'long run', Middleton's
A Game at Chess in August 1624, ran for nine consecutive days – an achievement so remarkable it was trumpeted on title pages. Plays, like actors, had
their exits and their entrances.

Revivals and reputations

Many of Shakespeare's plays remained in the repertory of the King's Men
for years. But revivals were no more static than any other aspect of playing.
Actors retired, or died, and had to be replaced; boy actors grew up. Costumes wore out, or ceased to be appropriately fashionable. Worcester's Men,
reviving the collaborative play *Sir John Oldcastle* in 1602–3, paid £15 10s
for new costumes – more than six times what they paid for revisions and
additions to the text.

But they did pay for changes to the text. 'New additions' were regularly
attached to popular old plays, like Kyd's *Spanish Tragedy*; any play that
stayed in the repertory long enough would almost certainly be subject to
textual change. Shakespeare himself added a scene to the original version of
Titus Andronicus. In 1606, Parliament passed a law 'to restrain the abuses
of players', which set heavy fines for actors who uttered the name of God on
stage; Shakespeare's earlier plays had been full of profanity, as defined by that
statute, and had to be retrospectively purged in revivals. Beginning in 1609,
older plays, designed for uninterrupted performance, had to be provided
with appropriate act breaks. In the edition of *A Midsummer Night's Dream*
published in 1600, the action is uninterrupted from the entrance of Lysander
(3.2.412.2) to the exit of Bottom (4.1.211.1), 263 lines later; in the 1623
edition, the play is divided into five acts, and an extra stage direction is added
at 3.2.460.1, just before the beginning of act 4, specifying that *'They sleep
all the Act'* (meaning, through the act interval). Shakespeare may or may
not have been responsible for this change, but he apparently did, in about
1610, revise the text of *King Lear* for a revival, and that revision includes
added act breaks. The added interval before what became act 4 coincides
with omission of the dialogue between two servants that originally ended
3.7; that dialogue was no longer needed, because the interval gave the actor
playing Gloucester time to exit, change clothes, put plasters on his eyes, and
re-enter at 4.1.6.1. Shakespeare could therefore end the scene (and the act)
with the devastating spectacle of Gloucester's blind exit while servants carry
out a corpse.

But after Shakespeare retired and died, any changes for revivals would have to be scripted by someone else. The King's Men appear to have hired Middleton to adapt *Macbeth*, in about 1616: two songs, the goddess Hecate and some spectacular effects were added, moving the play decisively in the direction of baroque opera – innovations later endorsed, and expanded, by Restoration adaptations. To make room for all the resulting extra parts for boy actors, the three witches were transformed from 'fair nymphs' (seen by play-goer Simon Forman in 1611) into the ambiguously gendered women-with-beards familiar to us, who can be played by adult actors. He was also probably responsible for cutting the play, giving it the elliptical tightness so characteristic of his own style (and so uncharacteristic of Shakespeare's more expansive dramatic style). Middleton's apparent success with *Macbeth* may have prompted the King's Men to hire him again, in 1621, to adapt *Measure for Measure*: he expanded the city comedy parts of Lucio, Overdone and Pompey, and transformed a play apparently originally set in Italy into one located in Vienna at the outset of the Thirty Years' War. He also reshaped the play's structure, originally intended for uninterrupted performance, to accommodate act intervals. He transposed the third and fourth scenes to end act 1 with suspense about Isabella's mission to Angelo; he also divided the play's original long central scene into two scenes, transposing two of the Duke's speeches, and adding the song and initial dialogue that begins act 4.[9]

Of course, no company would go to the expense of reviving a play unless it had once been popular, and might be popular again. Judging by allusions to his work, Jonson was the playwright most widely admired by critics in the seventeenth century, but he was only intermittently successful in the theatres. Judging by the number of reprints in the period 1580 to 1660, Shakespeare wrote nothing as popular as Kyd's *Spanish Tragedy*, Marlowe's *Doctor Faustus*, or the anonymous *Mucedorus*. He did write two of the ten bestselling plays (but so did Heywood). Shakespeare's most popular plays, in descending order, were apparently *1 Henry IV*, *Richard III*, *Pericles*, *Hamlet*, *Richard II* and *Romeo and Juliet*. With the exception of *Pericles* (a collaboration with Wilkins), all of these were written between 1593–4 (*Richard III*) and 1600–1 (*Hamlet*). During that period – when Marlowe, Kyd and Greene were dead, but Jonson, Middleton and Fletcher had not yet replaced them – Shakespeare was undoubtedly London's dominant playwright.

But that dominance did not last. The waning of his theatrical clout can be measured, in part, by the history of performances at court. In the Christmas season of 1604/5, seven plays by Shakespeare, and two by Jonson, entertained the royal family. This is the high-water mark of Shakespeare's popularity, accurately reflecting his theatrical dominance in the last decade of Elizabeth I's reign. In the scanty records of the next five years, the one known

Shakespeare play at court (*King Lear*) is matched by one known Middleton play (*A Trick to Catch the Old One*). In 1611/12, Shakespeare gets two, but so does Fletcher; in 1612/13, Shakespeare gets nine, and Fletcher eight, in addition to their first collaboration, *Cardenio*. Shakespeare's last three plays (*Cardenio, Henry VIII/All Is True*, and *Two Noble Kinsmen*) were co-written with Fletcher, handing the baton to his younger rival and obvious successor. Records for the next few years are scant, but after 1619 Fletcher was consistently more popular: fourteen recorded court performances (to Shakespeare's three) in the 1620s, thirty-one (to Shakespeare's ten) from 1630 to 1642. When the King's Men performed *The Taming of the Shrew* and then Fletcher's feminist reply to it, *The Tamer Tamed*, at court on 26 and 28 November 1633, Shakespeare's play was merely 'liked', but Fletcher's 'very well liked'.

Fletcher's dominance, established by 1620, continued for the rest of the seventeenth century, and not only at court. In the three decades after 1632, ten Shakespeare plays were reprinted, each in a single quarto; but Fletcher's *Comedies and Tragedies* were published in folio, and eighteen individual plays appeared in thirty-eight different quartos. In the 1640s and 1650s, actors trying to defy the parliamentary closure of the theatres reached for Fletcher, not Shakespeare. In London, five different attempts to reopen the theatres between 1647 and 1654 showcased Fletcher. No one was willing to take such risks for a play by Shakespeare. When the actors and the King did finally return, in 1660, two different companies performed seventeen revivals of Fletcher, but only four of Shakespeare.

But the Restoration is another chapter. This chapter of the relationship between Shakespeare's plays and the stage ends, instead, with small groups of itinerate actors, like those common in Shakespeare's childhood, scratching a living from minimalist performances in rowdy fairgrounds, halls and taverns. Deprived of their proud and ornate London theatres, in the lean years between 1642 and 1660 the acting companies reverted to their vagabond heritage, performing what Francis Kirkman called 'pieces of plays', excerpts of the most popular scenes from old reliables. Of the twenty-six such 'drolls' Kirkman collected, the greatest number (nine) came from the Fletcher canon, but Shakespeare did furnish three: 'The Merry Conceits of Bottom the Weaver', 'The Bouncing Knight', and 'The Grave-Makers'. All three came from plays – *A Midsummer Night's Dream, Henry the Fourth* and *Hamlet* – performed at court in the 1630s, suggesting that the court's taste in Shakespeare did not much differ from that of the general public. All three, too, come from Shakespeare's late Elizabethan glory days.

In the mid-1590s, a hand-picked company of professional actors, performing *A Midsummer Night's Dream* in their own large London theatre, had demonstrated their confident virtuosity by mocking the incompetence of amateur thespians. By the 1650s that dream was in pieces. In 'The Merry Conceits of Bottom the Weaver', nothing was left of Shakespeare's play but the scenes featuring the 'hard-handed men that work' in the city (5.1.72), and those were described as having been 'lately, privately, presented by several apprentices for their harmless recreation, with great applause'.[10] The mechanicals had taken over.

NOTES

1 Gāmini Salgādo (ed.), *Eyewitnesses to Shakespeare: First-Hand Accounts of Performances, 1590–1890* (London: Sussex University Press, 1975), 30.

2 Ernest Schanzer, 'Thomas Platter's Observations on the Elizabethan Stage', *Notes and Queries* 201 (1956), 465–7.

3 Gustav Ungerer, 'An Unrecorded Elizabethan Performance of *Titus Andronicus*', *Shakespeare Studies* 14 (1961), 102.

4 See Gary Taylor, 'Feeling Bodies' in *Shakespeare in the Twentieth Century: Proceedings of the Sixth World Shakespeare Congress*, ed. Jonathan Bate *et al.* (Newark: University of Delaware Press and London: Associated University Presses, 1998), 259.

5 Francis Bacon, *The Proficience and Advancement of Learning, Divine and Human* (1605), II, 13.

6 C. C. Stopes, *Burbage and Shakespeare's Stage* (London, 1913), 118.

7 'An excellent Actor' in Sir Thomas Overbury [and others], *His Wife. With Addition of ... divers more Characters* (1616), sig. M2.

8 Thomas Heywood, *Apology for Actors* (1612), sig. C4.

9 See Gary Taylor and John Jowett, *Shakespeare Reshaped*, 1606–1623 (Oxford: Oxford University Press, 1993), 107–236; Gary Taylor, 'Shakespeare's Mediterranean "Measure for Measure"', *Shakespeare and the Mediterranean*, ed. Thomas Clayton *et al.* (Newark: University of Delaware Press and London: Associated University Presses, forthcoming); and *Measure for Measure*, ed. John Jowett, in Thomas Middleton, *Collected Works*, general editor Gary Taylor (Oxford: Oxford University Press, forthcoming).

10 Gary Jay Williams, *Our Moonlight Revels: 'A Midsummer Night's Dream' in the Theatre* (Iowa City: University of Iowa Press, 1997), 38–40.

2

JEAN I. MARSDEN

Improving Shakespeare: from the Restoration to Garrick

After an eighteen-year hiatus theatres reopened in London in 1660, following the restoration of King Charles II. While the stages, audiences and taste of this age were markedly different from those for which Shakespeare wrote, his works were an important part of the theatrical corpus of the later seventeenth century, along with others by Ben Jonson and John Fletcher. In his diary, Samuel Pepys records numerous performances of Shakespeare's plays in the first years after the Restoration, including productions of *1 Henry IV* and *The Merry Wives of Windsor* within months of Charles II's return. From the 1660s through the end of the eighteenth century, Shakespeare's plays were a routine part of any theatre's offerings and made up a far larger proportion of the popular theatrical repertoire than they do today in London or New York. They appeared regularly every year, although not necessarily in a form that Shakespeare would have recognised. In particular, the Restoration staging of Shakespeare has become infamous for its creative reconfiguration of Shakespeare's plays, in which some tragedies are given happy endings and others made more tragic, while characters are eliminated – or added – to conform to contemporary taste, and in which entire scenes and acts are omitted, replaced in some cases by new scenes and rewritten dialogue.

London theatre after 1660

In the decades after the Restoration, performances not only of Shakespeare but of other early drama were determined as much by theatre politics as by popular preference. Two theatre companies, the Duke's and the King's, were awarded patents in 1660 to establish theatres in London, and as part of these patents, the stock of existing drama was divided between the two companies with each company having sole proprietorship of the plays allotted to it. The allotment of these 'old stock plays' was notably inequitable. Thomas Killigrew's King's Company received the bulk of Shakespeare's most popular plays, including *Othello*, *The Merry Wives of Windsor* and

Julius Caesar, along with almost all of Ben Jonson's plays. Sir William Davenant's Duke's Company managed to secure only *Hamlet* among the Shakespearean favourites. This unequal distribution may be one reason why many more of Shakespeare's plays were altered by the Duke's Company than by the King's; handed unfamiliar or seemingly outmoded plays, the Duke's Company sought ways to enliven and modernise its repertoire of old plays.

The changes to the Shakespearean text were not made out of contempt, or even out of a sense of Shakespeare's inferiority to new writers and modes. On the contrary, Shakespeare was almost universally revered by late seventeenth-century playwrights and critics. The common impression is perhaps most famously articulated by John Dryden in his *Essay of Dramatick Poesy* (1668), written in the first decade after the Restoration. Assessing Shakespeare's talents in comparison to the playwrights of ancient Greece and Rome, as well as contemporary France, Dryden wrote: '[Shakespeare] was the man who of all Modern and perhaps Ancient Poets, had the largest and most comprehensive soul. All the Images of Nature were still present to him, and he drew them not laboriously, but luckily: when he describes any thing, you more than see it, you feel it too', concluding that while he admired Jonson's learning, 'I love Shakespeare'.[1] The minor poet and satirist Robert Gould reiterated these sentiments, claiming that Shakespeare was 'more than Man', adding in a comparison to the greatest of classical poets, '*Homer* was blind, yet cou'd all Nature see; / *Thou* wer't unlearn'd, yet knew as much as *He*!'[2] By the time Gerard Langbaine wrote his *Account of the English Dramatick Poets* at the end of the seventeenth century, he could state: '[I] shall take the Liberty to speak my Opinion, as my predecessors have done, of his Works; which is this, That I esteem his Plays beyond any that have ever been published in our Language.'[3]

Despite their admiration for Shakespeare's genius, writers also admitted that his works were far from perfect and that his beauties were offset by a variety of 'faults'. The nature of these faults was to determine the form in which plays were staged and whether they were staged at all. Perhaps most immediate was the language in which Shakespeare wrote. Perceived by a new generation as barbarous and unrefined, it also contained an overabundance of figurative language, along with a tendency toward low humour and puns. As critics and playwrights observed, while Shakespeare's characters were natural, the words they spoke seemingly were not. In reality, people in the midst of passion, whether love, anger or joy, did not speak in strings of metaphors or explain their feelings by means of elaborate puns. *Macbeth*, *Richard II* and *Hamlet* were cited by Dryden, for example, as particularly egregious linguistic culprits, although when Dryden chooses a specific example of poor diction, he singles out the play-within-a-play in *Hamlet* as if unwilling to censure Shakespeare too harshly.[4]

As writers such as Dryden argued, the English language had been refined in the decades since Shakespeare's death; Shakespeare lived in a 'barbarous' age so it was no surprise that he wrote in an unpolished style. One effect of this disparagement of Shakespearean language was that playwrights felt free to replace his words with their own, more refined verse. Thus, many of the plays were trimmed of their figurative language before being staged. For example, the following speech from *Macbeth* loses what a late seventeenth-century audience might regard as unnecessarily obscure language.

> Come, seeling night,
> Scarf up the tender eye of pitiful day,
> And with thy bloody and invisible hand
> Cancel and tear to pieces that great bond
> Which keeps me pale. Light thickens,
> And the crow makes wing to th'rooky wood;
> Good things of day begin to droop and drowse,
> Whiles night's black agents to their preys do rouse.
> Thou marvell'st at my words, but hold thee still;
> Things bad begun, make strong themselves by ill.
>
> (3.2.46–55)

In Davenant's version, first staged in 1664, the speech appears in a much more straightforward form:

> Come dismal Night.
> Close up the Eye of the quick sighted Day
> With thy invisible and bloody hand.
> The Crow makes wing to the thick shady Grove,
> Whilst Night's black Agent's to their Prey make hast,
> Thou wonder'st at my Language, wonder still,
> Things ill begun strengthen themselves by ill.
>
> (3.3.47–54)

A second problem that was to affect the form in which Shakespeare's plays appeared on stage was the perceived moral and structural irregularity of his plotting. Following Jonson, writers praised Shakespeare as the poet of 'Nature', but commented that he lacked 'Art', in particular that his plays did not follow the so-called 'mechanical rules' or unities derived from Aristotle and espoused by French neoclassical writers. The rules specified that drama should maintain a unity of action (i.e., avoid unrelated subplots that could dilute the tragic effect), a unity of place and a unity of time, usually a 24-hour span. While Shakespeare's failure to follow these rules in most of his plays

(*Merry Wives* and *The Tempest* are notable exceptions) was easily excused because of his supposed lack of learning, these defects were often, although not always, corrected when the plays were staged. The sprawling plots of plays such as *Richard III* or *King Lear* were trimmed and extraneous characters eliminated, while in some cases egregious irregularities such as the sixteen-year gap between acts 3 and 4 in *The Winter's Tale* and the multiple changes of scene between Rome and Egypt in *Antony and Cleopatra* may have contributed to the plays not being staged. Even more problematic was Shakespeare's failure to observe poetic justice, the practice of rewarding virtuous characters and punishing wicked ones. The most notorious case of this misplaced justice was found in *King Lear*, where the virtuous Cordelia dies needlessly, although similar objections were made to other plays, such as *Troilus and Cressida*, in which, Dryden observes, 'Cressida is false, and is not punish'd'.[5] Serious drama should instruct as well as delight, and poetic justice reiterated to spectators the lesson that they too were subject to the same divine justice. Not to observe this moral law could lead to charges that drama was immoral.

In addition, Shakespeare's plays needed to be adapted to suit the theatres of late seventeenth-century London. The first theatres to open after the Restoration were small in comparison to the large public theatres of the Renaissance, with both companies originally converting tennis courts into stages before moving into somewhat larger quarters in the 1670s. These theatres, despite their size, were not unsophisticated. Sir William Davenant, manager of the Duke's Company, soon installed elements of the early seventeenth-century court stage such as movable scenery and machines, which allowed for special effects such as flying entrances and exits, waves for sea scenes and clouds for storms. While such spectacular effects were not essential for success, they did attract audiences, and managers and playwrights incorporated them into drama both old and new whenever possible (and affordable). Writing in 1708 of Davenant's *Macbeth*, first staged more than forty years earlier, early theatre historian John Downes describes the popularity and profitability that the use of spectacle in all its forms could confer. The play, 'being drest in all it's Finery, as new Cloath's, new Scenes, Machines, as flyings for the Witches; with all the Singing and Dancing in it . . . it being all Excellently perform'd, being in the nature of an Opera, it Recompenc'd double the Expence; it proves still a lasting Play.'[6]

The most important development in late seventeenth-century theatre, however, was the introduction of women on the stage, which occurred within months of the theatres reopening in July 1660. Actresses had played on the Continent for decades, and England's new ruler, who had spent years in exile, encouraged the patent companies to allow women's parts to be played by women. One of the earliest recorded appearances of an actress occurred on 8 December 1660. The play was Shakespeare's *Othello*, and a prologue announced, 'I saw the Lady drest; / The Woman plays to day: mistake me not / No Man in Gown, or Page in Petty-Coat.'[7] As these lines indicate, the practice of having women play women's roles was noteworthy and even exciting to a Restoration audience. Actresses quickly became an important part of a production's marketability; they were as much a part of theatrical spectacle as the fine scenery and special effects that the new playhouses allowed. As a result, substantial roles for actresses were essential in new plays, and the works of Renaissance playwrights were altered to introduce more female characters and to increase the importance of those women already present. Thus, in Thomas Shadwell's version of *Timon of Athens* (1678), Timon is provided with two mistresses while in Davenant's *Macbeth,* Lady Macduff assumes as much importance as Lady Macbeth, even though she appears in only one scene of Shakespeare's tragedy.[8]

Adapting Shakespeare's texts

These elements combined to shape the staging and inevitable alteration of Shakespeare's plays. Respect for Shakespeare's genius and his abilities as a playwright made his plays popular; however, in part because his language was seen as outdated and overly extravagant, the text of his plays was not considered inviolable. His plays, along with those of other Renaissance playwrights, could be altered to fit the demands of a different theatre and the tastes of a different audience. As a result, many, although not all, of Shakespeare's plays were rewritten. These adaptations accommodated the new theatres' technical capabilities as well as the later seventeenth century's theories of drama and topical issues such as contemporary politics and even the talents of specific actors and actresses.[9]

A key figure in these early productions was Sir William Davenant, playwright and manager of the company most associated with visual effects such as the use of scenery and special effects. Davenant was interested in increasing the spectacular possibilities of English drama and thus bringing it more in line with the theatre of the Continent; the changes he introduced into his Lincoln's Inn Fields theatre were popular with the small audience in the early years after the Restoration, and whenever possible he incorporated these components into the old plays revived and adapted for the stage. Although his company had been granted few of the popular 'old plays', Davenant was quick to modernise the plays he was allotted. He wrote one of the earliest Shakespeare adaptations, combining *Much Ado About Nothing*'s 'gay couple' of Beatrice and Benedick with the serious plot of *Measure for Measure* as *The Law Against Lovers* (1662). Such a conflation moved Shakespeare's comedy closer in style to the new plays being written by playwrights in the 1660s. The following year, he produced *Henry VIII* with magnificent new costumes, scenery and pageants, with the result that the play became the benchmark for subsequent uses of spectacle in the theatre.[10] A year later, Davenant revised *Macbeth*, adding spectacular new scenes of witches flying and singing to showcase the technical capabilities of his theatre. He achieved his greatest success with the adaptation of *The Tempest*, written with John Dryden and first staged in 1667. Like *The Law Against Lovers* and *Macbeth*, this new *Tempest* greatly increased the number of female roles: both Ariel and Caliban have mates, while Miranda has a sister. In addition, Prospero secretly cares for a male ward, a man, who, in an inversion of Miranda, has never seen a woman. This male role was customarily played by an actress, in one of the popular breeches roles which provided another kind of spectacle for theatre audiences by revealing the legs of actresses. The play also featured a variety of visual effects such as storms, showers of fire and spirits who appear and disappear. Thomas Shadwell subsequently fashioned an operatic version of the Davenant–Dryden adaptation, adding several songs, devils who sing under the stage, and a spectacular conclusion with Neptune, Amphritite, Oceanus and Tethys in a 'Chariot drawn with Sea-horses; on each side of the Chariot, Sea-gods and Goddesses, Titons and Nereides'. Aeolus appears and summons the four winds, and the *'Scene changes to the Rising Sun, and a number of Aerial Spirits in the Air, Ariel flying from the Sun.'* Finally, Ariel and the spirits sing 'Where the bee sucks there suck I' while hovering in mid-air. Enormously successful, this extravaganza was revived repeatedly throughout the later seventeenth century and into the early decades of the eighteenth.

Many playwrights experimented with adapting Shakespeare's plays in the final decades of the seventeenth century. In addition to *The Tempest*, Dryden revised *Troilus and Cressida* (1678), making the ending clearly tragic (both protagonists die), and revising Cressida's character so that she only appears to be false; she feigns love to Diomede in order to help her father. Dryden also used the story of Shakespeare's *Antony and Cleopatra* as the basis for his regularised drama of love and honour, *All for Love, or, the World Well Lost* (1677). While not an adaptation, this retelling of *Antony and Cleopatra* was more popular than Shakespeare's play and replaced it on the stage through most of the eighteenth century.[11] Thomas Otway, the playwright who was described as next to Shakespeare in his ability to move the passions, mingled the romantic tragedy of *Romeo and Juliet* with a dark picture of partisan politics in Rome. In *The History and Fall of Caius Marius* (1679), the inherent instability of a republic destroys the star-crossed lovers, an interpolation which played to great success in the political turmoil of the late 1670s. But Otway's most enduring contribution to the staging of Shakespeare occurred in the play's final act. Rather than follow Shakespeare and leave Romeo to die before Juliet awakens from her drugged sleep, he enlarges the scene so that after Romeo drinks the poison, Juliet awakens, and the two lovers bid each other a heart-rending farewell. This amendment was to remain in the staging of *Romeo and Juliet* for almost 200 years.[12] When Theophilus Cibber revived *Romeo and Juliet* in 1744, he retained Otway's version of the tomb scene, and Garrick used it as the basis for his own adaptation of the scene. Otway's addition emphasises pathos, recasting *Romeo and Juliet* not simply as political tragedy but as the personal, domestic drama for which he would become famous. Through the use of pathos, tragedies such as *Caius Marius* appealed to private emotion rather than the public heroics prominent in the serious drama of the previous decade; this more intimate drama was to become the dominant mode of tragedy by the end of the seventeenth century.

Productions of Shakespeare were inevitably affected not only by new forms of drama such as domestic tragedy, but by topical issues such as politics, especially at times such as the early 1680s when governmental crises loomed and the theatres suffered financially. Chief among these crises was contention over who would succeed Charles II as king. Although the father of numerous illegitimate children, Charles had no legitimate descendants, leaving his Catholic brother James as heir presumptive. Protestant forces in Parliament sought to exclude James from the throne. Anxiety about the succession was heightened by the so-called Popish Plot, a supposed conspiracy led by Catholics to overthrow the government. In the years between 1678 and 1682, when fears of Catholicism and another civil war shook England, the number of adaptations increased markedly, as playwrights found fertile ground in Shakespeare's histories and tragedies for commentary on the politics of the time. These adaptations use Shakespeare's plays to emphasise the anguish of civil war and the disasters that can result from the attacks of political factions. Edward Ravenscroft's *Titus Andronicus* (1678), for example, stays close to Shakespeare's plot, yet becomes topical by emphasising the horrible end of plotting and perjury, thus linking his play to the Popish Plot and the subsequent trial of Titus Oates, events which had occurred just months before. John Crowne used the trappings of horror common to much tragedy of the late 1670s to shape his adaptations of the *Henry VI* plays. *The Misery of Civil War* (1680) and *Henry the Sixth, the First Part. With the Murder of Humphrey Duke of Gloster* (1681) graphically display the evils of civil war brought on by rebellious factions and the dangers of a court filled with Catholic advisors. One scene opens with a pointed representation of the consequences of civil war, consequences still vivid in public memory, as the scene opens revealing a gruesome backdrop, '*Houses and Towns burning, Men and Women hang'd upon Trees, and Children on the top of Pikes*' (*Misery of Civil War*, p. 36). Similarly, Otway's *Caius Marius* portrays the chaos which factions and political ambition cause in private life, and Nahum Tate's *The Ingratitude of a Common-Wealth* (1682), an adaptation of *Coriolanus*, shows the dangers of a commonwealth where factions seduce the multitude, resulting in bloodshed, suffering and the eventual destruction not of Rome but of the faction itself. Alone among the adaptors, Thomas Shadwell, a staunch Whig, represents a bloodless and triumphant rebellion in his *Timon of Athens*.[13]

In most cases, the overtly political tragedy of the Exclusion Crisis died with the age, and plays such as Crowne's versions of *Henry VI* were rarely revived.[14] One play from this period that did endure was Nahum Tate's now notorious adaptation of *King Lear* (1681). Tate, a minor playwright and poet, later Poet Laureate, became infamous to later generations by providing Shakespeare's bleakest tragedy with a happy ending, but in many ways Tate's *Lear* epitomises the late seventeenth-century approach to Shakespeare. It clarifies the play's moral debate by reshaping the plot to conform to the expectations of poetic justice, expands the role of its central female characters – in the process increasing both the pathos and titillation value of the drama (Edmund tries to rape Cordelia and is seen in amorous dalliance with both Regan and Goneril) – and infuses the action with contemporary political debates. As Tate explains in his preface, he saw Shakespeare's tragedy as incomplete, 'a Heap of Jewels, unstrung and unpolist', yet 'dazling' nonetheless. His goal, as he explains it, was to 'restring' these jewels in a more acceptable form: ''T was my good Fortune to light on one Expedient to rectifie what was wanting in the Regularity and Probability of the Tale, which was to run through the whole, a Love betwixt Edgar and Cordelia, that never chang'd word with each other in the Original.'

Tate uses this interpolated love story to tie together Shakespeare's more loosely woven plot lines and to provide clear motivation for Cordelia, whose seemingly heartless lines to her father in the play's opening act seemed to him unnecessarily harsh. In Tate's version, Cordelia says 'nothing' because to say otherwise might force her into a loveless marriage. More conspicuously, Tate rewards his lovers with a happy ending, thus satisfying both poetic justice and the politics of the age. Lear and Cordelia both live at the ending of Tate's *Lear*, and the play celebrates 'the King's blest Restauration' (5.6.119), an appropriate sentiment in a play which substitutes an unsuccessful civil war for Shakespeare's successful French invasion, a touchy subject always, but especially so during the later seventeenth century, given the general anxiety concerning Charles II's close ties with France. Tate's new ending also assuaged uneasiness over *King Lear's* bleak final act, in which the virtuous perish along with the vicious, seemingly by chance. This violation of the laws of poetic and celestial justice shocked audiences and even readers; even as other elements of Tate's adaptation were removed from the stage, no theatre manager in the Restoration or eighteenth century replaced the happy ending with Shakespeare's final act. It is worth remembering Samuel Johnson's comment in his 1765 edition of Shakespeare that 'I was many years ago so shocked by Cordelia's death, that I know not whether I ever endured to read again the last scenes of the play until I undertook to revise them as an editor.'[15] Concluding triumphantly that 'Truth and Vertue shall at last succeed' (5.6.161), Tate's version allows Lear to regain his sanity and live, while Edgar and Cordelia marry and rule the kingdom.

Betterton and Cibber

In the early 1680s London's two patent companies were forced to unite, sharply reducing the number and variety of plays being staged. With the country caught in the political turmoil of the Exclusion Crisis, theatre attendance dropped, and for more than a decade London was limited to a single acting company. This situation continued until 1695, when Thomas Betterton, the greatest actor of his age, seceded from the United Company along with a number of other actors and set up a rival company in a small, older theatre at Lincoln's Inn Fields. Not having a cache of plays at his disposal, Betterton turned to Shakespeare's works to build up the repertoire of his company, reviving several plays not staged since the early seventeenth century. So strong was his reliance on Shakespeare that in a comparison of the two theatre companies, Charles Gildon represents Betterton as praying to Shakespeare for guidance, concluding '*Shakespear*'s Ghost was rais'd at the New-house, and he seem'd to inhabit it for ever.'[16] While Betterton was nearing the end of his long and distinguished career as the new century began, Colley Cibber, who would ultimately, like Betterton, become a manager as well as an actor, was just beginning his. Although one of the most influential figures in eighteenth-century theatre, Cibber is best known to Shakespeareans for his adaptation of *Richard III* (1699), the longest lived of all the Restoration and eighteenth-century adaptations of Shakespeare. Lines of Cibber, such as the famous 'Off with his head. So much for Buckingham' (4.4.188) and sometimes even the entire Cibber text survived throughout the nineteenth century and into the mid-twentieth century.[17] Cibber's *Richard III* is a streamlined version of the Shakespearean original, with numerous characters eliminated (including such major figures as Queen Margaret and Clarence), scenes transposed and material introduced from other plays. The result is a play that focuses closely on the central figure of Richard, a role Cibber himself played for many years.

Although adaptations such as those of *Richard III* and *King Lear* remained a standard part of theatre repertoires until well into the nineteenth century, opposition began to grow in the early decades of the eighteenth century. Joseph Addison was one of the first to condemn the rewriting of Shakespeare's plays, writing in *The Spectator* that '*King Lear* is an admirable Tragedy . . . as *Shakespeare* wrote it; but as it is reformed according to the chymerical Notion of poetical Justice in my humble Opinion it has lost half its Beauty.'[18] The play's beauty, he finds, lies in the 'pleasing Anguish' its tragic catastrophe provides and in the 'serious Composure of Thought' with which the audience leaves the theatre. Addison's views were to become increasingly popular in the coming decades, although they would not have the effect of stopping the adaptation of Shakespeare or of forcing the most popular altered plays off the stage. While audiences might agree with Thomas Wilkes that Tate's 'catastrophe sends away all the spectators exalting with gladness' (Wilkes, *General History of the Stage*, 31), others began to find the very act of altering Shakespeare problematic. Samuel Richardson, for example, attacked not only Tate's *Lear* but the entire practice of rewriting Shakespeare, commenting in the postscript to his novel *Clarissa*, 'Yet so different seems to be the Modern Taste from that of the Antients, that the altered *King Lear* of Mr Tate is constantly acted on the English Stage, in preference to the Original, tho' written by Shakespeare himself' (p. 1497). Richardson's words articulate concerns that would increasingly shape not only the general perception of Shakespeare and his reputation, but ultimately the form in which his plays were staged. Commenting in horror that Tate's *Lear* rather than Shakespeare's appears on the 'English' stage, he hints that Shakespeare is associated with an innate Englishness. This attitude became commonplace as Shakespeare was increasingly seen as the English national poet, England's answer to Homer. This nationalist loyalty sanctifies Shakespeare's 'original' works, so that even barbarous words and questionable justice are better than the more refined interpolations of an adaptor.

The eighteenth century

By the early decades of the eighteenth century more of Shakespeare's unaltered works were appearing on the stage. Sparked in part by Betterton's revivals and in part by the growing availability of Shakespeare in the editions of Rowe, Pope and Theobald, increasing numbers of plays were staged in the early decades of the eighteenth century, often advertised as 'not acted' in many years.[19] By mid-century almost every play had appeared on stage, however briefly, and almost inevitably played to a full house. Audience demand played an important role in these revivals, most notably that of the so-called Shakespeare Ladies Club.[20] Playbills for these productions announce that the plays are staged 'at the Desire of several Ladies of Quality', and prologues to the plays laud the ladies for returning Shakespeare's 'manly genius' to the stage, in contrast to the effeminate and un-English productions of Italian opera, which had taken London by storm in the first decades of the century. Shakespeare revivals were at their height in the 1740/41 season, when almost one in four of the plays staged in London was by Shakespeare.

By the 1740s the nature of the debate over Shakespeare and the staging of his plays had changed. Theatrical competition was increasingly expressed not in terms of including 'new scenes' or song and dance numbers, but rather in terms of who could restore the most Shakespeare to the stage. David Garrick, for example, claims in one prologue, ''Tis my chief Wish, my Joy, my only Plan, / To lose no Drop of this immortal man.' (Ironically, this prologue introduced Garrick's version of *The Winter's Tale*, which omitted the first three acts of that play.) In practice adaptations continued to be staged and even written. In their public rhetoric, however, theatres used the idea of restoring Shakespeare, of bringing more of his original text to the stage, as both a marketing ploy and a means of attacking rival actors and managers. Thus, Theophilus Cibber attacks Garrick not for his acting but for his meddling with Shakespeare's text, writing with hyperbolic indignation, 'Were *Shakespeare*'s Ghost to rise, wou'd he not frown Indignation on this pilfering Pedlar in Poetry who thus shamefully mangles, mutilates, and emasculates his plays? . . . Rouse *Britons*, rouse, for shame.'[21] The prospect of 'mutilating' and thus 'emasculating' Shakespeare by altering his text would never have occurred to the playwrights of the later seventeenth century. In contrast to the earlier plays, which revised Shakespeare in order to reflect contemporary politics, Cibber implies that meddling with Shakespeare represents an unpatriotic act, one that should arouse the indignation of all good British citizens. His words, like those of Richardson, reveal the extent to which Shakespeare had become accepted as England's native genius, an assumption that shaped not only the response to Shakespeare's works but also the way in which they appeared on the stage.

Garrick

The figure most strongly connected with restoring Shakespeare, and also with the image of Shakespeare itself, was David Garrick, actor, theatre manager and playwright. From his first performance in London as Richard III, Garrick self-consciously associated himself with Shakespeare, the writer he would later describe as 'the god of our idolatry'.[22] Many of his most famous roles were Shakespearean (Hamlet, Lear, Richard III, Romeo), and he literally dedicated himself and his theatre to the performance of Shakespeare's works, claiming in his prologue for the opening of Drury Lane in September 1750 that 'Sacred to Shakespeare was this spot design'd / To pierce the heart and humanize the mind.' One aspect of his homage to England's native genius involved staging a variety of Shakespeare plays, although frequently in altered versions. In this way, Garrick could bill himself as 'restorer' of Shakespeare on the large scale. Much to the annoyance of his enemies, Garrick was able to present himself as the saviour of Shakespeare's immortal words in these adaptations, even as he presented a text that was not necessarily Shakespearean. In his dual role as adaptor and restorer, Garrick could both produce a play that appealed to the tastes of his audience and appear to score a point for England's literary heritage, most nobly represented in Shakespeare. So strongly was Garrick associated with Shakespeare in the public mind that upon Garrick's death, in 1779, Shakespeare's image was represented by poet Samuel Jackson Pratt as watching over Garrick while his characters paid their final respects to his corpse.[23]

A prolific adaptor of Shakespeare as well as other playwrights,[24] Garrick produced nearly a dozen Shakespeare adaptations during his years at Drury Lane. In them Garrick shares his contemporaries' concern for restoring the Shakespearean text; while he altered the plays he revived, sometimes drastically, Garrick could still claim to return more 'Shakespeare' to the stage. Among his most popular adaptations were abbreviated versions of several plays that had been staged only occasionally over the preceding eighty years. One was his version of *The Winter's Tale*, which avoided the disconcerting sixteen-year gap between acts 3 and 4 by adding a narrative segment. Although entitled *Florizel and Perdita*, the play's emphasis fell on Leontes, the role Garrick himself played. This three-act adaptation was usually paired with another of Garrick's abbreviated adaptations, this time of *The Taming of the Shrew*, which appeared as the two-act afterpiece *Catharine and Petruchio*. Other playwrights at other theatres produced similar condensed versions of Shakespeare, such as MacNamara Morgan's *Florizel and Perdita* (1754), a broadly comic musical afterpiece in which the Leontes–Hermione story disappears almost entirely in favour of Autolycus and the rural clowns. Theatre politics often decided which plays were staged and where; while Drury Lane staged Garrick's version of *The Winter's Tale*, Morgan's appeared at Covent Garden.

Another means by which Garrick and his contemporaries claimed to restore Shakespeare to the stage was by adapting earlier adaptations, replacing rewritten portions of the plays with more Shakespeare. By mid-century, most of the adaptations current in the later seventeenth century had vanished from the stage. Cibber's *Richard III* and Tate's *Lear* remained popular, but even the operatic *Tempest* declined in popularity and by 1760 was replaced by the original. Even though adaptations of *Lear* retained their hold in the theatres with the Tate ending accepted as a necessary denouement, both patent houses experimented with introducing more of Shakespeare's text into performance. Garrick trimmed, but did not eliminate, the Edgar–Cordelia love story, shifting emphasis once again on to Lear and his relationships with his daughters. At Covent Garden, George Colman combined the first four acts of Shakespeare's *Lear* with the final act of Tate. (Neither playwright considered reintroducing the Fool, who had been cut from all productions since the Restoration. The Fool, like other comic characters such as the Porter in *Macbeth* and the grave-digger in *Hamlet*, was considered too absurd and even buffoonish to belong in a serious play.)

Sentimental Shakespeare

Instead of emphasising the sensational, as so many early productions of Shakespeare had done, the mid-century productions, with their restoration of the Shakespearean text, stressed the sentimental, a movement that had begun with Otway's introduction of Romeo and Juliet's poignant parting in the tomb. In these productions the spectacle is emotion, not special effects. An emphasis on emotional connection shaped the performance of both old and new drama of the mid to later eighteenth century – we are feeling with, rather than laughing at or judging, the characters we see upon the stage. It was an age of sensibility in which the dominant modes of drama were sentimental or 'weeping' comedy and domestic tragedy. Actors were evaluated on their ability to move audiences, and Garrick in particular was known for his ability to elicit emotion; his strength as an actor was not grandeur, but feeling. One example of such expressive emotion was the famous start with which his Hamlet recognised the ghost of his father. Another, perhaps even more definitive, was the pathos he brought to his rendition of King Lear. Certainly audiences came to the theatre prepared to shed sympathetic tears. James Boswell, for example, wrote in his London journal that he arrived two hours early at the theatre in order to get a seat to see Garrick play Lear: 'I kept myself at a distance from all acquaintances, and got into a proper frame. Mr Garrick gave me the most perfect satisfaction. I was fully moved, and I shed abundance of tears.'[25]

As the play texts and reviews of the mid to later eighteenth century indicate, Shakespearean performances emphasised domestic rather than imperial concerns. Viewed through this lens, Shakespeare's plays could be interpreted as relating the fall of family men rather than kingly crises. Thus the public and political tragedy of Otway's *Caius Marius* was replaced by the private pathos of *Romeo and Juliet*. Acting texts from throughout the mid to later eighteenth century reveal that managers routinely trimmed plays in order to accentuate domestic relationships. The staging of *King Lear* presents perhaps the clearest example of the changed approach to performing Shakespeare. With Lear once again the central focus of the play, Garrick, the age's greatest Lear, portrayed him as a man driven mad by the ingratitude of his children. Lear's distress and hence his pathos arise from his position as father rather than his status as fallen king, with the result that *King Lear* becomes domestic drama rather than royal tragedy. Thus, the play's emotional impact is embodied in Lear's feelings towards his children rather than towards his crown, and Lear is driven by the cruelty of his two eldest daughters to madness, a family situation which, claimed Arthur Murphy, produced 'the finest tragic distress ever seen on any stage'.[26] Cordelia's moving devotion to her father, composed of a melange of Tate, Garrick and Shakespeare, was second only to Lear's calamities in its ability to move an audience to tears. If Tate's adaptation incorporates the Restoration's fascination with women in romantic distress, Garrick's *Lear* represents his age's love of sentiment in the form of daughterly devotion. Shakespeare's Cordelia may be devoted, but she never vows to bind her father's feet with her hair or bathe his cheeks with her tears. The end result of this accentuation of father–daughter bonds, both good and bad, was a tragedy highly praised for 'the fine pathetic that melts the heart in every scene' (Murphy).

This emotional family dynamic can be traced in many late eighteenth-century productions. Just as earlier playwrights had used the plays of Shakespeare, their near contemporary, as the foundation for works of their own, recasting his old works to conform to the taste of a new age, so too did the theatre managers of the later eighteenth century. While their productions may have been textually closer to Shakespeare's works as we know them, they also reinvented the plays, bringing them in line with the popular theatre of a new generation. For this audience, emotion was drama's central action, and they sought to sympathize with the characters they saw upon the stage. Actors, playwrights and managers found that these goals could be fulfilled by sentimentalising Shakespeare's comedies and recasting his tragedies as domestic drama.

Subsequent generations found such meddling sacrilegious, and in the nineteenth and twentieth centuries it was popular to belittle audiences of the Restoration and eighteenth century for their seeming indifference to Shakespeare's genius. These 'stage perversions of Shakespeare', it has been claimed, were 'the only way in which Shakespeare could be preserved for frivolous audiences'.[27] Such attitudes towards the period persist (as in a review, which described the adaptations as 'Darwinian mutants'), but our condemnation of these earlier audiences is surely somewhat premature. We have our own Shakespearean musicals (Cole Porter's *Kiss Me Kate*) and operas (Britten's *Midsummer Night's Dream*) as well as our own socially and politically relevant Shakespeare, whether it is the Freudian bed of Olivier's *Hamlet*, the postmodern, MTV *Romeo and Juliet* of Baz Luhrmann, or the visual fantasia of Peter Greenaway's *Prospero's Books*. Film has provided a new medium for representing Shakespeare, with its own demands of compression and its own opportunities for new and surprising special effects. In our own way, we may be closer to the Restoration than we are willing to think.

NOTES

1 John Dryden, *The Works of John Dryden*, ed. H. T. Swedenberg, Jr., *et al.* 20 vols. (Berkeley: University of California Press, 1956–), XVII, 55, 58.
2 Robert Gould, 'The Play-House. A Satyr' in *Poems Chiefly of Satyre and Satyric Epistle* (1689), 177.
3 Gerard Langbaine, *An Account of the English Dramatick Poets, or, Some Observations and Remarks on the Lives and Writings of all those that have Publish'd either Comedies, Tragedies, Tragi-Comedies, Pastorals, Masques, Interludes, Farces or Opera's in the English Tongue* (Oxford, 1691), 454.
4 See 'The Grounds of Criticism in Tragedy' (1679), prefixed to Dryden's adaptation of *Troilus and Cressida*.
5 Dryden, 'Preface' to *Troilus and Cressida* (1679), in *Works*, XII, 226.
6 John Downes, *Roscius Anglicanus; or, An Historical Review of the Stage* (1708), 33.
7 Thomas Jordan, 'Prologue' to *Othello*, in *A Nursery of Novelties in Variety of Poetry. Planted for the delightful leisures of Nobility and Ingenuity* [1665], 22.
8 For a more extended discussion of the influence of actresses, see chapter 9 below.
9 For example, John Lacy, actor and playwright, was well known for his character roles playing Scots and Irishmen, and his *Sawney the Scot* reconstructs *The Taming of the Shrew* with a Scottish tinge, substituting Sawney (Lacy) for Petruchio's servant Grumio.
10 On 27 January 1664, Pepys mentions Dryden and Howard's *The Indian Queen*, 'which for show, they say, exceeds *Henry the 8th*'. *The Diary of Samuel Pepys* (1660–8), ed. Robert Latham and William Matthews, 11 vols. (Berkeley: University of California Press, 1970–83), V, 28–9.
11 *Antony and Cleopatra* was only staged once in London during the eighteenth century, when Garrick revived it in 1759.
12 Some productions retained Garrick's version of Otway's tomb scene as late as 1879.
13 Shadwell's representation of government by an élite versus the need for a governing body (Parliament), as well as his portrayal of a virtuous, non-violent uprising (in stark contrast to Crowne), set *Timon of Athens* apart from the Tory adaptations of the same era.

14 Only Otway's *Caius Marius* and Shadwell's *Timon of Athens* could be said to have had any continuing popularity amongst the political adaptations; *Timon* appeared on stage until 1745 and *Caius Marius* until 1735.

15 Samuel Johnson, *Johnson on Shakespeare*, ed. Arthur Sherbo (New Haven: Yale University Press, 1968), 704.

16 Charles Gildon, *A Comparison between the Two Stages*, ed. Staring B. Wells (Princeton: Princeton University Press, 1942), 45.

17 A. C. Sprague reports having seen almost the entire Cibber text performed in 1930. *Shakespearean Players and Performances* (Cambridge, MA: Harvard University Press, 1953).

18 Joseph Addison, *Spectator* 40 (16 April 1711).

19 Theatre companies sought to outdo each other by stressing the novelty of these revivals, advertising the number of years since the play was last staged.

20 See Michael Dobson, *The Making of the National Poet: Shakespeare, Adaptation and Authorship, 1660–1769* (Oxford: Clarendon Press, 1992), 146–61.

21 Theophilus Cibber, *Two Dissertations on Theatrical Subjects* (1756), 36–7.

22 David Garrick, *Jubilee Ode* (1769).

23 Samuel Jackson Pratt, *The Shadows of Shakespeare: A Monody, in Irregular Verse, Occasioned by the Death of Mr Garrick, in Miscellanies* (1785), II, 25.

24 One of his most successful adaptations was a revision of William Wycherley's bawdy *The Country Wife* (1675) as the much more chaste *The Country Girl* (1766).

25 James Boswell, *London Journal*, ed. Frederick A. Pottle (New York: McGraw-Hill, 1950), 257.

26 Arthur Murphy, *Gray's-Inn Journal*, 12 January 1754.

27 George C. D. Odell, *Shakespeare from Betterton to Irving* (New York: Scribners, 1920), I, 24, 89.

3

JANE MOODY

Romantic Shakespeare

Performing Shakespeare in the Romantic age became an intensely political business. The leading theatre critics – William Hazlitt, Charles Lamb, and Leigh Hunt – pepper their dramatic interpretations with deft, savvy and mischievous political shots. Reviews make frequent and pointed references to controversial topical events (the disorder which broke out after the mass meeting organised by radical leaders at Spa Fields in 1816, for instance, or the government's decision in February 1817 to suspend *habeas corpus*, thereby removing the accepted civil liberties of the English people); political concepts and institutions – anarchy, monarchy and aristocracy – pervade the discussion of Shakespearean performance. What is at stake in these accusations and counter-accusations, sly asides and ironic tirades? Why should the discussion of Isabella's chastity, or Coriolanus's condescension towards a Roman mob provoke charges of sedition and libel?[1] At the heart of this period is a battle for the political and moral possession of Shakespeare.

Do Shakespeare's plays celebrate monarchy and aristocratic government? Or might these dramas offer a much more ambivalent interpretation of political power and moral values? Is Shakespeare a natural aristocrat, or a closet radical? In the early nineteenth century, performers, managers and theatre critics relished the chance to offer polemical answers to these controversial questions, for in Shakespeare's representations of political power seemed to lie the key to Britain's political future.

The tug-of-war between the proponents of a conservative Shakespeare, and those who highlighted Shakespeare's moral scepticism and political subversiveness, is sometimes playful, invariably clever, and occasionally vicious. It is remarkable, too, for producing some of the most original and surprising interpretations of Shakespearean characters in any period: Edmund Kean's tragic Shylock, for instance, or Hazlitt's disturbing insights, in his essay on *Coriolanus*, into our imaginative complicity with tyrants. On stage and on paper, traditions about Shakespearean performance were being challenged, reinvented and also dismantled.

This was of course a time of enormous political upheaval. Between 1793 and 1815 England was at war with Napoleonic France; as we shall see, the actor-manager John Philip Kemble was quick to recognise the potential of *Coriolanus* and especially *Henry V* as nationalistic propaganda. Meanwhile, the government struggled to confront and suppress a rising tide of popular discontent and radical protest. Theatre managers shared the government's concerns about playhouses as sites of political excitement: the voluntary censorship of potentially dangerous speeches in Shakespeare's plays became a common practice. At a time when a succession of poor harvests had resulted in severe food shortages, for instance, Kemble was quick to remove all references to famine from his production of *Coriolanus*. During George III's long illness, the managers of Drury Lane and Covent Garden agreed to withdraw *King Lear* from the repertoire, so as to prevent comparisons being made between the madness of a Shakespearean king and that of the reigning monarch.

The Romantic age is also distinctive for the institutional battle that was taking place over who had the right to perform Shakespeare. At the beginning of the nineteenth century, only three theatres in London – Drury Lane, Covent Garden and the Haymarket – were legally entitled to stage the works of England's national playwright. According to these managers and their supporters, Shakespeare was the supreme example of an élite culture that must be protected from the grubby hands of the populace. Thomas Morton, whose job it was to read and select play scripts for Drury Lane, cleverly quoted the Prologue from *Henry V* ('A kingdom for a stage, princes to act, / And monarchs to behold the swelling scene!') in support of this *de facto* monopoly; Shakespeare, he declared, should be performed 'only in the noblest temples of the Muses'.[2]

Until the passing of the Theatres Regulation Act in 1843, dramatic regulation prohibited the performance of tragedy or comedy at the minor playhouses: these included the Coburg (now the Old Vic), the Surrey (in St George's Fields) and the Adelphi Theatres. By the time of the Regency, however, this ban – and in particular the illegal status of Shakespeare – was being challenged in earnest. In 1809, Robert Elliston produced 'a Grand Ballet of Action, with recitative, founded on *Macbeth*' at the Surrey Theatre, formerly the Royal Circus.[3] As the Prologue reveals, Elliston's production ironically highlighted the legal conditions under which *Macbeth* was being performed:

> Though not indulged with fullest pow'rs of speech,
> The poet's object we aspire to reach.
>
> . . .
>
> To prove we keep our duties full in view,
> And what we must not *say*, resolve to *do*;

Convinc'd that you will deem our zeal sincere,
Since more by *deeds* than *words* it will appear.[4]

By converting *Macbeth* into mime, Elliston cunningly avoided the ban on dramatic dialogue at the minor theatres. The Surrey production also created a series of linen flags or scrolls, which performers held up at the appropriate moment for the spectators to read. Inscribed on each of these scrolls was a phrase or sentence explaining the silent action: 'Macbeth ordains a solemn Banquet'; or, on Macduff's banner at Birnam Wood, 'Destruction to the Tyrant'.

Elliston's version of *Macbeth* was a commercial success, and demand surged around St George's Fields for cheap editions of Shakespeare's plays. Several critics, however, accused the manager of 'administering to the ignorance or depravity of the multitude'.[5] Like most of the metropolitan theatres outside Westminster, the Surrey was patronised by local artisans, apprentices, sailors and dock workers. Beneath the ironic condescension of some reviewers lurks a pervasive fantasy that performing Shakespeare for mechanics, butchers and chimney sweeps might hasten the disintegration of social and cultural hierarchies in England.[6]

In 1819 the Coburg Theatre engaged the celebrated tragedian, Junius Brutus Booth, to star in *Richard III*. Drury Lane prosecuted the manager and a court imposed a fine of £50 for this illegal production. William Glossop claimed that the Coburg's *Richard III* was not Shakespeare's play (as adapted by Colley Cibber), but rather a melodrama written by his house playwright, William Moncrieff. The Covent Garden spy who had been sent to observe the performance testified that, apart from the sound of an occasional and almost inaudible musical instrument, the Coburg play scarcely differed from that staged at the patent theatre. (The one exception was the murder of the Princes in the Tower, which, in defiance of stage tradition and public decorum, was staged in full view of the spectators, accompanied by music, allegedly 'to drown the cries'[7]).

The minor theatres circumvented the illegal status of Shakespeare at their playhouses in various ways. Theatres like the Adelphi and the Strand in the midst of Westminster dared not represent Shakespeare openly, but they cocked a snoop at dramatic legislation by producing travesties of Shakespeare's plays that included tongue-in-cheek allusions to the supposed illegality of the spoken word on their stages. In Charles Westmacott's *Othello, the Moor of Fleet Street* (Adelphi, 1833), for instance, Othello pointedly declares,

> Most potent – very reverend grave
> My noble and approved good masters,
> Rather than speak I'll sing a stave
> Relating to my strange disasters.

At the Coburg, the managers commissioned their house dramatist, Henry Milner, to adapt or 'melodramatize' Shakespeare's plays. The plays that were performed include *The Three Caskets; or, The Jew of Venice* (1827) and a Gothic version of *Hamlet, Prince of Denmark* (1828) in which Hamlet is put on trial for his father's murder and the attempted murder of his mother, but is absolved by the Queen's confession, and finally proclaimed king.

Shakespeare, then, was a controversial piece of cultural property. At the same time, another form of struggle was taking place for control over the nation's leading playwright. Here, stage was being pitted against the page, the material character of performance against the imaginative freedom of reading. Charles Lamb's essay, 'On the Tragedies of Shakespeare, considered with reference to their fitness for stage representation' (1811) sets out the Romantic critique of Shakespearean performance with eloquent tenacity. *King Lear*, he argues, 'is essentially impossible to be represented on the stage'. In the theatre, Lamb suggests, we see in Lear only 'what is painful and disgusting': 'an old man tottering about the stage with a walking-stick, turned out of doors by his daughters in a rainy night'. For the stage makes everything corporeal; the power of the senses completely usurps the power of the imagination. But 'while we read it, we see not Lear, but we are Lear, – we are in his mind, we are sustained by a grandeur which baffles the malice of daughters and storms'.[8] Whereas reading licenses a sublime identification with the character of Lear, representation abruptly destroys that process, producing little more than grotesque corporeality.

Lamb's argument may seem perverse to us: what kind of identity can a Shakespeare play have beyond performance? To some extent, we need to understand this point of view as a response to specific performance conditions: mutilated acting editions and vast, cavernous playhouses (Sheridan's Drury Lane Theatre could accommodate 3,611 spectators, whereas Garrick's had seated about 2,000) that demanded an extravagant and unsubtle performance style. Even the fairies in *A Midsummer Night's Dream*, Hazlitt complained, were 'full-grown, well-fed' and 'six feet high'.[9] But Romantic scepticism about performance must also be seen as a rearguard action that aspired to defend the nation's greatest playwright from the 'levelling' effects of stage production and those cheap, spectacular effects deemed necessary to attract large audiences. Such views represent an uneasy response to the emergence of a mass theatrical culture in which Shakespeare had become just one cultural commodity amongst many others in a rapidly expanding marketplace.

Despite these anxieties, this is an age marked by a rich symbiosis of criticism and performance. Leading performers, including John Philip Kemble and Sarah Siddons, wrote detailed and illuminating interpretations of the

Shakespearean characters they played on stage; Kemble's productions incorporated the advice and scholarship of many leading antiquarians and literary editors, including Edmond Malone and Francis Douce.[10] At the same time, Shakespearean criticism was being forged in the crucible of stage performance. Thomas Barnes's description of a cold, unpolished, almost barbaric Coriolanus, for instance, represents a bold challenge to Kemble's portrayal of a genteel Roman hero; Edmund Kean's characterisation of Shylock utterly transformed Hazlitt's conception of Shakespeare's Jew.

What fascinated Romantic theatre critics was the performance and interpretation of *character*. Character, here, connotes far more than what the language of the page discloses: reviewers also reflect on the way in which innovations in costume, gesture and stage business shape our attitudes towards Hamlet, Othello or Shylock. In an age of stage celebrity, Hazlitt and Leigh Hunt styled themselves as theatrical judges who made public their own critical verdicts on the originality or wilfulness of a particular actor's interpretation. In these judgements, nature (as opposed to the cold brilliance of neoclassical artifice) became the new touchstone of theatrical genius; for Hunt, too, what distinguished great tragic performance was that intricate fusion of familiarity and majestic elevation that characterised the interpretations of Sarah Siddons.

Despite the absence of photography or video, Romantic performance remains vividly alive for us today because of the skill with which these writers transformed the multifarious sounds and sights of Shakespearean performance into evocative critical texts. This is an age when, almost overnight, a Shakespearean character came to be seen in an entirely different light. Romantic criticism offers us a series of wonderful glimpses into the perplexity, confusion and indeed the sheer exhilaration these performances produced.

Kemble's Shakespearean monarchy

In 1783 a tall, stately young man made his début at Drury Lane in the character of Hamlet. Five members of Kemble's family played on the London stage that season. Kemble's elder sister, Sarah Siddons, had already made a name for herself portraying the wronged wife in dramas such as Thomas Southerne's *Isabella* and Nicholas Rowe's *Jane Shore*. Siddons's emotional intensity in these roles was remarkable: sobs and shrieks could be heard throughout the Drury Lane auditorium when she performed, 'and fainting fits long and frequently alarmed the decorum of the house'.[11] But despite his success as Hamlet, Kemble's career developed slowly: many of the great Shakespearean roles at Drury Lane still belonged to established actors such as Thomas Bensley and George Frederick Cooke. Five years later, however, at the age of thirty-one, Kemble became acting manager of Drury Lane.

As the Drury Lane manager, Kemble minutely supervised every aspect of Shakespeare production. Having abandoned the theatre's dog-eared prompt-books, Kemble began to establish his own acting editions of Shakespeare's plays; scenery, costume and stage properties also came under the manager's watchful eye. Many a supernumerary, happily accustomed to wandering on and off stage virtually at their own pleasure, suddenly found themselves being marshalled into specific positions for crowd scenes, battles and processions. The result was a spectacular series of revivals whose grandeur and opulence enthralled audiences; at the same time, Kemble brought into being a new kind of political Shakespeare.

Kemble immediately embarked on a hugely expensive and magnificent production of *Henry VIII* starring Sarah Siddons as Katherine of Aragon. By turns majestic, sorrowful, affectionate and scornful, Siddons's Queen Katherine took London by storm. Audiences admired in particular the psychological realism with which the actress depicted Katherine's final sickness: 'that morbid fretfulness of look, that restless desire of changing place and position, which frequently attends our last decay'.[12] In place of the 'motionless languor'which usually characterised stage pictures of sickness, Siddons highlighted Katherine's mental and physical irritability and her slow, gradual decline into death. So weighed down by sorrow did spectators become that, to the surprise of reviewers, no one dared to applaud until the Queen's body had finally left the stage.

In the seasons that followed audiences flocked to *Henry V* and *The Tempest* as well as to old favourites such as *As You Like It* and *Richard III*. But by 1802 the finances of Drury Lane were in a perilous state. Richard Brinsley Sheridan's political interests had left him little time to oversee day-to-day business at the theatre and salaries (including Kemble's own) had been left unpaid. Kemble and his sister therefore decided to abandon Drury Lane in favour of more secure employment at the rival theatre. By 1803, Kemble had become manager and part proprietor at Covent Garden, a position he would hold until his retirement in 1817.

'Were it not for Mr Kemble's exertions', remarked Leigh Hunt, 'the tragedies of our glorious bard would almost be in danger of dismissal from the stage.'[13] At a time when stock tragedies and comedies often played to half-empty pit benches (melodrama and pantomime, by contrast, drew packed houses), Kemble's successful production at Covent Garden of twenty-four Shakespeare plays seems a remarkable achievement. What is more, John Philip Kemble and Sarah Siddons became one of the great Shakespearean partnerships of the nineteenth century. They first starred as King John and

Constance, in a performance requested by George III, in 1783. Siddons revelled in the loftiness of Constance's character, her 'proud grief and majestic desolation'. 'Her elocution', remembered the biographer Thomas Campbell, 'varied its tones from the height of vehemence to the lowest despondency, with an eagle-like power.' So captivating was her interpretation, 'as grand as it is petrifying', that spectators came to see Sarah Siddons rather than the play, and often left the theatre as soon as Constance had left the stage.[14]

In *Coriolanus* (Drury Lane, 1789) Kemble's stiff, patrician Caius Martius perfectly complemented Siddons's towering maternity in the part of Volumnia. Such was the veracity of Kemble's performance that the female part of the audience would scream with horror as the Volscians approached Coriolanus from behind and appeared to pass their swords through his body. According to Walter Scott, the scene 'had the most striking resemblance to actual and instant death we ever witnessed'.[15]

Kemble and Siddons also played opposite each other in *Othello* (1785), *Measure for Measure* (1794) and *Macbeth* (1794). Kemble performed Shakespeare's Scottish hero dressed in a magnificent Highland dress and a bonnet decorated with tall black ostrich feathers; Scott praised his 'exquisitely and minutely elaborate delineation of guilty ambition'.[16] (The young Edmund Kean played a sprite during the incantation scene in act 4 but behaved so mischievously that he and his fellow-sprites were instantly dismissed by the furious manager.) But it was Siddons who stole almost all the glory, with her awe-inspiring portrayal of Lady Macbeth.

The famous eighteenth-century actress Hannah Pritchard had played Lady Macbeth as a savage, almost demoniac figure. By contrast, Siddons created a character who was both terrifying and yet, in her guilt and remorse, tenderly human. Above all, what spectators remembered was a vision of frightening power, 'little less appalling in its effects than the apparition of a preternatural being'.[17] Siddons's acting in the sleepwalking scene seems to have elicited similar reactions. Towards the end of the scene, Lady Macbeth despairingly murmurs to herself, 'Here's the smell of the blood still: all the perfumes of Arabia will not sweeten this little hand' (5.1). These words, recalled a spectator, were accompanied by 'a convulsive shudder – very horrible. A tone of imbecility audible in the sigh.'[18]

Dignity, grandeur and majesty were the hallmarks of Kemble's Shakespeare. Classical statues provided one important model for Kemble's and Siddons's stage gestures; they also drew inspiration from the *beau idéal* style of painting championed by Sir Joshua Reynolds. The actor William Macready later remarked on the painterly quality of Kemble's performances, which, 'like a Rembrandt picture . . . were remarkable for the most brilliant effects, worked out with wonderful skill on a sombre ground'.[19] His style of acting was slow, dignified and statuesque (Kemble's production of *Hamlet* allegedly lasted at least twenty minutes longer than anyone else's, and the actor's pauses were so long that Sheridan cruelly suggested that music should be played between the words); his characters remained cold, refined and full of *gravitas*. Kemble also liked to ponder the niceties of a Shakespearean text with obsessive exactness. His eccentric devotion to the antiquarian pronunciation of Shakespeare's language became legendary: the most celebrated examples included 'hijus' (hideous), 'varchue' (virtue) and, most notoriously, 'aitches' for aches. When *The Tempest* was performed, spectators seem to have packed the pit just to enjoy the pleasure of hissing Kemble's delivery of Prospero's threat to Caliban, 'I'll rack thee with old cramps, / Fill all thy bones with aches' (1.2).

Amidst the revolutionary fever of the 1790s, Kemble's Shakespeare productions represented a magnificent and spectacular advertisement for the political establishment. In Kemble's hands, *Coriolanus* became a parable about the rightness of patrician rule; *Measure for Measure* a drama about the paternalist care of rulers for their subjects, and *The Tempest* an eloquent justification of Prospero's benign authority. Kemble's production of *Coriolanus* reached the stage only a few weeks before the storming of the Bastille in 1789. As the revolution in France took shape, however, staging *Coriolanus* became an increasingly risky prospect; the play all but disappeared from the stage for several years. The playwright and critic Elizabeth Inchbald tellingly alludes to this voluntary censorship when she remarks, 'this noble drama . . . has been withdrawn from the theatre of late years, for some reasons of state . . . Certain sentences in this play are therefore of dangerous tendency at certain times'.[20]

Kemble recognised that *Coriolanus* was a play with an explosively topical plot. For this is a drama about the injustice of the patricians having storehouses 'crammed with grain' whilst the citizens starve, about the dependence of political leaders on the votes of the people – in other words, about the nature of popular power. The production Kemble created, however, quietly suppresses this aspect of Shakespeare's play. The actor-manager subtly amended the current acting edition of *Coriolanus* so as to magnify his hero's dignity and stature. What is more, Kemble's acting text got rid of all references to his hero's weaknesses (the 'O mother, mother!' speech disappears from act 5, scene 3, as well as Coriolanus's sudden change of mind in 5.4). Kemble also decided to omit Coriolanus's defiant arrogance in refusing to beg for the votes of the plebeians as well as the hero's decision to betray Rome by joining the Volscians.

Kemble's spectacular production featured 240 people, including dozens of soldiers, sword bearers, standard bearers, trumpeters and drummers.

These massed forces, seen to their best advantage in huge stage processions and dramatic tableaux, played an important role in the theatrical creation of majestic ceremony and regal power. At the same time, Kemble transformed Shakespeare's plebeians into ignorant, ineffectual and laughable characters whose protests against patrician luxury could therefore be dismissed as ridiculous and despicable. In Kemble's hands, *Coriolanus* was no longer a drama that anatomised in disturbing ways the nature of political power. On the contrary, it became a play that glorified authoritarian leadership. (See fig. 2)

For John Finlay, Kemble's Coriolanus 'was a matchless scenic exhibition; every sentence a lesson on elocution; every movement an attitude for the painter; ... it developed a panorama of patrician Rome; it was a glass for kings to dress at; it was a lecture for Lawrence and Canova'.[21] The majestic maternity of Siddons's Volumnia thrilled spectators. The actor Charles Young vividly recalled the moment when Siddons came down the stage at the triumphal entry of Coriolanus. Her dumb show 'drew plaudits that shook the building. She came alone, marching and beating time to the music; rolling (if that be not too strong a term to describe her motion), from side to side, swelling with the triumph of her son. Such was the intoxication of joy which flashed from her eye, and lit up her whole face, that the effect was irresistible.'[22] Reviews confirm that the dignity and 'haughty grandeur' of Kemble's Coriolanus seemed to legitimise his contemptuous dismissal of the plebeians. 'In the scene in which he rejects the votes of the people', wrote the *Times* reviewer (19 May 1814), 'his attack on the tribunes was a model of refined and lofty indignation.' Through these textual changes, as well as through characterisation and stage business, Kemble encouraged the spectators of *Coriolanus* to admire patrician authority and to despise those who questioned its foundation or legitimacy.

During a period marked by rumours of radical plots and murmurs of insurrection, Kemble's aristocratic Coriolanus became an important piece of unofficial propaganda for the conservative cause. (In April 1796 Aufidius's description of the Romans in *Coriolanus* was perceived to bear 'so strong a likeness to the savage barbarity of modern France, that it rushed through the House like lightning.'[23]) Kemble's adaptation of *Henry V*, staged later in the same year and pointedly subtitled *The Conquest of France*, similarly glorified English monarchy and English heroism. In this production, Kemble carefully omitted any discussion of the French battle plans, as well as deleting all traces of the French language from his acting edition. The *Times* reporter, who obviously relished the play's topical subtext, declared that *Henry V* served 'to convince our Gallic neighbours in the midst of all their triumphs that they are but mere mortals'.[24]

2 John Philip Kemble as Coriolanus. Painting by Sir Thomas Lawrence.

'This is a decorative era', proclaimed the *Oracle* (22 April 1794), and audiences flocked to Drury Lane and Covent Garden to enjoy the magnificent scenery, glorious pageantry and opulent costumes for which Kemble's Shakespeare productions became famous. The vast new stages at both patent theatres had rendered obsolete the old flats and wings: for Kemble, this loss presented a perfect opportunity to commission fresh scenery from leading antiquarian designers. At Covent Garden, the scene designer William Capon created a fine set of all-purpose wings and flats taken 'from exact specimens of the Gothic' in England and 'selected on account of their picturesque beauty'. Capon was fascinated by depicting the play of light upon stone; his scenery beautifully evoked the dramatic world of the Gothic sublime. Moreover, as the designs for *The Winter's Tale* reveal, Capon combined an eclectic variety of influences and historical periods: open Gothic arches in the style of Henry VIII's reign; a canopy modelled on the coronation throne in Westminster Abbey for the trial scene; a Corinthian antechamber for Paulina's chapel; and a prison design based on the nightmarish drawings of Piranesi.

Kemble's productions shrewdly exploited the visual attractions of Gothic mystery and the pleasures of modern sartorial luxury. Stage wardrobes were completely overhauled, old and familiar props abandoned, and new armour proudly designed. A sceptical Charles Lamb, watching the successive changes of costume that punctuated Kemble's *Macbeth*, was reminded of 'a Romish priest at mass'.[25] But many critics were delighted by this transformation of Shakespearean costumes and properties. '*Macbeth* and *King Harry*', commented one reviewer with obvious amazement, 'do not sit upon the same throne . . . while *Desdemona* has her own bed and damask curtains'.[26] Costumes for *The Tempest* (1789) were similarly lavish: the production featured Dorinda (Miranda's sister in John Dryden and William Davenant's adaptation of the play) and Miranda 'in white ornamented with spotted furs', whilst in *Richard III* Kemble made his appearance at the Battle of Bosworth Field 'arrayed in spotless silk stockings and long-quartered dancing shoes, adorned with the Rose of York'.[27]

The Romantic period was an age of expurgation, which saw the editor of *The Family Shakespeare* censor Juliet's speech of sexual longing for Romeo ('Gallop apace . . .') and describe *Othello* as 'unfortunately little suited to family reading'.[28] Kemble remained perfectly in tune with middle-class anxieties about Shakespearean morality, as his painstaking expurgation of *Measure for Measure* reveals. In our own time this drama continues to raise some thorny issues: can we forgive Isabella for valuing her chastity above her brother's life? And to what extent should the Duke of Vienna be held responsible for the sexual anarchy in his own city? The play's richly uncertain final scene, in which the Duke proposes marriage to Isabella ('I have a motion much imports your good') poses another challenge: should Isabella consent to this proposal, or, as we have seen in some late twentieth-century productions, violently reject him?

Kemble transformed *Measure for Measure* into a drama about the stern paternalism of a benign ruler; Isabella's innocence, purity and honour, meanwhile, are represented as the quintessence of modern womanhood. Covent Garden's austere revival pleased the reviewers who especially praised the Duke's 'dignity of deportment', 'sententious gravity' and 'just severity'.[29] Sarah Siddons's portrayal of the unrelenting Isabella also attracted warm praise: for the biographer James Boaden, her performance represented 'a model of cloistered purity, and energy, and grace'.[30] He remembered with particular admiration the scene between Claudio and Isabella, 'where she stood before him, as a searching, scrutinising spirit, to detect any quailing of feeble resolution, any even momentary preference of shameful life to lasting honour'.[31]

Kemble's acting edition of *Measure for Measure* removed the sexual undertow in Shakespeare's Vienna, its dark underworld of insinuation and half-concealed desires. Angelo's confession of his desire for Isabella – 'Never could the strumpet / With all her double vigour, art and nature, / Once stir my temper; but this virtuous maid / Subdues me quite' (2.2. 187–90) – disappeared completely; in Kemble's production, such a fantasy would fatally endanger both Angelo's moral authority and the audience's belief in Isabella's chaste purity.

Kemble quickly suppressed the Duke's duplicity and his moral failings. The acting text ruthlessly excised the speech of characters likely to compromise or endanger the heroism and political authority of the Duke and Angelo. Lucio's jokes about grace, pregnancy and venereal disease therefore disappear; the satirical Pompey (who stubbornly maintains that the life of a bawd is a 'lawful trade') becomes a clown, and Barnadine, whose famous refusal to be hanged until the morning constitutes one of the play's most subversive protests against Angelo's authority, is transformed into a harmless comic Yorkshireman.

Rather than repudiating or ignoring the Duke's proposal in the last scene, Isabella silently accepts its moral authority. During the Duke's final speech, written by Kemble himself, Isabella begins to fall to her knee. But the Duke prevents this act of humility and obedience by kissing her hands, whilst appealing to her as a 'sweet saint':

> Thy duke, thy friar, tempts thee from thy vow;
> In its right orb let thy true spirit shine,
> Blessing both prince, and people.[32]

As the language of this speech suggests, Kemble's Isabella is a woman more heavenly than earthly.

The radical, heterodox Shakespearean criticism of William Hazlitt is powerfully indebted to Kemble's spectacular, conservative productions. Often, Hazlitt seems to be writing in the margins of Kemble's performances, intent upon disputing their moral certainties and political values; performance thus provides the critical impulse for an audacious counter-interpretation. Hazlitt's controversial reading of *Measure for Measure* provides an excellent case in point. Whereas Kemble's production had been determined to silence Barnadine, Hazlitt goes out of his way to praise him as 'a fine antithesis to the morality and hypocrisy of the other characters of the play'. Moreover, in a move which scandalised many readers, he dared to question the morality of Isabella's decision: 'Neither are we greatly enamoured of Isabella's rigid chastity, though she could not act otherwise than she did' (Bate, *Romantics on Shakespeare*, 453). William Gifford was incensed by this interpretation and derided what he acidly described as 'Mr Hazlitt's notions of *natural morality*', especially Hazlitt's refusal to condemn characters such as Barnadine, Pompey and Froth.[33] As this controversy over *Measure for Measure* reveals, the uncompromising morality that had underpinned Kemble's production suddenly seemed dangerously fragile.

Similarly, Hazlitt takes Kemble's grandly patrician production of *Coriolanus* as the starting point for the exploration of a moral and political dilemma. Why is it, he asks in his review, that Shakespeare's play encourages us to admire the cause of the powerful (Coriolanus) against the interests of the powerless (the plebeians)? The uncomfortable answer, Hazlitt suggests, is that the 'insolence of power is stronger than the plea of necessity' (Bate, *Romantics on Shakespeare*, 283). The imagination is an aristocratic faculty which revels in turrets, crowns, blood and sacrifice; the miseries of starving multitudes cannot excite its admiration. What *Coriolanus* seems to prove, Hazlitt argues with bitter irony, is the legitimacy of oppression: 'The people are poor; therefore they ought to be starved. They are slaves; therefore they ought to be beaten ... This is the logic of the imagination and the passions: which seek to aggrandize what excites admiration and to heap contempt on misery' (Bate, *Romantics on Shakespeare*, 285). Whereas Kemble had presented Coriolanus's charismatic authority as the cornerstone of a stable political society, Hazlitt exposes Coriolanus as a tyrant whose power is founded upon the oppression of the Roman populace. Moreover, Hazlitt despairingly implies, the political logic of *Coriolanus* precisely reflects the savage injustices in contemporary English society.

Kean's illegitimate rebellion

The arrival of Edmund Kean on the London stage in 1814 shattered the calm aristocratic decorum of the Kemble tradition. The performances of this short, graceless, even uncouth actor in roles such as Shylock, Othello and Richard III shocked and entranced London. Spectators besieged Drury Lane on the nights when he was to perform, desperate to obtain seats to see London's most controversial actor; almost overnight, Edmund Kean had become the talk of the town. Two years later, William Hazlitt would write, with a mixture of irony and wistfulness, 'We wish we had never seen Mr Kean. He has destroyed the Kemble religion; and it is the religion in which we were brought up' (*Hazlitt* v, 345). This image of religious belief destroyed, of cherished convictions overturned, evocatively captures the significance of Kean's Shakespearean revolution.

Kean's arrival on the London stage coincided with a period of radical ferment and public disorder. In pamphlets and newspapers, radical writers questioned the divine right of monarchs and satirised the corruption of Britain's unreformed parliament; news of Luddite machine-breakers in northern cities and angry protests against the Corn Laws added to the atmosphere of political crisis. Kean's celebrity was inextricable from the maelstrom of Regency politics. In the eyes of his detractors, Kean was a plebeian actor whose lowly social origins, poor education and undignified deportment rendered him unfit to portray Shakespeare's great tragic heroes. But for critics like Hazlitt and Leigh Hunt, the iconoclasm of Kean's performances represented a theatrical form of that popular rebellion taking place against Liverpool's government.

Kean's violent, passionate, volcanic style seemed to challenge institutions and assumptions at the heart of the political and social order. As Hazlitt remarked, 'Mr Kean's acting is not of the patrician order; he is one of the people, and what might be termed a *radical* performer' (Bate, *Romantics on Shakespeare*, 289). For Kean's interpretations seemed to privilege anarchy over order, to delight in rebellion rather than to venerate the voice of authority. In other words, his portrayals of Shakespearean heroes powerfully disrupted the perceived identity between the national playwright and the nation's government. At Covent Garden, Kemble had presented the Shakespearean populace as a band of ignorant citizens or as an unruly mob; what seemed to characterise Kean's performances, by contrast, was a fascination with the power of oppression in a society, the insidious workings of prejudice.

Where can we see this revolution in practice? Kean's first role at Drury Lane was Shylock. Charles Macklin, who had played the part with great success for almost half a century, portrayed Shakespeare's Jew as a crafty, savage individual, contorted by rage. Kean was determined to abandon this tradition. Rather than adopting the worn-out clothes and trademark red beard customarily worn by stage Shylocks, he decided to play Shylock in a respectable black wig, loose gaberdine and Venetian slippers. 'It is an innovation; depend on it, it will never do', declared Raymond, the acting manager of Drury Lane, when he saw Kean's black wig. But the actor was adamant. 'I wish it to be an innovation', he replied.[34]

'When we first went to see Mr Kean as Shylock', remembered Hazlitt some years later, 'we expected to see, what we had been used to see, a decrepid old man, bent with age and ugly with mental deformity, grinning with deadly malice, with the venom of his heart congealed in the expression of his countenance ... and fixed on one unalterable purpose, that of his revenge' (*Hazlitt* IV, 323). Kean, however, quickly dispensed with this malevolent stage tradition, creating instead a Shylock who was intelligent, tender, vulnerable and grief-stricken. Though at one moment he wishes to see Jessica dead at his feet, at the next, Kean's Shylock recoils in revulsion from his own unnatural desires, burying his head in his hands and murmuring despairingly, 'No, No, No'. This is a Shylock whose desire for revenge becomes not only explicable, but disturbingly poignant.

Kean's Shylock is, above all, a tragic victim of Christian persecution; it is the oppression Shylock has suffered as a Jew in a Christian society that has made him a villain. The idea that we might sympathise with Shylock was a new and startling one in Regency Britain; still more surprising was the proposition that the prejudices and inequalities of Christian society might have nurtured Shylock's bitter hatred. Surely Shakespeare is a poet who staunchly defends Christian institutions? Is not Shylock an evil character justly punished for his savage cruelty and wrongdoing? Kean's interpretation broke new ground by inviting the audience to question the supposed civility of Venetian society, and to reflect on society's responsibility in creating the villain which Shylock becomes. Kean's performance thus raised what may seem to us very modern questions about the political consequences of social prejudice.

Spectators marvelled at Kean's dark and piercing eye and at a voice which, at moments of high emotion, sounded physically muffled by intense feeling. 'His style of acting', remarked Hazlitt, is 'more significant, more pregnant with meaning, more varied and alive in every part, than any we have almost ever witnessed' (*Hazlitt* V, 180). Above all, Kean's illegitimate style of performance brought about a revolution in Shakespearean acting. Kean had served his dramatic apprenticeship playing villains in Gothic melodrama and Harlequin in pantomimes. In these 'low' genres, the conventions that governed movement, gesture and expression had little in common with

3 Edmund Kean as Shylock; an engraving done from a painting, 1814.

the decorous gentility and statuesque hauteur characteristic of Kemble's Shakespeare productions. On the contrary, melodrama featured sudden, virtuosic transitions between such contrasting emotions as hate and re-morse. What is more, melodramatic speech dispensed with the formalities of classical rhetoric in favour of a far more colloquial language which was interspersed, at times of high emotion, with inarticulate cries and silent visual appeals for the intervention of heavenly powers. Kean's rebellion originates from his determination to appropriate the conventions of a plebeian aes-thetic for the theatrical representation of Shakespeare's great tragic heroes. Suddenly, the interpretation of Shakespeare was in the hands of a common man; illegitimate by birth and, in his gestures and expression, the visible embodiment of an illegitimate stage tradition.

Whereas Kemble's demeanour, even in moments of anger, had remained composed, even cold, Kean was an actor whose tempest-like emotions were written on his body. As Hazlitt remarked, 'it is in the working of his face that you see the writhing and coiling up of the passions before they make their serpent-spring' (*Hazlitt* VIII, 277). Kean's villains were often wickedly

4 Edmund Kean as Othello.

triumphant (Richard III rubbed his hands together in glee) or insouciantly matter-of-fact (the command, 'Chop off his head' in act 3, scene 2 would be delivered as if it were no more than a demand for the next meal). His extraordinary range of pantomimic gestures thrilled audiences, who wondered at Kean's sudden and unexpected transitions 'from the expression of the fiercest passion to the most familiar tones of conversation' (*Hazlitt* IV, 299).

Kean's Othello, regarded by many contemporary critics as his masterpiece, exemplifies the actor's transformation of Shakespearean characters. Kemble had played Othello as a neoclassical hero; 'grand', 'awful', and thoroughly European.[35] His choice of costume – a turban, combined with a British grenadier's uniform – drew visual attention to this magnificent confusion of oriental and British iconographies. What Kean did was to break the tradition of playing Othello as a blacked-up European tragic hero and to present instead a character driven by a romantic temperament and uncontrollable passion.

Kean's Othello startled audiences with his lightning transitions between 'delicious tranquillity' ('What sense had I of her stolen hours of lust?') and furious cries of 'wild and grinning desperation' ('I found not Cassio's kisses on her lips').[36] Similarly, his melodramatic gestures gave a new kind of emotional intensity to the portrayal of Othello's psychological pain: 'his joined uplifted hands, the palms being upwards, were lowered upon his head, as if to keep his poor brain from bursting'.[37] In the 'O, blood, Iago, blood!' speech (3.3), recalled the poet John Keats, 'the very words appeared stained and gory . . . His voice is loosed on them like the wild dog on the savage relics of an eastern conflict'.[38] Kemble's decorous, genteel Othello had given way to a far more unstable character whose emotions ruled his actions to an almost anarchic degree.

Kean's performances radically altered the stage history of many of Shakespeare's characters. As Hamlet, Kean abandoned the regal finery customarily worn for the part. To the surprise of his audiences (especially the *Times* reviewer, who regarded the actor's costume as an unjustified innovation), Kean portrayed Hamlet as a serious and introspective character, dressed in an undecorated garb of black velvet without insignia or ornament. What interested Kean about Hamlet was not his princely birth, but his state of mind. We can see this fascination with Hamlet's contradictory emotions in the actor's decision to return at the end of the nunnery scene, 'from a pang of parting tenderness' and kiss Ophelia's hand. The interpretation was soon being celebrated as one of Kean's finest 'new readings'; for Hazlitt, this poignant gesture of remembered love remained 'the finest commentary that was ever made on Shakespear' (*Hazlitt* v, 188).

Kean's performances exposed the powerful tensions between sympathy and moral judgements. Nowhere was this more true than in his portrayal of Richard III. Garrick's Richard had possessed a mixture of intrepid heroism and 'dreadful energy'; a decade before Kean's arrival on the London stage, George Frederick Cooke had portrayed Richard as a ferocious, gloating character whose humour put Charles Lamb in mind of 'the coarse, taunting humour, and clumsy merriment, of a low-minded assassin'.[39] But Kean's Richard combined recognisable features of melodramatic villainy – critics remarked with distaste on the character's violent beating of his breast – with a lofty, daring fearlessness: at Bosworth Field, Hazlitt declared, Kean 'fought like one drunk with wounds' (*Hazlitt* v, 182). This Richard was a Byronic hero whose intelligence, individualism and 'towering superiority' demanded spectators' admiration rather than their shuddering disgust: 'Why is this? because he seems to belong to a class above mankind: he is the destroying demon whom we regard with awe and astonishment, and not the mere murderer whose meanness and vulgarity almost rob crime of its horrors. Such

5 Edmund Kean as Richard III.

are the leading features of the character which Mr Kean has represented.'[40] As Thomas Barnes realised, the sheer power and charisma of Kean's Richard posed a moral dilemma: here the audience finds itself in satanic collusion with infamy against the forces of good. Just like Hazlitt in the essay on *Coriolanus*, Barnes was fascinated by the anarchic character of our dramatic sympathies, by the capacity of the imagination to be swept away into a world of amorality. Whereas Kemble's Shakespeare had offered a spectacular representation of monarchy and social tradition, Kean's characters seemed to revel in the sheer electricity of political disorder.

After Kean's revolution, Shakespeare could no longer be conceived of as the 'philosophical aristocrat' presented by Samuel Taylor Coleridge.[41] On the contrary, Kean's interpretations had revealed what we might call a radical Shakespeare, a playwright preoccupied by the nature of prejudice, by the workings of political oppression, and by the legitimacy of popular power. Kean's Shakespeare was chaotic, conversational, and, most disturbing of all, plebeian. Suddenly, the aristocratic monopoly of Shakespeare had begun to disintegrate: Edmund Kean's performances had fractured the moral and political certainties of the Kemble era.

NOTES

1 In his notorious review of *Characters of Shakespeare's Plays*, the critic William Gifford accused Hazlitt of having 'libelled our great poet as a friend of arbitrary power'. See *Quarterly Review* 18 (1817–18), 458–66, 464.

2 *Report and Minutes of the Select Committee on Dramatic Literature* (1832) in Parliamentary Papers, *Reports from Committees*, 18 vols., VII, question 3897.

3 *The Times*, 25 August 1809.

4 *The History, Murders, Life, and Death of Macbeth: and a full description of the Scenery, Action, Choruses, and Characters of the Ballet of Music and Action, of that name* (London: T. Page, 1809).

5 *Theatrical Inquisitor* 2 (April 1813), 136.

6 See further, Jane Moody, *Illegitimate Theatre in London, 1770–1840* (Cambridge: Cambridge University Press, 2000).

7 *British Stage; or, Dramatic Censor* 4 (March 1820), 141.

8 *The Romantics on Shakespeare*, ed. Jonathan Bate (Harmondsworth: Penguin, 1992), 123.

9 *Shakespeare in the Theatre: an Anthology of Criticism*, ed. Stanley Wells (Oxford: Oxford University Press, 1997), 44.

10 See John Philip Kemble, *Macbeth Reconsidered; an Essay: Intended as an Answer to Part of the Remarks on Some of the Characters of Shakespeare* (London, 1786). Sarah Siddons's notes on Shakespearean heroines were later incorporated into Thomas Campbell's biography. (See also chapter 7.)

11 James Boaden, *Memoirs of Mrs Siddons* (London: Gibbings & Co., 1896), 195. On Sarah Siddons, see chapter 9.

12 See Thomas Campbell, *Life of Mrs Siddons* (New York: Harper & Bros., 1834), 172.

13 *Leigh Hunt's Dramatic Criticism 1808–1831*, ed. Carolyn Houtchens and Lawrence Houtchens (New York: Columbia University Press, 1949), 38.

14 Campbell, *Life of Mrs Siddons*, 87; Houtchens and Houtchens, *Leigh Hunt's Dramatic Criticism*, 39.

15 Wells, *Shakespeare in the Theatre*, 34.

16 ibid., 33.

17 *The Complete Works of William Hazlitt*, ed. P. P. Howe, 21 vols. (London: Dent & Co., 1930–4), V, 373. Hereafter cited within the text as *Hazlitt*.

18 G. J. Bell, cited in Linda Kelly, *The Kemble Era: John Philip Kemble, Sarah Siddons and the London Stage* (London: Bodley Head, 1980), 48.

19 *Macready's Reminiscences, and Selections from his Diaries and Letters*, ed. F. Pollock, 2 vols. (London: Macmillan, 1875), I, 150.

20 Elizabeth Inchbald (ed.), *The British Theatre*, 25 vols. (London: Longman & Co., 1808), V, 5.

21 John Finlay, *Miscellanies* (Dublin: John Cumming, 1835), 280.

22 Campbell, *Life of Mrs Siddons*, 175.

23 *The Times*, 20 April 1796.

24 *The Times*, 2 October 1789.

25 Bate, *Romantics on Shakespeare*, 126.

26 *Bell's Weekly Messenger*, 19 February 1804, cited in George C. D. Odell, *Shakespeare from Betterton to Irving*, 2 vols. (New York: Scribner, 1920), II, 96.

27 John Genest, *Some Account of the English Stage, from the Restoration in 1660 to 1830*, 10 vols. (Bath, 1832), VI, 577.

28 *The Family Shakespeare*, ed. Thomas Bowdler, 8 vols., first published in one volume in 1807 (London: Longman and Co., 1827), VIII, 377. Bowdler's sister, Henrietta, took a significant editorial role in this project.

29 *The Times*, 22 November 1803.

30 James Boaden, *Memoirs of the Life of John Philip Kemble*, 2 vols. (London: Longman, 1825), II, 138.

31 Boaden, *Siddons*, 255.

32 *John Philip Kemble Promptbooks*, ed. Charles H. Shattuck, 11 vols. (Charlottesville: University Press of Virginia for Folger Shakespeare Library, 1974), VI, 68.

33 [Gifford], *Quarterly Review*, 463.

34 William Cotton, *The Story of the Drama in Exeter, During its Best Period, 1787 to 1823. With Reminiscences of Edmund Kean* (London: Hamilton, Adams & Co., 1887), 26–7.

35 Boaden, *Kemble*, I, 256.

36 *The Times*, 14 May 1814.

37 George Henry Lewes, *On Actors and the Art of Acting* (London, 1875), 152.

38 Wells, *Shakespeare in the Theatre*, 51.

39 Boaden, *Kemble*, I, 131; *Lamb as Critic*, ed. Roy Park (London: Routledge, 1980), 104.

40 [Thomas Barnes], *Examiner*, 27 February 1814, 138.

41 See Coleridge's comments on *The Tempest* in Bate, *Romantics on Shakespeare*, 528–34, 533.

4

RICHARD W. SCHOCH

Pictorial Shakespeare

The popular culture of Victorian Britain, as described by a contemporary observer, comprised heterogeneous 'exhibitions, galleries, and museums' devoted to 'popular education in the young and in the adult'.[1] These forms of respectable recreation became the 'libraries of those who have no money to expend on books ... [and] the travel of those that have no time to bestow on travel'. Among the 'amusements for mind and senses' which 'woo the world of London at every turn', the *National Review* counted 'lecture-rooms, dioramas, panoramas, cheap concerts, oratorios, public gardens, and innumerable other diversions, suited to every scale of purse and every variety of taste and cultivation'.[2] Informative entertainments such as the Diorama in Regent's Park, the Cosmorama (an indoor 'peepshow' gallery of famous sites from around the world) in Regent Street, and Wyld's Great Globe in Leicester Square exercised cultural governance over an imperial city whose population at mid-century passed 2,000,000. This thriving popular culture was nothing if not visual. From the *Illustrated London News* to stereoscope photographs (double images of the same subject which, when inserted into a viewer, create the illusion of three dimensions), and from the annual Royal Academy exhibitions to *cartes de visite* (small, inexpensive photographic portraits suitable for mounting in an album), the Victorians were insatiable consumers of pictures.

But for Londoners '[h]igh or low, rich or poor', enthused *Blackwood's Magazine*, theatre was their 'supreme delight' (51 (1842), 426). The 'upper, middle and lower classes' of the nation's capital could take their pick of 'theatres for the east, and theatres for the west; theatres for this side of the river, and theatres for that; theatres for performances equestrian and aquatic; theatres legitimate and illegitimate' (427).[3] The theatre was a central part of Victorian visual culture because its audience was predisposed to look at the stage as if it were a series of living pictures. Pictorial staging meant not only highly elaborate scenery, but also detailed costumes and properties, spectacular effects, and the frequent use of tableaux vivants – a static pose held by the acting ensemble at a climactic moment which made the stage look as if it were a painting.

While pictorialism covered the full range of theatrical productions from melodrama to pantomime, it was especially identified throughout the Victorian and Edwardian eras with revivals of Shakespeare. The actor-managers who dominated London's leading theatres during these years – W. C. Macready, Samuel Phelps, Charles Kean, Henry Irving and Herbert Beerbohm Tree – were all committed to a pictorial *mise-en-scène*. Alternatives to pictorialism, such as the pseudo-Elizabethan bare stage, found few buyers in the dynamic nineteenth-century theatrical marketplace. Pictorialism was not what actor-managers thought about when they staged their productions; it was *how* they thought. It was all but inconceivable to imagine a nineteenth-century production of Shakespeare as anything other than an animated painting.

Of course the theatre's steadfast devotion to a pictorial aesthetic need hardly surprise us, since this was precisely the aesthetic of its audience. Victorian theatre-goers were heirs to a century-long tradition of reading illustrated editions of Shakespeare's plays and looking at paintings, prints and engravings in which the playwright's characters were depicted sometimes as real people (e.g., portraits of Benedick) and sometimes as 'roles' impersonated by famous actors and actresses (e.g., Garrick *as* Benedick). From the 1709 publication of Nicholas Rowe's first illustrated edition of the complete plays to the opening of John Boydell's Shakespeare Gallery in 1789, the enduring popularity of Shakespearean iconography in the eighteenth century shaped and conditioned audience responses to the plays in performance. What people saw in picture galleries they expected to see upon the stage. The Victorians, building upon this union of theatrical and visual cultures, took as axiomatic that good Shakespeare meant illustrated Shakespeare, whether in Charles Knight's eight-volume *Pictorial Edition of the Works of Shakespeare* (1839–42), the richly detailed pre-Raphaelite paintings of characters from *Hamlet, King Lear, The Tempest* and *The Two Gentlemen of Verona*, or even the toy theatre 'sheets' of costumed actors and stage settings. Academically trained easel painters worked as scene designers throughout the nineteenth century, from Macready's collaboration with Clarkson Stanfield in the 1830s to Irving's association with Ford Madox Brown and Lawrence Alma-Tadema sixty years later. At the same time, the theatre continued to provide subjects for painters. Portraits of celebrated performers – one thinks of John Singer Sargent's painting of Ellen Terry as Lady Macbeth in a gown decorated with green beetle wings – certainly never lost their appeal. Some painters, however, depicted a complete 'stage picture' or tableau from memorable Shakespeare productions, as when Queen Victoria commissioned E. H. Corbould to paint a series of scenes from Kean's 1852 *King John*.

In keeping with the primacy of pictorial aesthetics, the text in performance was freely reshaped so that each act could end in a striking tableau. These culminating stage pictures, along with spectacular scenic and lighting effects, interpolated stage action, and lengthy set changes meant that nothing like a complete text could be performed. Although the plays were heavily abbreviated and often rearranged for performance, they were, from Macready onwards, usually based upon Shakespeare's own texts and not upon the adaptations and alterations that had dominated the theatre since the Restoration. While today we might not countenance Victorian acting versions of Shakespeare, nonetheless we should remember that the relationship between word and image on the Victorian stage was not a simplistic one. Although the period had its share of theatrical critics who were textual purists at heart, the most imaginative writings about the nineteenth-century stage affirmed the complementarity of Shakespeare's poetry and theatrical scenery. Indeed, theatrical editing was itself discussed in pictorial terms. Macready, in his 1838 *Coriolanus*, restored some of Shakespeare's lines which had been cut in previous productions. *John Bull* welcomed the textual revisions not so much because they did honour to the playwright, as because a more complete performance text 'enlarge[d] the historical canvas to statelier proportions'.[4] The text in performance had not a literary, but a pictorial function: to allow the stage to become a 'statelier' history painting.

The 'stateliness' of pictorial Shakespeare tells us something about its high moral tone. Never an illicit pleasure, Victorian theatrical pictorialism was intimately tied to the middle-class obsession with rational amusement: the education and instruction of mass audiences through popular culture. History was the ideal subject for the theatre to teach through its historically accurate scenery, costumes and stage properties. While Shakespeare's English and Roman chronicle plays were an obvious place to start, his tragedies, comedies and romances were all treated as opportunities for historical instruction. Performance was a powerful agent of historical consciousness in the nineteenth century precisely because it could realise the past with a 'bold and master hand', as one mid-Victorian journalist maintained, greater than that of literature, painting or even photography.[5] Indeed, the theatre's commitment to historical accuracy was the very sign of its modernity. To prefer anachronistic performances of Shakespeare, Charles Dunphy of the *Morning Post* argued, was to prefer 'the semaphore to the electric telegraph' or 'the stage-coach to the locomotive'.[6] And thus the measure of success for Shakespeare revivals became their ability to surpass the vivacity and precision of history novels, genre paintings, museum collections and architectural restorations. Archaeological eclecticism flourished throughout the century and a lively range of historical places, personages and events was recreated for eager and ever-expanding audiences.

In his brief managerial career at the two patent theatres, Covent Garden (1837–9) and Drury Lane (1841–3), Macready was renowned not only for expelling prostitutes from the theatre, but also for restoring the integrity of Shakespeare's texts and expanding the artistic control of the actor-manager in something approximating modern stage direction. While he made the expected overtures towards historical representation in staging *Coriolanus*, *Henry V*, *King John* and *Macbeth*, he did not regard the theatre principally as a means of historical illustration. He did, however, regard it as a means of literary instruction. For some of his contemporaries, Macready's steward-ship represented the last hope of the legitimate drama to banish melodrama, burlesque and even animal acts from the stages of the patent houses. As the eminent tragedian declared during his 1851 retirement banquet, a perfor-mance of Shakespeare should be 'one of the best illustrated editions of the poet's works'.[7] Of course, to accomplish that literary goal, the theatre had to perfect its own means of scenic display.

After the Theatres Regulation Act of 1843, abolishing the long-standing monopoly of London's patent theatres over the performance of scripted drama, Samuel Phelps and Charles Kean embarked upon their famed series of Shakespeare revivals. Phelps, during his lengthy tenure at Sadler's Wells (1844–62), was lauded for endearing a local audience to poetic drama, en-semble acting, textual restoration, ambition in performing nearly the entire Shakespeare canon, and ingenuity in making do with a paucity of stage re-sources. 'To that remote suburb of Islington', Macready noted approvingly of the north London theatre run by his former colleague, 'we must look for the drama if we really wish to find it.'[8] Whether because of the financial constraints imposed by managing a theatre with modest box-office potential, the supposedly less refined tastes of a suburban audience, or even because of his own uncompromising allegiance to textual purity, Phelps was content to leave spectacular and antiquarian *mise-en-scène* to his West End counterpart, Charles Kean. Although historical accuracy never held a singular interest for Phelps, his many revivals of Shakespeare were firmly placed within his cen-tury's tradition of pictorial staging.

Charles Kean remains the most ardent and aggressive historiciser of Shakespeare in the British theatre. In just nine seasons at the Princess's Theatre (1850–9), Kean recreated not merely the medieval and Tudor England of Shakespeare's history plays (*Henry V*, *Henry VIII*, *King John* and *Richard II*), but also eleventh-century Scotland (*Macbeth*), Renaissance Italy

(*The Merchant of Venice*), and classical Greece (*A Midsummer Night's Dream*, *The Winter's Tale*). The actor-turned-antiquary 'rummaged out old books', 'turned over old prints' and 'brushed the dirt off old music' in preparing historically correct revivals of Shakespeare.[9] His antiquarian spectacles were celebrated – and censured – for their sets, costumes and properties of unprecedented historical precision; adherence to the descriptions and illustrations in the works of prominent historians; re-enactment of events not dramatised by Shakespeare; interpolation of music of presumed authenticity; historical essays in the playbills; and the publication of quasi-academic editions of the plays. The 'present age demands that all dramatic representations must of necessity be accompanied by a certain selection of scenery, dresses, and music', Kean argued in one of his playbill manifestos, and '*truth* in these matters is preferable to *inaccuracy*'.[10] So fastidious was Kean in his insistence upon authentic stage accessories that his detractors at *Punch* dubbed him not the 'Upholder' of Shakespeare, but the 'Upholsterer'.

Kean's retirement from the Princess's Theatre marked the beginning of a twenty-year gap in memorable London productions of Shakespeare, a tedious interval relieved only by Charles Fechter's *Hamlet* (1861, 1864) and by Squire and Marie Bancroft's picturesque *The Merchant of Venice* (1874). Shakespeare was eventually restored to the London stage by Henry Irving, who famously managed the Lyceum Theatre from 1878 to 1902. Irving inherited from Kean not simply a repertoire of Shakespeare and gentlemanly melodrama, but also a taste for historical spectacle as evidenced in his productions of *Coriolanus*, *Henry VIII*, *King Lear*, *Macbeth* and *Much Ado About Nothing*. 'There is no conflict between dramatic truth on the stage', the actor-manager argued in 1888, and the 'externals which perfect illusion'.[11] Aided by the use of three-dimensional built scenery, Irving could present quite convincing historical illusions. But even this daunting archaeological display was more a case of aestheticism than historicism. Under Henry Irving, history was not so much restored as beheld. The past was refigured more as an object for contemplation at a distance – across a darkened auditorium and through a picture-frame proscenium arch – and less as a tangible physical presence, as it had been in Kean's revivals.

Irving's 1882 *Romeo and Juliet* is a case in point. For the play's final scene Irving used two sets, a churchyard for the duel between Romeo and Paris and then the Capulets' crypt. At the end of the first scene the audience was shown an exterior view of steps leading down into the burial vault. Then, after a pause for changing the scenery, it was presented with an interior view of the vault with Juliet asleep centre stage at the foot of the same flight of steps. Romeo, dragging Paris's corpse, appeared at the top of the stairs and slowly descended into the depths of the tomb (fig. 6). As Dennis Kennedy has related,

6 *Romeo and Juliet*. Artist's impression of the final scene, designed by William Telbin, from Henry Irving's 1882 production at the Lyceum Theatre, London. Romeo (Irving), Juliet (Ellen Terry) and Paris lie dead in the Capulets' crypt as Friar Lawrence descends the stairs. Note the suggestion of depth through the use of two staircases.

the thrill of the scene lay in the creation of pictorial seamlessness – Romeo leaves the churchyard and then enters Juliet's tomb – even though the second scene violates the spatial logic of the first scene.[12] What mattered less in this scene, as in the entire production, was the historical correctness of the sets and costumes. What mattered more was the correct realisation of dramatic space and time.

In so placing history in the service of pictorialism, Irving richly profited from the example and advice of prominent contemporary painters. His revival of *King Lear* was influenced by Ford Madox Brown's painting *Cordelia's Portion* (1866) and the artist's own involvement in the production more than a quarter-century later when he provided sketches of the Romano-British interior of Lear's palace, Albany's hall, and an exterior view of Gloucester's seat with a Roman temple in the background. Similarly, Irving's 1901 *Coriolanus* was staged from Alma-Tadema's designs completed twenty years earlier. Yet Irving's association with the most celebrated painters of his day never amounted to a collaboration, since the actor-manager's own production 'concept' determined all theatrical decisions – as his staging of the tomb scene in *Romeo and Juliet* indicates.

The pervasiveness of pictorialism in nineteenth-century Shakespeare depended not merely upon aesthetic tastes, but also upon evolving and expanding stage technology in scenery and lighting. Since major scenographic advances came only in the 1880s with the introduction of automated machinery, the productions staged by Macready, Phelps and Kean continued the time-honoured arrangement of wings and flats set into grooves cut into the stage floor. These basic units of two-dimensional painted scenery could be shifted in four directions simultaneously: wings were easily slid on stage and off, while drops were set and removed through a 'rise and sink'. In shifting a backdrop, the top half was flown up – or raised – into the fly tower while the lower half was pulled – or sunk – beneath the stage floor. To create the impression of off-stage space, a 'raking flat' would be set at a 45-degree angle to a backdrop. Kean used this device throughout his 1855 revival of *Henry VIII*. By placing the acting ensemble and the stage furniture parallel to diagonal raking flats, spectators could imagine the 'indefinite length' of the setting depicted.[13] Wing-and-drop sets were increasingly augmented by the use of three-dimensional set pieces such as platforms, furniture or even practical doors, windows, steps and bridges. Innovations in scenery really arrive with Irving, who favoured practical, architectural scenery through which actors could move, rather than illusionistic painted scenery in front of which actors stood. Over the course of the century actors began to inhabit three-dimensional environments and no longer arranged themselves in tableaux vivants in front of painted backdrops.

Gauze and trapdoors were frequently used as adjuncts to painted and built scenery. Commonly featured in vision scenes and associated with otherworldly phenomena, gauze was a staple item in any manager's repertoire of spectacular effects. In Phelps's *Macbeth*, the witches performed behind green gauze, thus permitting them to materialise magically or to vanish mysteriously as the gauze was either illuminated or darkened. In his *A Midsummer Night's Dream*, a seamless green gauze was hung on the stage for those scenes set in the forest. With the actors performing only from behind the gauze, the effect, according to contemporary observers, was appropriately dreamy.[14] Sudden appearances of isolated figures were achieved through the use of simple traps. In Kean's revival of *The Tempest*, Ariel was repeatedly seen to 'descend in a ball of fire'.[15] Such fancy stage business required nothing more than a trap, a groundrow (a low piece of 'cut-out' scenery placed on the stage floor) and focused light. As Prospero called 'approach now my Ariel', a stage hand shone a beam of red-tinted limelight on to a groundrow painted as a bush. Behind the groundrow, and thus masked from the audience's view, was an open trap through which Ariel emerged. As the actress was brought up through the trap, the red light was extinguished. The entire sequence thus created the impression that Ariel herself had emerged from within the flame – or, more exotically still – that she had metamorphosed from fire to matter.

Of course not all pictorial effects required an actor's presence. The theatrical diorama, for example, simulated the effects of clouds, sunrise, sunset and storms when light moved over a stationary painted canvas surface stretched across the back of the stage. Sometimes the diorama consisted of a series of images painted on a canvas which was unfurled across the stage. (Such a device was also called a Panorama.) Dioramas typically combined picturesque settings with strong narrative or historical situations in a particular play, thus demonstrating the Victorian theatre's conviction that pictorialism and dramatic action went hand-in-hand. The 'Grand Moving Panorama Representing London' in Kean's *Henry VIII* is a particularly opulent example. Kean's justification for exhibiting this painstakingly detailed diorama, copied from a 1543 drawing, was that the Lord Mayor would have travelled by boat to the christening of Princess Elizabeth at the Church of the Grey Friars, an event Shakespeare dramatises in the final act of *Henry VIII*. Kean thus used a moving diorama of London as seen from the Thames – featuring old St Paul's, London Bridge and the Tower of London – as the spectacular lead-in to his production's final scene. More exclusively picturesque dioramas, such as those found in Shakespeare's pastoral comedies, reveal not a thoughtless indulgence of pictorial effects but rather the close and enduring relationship between scene design and contemporary painting. Macready's dioramas for *Henry V* were created by Clarkson Stanfield, while the diorama 'A Wood near Athens' in Kean's *A Midsummer Night's Dream* was actually a copy of J. M. W. Turner's *Golden Bough* with the figures removed.

Whether depicting historical monuments or picturesque vistas, dioramas offered audiences the pleasure of scenic fluidity: a single location was shown under the passage of time or different locations appeared one after the other as the diorama was slowly unfurled across the stage. There was no need to ring down the curtains, interrupt the stage action, or even call for a 'rise and sink' to change the backdrop. When Henry Morley praised Phelps's *A Midsummer Night's Dream* for making 'one scene ... glide insensibly into another', he was praising the impression created by the moving diorama itself as the stage action moved from Athens to the woods and back again.[16] The optical 'trick' of the moving diorama was, however, the exact opposite of its technical execution. That is, although the scenery moved in front of the audience, the *effect* of the diorama was that the audience, along with the characters, moved through the scenery. '[S]o artistically are the different changes

7 *Much Ado About Nothing*. The church scene (4.1), designed by William Telbin, from Henry Irving's 1882 production at the Lyceum Theatre, London. Mezzotint after the painting by Johnston Forbes-Robertson. Note the ornate altar, organ loft, massive columns and wrought iron gates. Compare the same scene in Edward Gordon Craig's 1903 production.

of moonlight, fog, and sunrise produced', the dramatist Douglas Jerrold observed of Phelps's production, 'that you imagine you have been wandering through an entire forest, with a fresh prospect meeting you unexpectedly at every turn' (quoted in *Betterton to Irving*, II, 324). The prominence of the diorama as a perceptual standard led some Victorian reviewers to describe live stage action as if it were a painted illusion. For example, *John Bull* praised the moment in Macready's *Macbeth* when the soldiers disguised as Birnam Wood appeared from behind their 'leafy screen[s]' as having 'all the reality of a diorama effect'.[17] The diorama is at the heart of pictorial staging because its claims to create a reality effect point to what must be for us the central paradox of nineteenth-century theatre: that the 'perfect illusion of reality', as Martin Meisel has astutely observed, 'was an imitation of art'.[18]

As Shakespearean spectacles became increasingly lavish, scene changes became lengthy and cumbersome. The *Literary Gazette* complained that the 140 stage hands needed to run Kean's *The Tempest* prevented the audience from chatting during the intervals, because although the men 'working the machinery' were 'unseen', they were, alas, 'never unheard'.[19] Irving, thirty years later, faced even greater difficulties in moving massive three-dimensional set pieces without the benefit of a mechanised stage. One of the splendours of his *Much Ado About Nothing* was the chapel in a Sicilian cathedral used for Hero and Claudio's wedding (fig. 7). Designed by William Telbin (and memorialised in Johnston Forbes-Robertson's painting), the enormous set featured wrought iron gates 12 feet high and 4 feet wide and real columns 30 feet high supporting an ornamental roof. The architectural space was populated not just by the wedding party, but also by ecclesiastics bearing candles, torches and incense, whose movements were underscored by organ, choir and stringed instruments. As Dennis Kennedy observes, this scene alone required a quarter of an hour to be put in place (*Looking at Shakespeare*, 30).

The lighting for Victorian revivals of Shakespeare was neither as extravagant nor as unmanageable as the scenic displays, and perhaps this is why it was generally admired. Actor-managers really had no choice in the matter, since the lighting instruments typically available to them were the familiar range of gas lamps: footlights, overhead borders or battens, 'lengths' (short battens placed on the stage floor to illuminate low pieces of scenery such as rocks or ocean waves), sidelights and strip lights (vertical stands placed behind wings to illuminate upstage areas). Gas lamps were first installed in 1815, at Covent Garden and Drury Lane, quickly replacing oil lamps and candles because they were cheaper, easier to use and cast a brighter, more consistent illumination. Gaslight made more of the stage visible and could be regulated by the 'gasman' who controlled the rate at which gas flowed through an intricate system of pipes. Thus, for the first time in the British theatre a spectator's attention could be focused through sustained lighting effects. Such effects could hardly compare to the wonders produced with electric lights (introduced in 1881) and, far more recently, with computerised light boards. But gaslight, in its own time, was an artistic breakthrough.

Apart from gas lamps, the principal innovations in nineteenth-century stage lighting were limelight and the carbon arc. A block of quicklime, when heated by a combined flame of oxygen and hydrogen, produced a brilliant white light – called 'limelight'. The hand-operated lamp threw a larger and more powerful beam of light over a greater distance than had previously been possible. This intense light could be used for a general 'wash' of white light, while focused limelight (i.e., filtered through a lens, which could itself be coloured) functioned as a primitive follow-spot. Charles Kean is generally credited for its first theatrical use in the vision scene from *Henry VIII*, when a beam of light was focused upon the host of angels who visited Queen Katharine as she slept. Journalistic references before 1881 to 'electric' theatrical lights usually refer to the carbon arc: a light produced by the resulting 'arc' when an electrical current generated in a battery was slowly broken. Introduced in 1848, the carbon arc was frequently placed behind painted backdrops of sunrises and sunsets for enhanced illumination. Alternatively, the light could be directed upward towards figures suspended in mid-air. When Hans Christian Andersen described the Ariel in Kean's *The Tempest* as 'isolated by the electric ray', he was doubtlessly referring to the effect of a carbon arc focused on the actress playing Ariel.[20]

As the foregoing examples attest, the Victorian theatre applied every technological resource at its disposal to mount increasingly spectacular productions of Shakespeare. Yet spectacle was certainly not without its critics. Those who objected to pictorial Shakespeare – even when placed in the service of historical instruction – believed that stage pictures could only ever usurp the rightful pre-eminence of poetry and acting. *John Bull* thus assailed Macready's revival of *The Tempest*, which it likened to an 'Easter-piece' or holiday pantomime, for the scene in which 'Ariel is whisked about by wires and a cog-wheel, like the fairies in Cinderella'.[21] Similarly, at the end of the century, George Bernard Shaw denounced the sterility of Irving's 'decorative' Shakespearean revivals for replacing drama with 'the art of the picture gallery'.[22] Though such opinions were part and parcel of Victorian dramatic criticism, they were nonetheless out of step with prevailing theatrical styles and conventions – all of which embraced the visual, the pictorial and the magnificent. By looking in more detail at some of the justifications for pictorial Shakespeare made by nineteenth-century observers, we can construct a theory for this dominant stage practice – and thereby get a better sense of why it was able to withstand almost a century of critical opposition.

The principal argument on behalf of increasingly elaborate pictorial effects was that Shakespeare himself wanted such effects but his theatre did not possess the resources required to achieve them. Victorians read the Chorus's prologue in *Henry V* – which termed the Globe an 'unworthy scaffold' – not merely as Shakespeare's apology for the limitations of his theatre, but as an instruction to future generations to produce his plays with every possible scenic and technological advantage. Shakespeare's genius, confined by the inadequacies of his own theatre, could only be liberated on the nineteenth-century stage. The 'machinist' and the 'scene-painter' were Shakespeare's rightful 'ministers and interpreters', the *Leader* decreed in 1858, because the poet himself 'would desire to be represented before a nineteenth-century audience with all the means and appliances which art, learning and science of the nineteenth century can furnish'.[23] While we might disagree with that presumptuous assessment, we must nonetheless acknowledge that for most Victorian actor-managers, the pseudo-Elizabethan bare stage was *un*-Shakespearean precisely because it perpetuated not the best, but the worst of Shakespeare's own theatre.

The playwright's pictorial intentions, many Victorians argued, could also be inferred dramaturgically – that is, by reading the plays for clues as to how they should be staged. Such a strategy of reading clearly presumes that pictorialism already exists within the text (placed there by Shakespeare himself) and therefore is not capriciously imposed upon it by zealous actor-managers. *Henry VIII* – which Coleridge had termed a 'show play' and 'historical masque' – was the play most often cited as the example *par excellence* of how Shakespeare wrote pictorialism and spectacle into his texts. The 'appointments and accessories' of *Henry VIII*, pronounced the *Illustrated London News*, were 'manifestly intended by Shakespeare himself for spectacular display'.[24] Indeed, all Victorian and Edwardian productions of *Henry VIII* – and particularly those of Kean, Irving and Tree – capitalised on the many spectacular and ceremonial events which Shakespeare himself dramatised: Wolsey's banquet, Henry VIII dancing in a court masque, the ecclesiastical trial of Henry and Queen Katharine, Anne Boleyn's coronation procession, the angelic visitation during Katharine's dream, and the baptism of Princess Elizabeth. When Tree declared in 1910 that '*Henry VIII* is largely a pageantry play ... as such did we endeavour to present it', he effectively summarised more than a half-century's tradition of equating pictorial spectacle with Shakespeare's dramatic action.

These sorts of arguments are really about fidelity and faithfulness: that is, pictorial Shakespeare is true to the intentions of the playwright and true

8 *Henry V.* 'Historical Interlude' of Henry's return to London after the victory at Agincourt, from Charles Kean's production at the Princess's Theatre, London, 1859. The stage manager's promptbook lists more than 140 characters and supernumeraries required for this elaborate set piece, including a chorus of angels and a company of biblical prophets.

to the structure of his plays. Other, more daring arguments claimed that spectacular and illustrative stage effects compensated for deficiencies either in the audience's familiarity with the text or, indeed, with the text itself. A production of Shakespeare thus might require pictorialism in order for the production to be understood. Consider, for example, the dioramas painted by Clarkson Stanfield for Macready's *Henry V*. The dioramas, which accompanied the Chorus's speeches, depicted the voyage of the English fleet across the Channel, the English and French armies on the eve of battle, and Henry's triumphal return to London after victory at Agincourt.[25] According to Macready, such innovative pictorial effects were needed 'to render more palpable . . . the narrative and the descriptive poetry spoken by the Chorus'.[26] It bears remembering that Macready restored the Chorus in this production, and so he was doubtless aware that while his spectators might have read the Chorus's speeches, they had never before seen them performed. In consequence, then, his spectators indeed might have required pictorial adjuncts 'to render more palpable' those parts of the text that had not been performed for more than 200 years.

Similarly, Kean's astonishingly intricate 'Historical Interlude' of Henry V's triumphal return to London (fig. 8) demonstrates the escalating degree to which stage effects made up for perceived shortcomings in the script. Henry's entry, though alluded to by the Chorus, is not really part of the play. But Kean transformed a passing reference into a twenty-minute set piece with music, dancing and hundreds of extras. Kean was only too eager to 'regulate' this historical interlude according to the 'evidence of an eye-witness', because he could then provide the detailed living picture which Shakespeare neglected to paint – but which Kean's own audience was anxious to see.[27] The antiquarian supplements of this production redeemed Shakespeare's failure to document medieval history as exhaustively as a mid-Victorian audience would have liked. In these two examples from *Henry V* we can see, yet again, that pictorialism was the means of making Shakespeare's plays conform to the expectations and desires of nineteenth-century audiences.

But of course it is the nature of expectations and desires to change, even in the theatre. And by the end of the Victorian era Shakespearean revivals began to disown their long-standing traditions of pictorialism, spectacle and historical accuracy. The end of pictorial Shakespeare – at least in the theatre – was clearly in sight when the *Athenaeum*, in its 1900 review of Tree's *A Midsummer Night's Dream*, declared that the actor-manager 'has reached what may, until science brings about new possibilities, be regarded as the limits of the conceivable'.[28] The scientific 'new possibilities' which would enable the theatrically inconceivable to be born were not long in coming. These possibilities were not, however, theatrical; they were cinematic. This need scarcely surprise us for motion pictures, even in their earliest forms, promised to recreate scenes and scenery on a scale unimaginable in a playhouse. Cinema was the real successor to the nineteenth-century theatre because it, too, depicted an ever-changing series of pictures. The birth of Shakespeare on film was particularly well timed, since the stage seemed only too grateful to remand pictorial spectacle to the protective custody of the cinema. In so doing, the theatre freed itself to 'revitalise' Shakespeare's plays, as Dennis Kennedy has argued, by 'transforming the nature of their representation' from the real to the abstract or the symbolic (*Looking at Shakespeare*, 43).

In short, the emergent alternative to nineteenth-century visual spectacle was not realism but modernism. Edward Gordon Craig, applying the formal principles of Adolphe Appia, began to use light and scenery not to represent particular historical sites within Shakespeare's plays, but rather to create symbolic worlds in which the plays were enacted. In a contrasting instance of theatrical modernism, William Poel returned Shakespeare to his origins through the platform stage, curtains, and screens used by the Elizabethan Stage Society. Yet for all their evident differences, Victorian spectacle and twentieth-century theatrical modernism had this much in common: a belief that the vitality of a performance lay in the conscious arrangement of theatrical space to create a distinctive milieu. The wedding scene from *Much Ado About Nothing* in the productions of Irving (1882) and Craig (1903) is instructive on this point (see figs. 7 and 9). While the Victorian impresario, as we have seen, incorporated mammoth three-dimensional columns and wrought iron gates into his scenery, the young director-designer created the same dramatic space through a plain backdrop of folded grey curtains and a lone crucifix hung above a simple altar. In terms of form, these two productions occupy opposite ends of a visual spectrum; but in terms of concept, there is an ironic sympathy between them in a shared commitment to realise what one nineteenth-century theatrical observer called a 'complete impression'.[29] The sympathy is bitterly ironic, however, because the very theoretical premise of pictorial Shakespeare was eventually its own undoing.

Even so, it would be wrong to believe that the transition from pictorialism to formalism was also a transition from the artificial to the real or the vulgar to the pure. Such a simplistic view can only blind us to the value once accorded to pictorial Shakespeare – a value we are apt to overlook because it is no longer our own. As suggested earlier in this chapter, spectacular and pictorial *mise-en-scène* was how the nineteenth-century theatre manifested its commitment to historical instruction and 'rational amusement'. Through lavish Shakespeare revivals, the theatre educated a mass, metropolitan audience and thereby acquired respectability for itself as an agent of moral and social improvement. The theatre also demonstrated its much-lauded

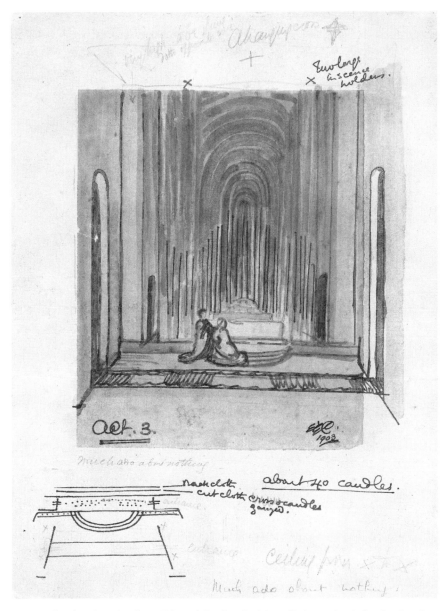

9 *Much Ado About Nothing.* Edward Gordon Craig's preliminary sketch for the church scene (4.1) in his 1903 production at the Imperial Theatre, London. Note the spare, simplistic look of the scenery. Compare with the same scene in Henry Irving's 1882 production.

progressivism by relying on the latest stage technology to create its visual splendours. All of these efforts meant that the theatre had to join forces with non-theatrical activities in the fine arts, historical culture, technology and innovation, education and social reform. While nineteenth-century Shakespeare revivals can thus boast a social conscience, they can equally boast a theatrical conscience. For the productions of Macready, Kean, Phelps, Irving and Tree were also critical statements about Victorian attitudes towards Shakespeare as the national poet. The elaborate pictorial accessories of the nineteenth-century stage, as this chapter has tried to demonstrate, were the means not of betraying Shakespeare but of realising what the Victorians took to be his true, yet previously unattainable goal: the detailed depiction of historical events, cultures and geographies.

The century-long obsession with pictorial Shakespeare – whether as an engine of social utility or the expression of the poet's unfettered genius – exposed a Victorian desire not for an 'authentic play', but for what Stephen Orgel calls 'an authentic Shakespeare, to whom every generation's version of a classic drama may be ascribed'.[30] In short, the nineteenth-century theatre did neither more nor less with the Bard than all theatres, including our own, have always done. It found a way to make him its own contemporary. We in the twenty-first century might wonder just how central a role Shakespeare could have played in the vibrant and robust popular culture of Victorian Britain. But that is our problem. For nineteenth-century audiences it was not a problem at all. They knew exactly which role Shakespeare played because they had cast him in it: the personification of every social and cultural enterprise which merited the proud name 'Victorian'.

NOTES

1 *Blackwood's Magazine* 51 (1842), 278.
2 *National Review* (January–April 1856), 412.
3 The terms 'legitimate' and 'illegitimate' refer to whether or not a particular theatre was licensed by the Lord Chamberlain for the performance of scripted – i.e., 'legitimate' – drama. For more information on theatrical licensing in the nineteenth century, see chapter 3 above.
4 *John Bull*, 19 March 1838.
5 *Tallis's Dramatic Magazine* (April 1851).
6 A letter to Charles Kean, 17 March 1857, Fol. Y.c. 830 (2), Folger Shakespeare Library, Washington, DC.
7 Quoted in E. B. Watson, *Sheridan to Robertson: a Study of the Nineteenth-Century London Stage* (Cambridge, MA: Harvard University Press, 1926), 184.
8 Quoted in the *Athenaeum*, 16 November 1878.
9 Review of *Henry VIII*, Princess's Theatre, London, *The Times*, 16 May 1855.
10 Playbill for *Pizarro*, Princess's Theatre, London, 1 September 1856.

11 Quoted in *Sir Henry Irving: Theatre, Culture and Society*, ed. Jeffrey Richards (Keele: Keele University Press, 1995), 279.

12 Dennis Kennedy, *Looking at Shakespeare* (Cambridge: Cambridge University Press, 1993), 30.

13 Review of *Richard II*, the *Builder,* 21 March 1857.

14 See, for example, the *Examiner,* 15 October 1853 and *Lloyd's Weekly,* 23 October 1853.

15 John Cole, *Life and Theatrical Times of Charles Kean, FSA.* 2 vols. (London: Richard Bentley, 1859), II, 220.

16 *Examiner,* 15 October 1853.

17 *John Bull,* 13 November 1837.

18 Martin Meisel, *Realizations: Narrative, Pictorial, and Theatrical Arts in Nineteenth-Century England* (Princeton: Princeton University Press, 1983), 438.

19 *Literary Gazette,* 4 July 1857.

20 Hans Christian Andersen, 'A Visit to Charles Dickens', *Temple Bar* 31 (1870), 39.

21 *John Bull,* 21 October 1838.

22 *Saturday Review,* 17 July 1897.

23 *Leader,* 9 June 1858.

24 *Illustrated London News,* 16 July 1859.

25 Review of *Henry V, The Times,* 11 June 1839.

26 *Henry V*, playbill, 10 June 1839, Covent Garden, London.

27 *Henry V*, playbill, 28 March 1859, Princess's Theatre, London.

28 *Athenaeum,* 20 January 1900.

29 Review of *Merchant*, Princess's Theatre, London, *Literary Gazette,* 11 September 1858.

30 Stephen Orgel, 'The Authentic Shakespeare', *Representations* 21 (Winter 1988), 25.

5

MARION O'CONNOR

Reconstructive Shakespeare: reproducing Elizabethan and Jacobean stages

Even from its inauguration early in Her Majesty's long reign, the Victorian pictorial mode of staging Shakespeare's plays generated its own reaction. At Covent Garden late in 1823 Charles Kemble (1775–1854) presented *King John* in early thirteenth-century decor, with (claimed the playbill) 'the whole of the Dresses and Decorations being executed from indisputable Authorities, such as Monumental Effigies, Seals, Illumined MSS, & c.'.[1] At the Haymarket in March 1844 Benjamin Webster (1798–1882) presented a production of *The Taming of the Shrew* in which the players who arrive in the Induction were made up to resemble Shakespeare, Ben Jonson and Richard Tarlton: however implausible the assembly of these individuals, their respective appearances were copied from old paintings and prints. The two productions were thus the result of the same kind of study of pictorial and plastic images that had survived for centuries; and in fact they had been designed by the same person, J. R. Planché (1795–1880).

The crucial difference between the two productions lay in the point of application of antiquarian research. The 1823 production represented the dramatic time and place in which a Shakespeare play was set, while the 1844 production represented the theatrical time and place in and for which a Shakespeare play was written. The first production since the Restoration to stage the Christopher Sly material, the 1844 *Taming of the Shrew* was applauded for 'reviving the play in the shape in which we find it in Shakespeare's work' (*The Times*, 18 March 1844, 5). And overall the Victorian project of reproducing Elizabethan and Jacobean stage conditions and conventions would be text-driven in several respects: it had been adumbrated by editors like Samuel Johnson (1709–84) and Edmond Malone (1741–1812);[2] it was most often justified by appeals to early printed books and manuscripts; and it was accelerated by the publication of facsimiles of the First Folio and several quartos. Yet its initial champions were not scholars, let alone academics, but theatre practitioners with antiquarian inclinations and associations.

Reconstructive Shakespeare started out as a mere change of scenery on proscenium stages. The initial efforts literally hung by threads. In the 1844 Haymarket production of *The Taming of The Shrew* (which Webster revived in 1847), the first scene of the Induction was

> played in the ordinary manner before a scene representing an inn; but when [Christopher Sly] is removed into the [Lord's] hall, there is no further change, but the play of the *Taming of the Shrew* is acted in that hall, two screens and a pair of curtains being the whole dramatic apparatus ... and all the exits and entrances are through the centre of the curtain, or round the screens, the place represented being denoted by a printed placard fastened to the curtain.
>
> (*The Times*, 18 March 1844, 5)

Downstage exits and entrances were obstructed by the placement of the on-stage audience in them, behind the proscenium line: an engraving published in *The Illustrated London News* (23 March 1844) indicates that the curtained proscenium stage of the Haymarket appeared to have been set with another curtained proscenium stage.[3] Decades later, in 1881, William Poel (1852–1934) announced his vocation: 'to obtain a more faithful representation of Shakespeare's plays upon the stage ... is the cause I have at heart'.[4] The first of his lifelong labours for this cause to receive much notice was Poel's production of the First Quarto of *Hamlet* in a single performance on 16 April 1881. The stage of St George's Hall was surrounded by red curtains, entrances and exits being effected through openings in them at upstage centre and downstage to either side. For the play-within-a-play, four chairs and a stool were placed before a small wooden platform at upstage left, adjacent to the line of curtains through which the Players made their entrances and exits in 'The Murder of Gonzago'. The Players' stage, with its backing of curtains, was thus a reduced version of the St George's Hall stage, with its curtain surround. Like Planché in 1844, Poel in 1881 gave his audience an on-stage image of themselves watching a stage-upon-a-stage which represented his notion of an Elizabethan stage and which consisted principally of curtains.[5]

For years reconstructive Shakespeare was swathed in curtains. They afforded an inexpensive and easily adjustable way of: (a) concealing some of the fixtures and fittings of proscenium theatres; (b) eliminating the need for representational scenery; (c) concentrating audience attention on the bodies of actors wearing Elizabethan costume; (d) situating points of access/egress to/from the stage; (e) demarcating acting areas in accordance with notions about divided or (later) zoned stages; and (f) keeping pace with broad shifts in scenic design. Their use is, indeed, a common term between the 'Elizabethan methodists' who imitated William Poel and the scenic avant-garde who echoed Edward Gordon Craig. (Poel intermittently restated his claim to have got there first.[6]) Thus they are conspicuous in photographs both from the early decades at the Maddermarket Theatre (see below) and from two of the three Shakespeare productions that Harley Granville Barker (1877–1947) staged at the Savoy Theatre in 1912 and 1914.[7] As permanent fixtures for reconstructive Shakespeare productions, however, curtains carry some disadvantages: they deaden sound and collect dust; to open or close curtains during performance is to run a double risk of distraction – by noise and by movement; they cannot incorporate different levels; unless anachronistic lighting effects are played upon them, their very neutrality risks visual tedium; and, rather like mail order slip-covers, they usually look like cheap and nasty makeshifts.

The 'Shakespeare Stage' built in the Munich Hoftheater in 1889 under the direction of Jocza Savits (1847–1915) was somewhat more substantial. The stage itself was extended over the orchestra pit: this curved apron was lit by footlights and was in that respect a thing of its time, despite its dimensions. What made the stage Shakespearean stood upstage, past the proscenium opening and curtain line: a backdrop represented an architectural façade with three levels, the uppermost a colonnade of arches, while the ground level contained functional openings – a central discovery space bracketed by doors. Poel saw *King Lear* played on this stage in 1890 and was 'not quite satisfied with the setting'.[8] So he said a quarter of a century after the fact; but nearer the time, he had been sufficiently satisfied with Savits's results to have adopted his method of using the scenery and scenic conventions of their own late nineteenth-century time to represent a then current notion of late sixteenth-century English theatrical building and stage. For a production of *Measure for Measure* in November 1893, Poel set the stage of the Royalty Theatre with a simulacrum of an Elizabethan theatre, complete with

> a practical rostrum and balcony and canvas painted cloths, representing galleries, boxes and amphitheatre, two entrances to Stage under balcony, a centre entrance, closed by pair of painted oak doors, two pillar supports, 18 feet high, to carry the roof or 'Heaven' to centre of stage, with facsimile ceiling piece of blue ground and gilt stars and covered by a lean-to tile painted roof joining on to tyring house, roof and wall, a pair of reproduction curtains, each 18 feet high by 9 feet, suspended on brass rods between the pillars, with ropes, pullies, etc.; also the back curtain in similar material of different design, each 8 feet square with ropes and pullies. There are also tapestry curtains for doors under balcony, matting for floor of Stage, painted canvas palisade for front of platform.[9]

Poel publicised this elaborate set as a model of the Fortune, a rectangular theatre for which the builder's contract of 1600 had been known to antiquarians

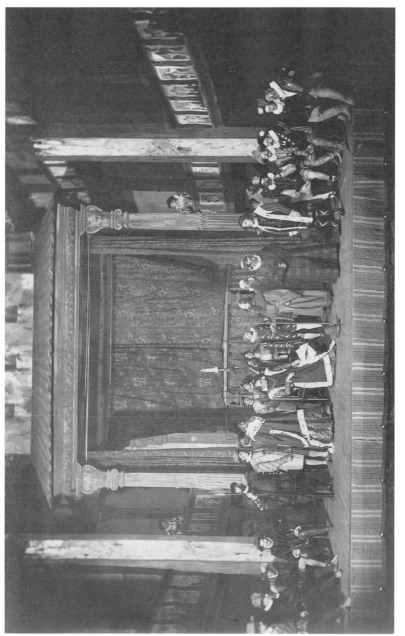

10 Fit-up stage, representing the Fortune Theatre, first used by William Poel in November 1893 for his production of *Measure for Measure* at the Royalty Theatre, London.

since 1790, when Malone published a transcription of it in the apparatus to his edition of Shakespeare's *Works*. However, photographs taken of the set in use at least six different times show that, in all but minor decorative details, it had been modelled on the amphitheatrical Swan, of which a (second-hand) sketch, the so-called De Witt drawing, had surfaced only in 1888. Whatever antecedents the model may have had among Elizabethan theatre buildings, moreover, some of its measurements and proportions were determined by the Victorian theatre building for which it was originally designed.

In the last decades of his life, Poel preached a new gospel of platform stages, but the theatrical practice of his theoretical notions was severely restricted, both by the architecture of the buildings in which he was able to pursue them, and even more by the extreme brevity of his occupancy of them. For just a single performance of *The Two Gentlemen of Verona* in 1910, for example, Poel extended the apron of His Majesty's Theatre far out over the stalls; while upstage, behind the proscenium, he set up scenery (possibly recycled from the Fortune fit-up) representing a tiring-house façade, its balcony complete with painted cut-out balustrades.

Simulacrum sets

Poel's painted canvas representation of the Fortune and his platform stages are the best-known instances of scenery temporarily transforming proscenium theatres into simulacra of Elizabethan amphitheatrical ones. Other, more obscure, instances abound, notably in North American universities: at Harvard in 1895 and again in 1904–8; at Stanford in 1902–5; at the Carnegie Institute of Technology in Pittsburgh from 1926; at the University of Washington in 1930; at the University of Illinois (Champaign-Urbana) from 1944; at Hofstra in 1951. Each was inflected by the particular preoccupations of individual members of staff: at Harvard, George Pierce Baker (1866–1935); at Stanford, Raymond Macdonald Alden (1873–1924) and Ben Greet (1857–1936), an erstwhile associate of Poel, temporarily holding a Californian chair of drama; at Carnegie Tech, Ben Iden Payne (1881–1976), Lucio in a 1908 Manchester revival of Poel's production of *Measure for Measure*, now successor to Thomas Wood Stevens as chairman of the first university department of drama in the USA; at Washington, John Ashby Conway (1905–87), with Payne as visiting director; at Hofstra, John Cranford Adams (1903–86), Shakespearean scholar turned university president. As with Poel's simulacrum of the Fortune, adjustments to notional dimensions were made in order to fit the available spaces. The Harvard reconstruction, based on the Fortune contract, made a 1/14 reduction of the measurements given in it. Both the Hofstra and the Illinois ones were based on a model of the first Globe which Adams propounded in his *The Globe Playhouse: its Design and Equipment* (1942), but the former was built to 5/6 scale and the latter to 3/4. In England, where English literature and, even more, drama were not recognised as degree subjects until long after they had been so institutionalised by the American academy, such pseudo-period venues for academic productions came later and were fewer. In 1926, however, at what is now Queen Mary Westfield College, University of London, Allardyce Nicoll (1894–1976) effected a similar transformation of a lecture hall into an eighteenth-century playing space, with doors of entrance (and balconies above them) on either side downstage of the proscenium.

Proscenium stages outside the academy were also given Elizabethan makeovers. In 1920, beginning his second stint at the Old Vic in London's Waterloo Road, Robert Atkins (1886–1972) by his own account

> insisted upon the building of a semi-permanent set, obeying the ground plan of the Elizabethan theatre, with inner stage and upper galleries ... a black traverse, hung where the supports of the Heaven might have been for the front scenes. The playing before the black drop was heightened by the restoration of ... the forestage ... The shape of the theatre made it impossible to be truly Elizabethan, but the forestage helped rapidity of speech and with staging obeying the author's construction of the plays, it was possible to catch the spirit of Elizabethan presentation.[10]

On becoming director at Stratford-upon-Avon in 1935, Payne tried something similar, but the shape of the Shakespeare Memorial Theatre (built in 1932 and irretrievably inflected by cinema architecture) was less amenable to an Elizabethan mask than the Old Vic (built in 1818 for melodrama and reconstructed in 1871 as a music hall). The height of the Stratford proscenium opening being very low, the upper level of Payne's Elizabethan set on stage could not be seen from most seats in the dress circle, let alone the balcony, of the auditorium. In 1976, after the Shakespeare Memorial Theatre stage had baffled a succession of architectural rescue efforts, John Napier and Chris Dyer attempted to erase its proscenium by *trompe-l'œil* means – primarily, by making the circle and balcony of the auditorium appear to continue the two galleries of the Elizabethan set on stage, and secondarily, by putting members of the audience into those galleries.[11] On both points, Napier's and Dyer's set had been anticipated by Poel's production of *Measure for Measure* in 1893, when the painted canvas palisade of the Fortune balcony was carried on to the stage boxes of the Royalty Theatre and costumed members of the Elizabethan Stage Society were seated on stage. These strategies were short-lived in 1976 and 1893 alike: the Stratford set proved permanent only through a single season, and Poel does not appear to have repeated either the use of an on-stage in-period audience or the assimilation of the Fortune model into an auditorium in which it had been erected.

Reconstructive Shakespearean staging, then, was initially a matter of setting the stages of proscenium theatres with scenery that represented an image of one or more of the public playhouses of Shakespeare's time. Putting simulacra of Shakespearean theatre buildings onto the stages of post-Restoration theatre buildings had two great disadvantages. One was practical: making inefficient use of space and time, such simulacra were not cost-effective. Apron stages displaced high-priced seats in the orchestra, while both these downstage extensions and also upstage facsimiles of tiring-houses often fell outside the sightlines from less expensive seats up in the 'gods'. Poel's 1910 set for *Two Gentlemen of Verona* covered one-third of the stalls and could not be seen from either the upper circle or the gallery: thus over half (54 percent) of the 1,319 seats in His Majesty's Theatre were temporarily unsaleable. Besides reducing seating capacities, such simulacra could be unwieldy in the extreme: the Hofstra one, for example, comprised 500 parts and required 800 hours for its assembly. (Unsurprisingly, the academic efforts were erected at most once a year.) The other disadvantage was perceptual: regardless of the material of which it was constituted – whether curtains, painted canvas, wooden structures or fibreglass flats – each was obviously the simulacrum of an old theatre set up within a modern one. Uncropped photographs indicate that, framed by the architecture and appurtenances of twentieth-century auditoria (fixed seating, proscenia, side stairs, safety exits, flies, lighting rigs), reconstructive Shakespearean stage settings always looked like what they were: stage sets pretending to be theatres other than the theatres which they occupied.

A solution to the inconvenience of the cumbersome simulacrum stages was to increase their flexibility, portability and ease of assembly. Poel's own work gave a cue. As noted above, his model of the Fortune was partly shaped by the London theatre, the Royalty in Dean Street, where it was initially used. Poel had the hire of this Soho firetrap for three performances only and, having cut his professional teeth on low-budget touring, he was well equipped for the theatrical transience that characterised his long career. Poel's model stage of the Fortune was a 'fit-up', designed to be portable from one theatre to another and to be adaptable to the fixed dimensions of different stages. In 1905, when the model stage was put up for auction, Poel wrote to a potential buyer: 'The Stage requires, for its erection, a space on the floor of thirty feet in length and twenty four feet in depth and a height of not less than twenty-three feet. The stage will all take to pieces and then consists only of lengths of timber and rolled cloths with one or two small flat pieces and takes very little room to store.'[12] The Fortune fit-up remained within Poel's control even after its sale in 1905, but by 1907 he could make only piecemeal, or provincial, use of it: new fire regulations, requiring the safety curtain to descend during every performance, meant that the complete fit-up could no longer be used for public performances in any licensed theatre in the capital. It continued to be used outside London – for example, at the Royal Gaiety Theatre in Manchester, where the 1893 production of *Measure for Measure* was re-vived by Annie Horniman's Company – 'following the Elizabethan method' and under Poel's direction – in April 1908. Meanwhile, and in London, Poel and his supporters continued to circulate another, smaller, fit-up stage that he had first used in 1899 for a production of Ben Jonson's *The Alchemist*. Unlike the Fortune fit-up, this one was no simulacrum of an Elizabethan the-atre building, but simply an enclosure of acting space, its stage raked, fronted by footlights and framed by wing pieces that formed a proscenium. And, again unlike the Fortune fit-up, the smaller one was non-representational: although it was covered with various bits of tapestry and painted canvas from the Fortune fit-up, it did not represent (nor was it presented as) an Elizabethan theatre, in general or in particular. Such structures recur in re-constructive Shakespeare across the twentieth century. Some were merely notional.[13] Of those that progressed past the drawing board, the best known was the first Mermaid Theatre of Bernard Miles (1907–91) and his wife Josephine Wilson. Built in 1951 in a schoolroom at the bottom of their garden in St John's Wood and then reassembled two years later on the floor of the Royal Exchange at the centre of the City, it was designed to be portable – and was eventually abandoned for bricks and mortar by Blackfriars Bridge.[14]

As for incongruity between Ye Olde simulacra and not-so-old auditoria, Poel's solution, as practised by himself, was capable of exacerbating the prob-lem. His productions of plays by Shakespeare and other early modern English playwrights were sometimes presented in spaces contemporaneous with the dramatic texts. Such spaces were afforded by the centuries-old halls that sur-vive in several of the Inns of Court and of the City Companies, at London palaces such as Hampton Court and Lambeth, and in the country houses of the Tudor élite. The screens in these halls provide the minimal features of Shakespearean public theatres: a permanent architectural setting, at least two doors of entrance on a level with a floor space cleared for playing, and, above, a musicians' gallery capable of serving as an upper level. Two halls had an advantage among Victorian antiquarians, because Shakespearean plays were known to have been played in them during Shakespeare's pro-fessional lifetime. Poel presented *The Comedy of Errors* at Gray's Inn Hall in December 1895, 301 years after its Elizabethan performance there, and then *Twelfth Night* in Middle Temple Hall in February 1897, 295 years after its Elizabethan performance there. Yet for his three performances of

Twelfth Night before the benchers of Middle Temple, Poel disregarded the elaborately carved oak of the hall screen in favour of his own Fortune fit-up, with its painted oak, lathe and canvas. This apparent indifference to the staging possibilities afforded him by the architecture of Middle Temple Hall was continued by Poel's theatrical successors in the performance of *Twelfth Night* there, notably Lillah McCarthy (1875–1960) in 1916, Donald Wolfit (1902–1968) in 1951, and the New Shakespeare Company in 1964. (Wolfit, for example, set up a low stage on the dais, *opposite* the screen, and indicated changes of scene thereon by turning the pages of a large property book.) Other period venues had more respectful visitors: at Crosby Hall in 1951, for example, C. B. Purdom (1883–1965) presented *Macbeth* on a bare platform stage.

Conversions

For inconvenience and incongruity alike, one solution, never available to Poel, was to abandon antiquarian claims to the possession or even the pursuit of authenticity, and to invent new structures that adapted the features of Elizabethan playhouses. This was at first a matter of converting extant buildings. In the Maddermarket area of Norwich, a late-Georgian Roman Catholic chapel, latterly used as a Salvation Army Citadel, was in 1921 converted into a theatre for the Norwich Players. Their leader, Nugent Monck (1878–1958), had stage-managed and acted for Poel in various productions across the first decade of the century. Late in 1904 he acted in the revivals of Poel's 1895 production of *The Comedy of Errors* and 1896 production of Marlowe's *Dr Faustus*. Poel's Fortune fit-up was used for these revivals, so Monck, having played Pinch and Robin on it in 1904, could draw on experience when in 1921 he resolved on 'keeping the gallery [of the chapel] where it was, to build at one end an Elizabethan stage ... modelled on that of the old Fortune theatre; where we could act Shakespeare's plays as he intended them to be played'.[15] In designing his stage, Monck sought the advice of Poel but proceeded to disregard it in the interests of financial exigency and practical advantage. For example, the Fortune contract specifies a stage projecting to the middle of the yard; but Monck, rather than reduce the seating capacity (only 220 at opening), kept the trapezoidal stage of the Maddermarket shallow: including an apron just over 2 feet deep, the maximum depth of the stage was 16 feet, half its maximum width. And Monck's architect, Noel Paul, devised a malleable space in which successive designers were able to create an illusion of upstage depth when it was wanted. Downstage, in diagonal walls at the level of the stage floor, there were two stage doors on either side, and by the insertion of a false proscenium just upstage of these doors,

11 Maddermarket Theatre, Norwich, February 1926: interior view, with gallery and front rows of chairs facing the stage set for a production of John Dryden's *Marriage à la Mode*.

Maddermarket designers were able to transform their Elizabethan stage into a Restoration one. The addition of a flight of steps (and sometimes rostra) could transform the balcony upstage centre into a second stage. In every one of the eighty years that it has been in use, the Maddermarket stage has offered between ten and twelve productions, usually including only two or three Shakespearean plays. Its long record has on the whole vindicated the principle – fundamental but no longer peculiar to reconstructive Shakespeare – that plays written for a particular kind of theatrical space are best staged in such a space or its semblance.

In reconstructing Elizabethan theatrical space within a Georgian chapel, the Norwich Players enjoyed several architectural advantages over subsequent attempts at converting buildings into Shakespearean playhouses: one was that the acoustics of the Maddermarket chapel were near perfect; another was that the chapel was so small that intimacy was almost unavoidable; a third, that its internal features – notably, the gallery that ran around three sides and the squared wooden pillars that supported it – were commensurate and correspondent with such features of the Jacobethan stage as were to be reconstructed in it. Other conversion efforts have been hampered on account of at least one of the following: acoustics, size and extant architectural features. Late in 1936 Atkins adapted a boxing venue, the Ring in Blackfriars Road, for three bare-stage productions of Shakespeare, and his performers had problems with audibility in an originally ecclesiastical building. The transformation in 1976 of yet another redundant church fallen by the wayside, St George's in Tufnell Park, was doomed on all three points. What particularly recommended this north London building to George Murcell (1925–98) and C. Walter Hodges (b. 1909) for conversion into an Elizabethan theatre was that it was polygonal, as the public playhouses on the south bank of the Thames are generally agreed to have been. St George's, however, was not just multisided but also multivaulted, multiarched and multipillared. Exaggerating the apparent volume of already capacious space, these manifold divisions distracted attention and distorted perception, and Hodges's stage – in itself a triumph of flexibility and mobility – was *in situ*, amid the expanses of Victorian Gothic, monumentally wrong.

By contrast, the most successful Elizabethan conversion in North America began with a building so neutral, and ruinous, as to be only an enclosure of space in rural Oregon. The building was a 'chautauqua', a single-storeyed, concrete-walled amphitheatre intended for culturally elevating and morally improving events. (The term derives from a place name in up-state New York, where the form was developed in the 1890s.) The chautauqua was 180 feet in diameter and had lost its roof by the time it was first used for reconstructive

Shakespeare performances; and it had never had a floor, having been built on a slope, which gave the auditorium a natural rake. At the lower end, the concrete circle of the chautauqua was broken by a 65-foot wide proscenium opening, its arch now reduced to 7-foot high bases. The transformation of the chautauqua into an Elizabethan theatre was the work of Angus Bowmer (1905–79), who as a student had worked on two productions that Payne guest-directed at the University of Washington in 1930. When he took over the chautauqua shell in 1934, Bowmer was himself teaching in higher education and had toured a student production of *The Merchant of Venice* on a fit-up Elizabethan stage. A revival of this production and a production of *Twelfth Night* constituted the first Oregon – and indeed, the first US – Shakespeare Festival, which played through July 4th week in 1935. Save for six years around the time of the Second World War, the Ashland festival has been held every summer since. The stage end of the chautauqua shell has been rebuilt in a succession of Elizabethan stages: the first was used from 1935 to 1940; the second from 1947 to 1958; and the third since 1959 (see fig. 12). There are constant elements across all three stages: a trapezoidal apron stage; upstage an architectural façade, including a central discovery space flanked by doors of entrance at ground level and at least one balcony above; a canopy supported by a pillar at either side downstage. However, each stage was more elaborate, and expensive, than its predecessor: the first was sketched by Bowmer on the back of an envelope and rapidly built with donated materials; the second was built, out of wood recycled from a US Army base, from plans drawn by Conway following the dimensions given in the Fortune contract; and the third was designed by the festival's scenic and technical director, Richard Hay, working from the models proposed by Adams and Hodges. The changes have served to increase and vary acting space, with shallow slipstages (and adjacent doors and windows) inserted on either side of the main stage, the balcony built out as a pavilion, and above it another gallery added to a heightened façade. Giving exclusive place to productions of Shakespeare's plays (between three and five every summer), the successive stages of Ashland's erstwhile chautauqua have proved enormously variable for the thirty-seven plays to which it is restricted.[16]

Reconstructive Shakespeareans have also built brand new theatres to serve their purposes. In Canada, Tyrone Guthrie (1900–71) convinced the organisers of the Ontario Stratford Shakespeare Festival to build 'the sort of theatre for which [Shakespeare's] plays were written' – by which he meant (a) an intimate amphitheatre and (b) a stage without a proscenium frame but with such permanent architectural features as a balcony and a trap.[17] These desiderata were approximated for three seasons under a tent before they were achieved in 1957 by the Stratford Festival Theatre, which holds just under

12 Oregon Shakespeare Festival, Ashland, July 1949: the chautauqua shell and the second Elizabethan stage.

2,300 seats, none more than 65 feet from the stage. The design was the work of Robert Fairfield (1918–94), a Toronto architect, and Tanya Moiseiwitsch (b. 1914), who had earlier assembled Elizabethan elements into a permanent set for the English history plays at Stratford-upon-Avon in 1951 (see chapter 6 below). The building in Stratford, Ontario set the standard for a series of new theatre buildings in the US and UK in the 1960s and 1970s. Most of these were not particularly intended for Shakespeare productions, let alone reconstructive ones. All, however, instantiated a shift in theatrical paradigms – from representational to indicative scenery, from proscenium to thrust or arena stages, and from rectilinear auditoria containing invisible viewers to surround seating whose occupants can be seen (even touched) by performers on stage – which reconstructive Shakespeare productions had initiated. One such theatre which *was* purpose-built specifically for the production of plays by Shakespeare and his contemporaries, the Swan in Stratford-upon-Avon, is astonishing in its beauty and energy alike.

Replicas

Besides new buildings that adopt elements of Shakespearean stages, there have been recurrent attempts to replicate the ensemble of a particular Shakespearean theatre. At the turn of the millennium a replica of the Rose

Theatre was being mooted in Massachusetts; but through most of the previous century imitative efforts had concentrated on the Globe. As a notion, this project like so much else goes back to Poel, of whom it was reported as early as 13 December 1894 in the gossip column of *The Stage*. By then he had designed a small model of the Fortune, and an identically scaled (1:24) model of the Globe soon followed, but Poel himself never managed to construct a bigger building. Both of his models, however, were probably consulted for the reconstruction of the Globe at the 1912 'Shakespeare's England' exhibition in Earl's Court, west London.[18] Here there was not just a simulacrum of the Fortune stage within one of the permanent exhibition buildings, but also a full, working replica of the Globe Theatre. The Earl's Court replica was the first Elizabethan playhouse to be erected in post-Restoration England. Like other buildings at 'Shakespeare's England' (most of them designed by the fashionable architect Edwin Lutyens (1869–1944)), the Globe replica was built to a slightly reduced scale, imperceptible because uniformly maintained. Over the six months' duration of the exhibition, from April to October of 1912, the Fortune stage at Earl's Court was used for demonstrations of morris dancing, while the Globe replica gave place, thrice daily, to thirty-minute performances of scenes from plays by Shakespeare and his contemporaries.

Subsequent replicas of the Globe were also built on exhibition grounds, but the soil was transatlantic. The 1934 Chicago World's Fair featured such a replica, which had been designed by Stevens and in which Payne directed Shakespeare productions. As at Earl's Court in 1912, the performers alongside Lake Michigan in 1934 were professionals, albeit junior ones, and the performance texts were pruned: in Chicago whole plays were staged in fifty-minute miniatures. The following year Stevens's 580-seat replica was rebuilt at the California Pacific International Exposition in Balboa Park, San Diego, and again it gave place to Payne's short-text productions. It was purchased by the local community theatre in 1937, after the exhibition had closed, and its long working life was ended only by arson in 1978. By then the replica was giving annual place to a summer season of two or three productions of Shakespeare's plays. Styled the San Diego National Shakespeare Festival, the season began with a production of *Twelfth Night* directed by Payne in 1949. The festival was initially an association between local academics (San Diego State College, now University) and amateurs (San Diego Community Theatre); but in 1954 the theatre shed its links with the college, and in 1959 the Shakespeare season became fully professional.[19]

Among the many North American Shakespeare festivals established after those at Ashland and San Diego, Globe replicas have been built on some surprising sites. A quonset hut in Los Angeles, California, accommodated a 99-seat replica Globe in which some seventy-five productions, mainly

Shakespeare, were staged across fifteen years from 1974.[20] At Odessa, Texas, the Globe of the Great Southwest was begun in 1958 and in use by 1966, and at Cedar City, Utah, the Adams Memorial Shakespeare Theatre was begun in 1971 and opened in 1977. The divergent fates of these two buildings may be in part attributable to differences in their genesis. Built to specifications (including the dimensions given in the Fortune contract) which a local English teacher had proposed in her MA thesis, the Globe of the Great Southwest was from the beginning its own excuse for being. 'The only exact replica to scale of Shakespeare's 1598 playhouse anywhere in the world', as its publicist wrote in 1976, it was erected in a town which 'hosts an annual rattlesnake hunt'.[21] Since the end of the 1970s, however, Odessa has not hosted a professional company, for however short a season, in its 418-seat replica of the Globe: the roofed building is now used mainly by amateur and touring groups. In Cedar City, by contrast, the Adams Memorial Shakespeare Theatre (capacity 881) was built for an established festival and by a production team who had a decade's experience of presenting Shakespeare plays on an outdoor platform stage backed by a tiring-house. The designer was, in his own words, 'armed with notes and drawings from past Festival seasons, comparative theatre descriptions of every major Elizabethan theater historian and critic, and a tentative vision of how it would fit into a harmonious setting'.[22]

From about the same time, unprecedented levels of research, design and construction work in London produced the replica theatre which calls itself Shakespeare's Globe but which is more accurately designated Southwark Globe 3.[23] The building is the result of a long series of scholarly best-guesses about the first Globe, its orientation, number of sides and disposition of staircases having been particularly contentious topics. Expert ideas about the original had to concede some points to safety requirements (which necessitated an increased number of exits for the audience) and to theatrical priorities (which demanded evening performances and therefore the use of floodlighting) for the replica. On still other points, the experience of each season has dictated changes for the next, with major modifications made to: the placement, size and shape of the pillars supporting the roof over the stage; the articulation of the tiring-house façade; and the kind of fixtures closing the stage entrances. The ur-version of Globe 3 went on under a tent on Bankside in the early 1970s; after years of international fund-raising as well as legal and political manoeuvring, ground was broken for the replica in 1988; two bays were built in 1992; a mock-up stage was used briefly in 1996; and, with Mark Rylance (b. 1959) as artistic director, the first full season played May–September 1997.

The subsequent commercial success of Globe 3 is against historical odds. Potential audiences for a presumptively élite entertainment are sufficiently

13 A production of *The Tempest* at the Southwark Globe, 2000. Jasper Britton as Caliban.

finite that there has rarely been much prospect of running one long enough to recover expenses. (Professionally active for more than half a century, Poel managed to make a profit on only two productions – *Everyman* and Milton's *Samson Agonistes*.) Those expenses are incurred early on in the process of production and are heavy. Often requiring specialist techniques as well as knowledge, period costumes and properties are expensive to make; and although they can be used in one production after another, recycling carries costs of storage and maintenance. Purpose-built stages and even theatres likewise both require massive outlays for construction and also incur heavy overheads to use or merely to keep in working order. Reconstructive Shakespeare has generally been a gamble for low stakes and with high risk, both sometimes reduced by inclusion within a more widely and reliably attractive exhibition.

The site of Globe 3 – on the south bank of the river Thames, close to where the foundations of Shakespeare's Globe have been found and closer still to where they were formerly thought to lie – is in itself a magnet for bardolators, but Globe 3 is not just an isolated shrine for their devotions. From early on, the site was envisaged as offering multiple attractions – a museum, a pub, a restaurant, a lecture hall and reception area, an audio-visual archive library, a second theatre, a piazza with shops and flats. Some of these have yet to happen, but additional attractions have appeared around Globe 3 anyhow: just up river, an abandoned power station has reopened as Tate Modern and a new footbridge has sprung across the Thames to St Paul's Cathedral. Located in an area that was derelict for decades but has now turned into tourist territory, Southwark Globe 3 is enviably positioned as a stop on the culture-vulture circuit. It thus enjoys one of the advantages of the replicas which were built on exhibition grounds, without having turned itself into a theme park.

Acting

Alongside the economic difficulties of funding and marketing reconstructive Shakespeare, there have been recurrent problems of theatrical practice. Rates of pay are unlikely to be attractive, while the professional marginality and seasonal timing of reconstructive productions can repel a performer good enough to go elsewhere. Moreover, reconstructive productions require special performance skills. The most basic may be the most difficult – skill in the utterance, on stage and in character, of Shakespearean blank verse and prose cadences. A few reconstructive productions have gone so far as to demand that pronunciation, inflection, pace and phrasing mimic some notion of how Shakespeare himself would have sounded. Poel's very strong opinions on this point were less persuasive, and proved less productive, than other parts of his doctrine. There have, however, been intermittent attempts to make performers sound Elizabethan: the extreme instance is perhaps Miles's production of *Macbeth* on his Mermaid stage in 1952. English-language specialists at University College, London were recruited to make both a phonetic transcription of the text in Elizabethan pronunciation and then a sound recording of the transcription. The performers learned their parts by ear, from the recording, which they attempted to reproduce. Moreover, they delivered their lines with gestures and in postures taught them by Bertram Joseph, whose *Elizabethan Acting* (1950) had recently argued that the visual stock-in-trades of the Chamberlain's Men could be inferred from rhetorical handbooks.

Less extreme in demands but far more common in occurrence are the adjustments that performers have had to make to the spaces of reconstructive Shakespearean productions. The novelty was discernible from the very beginning: the *Times* reviewer of the 1844 Haymarket *Taming of the Shrew* noted that the arrangement of the stage 'tended to give closeness to the action, and by constantly allowing a great deal of stage room, afforded a sort of freedom to all the parties engaged'. The parties so engaged have not always enjoyed that sort of freedom. Well into the twentieth century, most classical acting took place on proscenium stages, where the optimum use of space is at variance with the situation on a platform stage: anyone trained for and accustomed to playing behind a proscenium is habitually disinclined to play to more than one point on the compass (plus up and down), let alone to turn away from some part of the audience – as she or he may do on an apron and must do on a thrust stage. A trade press review of Poel's performance of *The Two Gentlemen of Verona* at His Majesty's Theatre registered the implications of a platform stage built out into the orchestra:

> The structure of this stage was in the old times conditioned by the playing in inn-yards and similar places, where the spectators wanted to see from at least three sides. Such primitive arrangements ... require an optique of their own, in which our actors are not trained. The actors are practically acting amongst the audience, and this very intimate art has a new and difficult technic. It cannot be said that last night's actors showed much proficiency in it.
>
> (*The Stage*, 21 April 1910, 17)

The verdict still holds more often than not, even though at the beginning of the twenty-first century experience of 'practically acting amongst the audience' is usual in an acting career (especially the early years) on either side of the Atlantic. For what is also common is experience of television work, which seems to erode the ability to fill a stage, perhaps due to the difference in scale. It certainly produces performers who are unaccustomed to, and appear ill at ease with, interactive audiences. At Southwark Globe 3, the capacity to play to and with live audiences of 1,500 people, nearly half of them milling around three sides of a deep thrust stage, is what distinguishes performers in their second (or subsequent) season from the novices there. What further distinguishes the best of the veterans is their ability to do this without mugging.

The difficulties registered by actors are of consequence for repertoire. While reconstructive Shakespearean ventures sometimes set out through the entire dramatic canon, the less determined drift is to the comedies, particularly *Twelfth Night*. Tragedy, by contrast, has almost always proved trickiest. Across more than half a century Poel staged several full productions of *Hamlet* but none of *Othello*, *King Lear*, *Antony and Cleopatra* or *Timon of Athens*. With the arguable exception of a visiting production (*Umabatha: the Zulu Macbeth*), no Shakespeare tragedy was attempted at Southwark Globe 3 until the third year of full operation, 1999, which saw all-male productions of *Julius Caesar* and *Antony and Cleopatra*. The acting honours for the latter, and again for *Hamlet* in 2000, went to Rylance – the one actor at Globe 3 who consistently and comfortably acknowledges the omnipresence of his audience. While Rylance's veteran colleagues do as much in comedies and histories, during tragedies even they have so far tended to ignore the spectators who surround them on three sides.

Audiences also often lack experience of the space and the playing relationships of reconstructive Shakespeare. Most lack knowledge of the visual signification operative in productions that adopt early modern English costumes, properties and gestures: that a man wearing a crown is a king may be universally recognised, but that a civilian bearing a sword is at least a gentleman, or a gentleman's servant, is illegible to anyone unacquainted with Elizabethan sumptuary legislation. Programmes can decode such points of iconography and elucidate much else as well, but they can never reconstitute the whole frame of reference. Indeed, in a theatre distinguished by spatial proximity, annotations and explanations highlight temporal distance. They are only reminders that reconstructive Shakespearean performances are plays-within-plays, representations late in the reign of Victoria or Elizabeth II of representations late in the reign of Elizabeth I or James VI & I. The audience of the former are asked to impersonate the audience for the latter: the invitation may be directly cued by actors in costume and character as groundlings, or it may be implicitly issued by the period environment, but the demand insistently interrupts the immediacy of performance in that space and structure.

Thanks to archival projects such as the University of Toronto Press's Records of Early English Drama (REED) and to archaeological ones like the Rose and Globe excavations, the sum of factual, physical knowledge about early modern English theatre is greater than it ever has been; but each access of information has exposed another area of ignorance or, at best, uncertainty. The scholarly consensus upon which reconstructive Shakespeare builds today will change tomorrow: the blueprints go out of date before the ground-breakings. Moreover, that building does not occur in a vacuum. Even if the physical structures of the theatre buildings and all the material chattels of the theatre companies were somehow to spring up again from the Bankside, the economics and the organisation of any theatrical enterprise there would be irretrievably different, as would the assumptions and attitudes of all its customers.

Thus the ambition of Poel's life, and of reconstructive Shakespeareans ever since – 'a more faithful representation of Shakespeare's plays upon the stage' – sets sights on a chimera. The ostensible goal is unreachable, and the actual achievements lie elsewhere, along an uncompleted route. Reconstructive Shakespeare projects have helped to shape Anglo-American theatre at the end of the second millennium. On both sides of the Atlantic such projects have anticipated paradigm shifts in theatrical practice: their architectural settings indicated an escape from representational scene design, and their perforation of the proscenium arch pointed the direction for stage design. In England reconstructive Shakespeare was from the start associated with the movement that eventuated in a National Theatre by 1963 and a purpose-built house for it in 1976. Leading that movement were William Archer (1856–1924) and Granville Barker: relative to Poel, the one was a sceptic who championed allied causes, the other a disciple who went his own way. According to their *Schemes and Estimates for a National Theatre* (written and privately circulated in 1904, published in 1907), a National Theatre was needed both as museum, preserving drama, Shakespeare's especially, and as nursery, training theatre personnel and educating audiences. The record of reconstructive Shakespeare shows both how quickly theatre-as-museum itself becomes a museum piece, and yet also how irresistibly theatre-as-nursery fosters change.

NOTES

1 Playbill for 19 January 1824, reproduced in George C. D. Odell, *Shakespeare from Betterton to Irving* (New York: Scribner, 1920), II, 171–2.
2 See Franklin J. Hildy, 'Rebuilding Shakespeare's Theatre' in F. J. Hildy (ed.), *New Issues in the Reconstruction of Shakepeare's Theatre* (New York: Peter Lang, 1990), 1–37, and especially 1–8.

3 Reproduced by Jan McDonald in 'The Taming of the Shrew at the Haymarket Theatre, 1844 and 1847' in Kenneth Richards and Peter Thomson (eds.), Nineteenth-Century British Theatre (London: Methuen, 1971), 160.

4 Letter dated 2 May 1881 to F. J. Furnivall, quoted by Allan Gomme in introduction to his bibliography of William Poel. A small portion of this bibliography, plus Gomme's chronology of Poel's productions, were published as appendices to Robert Speaight's William Poel and the Elizabethan Revival (London: Barrie & Rockliff, 1953). The original typescripts survive in the Theatre Museum.

5 See J. L. Styan, 'Mr Poel's Hamlet' in The Shakespeare Revolution (Cambridge: Cambridge University Press, 1977), 47–63; and Marion O'Connor, William Poel and the Elizabethan Stage Society (Cambridge: Chadwyck-Healey, 1987), 18–22.

6 William Poel, 'The Platform Stage' (1912), reprinted in his Monthly Letters, ed. A. M. T. (London: T. Werner Laurie, 1929), 81–6.

7 These were The Winter's Tale and Twelfth Night in 1912 and A Midsummer Night's Dream in 1914. Norman Wilkinson, who designed all three productions, hung the first and (even more) the last with curtains. Numerous photographs testify to the beauty of Norman Wilkinson's mise-en-scène and Granville Barker's stage management alike, yet also to the remoteness of these productions from Poel's reconstructive project.

8 Poel, Monthly Letters, 92. For Savits and Poel's debt to him, see Jill L. Levenson, 'The Recovery of the Elizabethan Stage' in G. R. Hibbard (ed.), The Elizabethan Theatre IX (Port Credit, Ont.: P. D. Meany, 1986), 205–29, especially 217–18.

9 Catalogue of the Elizabethan Stage Society sale by auction at 90 College Street, Chelsea, 5 July 1905, Lot 1, in the Shakespeare Centre Library, Stratford-upon-Avon. See Arthur Harris, 'William Poel's Elizabethan Stage: the First Experiment', Theatre Notebook 17 (1963), 111–14; and O'Connor, William Poel, 26–32.

10 Robert Atkins, An Unfinished Autobiography, ed. George Rowell (London: Society for Theatre Research, 1994), 103–4.

11 See Sally Beauman, The Royal Shakespeare Company: a History of Ten Decades (Oxford: Oxford University Press, 1982), 138–63 for Payne's directorship, and 331–2 for the 1976 set. A photograph of the set is reproduced in Payne's autobiography, A Life in a Wooden O (New Haven: Yale University Press, 1977).

12 Draft letter dated 3 June 1905 from Poel to W. S. Brassington, Librarian of the Shakespeare Memorial Theatre, Stratford-upon-Avon, in the Theatre Museum.

13 See Harley Granville Barker, 'A Village Shakespeare Stage', Drama 43 (December 1924), 57–8.

14 See Bernard Miles and Josephine Wilson, 'An Elizabethan Theatre in a London Garden', Radio Times (5 October 1951), 7; Roy Walker, 'Back to Shakespeare: Macbeth at the Mermaid', Theatre 156 (27 September 1952), 10–3; Bernard Miles and Josephine Wilson, 'Three Festivals at the Mermaid Theatre', Shakespeare Quarterly 5:3 (summer 1954), 307–10.

15 Nugent Monck, Tuesday 27 December [1932] radio broadcast, typescript in Norfolk Record Office, Norwich Central Library. This quotation, p. 8. On Monck, see Franklin J. Hildy, Shakespeare at the Maddermarket: Nugent Monck and the Norwich Players (Ann Arbor: UMI Research Press, 1986); O'Connor, William Poel, 101–11; and Franklin J. Hildy, 'Playing Places for Shakespeare: The Maddermarket Theatre, Norwich', Shakespeare Survey 47 (1994), 81–90.

16 Full accounts of the early decades at Ashland were written by Bowmer, lavishly illustrated with photographs and published by the Oregon Shakespeare Festival: *As I Remember, Adam: an Autobiography of a Festival* (1975); *The Ashland Elizabethan Stage* (1978); and *Acting and Directing on the Ashland Elizabethan Stage* (1979). I am grateful to Alan Armstrong of Southern Oregon University and to Kit Leary and Amy Richard at the Festival for their generous assistance.

17 Tyrone Guthrie, 'First Shakespeare Festival at Stratford, Ontario' in Tyrone Guthrie and Robertson Davies, *Renown at Stratford: a Record of the Shakespeare Festival in Canada* (Toronto: Clarke, Irwin, 1953), 6. See also Guthrie's account of Stratford in his autobiography, *A Life in the Theatre* (New York: McGraw-Hill, 1959), 314–37.

18 See Marion O'Connor, 'Theatre of the Empire: "Shakespeare's England" at Earl's Court, 1912' in Jean E. Howard and Marion F. O'Connor (eds.), *Shakespeare Reproduced* (London: Methuen, 1987), 68–98; Hildy, 'Rebuilding Shakespeare's Theatre', 18–25; and Martin White, 'William Poel's Globe', *Theatre Notebook* 53:3 (October 1999), 146–62.

19 On the San Diego Globe, see Felicia Hardison Londré and Daniel J. Watermeier, 'Old Globe Theater' in Ron Engle, Felicia Hardison Londré and Daniel J. Watermeier (eds.), *Shakespeare Companies and Festivals: an International Guide* (Westport, CT: Greenwood Press, 1995), 46–53.

20 See Daniel J. Watermeier, 'Globe Playhouse of Los Angeles' in Engle, Londré and Watermeier (eds.), *Shakespeare Companies*, 31–4.

21 Letter dated 1 April 1976 from Wanda Snodgrass, publicity director of the Globe of the Great Southwest, in the Shakespeare Centre Library, Stratford-upon-Avon.

22 Douglas N. Cook, quoted in unattributed article, 'Scholarship Governed Theatre', *Daily Spectrum* (Cedar City), 10 July 1983.

23 See Andrew Gurr with John Orrell, *Rebuilding Shakespeare's Globe* (London: Weidenfeld & Nicolson, 1989); Barry Day, *This Wooden 'O': Shakespeare's Globe Reborn* (London: Oberon Books, 1996); J. R. Mulryne and Margaret Shewring (eds.), *Shakespeare's Globe Rebuilt* (Cambridge: Cambridge University Press, 1997); Gabriel Egan, 'Reconstructions of the Globe: a Retrospective', *Shakespeare Survey* 52 (1999), 1–16.

6

ROBERT SMALLWOOD

Twentieth-century performance: the Stratford and London companies

In the early months of 2001 the Royal Shakespeare Company brought together productions of all eight of Shakespeare's Lancastrian history plays (with a rehearsed reading of *Edward III* thrown in for good measure). This ambitious endeavour, to which I shall return at the end of this chapter, long planned as the Millennium Project of a large and permanent theatre company, offering the plays in a variety of styles and periods, involving four directors and around 100 actors, and depending absolutely for its existence on subsidy, public and private, national and international, may usefully stand as the final milestone on the journey that Shakespeare theatre production has taken through the century with which this chapter is concerned. Many of its assumptions and characteristics are part of what we now take for granted in the performance of Shakespeare's plays; the evolutionary process that produced it is the subject of this chapter.

Stratford and London before the First World War

On 10 January 1900 Herbert Beerbohm Tree's notorious production of *A Midsummer Night's Dream*, with Oberon played (and sung) by Julia Neilson, and the rabbits of the wood near Athens played, inexorably (and, so far as theatre history records, unsung) by themselves, opened at Her Majesty's Theatre in London. Three months later, a Frank Benson company arrived in Stratford for what had, since 1886, been their virtually annual provision of the short festival season, and would continue to be so until 1919. At the turn of the century the two-week Stratford season was twice the length it had been when the Memorial Theatre opened in 1879 and offered a surprisingly broad repertoire of up to eight or nine plays, each seen only once or twice before Benson and his company left on their endless provincial tours. In spite of the brevity of these seasons, however, and of the predictability of their sets and costumes, there was acting that seems, intermittently at least, as in Benson's much praised Richard II, to have achieved real quality, while the Stratford festivals offered, to their largely local audience, a wider range of Shakespearean revivals (even extending, in 1906, to the three parts of *Henry VI*) than could be seen anywhere in British theatre. London, in these years before the First World War, offered the twilight of the Victorian actor-manager's spectacular tradition, the experiments in Elizabethan staging of William Poel (discussed in chapter 5 above), and, pointing the way forward, three productions by Harley Granville Barker that marked a major turning point in the performance history of Shakespeare's plays.

The importance of Barker's Savoy Theatre productions of *The Winter's Tale* and *Twelfth Night* in 1912 and *A Midsummer Night's Dream* in 1914 can scarcely be exaggerated.[1] They brought together a whole range of ideas from the preceding decade or so – Poel's on the open, unlocalised stage, Edward Gordon Craig's on abstract, non-representational designs, the advances in lighting achieved in Max Reinhardt's productions in Germany – and they did so in theatrical service of the text that marked a total break with the pictorialist tradition. 'I abide by the text and the demands of the text, and beyond that I claim freedom' wrote Barker in a letter to the *Daily Mail* coincident with the first of these productions; and though the critical response to them (a wonderful mixture of outraged hostility and enthusiastic welcome) was overwhelmingly to their visual aspects – to the eclectic, timeless Sicilia of *The Winter's Tale*, the stylised, vividly coloured abstractions of *Twelfth Night*, the golden fairies in their white-lit, un-Mendelssohnian wood near Athens – it is above all for their emancipation of Shakespeare's language that Barker's productions are lastingly important. The escape from the tyranny of painted canvas imposed by pictorialism, the use of patterned curtains and drapes economically to suggest mood and atmosphere, the replacement of the literal and archaeological by the abstract and emblematic and the consequent elimination of interminable scene changes, allowed scenes to flow from one to the next and for a speed of playing that put an end to the massive textual cutting that had been such a feature of the pictorial tradition.

This revolution in the aesthetics of Shakespearean performance was occurring around the same time as significant changes in the organisation of what would quickly become the century's most significant Shakespearean performance spaces. Archibald Flower had taken over the chairmanship of the Shakespeare Memorial Theatre in Stratford in 1903 and by the time of Barker's Savoy productions the process that would move the Stratford theatre from a brief annual provincial festival to a site of international theatrical pilgrimage was beginning to emerge. Lilian Baylis had taken control of the business affairs of the Royal Victoria Coffee Music Hall in 1898; just as the war began, she set up the Old Vic's first regular Shakespeare company. From that point on through the century it was, with a satisfying appropriateness to Shakespeare's own career, to Stratford and to the South Bank that one looked first for the consistently sustained energies of English Shakespeare performance.[2]

At Stratford, Flower's early changes involved the addition of a summer season to the few weeks around the birthday; moves towards an American tour, in the hope of keeping a Stratford company together between seasons; invitations to major actors from London to give a few performances each year in Stratford; persuading William Poel to bring his productions of *Measure for Measure* to Stratford in 1908 and of *Troilus and Cressida*, with the young Edith Evans as Cressida, in 1913 – both of them daring additions to the Edwardian Shakespeare repertoire; inviting Nigel Playfair, in 1919, to direct *As You Like* It in what turned out to be a completely redesigned and rethought version, famously without the moth-eaten stuffed stag from Charlecote Park that had appeared in all Stratford productions of *As You Like It* since the first festival seasons. And in 1919 he appointed William Bridges-Adams, then only thirty years of age, a firm adherent of the ideas of Granville Barker, to take over direction of the Stratford company. The appointment of Bridges-Adams, a director,[3] not an actor-manager as all those in charge of the Stratford festival had hitherto been, with a full-time, year-round contract to direct a company whose sole purpose was the production of Shakespeare's plays and who was no longer to be dependent on the comings and goings of touring companies, is a significant turning point in the history of Shakespeare production in Britain.

It was five years earlier, in 1914, that Lilian Baylis had brought Ben Greet to the South Bank to create a Shakespeare company that included the young Sybil Thorndike as its leading lady and which, by the end of the war, had presented twenty-five of Shakespeare's plays in simple makeshift sets that permitted the use of distinctly fuller texts than the old actor-managers' pictorialism; they had also presented the 1916 Stratford festival, beginning that process of interchange between the South Bank and Stratford that still survives and prospers.

From the end of the First World War to the beginning of the Second, the work of the Old Vic and Stratford companies developed along interestingly related, yet contrasting, lines. Bridges-Adams's appointment at Stratford was much connected with, and his company for the first few years partly financed by, the London-based committee dedicated to the creation of a national theatre. Nearly half a century later the nascent National Theatre was to have its first home at the Old Vic, its founder governors having been in close discussions with the governors of the Royal Shakespeare Company (RSC) about formalised collaboration almost down to the eve of its birth as a quite separate organisation, as they had been intermittently through the preceding decades.[4]

Stratford between the wars

Bridges-Adams's work at Stratford was always confined, if not altogether cribbed and cabined, by the conservatism of governors who insisted on retaining the pattern, established when the theatre was first opened, of many productions opening in quick succession, usually on consecutive nights, at the beginning of each festival season, with too little rehearsal time. There was also a continuing reluctance to allow adequate production budgets, in spite of the fact that the rapid development of tourism to Stratford meant steadily rising revenues for the theatre. The opening of the new theatre in 1932, following the fire that had, six years earlier, destroyed the 1879 building, should have been a glorious new beginning, but the building never quite lived up to the high hopes at its inauguration. Despite all its technical equipment, playing on its stage was famously described by Baliol Holloway, an experienced Stratford actor, after his first attempt at it, as being 'like acting to Calais from the cliffs of Dover'.[5] The problem that Holloway so poignantly describes has resulted in two major rebuilds and innumerable modifications over the past seventy years, but the century has ended with the difficulties still defiantly there and ideas for a new theatre being energetically discussed.

Bridges-Adams's resignation two years after the new theatre opened, and his succession by Ben Iden Payne, with his commitment to pseudo-Elizabethan productions on a semi-permanent stage, condemned Stratford increasingly through the 1930s to the status of a provincial museum theatre – with the important exception, however, of the work of the emigré Russian director Theodore Komisarjevsky. Between 1932 and 1938 he directed a number of plays at Stratford in innovative (and usually controversial) productions remarkable for their non-representational designs and atmospheric lighting, thus bringing to the Stratford stage an irreverent energy and exuberant theatricality hard to find in much of the other work there.[6] Financially, on the other hand, the lengthening season, the larger auditorium, and the constantly rising numbers of visitors to the town meant that the theatre reached the 1940s in an unprecedented (and unrepeated) state of affluence.

The Old Vic, the West End and Barry Jackson

At the Old Vic, meanwhile, the twenties and thirties were years of extraordinary theatrical achievement, under a succession of directors who could depend on the loyalty of a regular audience to allow a remarkable range of plays to be explored. Between 1920 and 1925 Robert Atkins presented every play in the Folio (with the exception of *Cymbeline*), plus *Pericles*, in simple, direct, textually full versions that established the theatre's Shakespearean reputation and prepared the way for the achievements of Harcourt Williams (from 1929) and Tyrone Guthrie (from 1933) and the succession of players whose names still seem to dominate the theatrical century: Edith Evans in the mid-twenties as Cleopatra, Katharina, Beatrice, Rosalind, the Nurse; John Gielgud from 1929 in a great list of major roles including the first of many Hamlets; Ralph Richardson, Peggy Ashcroft, Michael Redgrave, Charles Laughton, Flora Robson, Alec Guinness, and, in 1937, Laurence Olivier in a production of *Hamlet* in which Guthrie famously presented a 'reading' of the play (the term seems apt, if a little before its time) based on the psychiatrist Ernest Jones's 'Oedipus complex' theory of Hamlet's behaviour. By the end of the 1930s the Shakespearean reputation of the Old Vic was unchallenged.

To imagine that all the important Shakespeare productions in London happened in that theatre, however, would be to oversimplify the story. There was, throughout the twenties and thirties, a surprising amount of Shakespeare in the West End, including some of the more significant productions of the period, some deriving from Old Vic productions, others independent: Gielgud's most celebrated *Hamlet* of the decade ran for 155 performances at the New Theatre (now the Albery) in 1934; also at the New, the following year, was his production of *Romeo and Juliet*, with himself as Mercutio, Laurence Olivier as Romeo (they exchanged roles after six weeks), and Peggy Ashcroft as Juliet; Gielgud's remarkable *Richard II* was at the Queen's Theatre in 1937, and it was at the New Theatre, also in 1937, that Edith Evans gave her last version of Rosalind, opposite Michael Redgrave's Orlando; her performance was still being used by reviewers twenty years later as the standard for comparison for later attempts at the role.

Important innovation, too, came from the provincial theatre. In 1923, at Birmingham Repertory Theatre, Barry Jackson shocked audiences with a device that seemed at the time astonishing and revolutionary, though it has since become a regular part of the Shakespeare director's range of choices: his production (directed by H. K. Ayliff) of *Cymbeline* in modern dress was followed by modern-dress versions of *Hamlet* in 1925, *Macbeth* in 1928, and *The Taming of the Shrew* in 1930, the last three all presented in London. It was above all the 'Hamlet in plus-fours' that crystallised the responses of reviewers – on a spectrum that ranged from outrage to revelation.[7] The freedom of directorial choice about the historical period in which to set a Shakespeare play, something that we now take for granted, has its origin in the daring simplicity of Jackson's experiment.

Post-war Stratford

It was to Barry Jackson that Fordham Flower, the new chairman at Stratford, turned in 1945, with the Memorial Theatre in a curious mixture of financial strength and artistic weakness. Jackson brought with him the 21-year-old Peter Brook, whose first production at Stratford, in 1946, a version of *Love's Labour's Lost* in Watteauesque designs, gave the play an artistic coherence that, in retrospect, may be seen to mark the beginning of its theatrical rehabilitation. Jackson also brought in a group of young actors – Paul Scofield, Robert Harris, Donald Sinden and others – whose contributions to future seasons would be of increasing significance. Guest directors under Jackson included Michael Benthall, Nugent Monck, Godfrey Tearle and, more particularly, Anthony Quayle, who, in 1948, succeeded Jackson as director – the first actor-director since 1919 (and, to date, the last) – and energetically pushed forward Jackson's work in widening Stratford's horizons. Over the next few years a succession of big-name directors (Brook, Byam Shaw, Devine, Gielgud, Guthrie) and big-name actors (Ashcroft, Gielgud, Olivier, Redgrave, Richardson) were to work at Stratford. The aim was clear, overt and determined: bring the famous names to Stratford and build the plays, and the seasons, around the stars; continuity from season to season, the creation of any sense of coherent 'company', were not on the agenda. One of the highlights of this period, the second tetralogy of history plays in the Festival of Britain season of 1951, is a case in point: with Michael Redgrave as Richard II and Hotspur, Harry Andrews as Bolingbroke and Henry IV, Richard Burton as Prince Hal and Henry V, and Anthony Quayle as Falstaff, and a more or less permanent, non-localised and much admired set designed by Tanya Moiseiwitsch, the season achieved enthusiastic critical acclaim; yet it really led nowhere, and none of its actors except Quayle himself were in the following season's company.

The Quayle directorate was immensely important, however, in placing Stratford firmly on the global theatrical map and in swinging the pendulum decisively away from London as far as Shakespearean theatre was concerned. When, in 1955, Laurence Olivier and Vivien Leigh starred (the word is unavoidable) in Peter Brook's production of *Titus Andronicus*, the Memorial Theatre at last completed the Shakespeare canon in a production that flamboyantly epitomised this period of confident expansionism.

Peter Hall at Stratford

The great gear-change at Stratford came at the end of the 1959 season, with the appointment of the 29-year-old Peter Hall as artistic director in succession to Glen Byam Shaw, who had followed Anthony Quayle and pursued, with much success, a similar star-based production policy. Hall's Shakespearean experience was limited and he was better known for his work with new writing, in particular his famous 1955 production at the Arts Theatre in London of Beckett's *Waiting for Godot*. The mid-1950s had brought enormous changes to British theatre. The first visit of the Berliner Ensemble in 1956 had demonstrated what could be achieved with a coherent company working together over a long period with ample rehearsal time and within a consistent, non-illusionist production ethic. The impact of Beckett's plays and of that whole wave of post-war actors, directors and writers, epitomised, perhaps, in the production in 1956 of John Osborne's *Look Back in Anger*, were changing all the theatrical landmarks.[8] It was in this new theatrical context that Hall took over the Stratford directorate.

Hall's two most fundamental aims, a London base and a permanent company, were interdependent. The Stratford season was by now continuous from spring to autumn, but occasional and irregular tours of parts of the Stratford repertoire had never achieved more than limited success in holding companies together. The lease of the Aldwych Theatre in 1960 and the introduction of three-year contracts for actors would allow a committed company to work on Shakespeare in Stratford and on new writing in London, and provide a regular opportunity for the transfer of successful Stratford work to the West End. It was also in 1961 that the Shakespeare Memorial Theatre became the Royal Shakespeare Theatre and its actors the Royal Shakespeare Company. The new name and the London base lasted the century; three-year actors' contracts were quickly given up in recognition of the impossibility of holding actors on salaries that could not compare with offers from the commercial theatre or film and television; the same situation remains to this day.

The Old Vic and the West End after the war

The Shakespearean theatrical scene in London that the newly named Stratford company joined at the beginning of the 1960s had changed a great deal since the celebrated Old Vic and West End productions of the late 1930s. The immediately pre-war years at the Old Vic had seen Olivier as Macbeth in a Michel Saint-Denis production, as Coriolanus with Sybil Thorndike as Volumnia, and, opposite the Othello of a Ralph Richardson said to have been unaware of the interpretation, as Iago in Tyrone Guthrie's exploration of another Ernest Jones theory, the homosexual explanation of Iago's motives. The Old Vic suffered bomb damage in 1940 and London became, during the war, to all intents and purposes a touring date for Shakespeare productions, though Sir Donald Wolfit's company offered a series of Shakespeare productions at the Strand Theatre through the first years of the war and there were occasional Old Vic productions at the New. Almost the last production before the Old Vic's closure had seen the return of Harley Granville Barker to co-direct John Gielgud as King Lear: the most important single influence on twentieth-century Shakespeare production and one of the century's greatest Shakespearean actors symbolically in partnership as war was about to close a theatre that had presented the most sustained and concentrated exploration of Shakespeare's plays to be seen in London during the preceding three decades.

The search for symbolic moments might take one to the last but one year of the war when, in the summer and autumn of 1944, London saw the mid-century's three most celebrated Shakespearean actors in three of their most famous roles. At the Scala, Wolfit was giving his King Lear, the old actor-manager tradition still at full throttle; at the Haymarket, Gielgud was Hamlet once again, but on this occasion directed by George Rylands, Fellow of King's College, Cambridge, several of whose pupils, among them Peter Hall and John Barton, would have a profound influence on the directions taken by Shakespeare production in the later decades of the century; and at the New Theatre, Laurence Olivier, fresh from making of one of the most successful Shakespeare films of the century, *Henry V*, was playing the title role in a John Burrell production of *Richard III* for the Old Vic company, a performance acclaimed as one of the most brilliant of a distinguished Shakespearean career and one that would itself lead to a celebrated film.

The immediate post-war years in London saw the Old Vic company continuing at the New Theatre under the joint direction of Olivier, Burrell and Ralph Richardson and offering two or three Shakespeare productions a year, notably the two parts of *Henry IV* in 1945–6, with Richardson as Falstaff and Olivier in his famous double of Hotspur and Shallow; *King Lear* in 1945–7, with Olivier as Lear and Alec Guinness as the Fool; *Richard II* in 1947–8, with Alec Guinness as Richard; and *Love's Labour's Lost* in 1949–50, with Michael Redgrave as Berowne and Diana Churchill as Rosaline. The establishment of the company at the New Theatre had been with the help of a grant from CEMA (the Council for the Encouragement of Music and the Arts, later the Arts Council of Great Britain), the beginning of that system of public subsidy that would come to dominate the Shakespearean stage (and the time and energy of those seeking its support for their work) for the rest of the century.

In the 1950/1 season the Old Vic company finally returned to the Waterloo Road and, from 1953, embarked on an ambitious five-year plan to stage all of Shakespeare's plays, culminating in 1958 with a production of *Henry VIII* in which John Gielgud and Edith Evans returned to the company to play

Wolsey and Queen Katherine. Nearly half the productions were directed by Michael Benthall, but Guthrie, Hugh Hunt, Robert Helpmann and others all contributed and some productions came from elsewhere, such as Douglas Seale's celebrated version of the three parts of *Henry VI* from the Birmingham Repertory Theatre and Denis Carey's of *The Two Gentlemen of Verona* from the Bristol Old Vic, with the young John Neville, who would go on to play many major roles at the Old Vic, as Valentine. Apart from Neville, the Old Vic company during this period regularly included Claire Bloom, Richard Burton, Robert Helpmann, Michael Hordern, Barbara Jefford, Paul Rogers, and, towards the end of the decade, Joss Ackland, Judi Dench, Alec McCowen and Maggie Smith. Many of these names were as familiar beside the Avon as on the Waterloo Road, as commuting, from season to season, between London and the increasingly more glamorous theatrical scene in Stratford, became more regular. To see the Stratford and the South Bank companies as holding a monopoly on twentieth-century Shakespeare production in Britain is something that this chapter has already warned against, but it becomes a little more justifiable from the 1950s onwards. Important touring companies would continue to offer significant work – Wolfit in the early years, the English Shakespeare Company, Kenneth Branagh's Renaissance Theatre Company, Cheek by Jowl and others, later on: the annual summer productions in Regent's Park would outlast the century and usually offer something of interest, as would some of the provincial Shakespeare festivals, such as those at Ludlow and Stamford; there was good Shakespearean work still to be found at some of the provincial repertory theatres; but it was on the banks of the Avon and of the Thames that continuous Shakespearean endeavour came increasingly to be concentrated.

Particularly noticeable after the middle of the century is the decline of Shakespeare in productions originating with West End theatre managements. Admittedly the half-century begins with a spectacular production by Michael Benthall of *Antony and Cleopatra* at the St James's Theatre in 1951, with Laurence Olivier and Vivien Leigh in the title roles, and ends with a *Macbeth* directed by John Crowley at the Queen's Theatre in 1999, with the popular film and television actor Rufus Sewell as Macbeth. But such revivals are rare, and become rarer as the decades pass, and like these two are usually founded upon the assumed box-office vendibility of their principal actors. Occasional Old Vic or Stratford Shakespeare successes made their way to the West End in the fifties and sixties, but it is a chastening fact that for at least the last quarter of the century all RSC and National Theatre transfers to the West End have been of non-Shakespearean work (though transfer of Shakespeare productions to that other commercial medium, videotape, has, of course, developed simultaneously).

The vendibility of star actors in Shakespeare has, of course, in the later decades of the twentieth century, moved, along with the pictorial tradition, from the theatre to the cinema. For, with the CEMA subsidy to the post-war Old Vic company and with the major changes to the established theatrical world that we have already observed in the 1950s, the pendulum of Shakespeare production in Britain starts its decisive swing from the actors to the directors. For the sake of convenience, I have throughout this chapter been using the modern term *director* for the person who casts and rehearses the play (to assign to the role its most basic functions), but it is only at around this time that it begins to replace the older term *producer*. Argument about the nuances of the semantics would take more space than is available to me here, but even the briefest of pauses on the words cannot fail to observe the significance of the change: the provider of means is replaced by the maker of decisions.

Director's theatre

The appointment in 1959 of Peter Hall to run the Stratford company set a precedent that has not been broken: none of the RSC's artistic directors since that date has begun his (they have all been men) theatrical career as an actor and all of them have had university degrees in English.[9] Things were slightly different as the Old Vic moved towards reincarnation as the National Theatre. As Hall was establishing himself in Stratford and the young Judi Dench was being lauded by reviewers for her Juliet in Franco Zeffirelli's production at the Old Vic, the project to create an English national theatre – the subject of discussion and debate for a century and more in committee after reconstituted committee, of occasional government action (but mostly inaction), of an Act of Parliament in 1949 and the laying of a foundation stone by Queen Elizabeth (now the Queen Mother) in 1951, of circumspect negotiation, sometimes eager sometimes mistrustful, between Stratford and London – all this was at last moving towards a solution. By 1962 all the decisions were made and the basic shape of the major national companies in this country for the rest of the century had emerged: the RSC would operate from Stratford, but with a permanent London base for new work and transfers, while the National would remain on the South Bank (temporarily at the Old Vic until the new theatre at the end of the Waterloo Bridge should, in 1976, be adjoined to the foundation stone that had waited so patiently since 1951); both would receive substantial public subsidy, the National at a vastly higher level than the RSC; both would produce the plays of Shakespeare as well as other work, including new writing, but for the National Shakespeare would be occasional while for the RSC it would be the stock-in-trade. And so it has remained.

The National Theatre's opening production in 1963, not altogether surprisingly, was *Hamlet*. It was directed by the new company's first artistic director, Laurence Olivier, with Peter O'Toole as Hamlet. The appointment of Olivier, long foreseen and essential in providing the high profile the new enterprise required, was nevertheless an interesting survival of that earlier actor-manager tradition that most Shakespeare production was leaving behind. For all its future principals the National would follow the RSC and appoint a professional director; indeed two of Olivier's successors, Peter Hall (1973–88) and Trevor Nunn (1997–2001), have come to the National by way of the top job at the RSC; Richard Eyre (1988–97) fills the gap between them. The NT's fifth Director, Nicholas Hytner, has had considerable RSC experience. In 1964 came John Dexter's production of *Othello*, with Olivier in the title role. The film of this production has by now been seen by millions more persons than had the chance to see it on the stage; many will feel surprised that Olivier's performance, which can seem so overstated and indulgent on film, was so highly praised when it opened in the theatre. Memory is a treacherous faculty, but power, energy, and grandeur, not overstatement, are what remain in mind from the theatre experience.

The last forty years of Shakespeare production by the National Theatre under this quintet of directors, and by the RSC under its quintet of directorates – Peter Hall (1960–68), Trevor Nunn (1968–78), Trevor Nunn and Terry Hands (1978–86), Terry Hands (1986–91), and Adrian Noble (1991 to the present) – have inevitably seen a great cross-section of success and failure, of triumph and disappointment. Nevertheless, the basic structures, after all the changes and fluctuations with which much of this chapter has been concerned, have remained remarkably stable, and they are the structures of subsidised directors' theatre. In the most basic of terms these mean that the director has more or less full control over the choice of the creative team – designer, composer, lighting designer, fight director, etc. – and, normally, a very high degree of control over the budget that has been assigned to the production. That budget, and the salaries of the actors and others concerned with the performance of the play, are, in theory at least, guaranteed through the system of subsidy for the initially announced run of the production, regardless of its reception at the box-office; the system thus gives to directors, in the well-worn phrase, the 'right to fail'. A director's control over casting, until Trevor Nunn's creation of the National 'ensemble' at the end of the 1990s, has usually been a little more complete at the National, where most productions have been independently cast, than at the RSC, where casting is from a large company – something between seventy and ninety actors – brought together to cover up to a dozen plays in a season. But even at the RSC, directors are unlikely to go ahead with a production unless they can get the actors they want in the leading roles, for it has to be remembered that the opportunity to direct a particular Shakespeare play for one of the two national companies is likely to come only once in a career, so postponement will usually seem preferable to compromise. For actors, too, to play one of the major Shakespearean roles at Stratford, or at the National, will probably also be a unique opportunity; to find oneself as Viola, say, in a production that has exercised, in the opinion of reviewers and audiences, its director's right to fail, and, with Orsino, to lament, at every performance, that 'women are as roses whose fair flower, / Being once displayed, doth fall that very hour' must be a peculiarly poignant experience. Still, director's Shakespeare has brought us a very long way from the massively cut texts, generously interrupted with intervals, and from the Shakespeare of the scene painters, with which the century began. Wholly uncut Shakespeare is rare (though not unknown), but a text subjected to only modest pruning, its extent confessed in a programme note, we now all take for granted – and even the single brief interval, so vital to the theatre manager's accounts through the bar franchise, has occasionally been dispensed with in recent years by bold directors of, for example, *Macbeth* or *Julius Caesar*.

Verse-speaking

One thing that has not changed, though, is debate about the appropriate speaking of Shakespeare's verse. Pictorial Shakespeare, in its twilight years in the first decade of the century, the Shakespeare of a theatre of illusion, seems, rather paradoxically, to have been accompanied by a curiously unrealistic delivery of the lines, slow and ponderous, incantatory and portentous, or so the old recordings would lead one to suppose. Granville Barker's revolution, as we have seen, was a revolution in the speaking of Shakespeare: all his productions were greeted with hostile comment on the speed of speaking, with accusations of 'gabbling'. 'Be swift. Be alert. Be dextrous . . . Be swift. Be alert', reads one of Barker's notes to the Autolycus of his 1912 production of *The Winter's Tale*,[10] and that insistence on swiftness and dexterity of delivery was inherited by Barker's disciples. Taking over the Old Vic, Harcourt Williams determined 'to break down the slow, deliberate method of delivering the verse and the absurd convention of the Shakespearean voice'; Sally Beauman chronicles the on-going battles between Bridges-Adams and his critics, some of them governors of the Stratford theatre, about stage speaking that was alleged to destroy what was called the 'music', sometimes even the 'romance', of the verse; and in all the furore surrounding Barry Jackson's modern-dress productions the accusation that modern dress was causing actors to speak the language in a modern way was much to the fore. ('Words lose none of their beauty through being spoken as though the actors understood them', Jackson responded.[11]) Styles of theatrical speaking change as all styles of speaking change – listen to a cricket commentary of twenty years ago and compare it with a current one, for the simplest of examples of that; every group of actors, in every generation, like any group of human beings, will include some who speak more crisply, more briskly, than others. Evolution and variation are thus necessarily built into the equation; but an argument more fundamental than that about the appropriate way to speak Shakespeare's verse does not go away. Discussing his performance of Romeo in the New Theatre production of 1935, Laurence Olivier contrasted his own delivery of the lines with that of Gielgud, with whom he exchanged the role: 'John, all spiritual, all spirituality, all beauty, all abstract things; and myself as all earth, blood, humanity ... I've always felt that John missed the lower half and that made me go for the other ... But whatever it was, when I was playing Romeo I was carrying a torch, I was trying to sell realism in Shakespeare.'[12] Many actors who were with the RSC in the 1960s look back with nostalgia to the verse-speaking classes of John Barton, classes remembered for giving them what they think of as 'rules' – about line endings, caesuras, feminine endings, and so on – to be applied through a career. An understanding of the technicalities of Elizabethan verse is of course indispensable to a career that involves speaking it at length every night of the week, but this does not mean that the rational, intellectual, perhaps rather cool approach to verse-speaking that one hears on RSC recordings from the early 1960s is what actors want to imitate or audiences to hear today. Sir Peter Hall, for his insistence on constant observation of verse line endings, has been dubbed an 'iambic fundamentalist' by some of those who have worked with him. Verse-speaking at the RSC over the last couple of decades has been under the direction of Cicely Berry, whose work seeks primarily to connect actors with the physical energies of the language they are speaking, energies supported and carried by the patterning of the verse itself – for the idea that there is a conflict between observing the verse form and finding the meaning of the words is a popular heresy that is inimical to the satisfactory performance of the plays.[13] But the tension between artifice and naturalism in the approaches to the speaking of Shakespeare's verse has been with us throughout the century and remains as contentious as ever – which is an excellent thing, for it is the very tension itself that prevents what might otherwise be the calamitous victory of either extreme.

Choosing the period

Attitudes to the appropriate setting for a Shakespeare play seem to have developed less contentiously than have those to the issue of its appropriate vocal delivery. When the century began the rule was plain: the play was set, often with an extraordinary care for detail, in the historical period of its story, Roman, medieval, Elizabethan or whatever. Granville Barker's unlocalised settings for his Savoy productions, the concept largely followed in the early years at the Old Vic, then Barry Jackson's modern-dress experiments of the 1920s, blew all this away and blazed the trail to the situation of complete freedom that has pertained since the war. The efforts of Komisarjevsky and Guthrie and their contemporaries in the 1930s were directed towards the creation of settings that were unlocalised and timeless but offered an appropriate aesthetic context for the presentation of the director's approach to the play. The contribution of the designer to the effect and purpose, the very ethic, of the production, became crucial. The new design team Motley created the set for John Gielgud's first London production, *The Merchant of Venice*, in 1932; Gielgud provided a programme note:

> The costumes are inspired by many periods, but are actually of no known historical fashion. They are conceived in relation to the characters they are to clothe, and to the general scheme of colour and design. The entire pictorial and musical side of the production is frankly decorative and unrealistic. I believe this treatment to be a good one, preserving the fantasy of the Portia story and throwing into strong relief the realism of the character of Shylock.[14]

One can hardly imagine a present-day designer feeling uneasy with any of that – but, then, one can hardly imagine a present-day director feeling the need to provide a similarly self-defensive programme note. And from unlocalised space and timeless costumes, the route is direct to the empty space, ostentatious in its guilelessness, the brilliantly lit white box, the trapezes, and the circus-based costumes of Peter Brook's famous production of *A Midsummer Night's Dream* for the RSC in 1970.[15]

The present-day director's range of options now covers the entire gamut; even the old precision of period setting is still with us, as Gregory Doran's 1996 *Henry VIII* at Stratford, with its meticulously precise mid-Tudor costumes, revealed – and highly successfully. It is hard to think of any of the plays that one has not seen in modern dress, and hard to count the number of 'timeless' versions of many of them that have come one's way. When, in 1938, at the Old Vic, by way of bidding farewell to the whole Mendelssohnian way of doing the play, Guthrie set a production of *A Midsummer Night's Dream* in a pastiche Victorian world, he started another tradition of setting that remains much in evidence: the presentation of a play in a carefully re-alised historical period between Shakespeare's and our own. Peter Brook's Watteauesque *Love's Labour's Lost* in 1946 and Michael Benthall's 1948 *Hamlet*, alternating Robert Helpmann and Paul Scofield in the title role and presented in early Victorian costume, seem to have been its first manifes-tations at Stratford. There and at the National Theatre over recent decades this approach has allowed some extraordinarily powerful and effective read-ings of many plays: Jonathan Miller's late nineteenth-century *Merchant of Venice* at the National in 1970, Trevor Nunn's graciously Chekhovian *All's Well That Ends Well* at Stratford in 1981, David Thacker's French Revolution *Coriolanus* at Stratford in 1994, or Sam Mendes's *Othello*, set in a 1930s colonial world for the National Theatre in 1997, are examples from a long list. And if a director and designer can create one histori-cal period to provide a context for their production, they can also cre-ate several: deliberate anachronism, an historical eclecticism that sharpens an audience's response to the continuous relevance of the issues the play is exploring, has been a feature of much recent Shakespeare production: Sam Mendes's *Troilus and Cressida* at Stratford in 1990, for example, gave us images of warfare from the classical, the Elizabethan, and the modern worlds.

Playing spaces

If the search for effectiveness of setting has been a constant process of exploration, so too has been the search for appropriate playing spaces. The disappointment of the high hopes at the opening of Stratford's new Memorial Theatre in 1932 has been noted. In the years immediately follow-ing, Guthrie's work with Shakespeare at the Old Vic was provoking that in-creasing dissatisfaction with proscenium-arch staging that was ultimately to lead him, with Tanya Moiseiwitsch, and via the Assembly Hall in Edinburgh and the big tent at Stratford, Ontario in which the Shakespeare festival there began, to the open-stage, three-quarter-round arena theatre design of the permanent Ontario building in 1957. Directly descended from that the-atre were the Chichester Festival Theatre in 1962, and the Guthrie Theatre in Minneapolis in 1963 – and, in modified form, and somehow grander and more impersonal and much more difficult to fill with theatrical energy, the Olivier auditorium of the National Theatre complex, opened in 1976. The search for open-stage playing spaces has been driven by, and frequently gone hand in hand with, the desire for a return to something more akin to Elizabethan conditions of performance; the purist version of this movement, and its culmination in the opening of the replica Globe Theatre on Bankside in 1996, is the subject of chapter 5 above. What effect the arrival of the Globe will have on styles of playing in other Shakespearean theatres, and whether, indeed, its propensity to pander to the lowest common denominator of taste in its audiences is a passing phase or an incurable malady, it is too early to say.

The quest for ideal playing spaces might be indulged in elsewhere; Stratford, meanwhile, had to live with its 1932 Memorial Theatre; and here the periodic attempts at modification of the house, and the addition of various forms of apron stage across the old orchestra pit, continued to the end of the century (and beyond). In 1974, and in tune with the growing interest in 'alternative', small-scale theatre, the RSC turned a metal hut in Stratford, formerly a rehearsal room, into a studio theatre, the Other Place. Here began a series of explorations of Shakespeare's plays in simple, intimate productions in a versatile space that could be played in the round or end-on, or anything between the two, and which, in its original form and in the rebuilt replica, gave the RSC some of its most memorable and satisfying productions, including, as examples from a long list, Trevor Nunn's *Macbeth* in 1976 and his *Othello* in 1989, Ron Daniels's *Timon of Athens* in 1980, and Tim Supple's *The Comedy of Errors* in 1996. The studio theatre at the National, the Cottesloe, part of the main 1976 complex, has also staged some of the company's most effective and powerful Shakespeare work, including Peter Hall's 1988 versions of *Cymbeline*, *The Winter's Tale*, and *The Tempest* and the more recent trio of *King Lear* (Richard Eyre, 1997), *Othello* (Sam Mendes, 1997), and *The Merchant of Venice* (Trevor Nunn, 1999). Perhaps the most successful space for recent Shakespeare productions for either the RSC or the National, however, has been the Swan Theatre in Stratford. Built within the shell of the burnt-out Memorial Theatre and with three tiers of seating round a thrust rectangular stage and an audience capacity of some 400, it offers something of the intimacy of studio space but with more capacity for that degree of ritual that is a vital element in much Shakespearean theatre. From Deborah Warner's astonishing *Titus Andronicus* in its second season (1987) to the millennium cycle of history plays, its value and significance in the work of the RSC have been enormous.

Repertoires

The millennium cycle of history plays brings us back to where this chapter began, and to some final reflections on repertoire in general and the history plays in particular. The fluctuations in the currency of Shakespeare plays are a matter of theatrical fashion to some extent, but also of political and social mood. Until the Old Vic and Stratford productions of the thirties, *King Lear* had been little done; the same is largely true of *Richard II*; the revival in the theatrical fortunes of *Love's Labour's Lost* dates from Brook's 1946 Stratford production. The post-war Shakespearean theatre has come back again and again to *Measure for Measure* and *Troilus and Cressida*, plays hardly touched, except in Poel's experiments, in the first half of the century – but that a play about corruption at the top of government and a play about the endless futility of war should be of abiding interest to late twentieth-century theatre-goers is not altogether remarkable. More surprising, perhaps, is that, in spite of notable revivals of *All's Well That Ends Well*, including Guthrie's in 1959 (with Edith Evans as the Countess), and Nunn's in 1981 (with Peggy Ashcroft in the same role), a play that centres on its heroine's proto-feminist defiance of social and political conventions in her search for self-fulfilment has not managed to establish itself with any regularity in the repertoires: in spite of its thirty-eight years of Shakespeare productions, the National Theatre has yet to present it. The list of the twenty-four Shakespeare plays thus far produced at the National Theatre is, indeed, rather instructive. The 'big' plays are there in force: five versions of *Hamlet*, four of *Macbeth*, three each of *King Lear*, *Othello*, and *As You Like It*, and two of *Antony and Cleopatra*, *Coriolanus*, *Measure for Measure*, *The Merchant of Venice*, *A Midsummer Night's Dream*, *Romeo and Juliet*, *The Tempest* and *Troilus and Cressida*. There are the predictable absences, such as *Timon of Athens* and *The Two Gentlemen of Verona* (the latter along with the other early comedies *The Comedy of Errors* and, surprisingly perhaps, *The Taming of the Shrew*); the only *Titus Andronicus* is Gregory Doran's production in collaboration with the Market Theatre, Johannesburg; and, presumably only through an odd quirk of chance, the only versions of *Twelfth Night* have been of small-scale productions for educational tours. But the really noticeable absentees are the history plays. Only two of the ten have been offered: *Richard II* and *Richard III*, with a production of each in the seventies and, more recently, the highly conceptualised productions of *Richard II* (1995) by Deborah Warner, with Fiona Shaw in the title role, and of *Richard III* (1990) by Richard Eyre, with Ian McKellen's Richard seizing power in a vivid evocation of a fascist state of the 1930s. But the big history cycles have been left to Stratford – and, at the height of its strength in the 1980s, to Michael Bogdanov's and Michael Pennington's English Shakespeare Company.

History cycles

The work of the English Shakespeare Company (ESC) (see also chapter 11 below) is mentioned here only in corroboration of the fact that the production of a big cycle of history plays can emerge only from a company committed over a long period to the performance of Shakespeare; the ESC achieved its zenith with the history cycle and, once it was completed, began a decline. To look for other history cycles in the past century is always to find a fully established company creating them. Frank Benson, after several seasons building up the repertoire, did all eight histories of the two tetralogies across the two Stratford festival seasons of 1905–6, with all three parts of *Henry VI* in 1906; his company by then had been on the road for more than two decades. The three parts of *Henry VI* were not to be seen again until 1951, when Douglas Seale directed them at the Birmingham Repertory Theatre; it was these productions that came to the Old Vic to complete that theatre's five-year Shakespeare programme, a closely knit provincial repertory company providing what even the Shakespeare-dedicated, but still seasonally changing, Old Vic company could not. As his success grew at Stratford in the late forties it was to the histories that Anthony Quayle turned in 1951, a landmark on the journey which his work at Stratford had accomplished; but the annual changes of company at that time permitted only the second tetralogy.

Following Peter Hall's creation of the RSC in 1961, history cycles, and, more particularly, attempts on the hugely demanding, actor-hungry first tetralogy have, every dozen years or so, punctuated the company's progress. In 1963/4 came Peter Hall's and John Barton's seven-play version, known as 'The Wars of the Roses' (the three parts of *Henry VI* compressed into two plays, with much link writing by Barton), their reading of Jan Kott's *Shakespeare our Contemporary* much in evidence in their presentation of the political power structures of history, the production's metal and wood designs by John Bury strongly influenced by the work of the Berliner Ensemble. Through the late seventies, across several seasons, came Terry Hands's productions of the eight Lancastrian histories, with Alan Howard as all the kings except Henry IV, in readings much more willing to accept the inconsistencies and ambiguities of the *Henry VI* plays than the adapted versions of the 1963/4 cycle had been. Adapted again – and reduced to two plays which, with *Richard III*, formed a trilogy to which the title 'The Plantagenets' was given – and rather more pictorially staged, were Adrian Noble's productions of 1988, preceded by *Henry V* in 1984 and followed by the two parts of *Henry IV* in 1991, the latter marking his appointment as artistic director of the company. And so to the end of the century, the statutory decade or so again having passed, and another history cycle, the most ambitious in the company's history. It stretched across two seasons, with a studio version of *Richard II* directed by Steven Pimlott in 'modern-eclectic' style to produce a startling immediacy in the play's political questioning. The two parts of *Henry IV*, at the Swan in their first season, scaled up for the Barbican in their second, were directed in 'timeless medieval' costumes by Michael Attenborough and presented with searching clarity the plays' juxtaposition of personal and political issues. A boldly modern *Henry V* by Edward Hall included English recruits reminiscent of football hooligans and images of battle derived from the two great world conflicts of the twentieth century. A few months later, with a second company, at the Swan, the first tetralogy, with all three parts of *Henry VI*, was performed for the fourth time in modern theatre history (three of them at Stratford), in exhilaratingly energetic versions by Michael Boyd in 'medieval-eclectic' style, with a young company whose physical skill in rope and ladder work provided extraordinary theatrical excitement to the plays' long succession of sieges and battles and wall-scalings. In April 2001, at the Barbican Theatre, the Pit, and the Young Vic, all eight plays appeared in repertoire together for what was almost certainly the first time in the history of the professional theatre in this country; an achievement that brought together at the beginning of the twenty-first century most of the twentieth-century Shakespearean theatre's concerns with issues of direction, design, playing space, and company coherence that have been the subject of this chapter and that ought to have provided an appropriate point at which to conclude it. It is a little ironic, therefore, that only a few months after the remarkable achievement of this Millennium History Cycle, the RSC came to the decision, apparently for economic reasons, to dismantle the company structure so painstakingly built up over forty years and to introduce in its place a system of short-term contracts and independent productions. Although it will bear the RSC 'brand', such work will be essentially different from that of an ensemble company. The evidence of Shakespeare productions in the century with which this chapter has been concerned – though it holds true, in fact, right back to the Chamberlain's Men – is that the most satisfying performances of Shakespeare come from ensemble companies working together on a repertoire of plays over a long period. The RSC's decision to suspend support of Britain's only significant ensemble Shakespeare company, coinciding, strangely but appropriately, with the end of a century, has something of the passing of an era about it.

NOTES

1 Granville Barker's work has been widely discussed; convenient starting points are Dennis Kennedy, *Looking at Shakespeare: a Visual History of Twentieth-Century Performance* (Cambridge: Cambridge University Press, 1993) and J. L. Styan, *The Shakespeare Revolution: Criticism and Performance in the Twentieth Century* (Cambridge: Cambridge University Press, 1977). For a fuller account see Dennis Kennedy, *Granville Barker and the Dream of Theatre* (Cambridge: Cambridge University Press, 1985).

2 For general accounts of the history of Shakespeare performance at Stratford and at the Old Vic, see Sally Beauman, *The Royal Shakespeare Company: a History*

of *Ten Decades* (Oxford: Oxford University Press, 1982), George Rowell, *The Old Vic Theatre: a History* (Cambridge: Cambridge University Press, 1993), and J. C. Trewin, *Shakespeare on the English Stage, 1900–1964* (London: Barrie & Rockliff, 1964).

3 For the sake of consistency, and to avoid confusion, I use the term *director* throughout this chapter, though for the first half, at least, of the century, the usual term was *producer*.

4 Developments in the history of Stratford–London theatrical politics are chronicled by Beauman, *Royal Shakespeare Company.*

5 Quoted ibid., 113. On the design and construction of the theatre, see Marian J. Pringle, *The Theatres of Stratford-upon-Avon, 1875–1992* (Stratford-upon-Avon: Stratford-upon-Avon Society, 1993).

6 On Komisarjevsky's work at Stratford see Ralph Berry, 'Komisarjevsky at Stratford-upon-Avon', *Shakespeare Survey* 36 (1983), 73–84.

7 On Jackson's modern-dress productions, see Styan, *Shakespeare Revolution*, 139–59; also Claire Cochrane, *Shakespeare and the Birmingham Repertory Theatre, 1913–1929* (London: Society for Theatre Research, 1993).

8 On these and other influences on Shakespeare production in the 1950s and beyond, see the essays by Inga-Stina Ewbank ('European Cross-Currents') and Russell Jackson ('Shakespeare in Opposition') in *Shakespeare: an Illustrated Stage History,* edited by Jonathan Bate and Russell Jackson (Oxford: Oxford University Press, 1996), 128–38 and 211–30. Peter Brook's 1962 production of *King Lear* for the RSC offers a particularly good example of the influence of the Berliner Ensemble.

9 For a discussion of some aspects of 'Director's Shakespeare', see my essay of that title in Bate and Jackson, *Shakespeare: Illustrated Stage History,* 176–96.

10 Quoted in Trewin, *Shakespeare on the English Stage,* 53.

11 For Harcourt Williams, see ibid., 115–16; for arguments at Stratford, see Beauman, *Royal Shakespeare Company,* 108, 131, etc.; for Barry Jackson, see Styan, *Shakespeare Revolution,* 146.

12 BBC interview with Kenneth Tynan, printed in *Great Acting,* edited by Hal Burton (New York: Bonanza, 1967), 17.

13 Cicely Berry, *The Actor and the Text,* 2nd edn (London: Harrap, 1992).

14 Quoted in Trewin, *Shakespeare on the English Stage,* 141. For a full (and well-illustrated) survey of twentieth-century Shakespearean design, see Kennedy, *Looking at Shakespeare.*

15 For a brief account of the production, see Beauman, *Royal Shakespeare Company,* 301–8. The book-length version is David Selbourne, *The Making of 'A Midsummer Night's Dream': an Eye-Witness Account* (London: Methuen, 1982).

7

SIMON WILLIAMS

The tragic actor and Shakespeare

In a searching essay on the principles of acting, the French actor François-Joseph Talma writes that the tragic actor must preserve the characters imagined by the playwright 'in their grand proportions, but at the same time he must subject their elevated language to natural accents and true expression; and it is this union of grandeur without pomp, and nature without triviality – this union of the ideal and the true, which is so difficult to attain in tragedy'.[1] Although Talma is writing of French classical tragedy, his understanding of acting as the representation of the grand through the embodiment of the natural articulates well the basic dynamic of Shakespeare's tragic heroes. We might add that in tragedy we see the general through the lens of individual experience and the symbolic through that of the personal, a series of perspectives perhaps more effectively realised by Shakespeare than by any other tragic playwright. But to fulfil the task set by Shakespeare is no easy undertaking.

On the one hand, the tragic actor must be able to penetrate the inner life of the character. Shakespeare's tragic hero has an intricate yet resonant emotional life and within it much of the dramatic action unfolds. Conflicts at the heart of the tragedies are so private that critics have argued they are best left unperformed, because stage representation violates and coarsens them. Charles Lamb famously claimed that when we read the tragedies 'we think not so much of the crimes which [Shakespeare's villainous heroes] commit, as of the ambition, the aspiring spirit, the intellectual activity, which prompts them to overleap these moral fences'. He goes on to argue that 'what we see upon a stage is body and bodily action: what we are conscious of reading is almost exclusively the mind and its movements'.[2] While we may object that the body in action can give access to the mind, we might agree that when an actor cannot provide this access, the performance of a tragedy by Shakespeare lacks interest.

But however effectively the actor takes us into the mind of the hero, the performance will lack stature if we do not understand how it applies to ranges of experience lying beyond the character. The tragic heroes' conflicts should be sensed as representative of more than themselves, as applying to life on social, political or metaphysical planes. It is this added dimension to the role that G. Wilson Knight, borrowing from Granville Barker, labelled its 'poetry'. When the actor plays the poetry, he plays both what is known to the character and what is not known. What is not known provides the symbolic content of the role, but as the action advances the hero comes to know more of this symbolic plane and the actor should therefore increasingly point towards general truths rather than only to individual experience. 'The heroes not only see themselves as the action matures with a new clarity, but also become more objectively philosophic and self-less'.[3] Hence, as they approach their ends, figures such as Romeo and Hamlet acquire a confidence, wisdom and self-mastery they had previously lacked. Schiller named this state of mind the 'Sublime', a condition that allows the hero and the audience watching him to rise above contingent circumstances, which leads them to understand the larger pattern of things that explains and possibly mitigates the harsh conditions of existence. While not all of Shakespeare's tragic characters reach 'sublimity' – neither Lear nor Othello appear to have grown that much either in knowledge of themselves or the symbolic world – the tragic actor must always keep in careful balance the personal and symbolic aspects of the role. If the balance is disrupted the performance will strike us either as insufficient, as it will be concerned only with the psychological details of the role, or overblown, as it is not founded on concrete human experience.

One of the prime expressive materials the theatre offers the actor is space, and in order to maintain the symbolic dimensions of the role, the actor must give the illusion of filling the space of the stage so that the role can be felt as a physical presence. This will influence other characters and the audience itself. It was such 'presence' that Sheridan Knowles felt when he wrote of Sarah Siddons's celebrated sleepwalking scene in *Macbeth*, 'the chill of the grave seemed about you while you looked on her; there was the hush and damp of the charnel house at midnight ... your flesh crept and your breathing became uneasy ... the scent of blood became palpable to you'.[4] The stage incarnated her guilt. So massive are the symbolic dimensions of some of Shakespeare's roles that the power to fill the stage to use it as an expression of the symbolic power of the hero often seems beyond the capacity of a single individual. It is hard when acting Antony to play the triple pillar of the world; the strumpet's fool is relatively easy.

The actor must also be alert to the moral dimensions of tragedy. Tragedy invites us to reach judgements about conduct in private, social and political life, but it does not do so directly. Melodrama encourages actors to portray characters in a manner inviting moral approval or rejection by audiences, but tragedy provides no such facile guidelines. As we become absorbed in the careers of tragic heroes, our sympathy is drawn to them despite the outrages they commit against themselves and others. Indeed, our concern for the moral implication of their actions is aroused primarily because we have learnt to value them, even empathise with them, as human beings. The intensity of impact aroused by this concern is dependent upon the degree to which we, as audience members, have come to identify with them. Hence, tragic actors should not overtly invite us to come to moral judgements through their representation of the role. When they do indicate a moral attitude for us to adopt, we sense the tragic impact to be irreparably weakened.

Tragic acting is a contradictory enterprise. If actors devote their energies primarily to a full embodiment of the character, in order to make an impact on the audience, they must also craft a symbolic dimension to the role that has the potential to sap the power of their characterisation. If they are drawn primarily to the symbolic dimensions of the role, what Wilson Knight referred to as 'philosophic' acting, they must also ensure that their acting is still grounded in sensuous experience. These approaches so easily cancel each other out that complete success in acting one of Shakespeare's tragic heroes is relatively rare. Nevertheless, it has been argued that the full import of the tragedies can only be grasped through the medium of the actor. John Barton observes that 'most people [don't] really listen to Shakespeare in the theatre unless the actors make them do so'.[5] T. S. Eliot saw the actor as the prime interpretive figure in the theatre, when he wrote that however rich the verbal text, it points to a beauty beyond the words. 'The spoken play, the words which we read, are symbols, a shorthand, and often, as in the best of Shakespeare, a very abbreviated shorthand indeed, for the acted and felt play, which is always the real thing. The phrase, beautiful as it may be, stands for a greater beauty still.'[6] It is primarily the actor who achieves that greater beauty.

Acting theory does little to help us understand the process by which an actor can combine the contradictory aspects of tragic representation. The theory of the humours, which provided some of the fundamental principles of Elizabethan acting, lost currency in the seventeenth century, and 400 years of changing assumptions about human physiology and psychology have led to varying theories of the actor's art. None, however, indicate how to represent the full complexity of the Shakespearean tragic role. Most attempts to theorise Shakespearean tragic acting focus on the specifics of diction, characterisation and interpretation, rather than on the means by which the actor embodies those facets of the role that seem to be contradictory.

Changing conditions and concepts of tragic acting

Shakespeare's tragedies have demonstrated an unusual capacity to appeal to successive generations and disparate peoples; they have been notably performed not only in English-speaking countries, but wherever theatre is a component of cultural life. This does not argue that they embody timeless truths; it suggests that the parameters of the plays are so flexible that different cultures and generations can find their own meanings within the tragedies. Certainly, these plays allow a wide range to the imagination of actors who are free to shift emphasis between several aspects of their roles so as to give them complexions and meanings that either speak to or challenge audiences' expectations.

When discussing the history of tragic acting, we should keep in mind the varying circumstances under which actors from different generations have had to work. For example, in the contemporary English-speaking theatre most Shakespeare productions are staged under the auspices of repertory companies or festivals, who sponsor a production that will usually be acted by a single cast over several weeks or months, after which the production will be taken off. This means that most actors will have the opportunity to play a major Shakespearean role only once or twice in their lifetime. In earlier centuries, however, the structure of the repertory dictated that actors should accumulate a personal repertoire of roles, any one of which they would expect to perform at any time in their career, regardless of their age. The pre-twentieth-century actor was therefore able to develop and mature the tragic roles of Shakespeare over a lifetime.

The modern theatre also places value on originality. Shakespeare festivals such as those at Stratford-upon-Avon, Stratford, Ontario, or Ashland, Oregon attract audiences in part by assigning well-known directors to a production and casting famous actors in the lead roles, hoping audiences will be curious to see how different their work is from that of others. Yet until the latter part of the nineteenth century, difference and originality in the interpretation of a role were liable to earn an audience's displeasure; actors were expected to repeat stage business and by-play that had been sanctioned by time. Deviations from established custom, be they details such as Kean's abstracted drawing of patterns with his sword in the sand at the end of *Richard III*, questions of presentation like Macklin's assumption of traditional Scottish garb in *Macbeth*, or total reinterpretations such as Kean's Shylock, succeeded and acquired historical significance only if they caught an audience's imagination. Then the innovations, in their turn, became part of the sanctioned business. We should also bear in mind that no two actors used exactly the same texts. In the seventeenth and eighteenth centuries, Shakespeare was regularly rewritten to make the action more accessible and entertaining, and the horror of the tragic events was moderated, often with the intent of emphasising the moral dimensions of the action. Sometimes even the deaths that usually conclude a tragedy were avoided. Hence, Davenant's adaptation of *Macbeth*, performed in London in the latter half of the seventeenth and first half of the eighteenth century, involved an operatic chorus of comic witches, cuts to the role of Lady Macbeth for reasons of decorum, and vastly increased parts for Macduff and his Lady, who stood for the forces of good against the unmitigated evil of Macbeth. Macbeth did still die, though King Lear did not in Nahum Tate's famous adaptation of that tragedy, as he was not considered morally to have deserved his death. Tate's version was played in London, with variations, from the end of the seventeenth to the first half of the nineteenth centuries. Today we pride ourselves on being 'faithful' to the 'original' texts of Shakespeare, but we are not entirely certain what these are, while the exigencies of stage performance mean that all of Shakespeare's works are subject to cutting, leading to radical differences between one performance text and another.

In the history of acting, actors tend to be gauged by where they can be placed on a spectrum between the poles of formalism and apparent naturalness. Periods in which one pole is emphasised are often followed, it is assumed, by a reaction that emphasises the other. Furthermore, certain nations, such as the United States, are believed to favour realistic acting in contrast to others, such as Great Britain, that are supposed to practise a more formal style. In actuality, such distinctions are over-schematic; elements of formalism and naturalness can be identified in the work of most representative actors and, while there might be some truth in the claim that one age's naturalness becomes another's formalism, the preoccupations and styles of one age can continue indefinitely as a stratum in the performance culture of subsequent ages.

Macbeth as a tragic role

To ensure specificity in our discussion of Shakespearean tragic acting, I shall focus on just one of his roles, Macbeth, and trace how actors have approached it in different periods of history. It has been dismissed as impossible. The immensity of the conflict that the murder of Duncan releases within the hero has caused some to claim that no actor can adequately represent it. Hamlet, Coriolanus, Romeo, Othello, even Lear, seem to lie more readily within the actor's grasp than Macbeth. Nevertheless, *Macbeth* is among the most frequently performed tragedies, and even though few productions are entirely satisfactory, its central role highlights aspects of tragic acting more saliently than other Shakespearean tragic heroes.

The main difficulty lies in persuading audiences to identify with a downright brute. Macbeth has the most appalling career of any Shakespearean tragic hero, and the murders he commits reveal a spiritual landscape whose horror is unparalleled in tragic theatre. But he is also the most interesting and sympathetic of heroes. His speeches on all he has lost in life are widely acknowledged as some of the most moving expressions of disenchantment in our culture. But though we identify with Macbeth, we never lose our terror at what he has done; indeed that terror feeds our sympathy. The actor must not only remind us constantly that Macbeth is a heroic villain, he must convince us he is a normal man, his scenes with his wife being among the most intimate in all Shakespeare. His closeness to his wife draws us closer to his predicament, and the release of emotions we experience at the end is accordingly more complex, even painful.

Macbeth highlights the inwardness of tragic experience. More than other Shakespearean tragedies, the action centres on one character, and the stage world often becomes an embodiment of his inner consciousness, a projection we now call 'expressionistic'. In *Hamlet* and *Othello*, we are taken into the minds of the central characters, but these plays largely involve the hero in conflict with the world on stage. Macbeth is opposed by the forces of Malcolm and Macduff, but they are represented with less fullness than is common in Shakespeare, throwing into sharper profile the stage world as a hideous projection of Macbeth's mind. How can an actor develop a 'presence' large enough to exercise that immense function? Also, as a performance of *Macbeth* rarely takes more than two and a half hours, how can the actor condense a lifetime's experience into the brief span allotted him on stage?

Enlightenment and Romanticism

The popularity of *Macbeth* in the theatre of the eighteenth century is surprising. As purveyors of the ideals of the Enlightenment, the primary mission of standing theatres in Britain and Europe was to craft a repertoire, mainly of classic but some modern works, which educated citizens by cultivating their sensibilities and awakening their moral sense. 'The proper business of the stage and that for which only it is useful', declared Lord Chesterfield, 'is to expose those vices and follies, which the laws cannot lay hold of; and to recommend those beauties and virtues, which ministers and courtiers seldom either imitate or reward'.[7] In Europe, where theatres were often under the aegis of royal patrons, they also encouraged respect for authority. *Macbeth* was difficult to incorporate in such a theatre because of the 'mixed' nature of its hero, by which was meant the ambiguous moral appeal of the role and the blurred distinctions between right and wrong. Yet this was the time when Shakespeare's tragedies were moving to the centre of the repertoire in England and were being introduced on the European, especially the German stage, so *Macbeth*, one of Shakespeare's greatest works, could not be ignored.

Enlightenment philosophy was based upon John Locke's assumption that human beings were instinctively good. As humans were innocent, evil could only come from outside and must therefore be represented as a power driving them against their nature, a deviation from the norm, to be eradicated. Therefore Macbeth became, as Joseph Donohue puts it, 'a figure for all virtuous men seduced and irredeemably betrayed by outside influences and, paradoxically, by their own innate sensibilities'.[8] The stage paradigm for an Enlightenment Macbeth was provided by David Garrick, who acted the role at Drury Lane between 1744 and 1768. Until Garrick, *Macbeth* was not highly regarded, because the predominantly rhetorical style of acting made little sense of it. Garrick focused on the inner life of the character by embodying a man vacillating between good and evil, emphasising an innocence in his character, a strategy made possible by the strong-minded Lady Macbeth of Mrs Pritchard. Garrick attended to the minutiae of bodily and vocal expression with a closeness unparalleled in his day. After the murder, he delineated the workings of conscience and the growth of horrified guilt so precisely that his Macbeth was bereft of all action. When the murder was discovered, his body and tongue were paralysed, as if his mind was abstracted from the world around him. Throughout the events of act 2, Garrick maintained the illusion of Macbeth observing himself, as if part of his character had remained untouched by what he had done. As the action progressed, the sufferings caused by his tortured mind refined him into a man of sensibility, rather than coarsened him into a tyrant. His death was marked by a moralistic speech he had composed himself, which highlighted the error of his ways. It was, according to the French/Swiss choreographer Jean-George Noverre, an exemplar of the workings of remorse. 'His gestures without losing their expression revealed the approach of the last moment; his legs gave way under him, his face lengthened, his pale and livid features bore the signs of suffering and repentance'.[9] Garrick focused on the moral thrust of the play, holding his audience by insisting that part of Macbeth's consciousness observed his actions. Consequently he maintained an innocence that mitigated the horror of his deeds and endowed the role with that 'philosophy' which extends beyond the purely personal (see fig. 14).

John Philip Kemble, the pre-eminent actor in London at the turn of the eighteenth century, is considered the antithesis of Garrick because his statuesque demeanour, laboured delivery and tendency to reduce characters

14 David Garrick as Macbeth, in the dagger scene.

to a single trait contrasted strongly with Garrick's complex litheness. Descriptions of Kemble's Macbeth, however, suggest that he tended to refine and highlight central features of Garrick's interpretation. Kemble played the role from 1778 until his retirement in 1817. His Macbeth was initially noble, brave and stoic, indifferent to the witches, and his development of the character was subdued. Macbeth's remorse after the murder was delivered quietly, as if he were in a dream; he stood 'motionless; his bloody hands near his face; his eyes fixed; agony on his brow; quite rooted to the spot'.[10] He was goaded to action by Lady Macbeth, usually played, in a celebrated interpretation, by his sister Sarah Siddons, who because she acted out of love for Macbeth, deflected from him full responsibility for the carnage of the action. Indeed, Siddons's majestic Lady Macbeth usually dominated the performance; she was, according to Hazlitt, 'the apparition of a preternatural being'.[11] Only after Lady Macbeth's death did Kemble take over the stage, erupting into furious action and effecting fine contrasts as he oscillated between anger and nostalgia for a world that could have been. 'His voice trembled and fluttered among the fond images of decay and clung with melancholy grace to the blessings.'[12] Like Garrick, though with greater pathos and less moral comment, he sustained the innocence of Macbeth, of a man contemplating the horrible manifestations of a world he does not understand and is not, in the last count, responsible for.

Actors contemporaneous with Kemble, but associated with Romanticism, also represented the divisions within Macbeth, though with even less clear moral intent. The two most representative were Ferdinand Fleck and Edmund Kean. According to Ludwig Tieck, Fleck, who from 1786 until his death in 1801 acted at the Berlin National Theatre, was the first German to represent Shakespeare's tragic roles in all their fullness. Kean, the leading tragedian at Drury Lane from 1814 until the late 1820s, brought to the English stage the volatility of Byronic Romanticism, giving roles such as Shylock, Richard III, and Othello a vitality that audiences, accustomed to morally oriented performances, found strangely exciting and disturbing (see also chapter 3 above).

Fleck first played Macbeth in 1787, when the play was virtually unknown in Germany. He presented a noble, warrior-like figure, but whereas Garrick and Kemble established Macbeth's nobility and courage from the start, Fleck became powerful only after the murder of Duncan, as if the crime validated rather than confounded his virtues. From then on his presence grew, though he undermined Macbeth's confidence by subtle indications of uncertainty, above all in the way he walked. A telling contrast occurred in the banquet scene. Initially divided between fury and fear, the less sterling aspects of his personality took over and he ended the scene babbling like a child. Tieck claimed his main contribution lay in his capacity to explore and explain the furthest reaches of Shakespeare's tragic heroes better than any English commentators.[13] He created the illusion that these furthest reaches of the character ultimately complemented each other and, as he died, Macbeth's evil was sensed as being incorporated into the benign wholeness of the universe. In 1800, Schiller produced an adaptation of *Macbeth* in which the universe is posited as essentially benign, an idealised version of the Enlightenment view of evil as aberrant. Although Fleck's performance of Macbeth was unsettling, it preserved the Enlightenment view of the character later echoed in Schiller's version of the tragedy. Schiller's *Macbeth* was performed universally in Germany for most of the nineteenth century.

Kean's Macbeth was more disturbing. With its excursions into emotional extremes, the role should have been natural for Kean, but tellingly he failed in it. Hazlitt identified the tragic dimension of the role by comparing Richard III to Macbeth. Richard, he argued, is cruel by will, Macbeth from 'accidental circumstances'. Richard acts out of misanthropy and love of mischief, while Macbeth is full of humanity and sees 'sights not shown to mortal eye and hears unearthly music' (*Hazlitt*, v, 205–6). These dimensions, itemised by Hazlitt in detail, compose the poetry of the part and give it greatness. But they eluded Kean. His Macbeth, like his Richard, was 'tight and compact'. His performance was noted for contrasts between terror and, at the end, a brave defiance at the forces massed against Macbeth, but he captured none of these poetic dimensions. More than a psychological representation with a common touch was needed to project Shakespeare's hero across the footlights.

Nevertheless, Kean's reduced Macbeth paved the way for the most celebrated Macbeth of the nineteenth century, that of William Charles Macready. Macready's growth in the role argues persuasively in favour of the old star system of acting, for he first played it at Covent Garden in 1820 but claimed only to have perfected it thirty years later at his retirement performance. He was the most deliberate of actors, preparing each moment with careful study. Over the years his Macbeth changed, though certain aspects were constant. The spectacle of the production, involving several elaborate royal processions, emphasised strongly the legitimacy of the royal rule that Macbeth has overthrown. But he was never set in melodramatic opposition to it. Macready always maintained a tension between the idealistic aspects of Macbeth's character and its weaker and more venal aspects, at different phases of his career emphasising one dimension in favour of the other. Hence both Hazlitt and George Henry Lewes found him modern and prosaic, while for others his performance, especially in the final act, reached peaks of intense excitement. He bridged the generations. His admiration for Kemble led him to project dimensions of heroism and innocence. His first appearance dressed as a highland chief has been nicely described as Wordsworthian,[14] but in the scenes with his wife, he represented with painstaking accuracy a man vacillating between horrified fascination at evil – his Macbeth does not seem to have been moved by ambition – and a highly active moral sense that left him in no doubt as to the dreadful fate to which he was consigning himself. Although Macready's delivery of Shakespeare's verse was often less than musical and struck many as mannered, he endowed the role with poetry by making Macbeth's 'imaginative terror' at the emanations of the supernatural unnervingly palpable. Throughout, he also kept in touch with a stratum of normality. He was never alienated from Lady Macbeth, her love gave him impetus and support, and his reaction to her death was not sentimental, but one of cold despair and desolation. Although Macready may have lacked Kemble's nobility and Kean's vitality, he managed to combine

15 William Charles Macready as Macbeth. Engraving taken from the edition
of Shakespeare published by John Tallis & Company, *c.* 1855.

the conflicting dimensions of tragic acting in a way that gave the role an
unusual wholeness and, as it borrowed from tradition as well, it struck audiences as innovative and vigorous. Macready's Macbeth was of epochal
significance.

Fin-de-siècle Macbeth

English Shakespeare performance in the late nineteenth century was dominated by actor-managers, who performed leading roles against tailor-made
romantic scenery poetically evoking an aura of historical authenticity, designed to set off their performance to maximum advantage. In Germany actors toured from one theatre to another, fitting into pre-existing productions.

The prominence of the virtuoso actor, combined with the rising interest in psychology, led to a growing fascination with the mental dynamics of Shakespeare's tragic heroes. While this gave fresh life to familiar roles, some complained it caused a decline in the stature of tragedy. Actors emphasised idiosyncrasies of personality rather than symbolic dimensions and audiences were uncertain about what was being represented on stage. Above all the sense of innocence, characteristic of Enlightenment interpretations, had dissolved.

The tenor of late nineteenth-century tragic acting can be grasped from strikingly similar performances by two actors pursuing entirely separate careers. Henry Irving, the most successful actor-manager in London, made his reputation primarily in Shakespeare and melodrama, eschewing modern developments, while his contemporary, the German Friedrich Mitterwurzer, was celebrated for 'broken characters' and became the first great German interpreter of Ibsen. Irving performed Macbeth in two separate productions, in 1875 and 1888, noted for the poetic wildness of their settings; Mitterwurzer performed the role from 1877 in several venues. Neither can have known of the other beyond general reputation.

Critical reaction makes it clear that the sense of an inherited tradition of interpretation had disappeared, and there was no critical consensus as to the meaning of Irving or Mitterwurzer's work. Some saw their Macbeths as series of disconnected episodes, others found continuity and momentum. Both actors were noted for the psychological acuity and gloominess of their portrayals, with no compensating sense of nobility. Unmistakably, both had the murder of Duncan in mind prior to meeting the witches and neither was bothered by conscience. Rather, they feared only the dreadful images flung up by their imagination, which they took as indications that they were subject to dreadful retribution. Irving claimed that Macbeth was a brave soldier, but a moral coward, 'a poet with his brain and a villain with his heart'.[15] The same might be said of Mitterwurzer. These Macbeths did not curry favour with audiences.

Psychological credibility was the prime concern for both actors, but this resulted in performances marked by luridness more than subtlety. There was, for example, a livid quality to their banquet scenes. In contrast to the customary ravings, the moment Banquo's ghost appeared, both Irving and Mitterwurzer were tongue-tied. This led to the high point of Mitterwurzer's performance. His body was temporarily paralysed and his lips could do nothing but mutter 'incomprehensible babbling'. Then his fury burst out with astonishing suddenness and he attacked the ghost violently, flinging plates, goblets, even food at him in his frenzy. As the ghost disappeared, Mitterwurzer's Macbeth burst into laughter.[16] Irving reserved his crowning effort to the end when he ranged the stage like a 'great famished wolf', heroic in his exhaustion.[17] The actors differed in their relationship to Lady Macbeth. Irving acted with Ellen Terry, a famously exotic Lady, who wore pre-Raphaelite dresses and worked on the world through charm, even while sleepwalking. Mitterwurzer, who rarely acted extensively with one company, played opposite various Lady Macbeths and seems to have paid little attention to them.

The persistent criticism of *fin-de-siècle* acting was that it lacked the stature necessary for tragedy. But some could invest Macbeth with heroic dimensions, though again at the cost of subtlety. The Italian virtuoso Tommaso Salvini, who toured Europe and America from 1869 to 1890, represented Macbeth as towering over all around him. His intent was to arouse admiration for Macbeth until the very end. Robert Louis Stevenson referred to his 'royalty of muscle',[18] arguing that he gained his courage from good circulation. Salvini did little to represent the negative aspects of Macbeth, consequently, he could only end with 'an indescribable degradation, a slackness and puffiness'. Equally imposing was the leonine German virtuoso Adalbert Matkowsky, who played the role in Berlin between 1901 and 1909. He too failed to capture the divided aspects of the character. Playing in a costume reminiscent of a Wagnerian warrior, Matkowsky's Macbeth was a man of action, all promptings of conscience being consumed by his overwhelming ambition for the throne.[19] His Macbeth had a headlong quality, as his ambition gave him confidence in everything he did. Even the death of Lady Macbeth was something he had no time to worry about. Only when the deceptiveness of the prophecies became apparent did his confidence collapse, but even then it was momentary as he raised the final moments to ones of massive defiance. The Macbeths of Matkowsky and Salvini demanded awe and fear, but elicited little pity.

Macbeth in the twentieth century

Shakespeare's tragedies in the twentieth century have been staged in many different environments, under a variety of auspices, and in virtually every theatre culture, so his heroes have been subject to a wide range of different acting approaches. Three have been particularly influential. Stanislavsky's theories have led actors to focus on unconscious impulses, in particular those suggested by the irony and imagery of the text. More influential in the performance of Shakespearean drama has been Brecht's theory of alienated acting, a style that emphasises the interdependence of individual action and sociopolitical life. The theories of Artaud inspire the actor to incarnate forces lying beyond immediate sensate experience and so materialise the numinous universe revealed by the tragic hero's career. Each theory has broadened the expressive range available to the actor.

Macbeth has not always fared well on the twentieth-century stage, but it is still among the most frequently performed of Shakespeare's plays. In recent decades it has acquired renewed interest, as it provides an opportunity to explore the psychic intricacies of that grimmest icon of the twentieth century, the dictator. This makes Macbeth difficult for us to accept as a tragic hero. We are not prepared to see any ideal sides to Hitler, Stalin or Idi Amin, all of whom have been referred to in recent productions of the play. The concern of contemporary directors with dictatorship can be disconcerting, as the methods of assault by which the dictator has gained his power are all too often transformed into the artistic means by which the production makes its impact, a technique making some modern productions of *Macbeth* close to unbearable. Nevertheless, there have been performances as fine as any in previous centuries. By common consensus, in the English-language theatre, there have been three interpretations that have struck a particular chord with modern audiences, all of which were first seen at Stratford-upon-Avon: Laurence Olivier in 1955, Ian McKellen in 1976, and Antony Sher in 1999.

Olivier's Macbeth was instantly proclaimed a masterpiece, calling forth comparisons with Garrick and other noted interpreters. In historical perspective, his interpretation is reminiscent of the eighteenth century, though with a post-Romantic lack of moral dimension. From the start, his Macbeth had a magnetic quality, without the abnormal psychology popular earlier in the century. He could depend on the loyalty of all around him, but through fear rather than love. The witches did not implant the idea of Duncan's murder in him, but, with a distinct air of weariness, he recognised them as part of his mental landscape. This endowed him with an innocence, especially reminiscent of Kemble, but innocence complicit in evil. 'He radiates a kind of brooding sinister energy', wrote Richard Findlater, 'a dazzling darkness . . . one glimpses the black abysses of the general's mind'.[20] The early passages were restrained, though their dark fascination kindled one's imagination. By suggesting that basic motives were beyond his immediate control, Olivier secured the symbolic dimension of the role.

Kenneth Tynan claimed that Olivier succeeded because he built the role to a climax of energy at the end, whereas other actors spent all they had in the first two acts. Olivier's Macbeth was scrupulously constructed; the events surrounding Duncan's murder were subdued, Macbeth spoke the dagger monologue as if drugged, was indifferent to the murder itself, and not much worried by supernatural promptings. What did destroy him, to his surprise, was his failure to find security, as if his supernatural familiars had betrayed

16 Laurence Olivier as Macbeth, with the witches, from Glen Byam Shaw's 1955
Stratford-upon-Avon production.

him. This rather than guilt drove him to further violence and gave psychological acuity to the interpretation. He was successful as king, but the height
of his assurance was complemented by an equally deep descent into despair
and madness, first when he saw Banquo's ghost – his reaction was as strong
as that of any nineteenth-century actor – and in the battle, which brought
the role to a massive climax.

Ian McKellen performed in an unfamiliar theatre for tragedy, The Other
Place, a small performing space in Stratford. Since then, productions of the
tragedies reduced in scale have become common. In an intimate setting, the
large gestures expected of tragic acting must be abandoned, as the role speaks
to the audience through personal emotion. Such closeness reveals dramatic
character to be composed of individual personality and of relationships with
others. There was nothing noble about McKellen's Macbeth; indeed, with it
he made us aware that nobility may no longer be part of our theatrical landscape. There was little that was even likeable about him, let alone admirable.
From the start he was an astute politician manipulating circumstances to his
advantage. The world in which he lived operated on manipulation: in the
political vacuum created by a distastefully pious Duncan, Malcolm had an

17 Ian McKellen as Macbeth, with the witches, from the 1976 production
at The other Place, Stratford-upon-Avon.

eye on the political chance, Banquo did not lack ambition, and Macduff was
a bully at heart. Macbeth was a product of his world, not an exceptional
personality within it. The one touch of warmth in Macbeth's life came from
his wife, played with concentrated passion by Judi Dench. As Macbeth waded
further in blood, their relationship atrophied, which only added to the bitter
chill of the production (see also chapter 9 below). Performed by a small cast

within a simple circle, the focus of the production was on relationships and the dynamics of the mind. Macbeth's contacts with the supernatural gave no evidence of poetic insight. He saw Banquo's ghost in an epileptic fit, while his confidence in the witches' prophecies did not arise from faith in providence, but from dementia. The visions the witches had shown him were only dolls, which he clung to like a cringing child until his death. While the scale of the role was reduced, the association of mental and physical disease with ruthless ambition provided disturbing insights into the workings of political power.

Although the stage world of Sher's Macbeth was more violent and harsh than McKellen's, authority was not represented as corrupt by nature. Duncan was genuinely benign, his court and army seemed reliable and honest, the costumes from the Second World War had an air of comforting familiarity, and the sparse Christian symbolism was employed without irony. Macbeth's regicide therefore made him more a deviant than a representative of the world he ruled. Sher's Macbeth began unambiguously as a popular leader and the witches' prophecy seemed genuinely to surprise him, so that the central focus of his performance was on the conflict between his new-found fascination with evil and his longing for the moral integrity of the world from which he had excluded himself. It was manifested physically by Macbeth's constant struggle to hold hysteria at bay, which resulted in an exaggerated clarity in speech and demeanour. It also created the sense that, after the murder, Macbeth was essentially an actor whose guises of authority, cruel play, and bonhomie appeared rather to be ploys used to fend off encroaching madness than means of exercising rule. He was deeply dependent on his wife, played with striking sophistication and sexual allure by Harriet Walter. His affection for her never abated, so even after he took over as the prime agent of evil, the warmth of their feelings for each other sustained our pity for them. Sher's Macbeth was far from heroic; after a brief moment of pathos when he heard of his wife's death, he degenerated into an obscene and childish terror. Ultimately Sher had little to say about the political world, but as a representation of psychological collapse, the performance carried great power.

Spectacle is often avoided or contained in productions of tragedy in contemporary western theatre, primarily because its use as a manifestation of power in the political world has undermined trust in its integrity. Elsewhere, notably in eastern Asia, spectacle has survived as an essential component of production, making us aware of what tragic performance in western theatre might be losing. Spectacle provides the hero with a setting that allows him to develop the larger dimensions of the role, as is apparent from the Macbeth of Masane Tsukayama, directed by Yukio Ninagawa in Tokyo in 1980. Set during the Japanese civil wars of the late sixteenth century in scenery reminiscent of a Buddhist shrine, military and religious aspects of the action were to the fore. The use of *mie* (gestures and poses) from *Kabuki*, as well as sliding screens and two *hanamichi* (raised entrances through the audience), created a Japanese setting, but this was strangely contrasted with passages of western classical music, notably the 'Sanctus' from Fauré's *Requiem* and Samuel Barber's 'Adagio for Strings', whose serenity suggested reconciliation beyond the violence of the dramatic action. This gave Tsukayama a broad range of symbolic experience within which to craft his Macbeth. The sharply articulated *mie* and the abrupt contours of the *Kabuki* speech patterns enabled him to represent Macbeth's torments with great intensity and breadth, giving his interpretation a size difficult to achieve in western theatre today. The most remarkable part of the performance, though, came in the final act, as Macbeth lamented over all he had lost in life with a slowness and deliberation rarely seen in western theatre. This lent him immense stature, confirmed by the supernal ease with which he dispatched all who attacked him in the subsequent battle. Two or three times the rage of the battle was suspended, and all that could be heard was the peace of Fauré and Barber's music, as if Macbeth would be part of a universe in which even his violence would be assuaged. His death on stage, from one massive blow by Macduff, was breathtakingly sudden, but the play ended with a sense of peace restored.

The blood and bile of contemporary productions of *Macbeth* seem far from the comparatively restrained performances of the eighteenth century. They reflect, perhaps, our doubts about the innate goodness of humanity and the benign order of the universe. Under such circumstances, it is not always easy for the actor to achieve the union of 'grandeur without pomp and nature without triviality'. But Olivier and Tsukayama did this, recalling the heroic restraint that characterised the representation of *Macbeth* until the mid-nineteenth century. But even Antony Sher, acting at the end of the twentieth century, could not give us a totally degraded hero. His Macbeth never lost sight of the innocence that had once been his, and so he did not seem totally complicit in his crimes. Accordingly there was a pathos in his death that reminded us of the goodness from which he had fallen. It suggested too that human nature is never beyond self-redemption, which may be the ultimate message that tragedy brings us.

NOTES

1 François-Joseph Talma in Toby Cole and Helen Krich Chinoy (eds.), *Actors on Acting* (New York: Crown, 1970), 183.
2 Charles Lamb, 'On the Tragedies of Shakespeare' in *Complete Works* (Philadelphia: Amies, 1879), 535.

3 G. Wilson Knight, *Shakespeare's Dramatic Challenge* (London: Croom Helm, 1977), 48.

4 James Sheridan Knowles, *Lectures on Dramatic Literature* (London: F. Harvey, 1875), 21–2.

5 John Barton, *Playing Shakespeare* (London: Methuen, 1984), 7.

6 T. S. Eliot, *Selected Essays, 1917–1932* (New York: Harcourt, Brace, 1932), 53–4.

7 David Thomas (ed.), *Restoration and Georgian England, 1660–1778*, Theatre in Europe (Cambridge: Cambridge University Press, 1989), 213.

8 Joseph Donohue, *Dramatic Character in the English Romantic Age* (Princeton: Princeton University Press, 1970), 150.

9 Jean-George Noverre, quoted in George Winchester Stone and George M. Kahrl, *David Garrick* (Carbondale: Southern Illinois University Press, 1979), 559.

10 Brander Matthews, *Papers on Acting* (New York: Hill & Wang, 1958), 90–1.

11 William Hazlitt, *The Complete Works of William Hazlitt*, 21 vols. (London: Dent, 1930–34), V, 373. Hereafter cited within the text as *Hazlitt*.

12 Leigh Hunt, *Dramatic Essays* (London: W. Scott, 1894), 232.

13 Edgar Gross, *Johann Friedrich Ferdinand Fleck* (Berlin: Gesellschaft für Theatergeschichte, 1914), 145.

14 Dennis Bartholomeusz, *Macbeth and the Players* (Cambridge: Cambridge University Press, 1969), 159.

15 Henry Irving, quoted in Alan Hughes, *Henry Irving, Shakespearean* (Cambridge: Cambridge University Press, 1981), 101.

16 Eugen Guglia, *Friedrich Mitterwurzer* (Vienna: Gerold, 1896), 86–7.

17 Ellen Terry, *The Story of My Life* (London: Hutchinson, 1908), 306.

18 Robert Louis Stevenson, quoted in Bartholomeusz, *Macbeth and the Players*, 210.

19 Philipp Stein, *Adalbert Matkowsky* (Berlin: Schuster & Loeffler, n.d.), 64.

20 Richard Findlater, quoted in Anthony Holden, *Laurence Olivier* (New York: Athenaeum, 1988), 294.

8

PETER THOMSON

The comic actor and Shakespeare

During the summer of 2000, *The Tempest* was staged at Shakespeare's Globe in London. There was an implicit challenge to traditional readings of the play in the casting of Vanessa Redgrave as Prospero, but her presence was as imposing and her voice as rich as any man's need have been. Perhaps this Prospero was more completely Miranda's parent, less securely the colonialist patriarch, than Michael Redgrave was at Stratford in 1951, but there was never any sense that allowances were being made. This was our Prospero, and we respected him. A cultural shift of great significance is even more evident here than in the reaction to Fiona Shaw's playing of Richard II, because the crossing of gender quickly ceased to be the audience's focus. For one thing, Redgrave's performance of the role brushed lesser considerations aside; for another, Prospero's fecundity is peculiarly genderless; and for a third, there was Caliban.

Actors of comedy and comic actors

The ability to sustain a role in a comedy was no less a routine requirement for professional actors in Elizabethan England than it is now. A genuine comic actor, though, is comparatively a rarity. We do not know who created the role of Caliban, but Shakespeare had someone in mind when he wrote it as an extreme stylistic contrast to Prospero. Prospero is at the very least a Tudor grandee, Caliban a clown in the original, non-theatrical sense – a rough, rustic peasant. Elizabethan audiences would scarcely have doubted Prospero's claims to ownership of the island, whatever post-colonial questions we may now wish to pose. Not until towards the end of the nineteenth century did the theatre express any sympathy for Caliban, and Herbert Beerbohm Tree's decision to make him *the* centre of attention in his 1904 production at His Majesty's Theatre was a bold initiative. Despite his occasional forays into tragedy, Tree was essentially a comic actor, at his best only when he could indulge his delight in the playfulness of plays. In his own theatre, he as Caliban competed with Prospero for the ownership, not only of the island, but also of the play. He did so by padding out the written text with stage business, emphasising Caliban's sensitivity (to music in particular, and to the world at large), and by featuring the repossession of *his* island in a final tableau of calm beauty. Tree's Caliban was no longer a comic butt. Jasper Britton's Caliban at the Globe in 2000 had no more sensitivity than a football hooligan, and was tonsured and dressed/undressed to emphasise the contemporary association. What was astonishing was his hold on the audience. He spat fish at them, singled some out for humiliating personal encounters, made no evident attempt to endear himself to them; and they loved him. When he incited them to join him in a tribal chanting of his name ('Ban-Ban-Caliban' shouted with a thumping rhythm like the football fans' 'Ar-sen-al'), they did so with relish, and certainly with more spontaneity than did Stephano and Trinculo. The audience at large, and the standing groundlings above all, may have admired Prospero, but the comic/grotesque Caliban was their man. I do not know whether this fealty was evident at every performance, but the engagement was so absolute at the one I attended that I was forced into a reappraisal of the likely nature and impact of comic acting on the Elizabethan stage (see fig. 13, p. 91).

There is, above all perhaps, an issue of proximity. It is a natural tendency, on the open stage, for the player of a dignified character to keep at a distance from the groundlings. Vanessa Redgrave did so: Jasper Britton did not. The comic actor enjoys the encounter with an audience: he milks laughter from it. For the Duke of Milan, even when he is in lonely exile, hierarchical consciousness inhibits interaction with the multitude. Whereas through the convention of soliloquy Hamlet can talk directly to us, Prospero has almost always an on-stage audience to illustrate and authenticate his authority. He is, in his island fastness, still a public man. The text allows him a handful of brief asides, but not until the epilogue can he fully share his presence with us. Standing spectators may be accepting of this emblematic distance, but they are quick to feel the privilege of direct address, and eager to reward the actor who notices them. Tree's Caliban contested the central stage with Prospero. Britton's Caliban willingly surrendered it for the mutual gratification of intimacy with the audience. The proscenium arch has introduced to the English language the concept of 'upstaging' – grabbing the attention of the audience by indulging in by-play behind a fellow-actor's back: its equivalent in the original Globe may well have been 'downstaging'. It is not difficult, on the open stage, to disconcert a fellow-actor by making contact with the groundlings. It would not surprise me if Will Kemp's irresistible urge to 'downstage' his colleagues in the Chamberlain's Men lay behind his abrupt departure from the company in 1599.

The 'comic' actor, then, distinguishes himself by a rapport with the audience which is denied to the 'serious' actor, and which is altogether different from that of the 'tragic' actor. (Hamlet or Macbeth may confide in us, but they cannot play with us.) Elizabethan drama was too close to its roots in communal festivity to underrate the value of goading the audience into laughter, and it would be misplaced reverence to suppose that Shakespeare resented an audience's demand for instant pleasure. In all his plays, there are written-in opportunities for actors to invite responses from the floor, and clear indications of his sensitivity to the variable resonances of locations on the platform stage. It might be argued that Ben Jonson was more astute in exploiting the sheer physicality of the theatrical space, but Jonson never risked anything as dangerous as *Othello*. That is a play in which the tragic protagonist is held at the centre of the stage, whilst his scheming antagonist can wander at will. The player of Iago has the freedom of a comic actor and can use it, as many actors (some intentionally) have in history, to undermine Othello's authority. When a comic actor is placed in apposition to a tragic actor, it is rarely the comic actor who forfeits the audience's attention.

Character and comedy

It is only in his freedom to wander that Iago invites the interest of a comic actor. He is, in all other respects, bound by his service to the plot. It is almost a journeyman role, within the range of most, if not all, of Shakespeare's colleagues in the Chamberlain's and/or King's Men, a test of competence which theatrical circumstance may convert to excellence. It would be a threat to the tonality of *Othello* to entrust it to the kind of virtuoso comedian for whom Shakespeare created Caliban, Bottom, Shylock, Malvolio, Richard III or the Porter in *Macbeth*. It is worth remembering that Elizabethan actors learned their parts from pasted copies that presented those parts as a whole, interrupted only by brief cues. It was evidently not the custom to identify the speakers of the cue lines, nor to provide any descriptive account of the dramatic context (the preparation of the 'parts' being laborious enough to discourage further scribal elaboration). If we add to that the fact that there was very little time for formal rehearsal before the plays opened, we are left with questions to ask about the nature of Elizabethan acting.[1] The actor who learned his part from a cue script necessarily developed skills in responding to verbal demand. The cue, however scant, is the trigger for the memorised response. For every comic actor, alertness to the line before he speaks and an ability to lead on to the line that will follow when he has finished speaking are essential qualities. He is part of a theatrical continuum whose effectiveness is dependent on interaction. An actor who finds it difficult to play off another actor may just cope with the demands of tragedy, but he should steer clear of comedy. 'You may humbug the town some time longer as a tragedian', Garrick once advised Charles Bannister, 'but comedy is a serious thing.'[2] In the modern theatre, the timing (in association with, but distinct from, the speed) of response is an insistent theme of experiment and interrogation in the rehearsal of comedies. But timing is only one of several constituents of comedic exchange. The original actors of Shakespeare's plays had to determine much more – tone, volume, direction of gaze, etc. – improvisationally than is generally permitted in today's theatre. The quality of the Chamberlain's Men is inherent in the texts. Shakespeare was not writing plays for posterity, but texts for performance by people he knew well. He relied on their competence, composed towards their capacity, and where there was egregious talent, he wrote for that, too.

The most striking development in the approach to comic acting during the reign of Elizabeth I was Ben Jonson's resourceful application of humours theory. The proposal that the thought patterns and behaviour of an individual are determined by the dominance of one 'humour' over the others was likely to be attractive to actors, because its blending of what we would now call psychology and physiology provided lucid performative guidance. It was attractive to Jonson, working often at arm's length from the actors, because it gave him greater control over the performance of his plays (at all times, a 'humour' is an adverbial stage direction). Just what hold Shakespeare, as a member of the company that presented his plays, had over their staging will remain a subject of debate, but his mode of writing comic roles is less dictatorial than Jonson's. There is, after all, more than one way of reading Prospero. This is not to say that Shakespeare knew nothing of the humours until the production of *Every Man in His Humour* in 1598. *Love's Labour's Lost* is not the only one of his early plays on which Jonson's imagination might have fed. But the idea of peopling a whole play with characteristics rather than personae was the product of Jonson's own delight in systems. Had Jonson written Caliban, he would not have furnished him with the brief aria of 'Be not afeard, the isle is full of noises'. It is a tendency of Shakespeare's major comic creations to break the rules of stereotyping that they seem initially to have accepted. This is a quality easily confused with the post-Shakespearean idea of dramatic character: Caliban has raped the child Miranda but loves nature; Shylock covets his daughter and his ducats; Falstaff disguises his frailty almost to the end from everyone but the audience. Such invitations to ambitious actors to personalise dramatic functions have proved irresistible in the stage history of Shakespeare's comedies, and may have been almost as strong a factor in their survival as the complexities of the tragic leads have been in the survival of his tragedies. It would be over-solemn to bemoan this historical distortion of the impetus that led to the making of the comedies, but there is no harm in reminding actors that their essential task is to serve the story. Much more obviously than his tragedies, Shakespeare's comedies depend on teamwork. The intelligent reading of a cue script calls for a pursuit of *purpose*. How does this speech drive the play forward? What function does it serve? What is being communicated to the audience? How directly? If the 'character' is not in the lines, how was the lonely memoriser of a cue script to discover it? If the 'part' was not almost as clearly notated as a musician's part in an orchestral score, it could not be accurately played. There needs to be a clear indication of the social standing – the likely position in the pecking order of power – but the moral flavour and the basic temperament (a more appropriate word than 'character' in the understanding of Elizabethan dramaturgy) of the part can be read in the lines. There is no Chekhovian subtext in Shakespeare, only text plus context.

Soloists, clowns and fools

Nearly all the 'great' Shakespearean actors have established their greatness through their playing of one or more of the major tragic roles (Shylock is scarcely an exception here), and yet the repertoire of most theatre companies through history implies an audience preference for the comedies. There is nothing surprising about this apparent inconsistency. It reflects the popular choice ('I like a good laugh') alongside a real, but lesser, delight in monumental acting. Shakespeare did not build comedy round a towering central figure, as Jonson built *Volpone* and as Molière would build many of his plays. His one attempt to do so, *The Merry Wives of Windsor*, was possibly a response to royal command, and not a particularly successful one. Actors in Shakespeare's comedies, however excited they may be at the opportunities provided by a particular scene, know that they must give way to other actors with equally exciting opportunities. The scene (not the act, and certainly not the play) is the unit of display. The distinction I have already drawn between actors in comedy and comic actors is crucial here. The comic actor is always in collusion with the spectators. His primary response, whatever the cue sheet may suggest, is to them. Shakespeare's model may have been Richard Tarlton, whose death in 1588 deprived the emergent professional theatre of its first great 'clown'. Tarlton was a solo artist whose accommodation to the etiquette of the playhouse was never more than partial. Provocatively plebeian in an era of deference, he might have made a notable Caliban. It was probably Tarlton who established the primacy of the specialist clown in the comic hierarchy of the early Elizabethan theatre, but it was Will Kemp whom Shakespeare inherited when he joined the Chamberlain's Men in 1594. What evidence we have suggests that Kemp was *the* crowd-puller during the formative years of the new company, but that his expertise was not that of a team player. When *A Knack to Know a Knave* was staged by Strange's Men in 1592, there was a self-contained episode, 'Kemp's applauded merriments of the men of Gotham in receiving the King into Gotham'. In such knockabout scenes, the discipline of the cue sheet might be legitimately displaced by the spontaneity of improvisation, with tempo and duration determined by audience response.

Kemp was probably in his late thirties when he joined the Chamberlain's Men. We know that he played Peter in *Romeo and Juliet*, on the face of it a surprisingly small (and largely self-contained) role for a star performer. We do not know who played Juliet's nurse, but, if it was an adult role, it is surprising that Kemp did not claim it. We must remember, though, that the clown had always the post-play jig to look forward to, and Kemp was one of the great jig-makers. Jigs were set pieces for comic actors, and there were sections of the Elizabethan audience that rated them much higher than plays. The other role to which Kemp's name can be firmly attached is that of Dogberry in *Much Ado About Nothing*. Shakespeare has again provided his clown with a largely isolatable role – a double act with Verges that can accommodate ad-libbing. Costard was surely Kemp's role in *Love's Labour's Lost*. The part of Launce in *The Two Gentlemen of Verona* was probably written specifically to exploit Kemp's skill as a stand-up comedian, and Launcelet (little Launce?) Gobbo, as soloist and part of a double act, is Launce's exuberant counterpart in *The Merchant of Venice*. Did the company let Kemp play Bottom? He was, despite his fame as a dancer, a heavily built man, and may, like John Liston two centuries later, have made a theatrical feature of his buttocks. If the actor who created the role of Pompey Bum in *Measure for Measure* was already in the company, he may well have been the preferred casting, although Bottom, even when entangled in the plot of *A Midsummer Night's Dream*, remains sufficiently a soloist to have suited Kemp. Falstaff, proposed by David Wiles as Kemp's last and greatest Shakespearean creation,[3] is more problematic. This is a role in which a selfish actor can overwhelm lesser talents and betray the plot. Was Kemp's 'downstaging' Falstaff the final straw in his uneasy relationship with the Chamberlain's Men?

Clowns like Tarlton and Kemp relied on their extratextual theatricality to captivate an audience. Since it is texts that survive, we are forced into speculation when we try to recover their comedy. They specialised in farcical set pieces, not all of them preserved in the texts that have come down to us. No 'low' comedian before the twentieth century would have felt constrained by the words set down for him, and all Elizabethan comic routines, whether solo pieces or double acts, should be read as *a* version, not *the* version, of what might have happened in a particular playhouse at a particular time.

Even so, as has been widely recognised, Kemp's departure brought about a shift in the comic emphasis of Shakespeare's plays. The fool is very different from the clown, and has a more complicated cultural pedigree. Educated Elizabethans were familiar with the contradictory Christian diptych of the Pauline 'fool for Christ' and the fool of Psalm 14 who 'hath said in his heart, there is no God', as well as the contrasting intelligences of the 'natural' and the 'artificial' fool. Robert Armin, who joined the Lord Chamberlain's company around the time that Kemp left it, was a student of folly. He was certainly not taken on as a replacement for Kemp: he was a singer, not a dancer, and he was diminutive, even dwarfish. Like Feste, whose role in *Twelfth Night* he probably created, he was 'wise enough to play the fool', and if Lear's fool, as well as Feste, was written for him, he had evidently a special line in social alienation. There is not much meat for an ebullient comic actor in the parts normally ascribed to Armin (Lavache in *All's Well That Ends Well*, for example, and even Pandarus in *Troilus and Cressida*), nor is there any justification in the claim that Shakespeare cut out the clowning when Kemp left. He did, however, keep tighter control of it. The comic set pieces of the plays dating from after *As You Like It* are generally more fully written into their dramatic context. The single-scene clowns of *Othello* and *Antony and Cleopatra*, for example, have none of the freedom to invent that was permitted to Kemp as Peter in *Romeo and Juliet*. Even the most opportunistic of Shakespeare's later comic creations, Autolycus in *The Winter's Tale*, is bound in by the plot to a degree that Launce, Gobbo, Bottom and Falstaff were not. Autolycus is a knave rather than either clown or fool, a comedic brother to Iago. Not that Shakespeare would let slip a comic opportunity: if the tiny Robert Armin played Autolycus, his exchange of garments with a much larger Florizel would have been a bizarre episode, allowing Florizel a rare moment of high humour on 'Should I now meet my father / He would not call me son', and Camillo at least a snigger on the succeeding 'Nay, you shall have no hat' (4.4.657–8).

Ensemble acting in comedy

Just which roles belonged to established comic actors in the plays that Shakespeare wrote for the Globe and the Blackfriars is not always clear. You could argue for Casca or the Soothsayer, as well as the drunken poet, in *Julius Caesar*, but not without risk to the traumatic impact of the assassination. If it was a comedian who created the role of Iago, the same man might have played Enobarbus in *Antony and Cleopatra*. He is dead in good time to double as Cleopatra's worm-bearing clown. Belch and Aguecheek were clearly enough a fat man–thin man double act in *Twelfth Night*, but, given a choice, the leading comedian would have plumped for Malvolio. Shakespeare would not have constructed this play as he did unless the company had at least three comic actors, in addition to Armin as Feste. But, unlike the clown, they were not confined by audience expectation to broadly comic roles, as is evident from the *dramatis personae* of Shakespeare's near contemporaneous plays. It is the versatility of Elizabethan actors and the ductility of Elizabethan audiences that need to be recognised. If Malvolio was first played by a great comic actor, there is no reason why he should not have gone on to create the roles of Edmund in *King Lear* and Iachimo in *Cymbeline*. Richard Burbage and Edward Alleyn were considered sublime tragedians, but playhouse economics ensured that they were not confined to tragedy. Robert Armin, who seems to have specialised in quick changes and disguise, might, after all, have played Edgar, not the Fool, in *King Lear* (Poor Tom, like Caliban, is 'unaccommodated man'). It was only in the later eighteenth century that middle-of-the-road actors, and such particular stars as Sarah Siddons and John Kemble (tragedians) or Joseph Munden and Dorothy Jordan (comedians), came to be squeezed into categories. Shakespeare's comedies are so constructed as to limit the scope for radical reinterpretation of individual roles. An actor cannot perform the Orlando of *As You Like It* as a bisexual fop without affecting our attitude to his Rosalind. It can reasonably be argued that the finest comedic scenes Shakespeare ever constructed are the finest precisely because they challenge the ensemble at the same time as they submerge the individual.

This is a point interestingly developed by Harley Granville Barker in his review of a production of *Twelfth Night* by Jacques Copeau and the Vieux-Colombier company:

> One has only to face the simple fact that Shakespeare's Malvolio, Feste, Maria, Sir Toby, and Andrew will last out the play, whereas the arbitrary funniments of actors will probably not. Shakespeare, for all his faults, M. Copeau, did know his business as a playwright, and as long as he enjoyed writing a character we may be pretty sure that the actor has more to gain by interpreting it than by using it as a peg upon which to hang his own, or anyone else's, ideas.[4]

Granville Barker, above all through his productions of Shakespearean comedy at the Savoy Theatre, London (1912–14), had already done more than any other single person to break the hold of the actor-managers on the theatrical establishment in England. He is writing here about a production, in French, first staged in 1914 by the great innovator of ensemble performance in France, and he is criticising what he sees as a breakdown of the ensemble intention. When the review was published in the *Observer* (1 January 1922), Granville Barker had already finished writing *The Exemplary Theatre*

(1922), a book in which he sought to explain 'the need for a creation in the actor of something like an integral sub-conscious self ... this mysterious second personality, which will be not himself and yet will be a part of himself', and concluded that 'these wedded beings born of the actor's art live for their one purpose only'. Copeau would probably have agreed with Granville Barker that the greatest actors are those who surrender themselves to 'the possession for the time of the obedient body by the changeling idea'.[5] Both men were pursuing through comedy an elusive, and ultimately spiritual, vision of theatre as an act of unification; a pursuit that has galvanised most of the major innovators since Stanislavsky. Although actors have been caught up in it, it is usually directors who have led the pursuit, and it is no longer as easy to determine the individual contribution of actors as it was before 1914.

Particularly in comedy, perhaps, it is the director who now establishes the frame within which rehearsals will be set. Like the conductor of a symphony, the director of a Shakespearean comedy must harmonise the parts. Shakespearean tragedy more blatantly requires an accommodation between director and protagonists, something like that of conductor and soloists in a concerto – though who is it who determines set and costume? When Henry Irving made his entrance, whether in tragedy or comedy, he instructed the limelight men at the Lyceum (there were twenty-two for the production of *Faust*) to direct the focus on him. The great comic entrances now are ensemble creations. When Malvolio interrupts the revellers in act 2, scene 3 of *Twelfth Night*, the weight of humour is equally distributed. When Sebastian makes his eye-opening incursion on to the stage in the final act of the same play, the impact on those around him is what matters. At Antonio's trial, it is the interventions of onlookers that provide the emotional orchestration for the solo parts of Shylock and Portia. Orlando's hilarious invasion of the alfresco feast in the Forest of Arden (*As You Like It*, 2.7) is hilarious only if the actors make it so. (In the Stratford production of 1973, Richard Pasco's wonderfully seedy Jaques broke the silence following Orlando's command to 'eat no more' by carefully selecting a morsel as he answered, 'Why, I have eat none yet', with a disregard of Orlando's threat that was, at the same time, a disregard of death.) The outstanding feature of Peter Brook's extraordinary production of *A Midsummer Night's Dream* at Stratford in 1970 was its trust in ensemble acting. If Bottom is a part for an exceptional comic actor, David Waller seemed unaware of it. His serious endeavour was to make a success of *Pyramus and Thisbe*. All the work of the production was carried out in full view of the audience, and the effect was as much of something shared as of something shown. I am persuaded that Granville Barker would have recognised in this production the presence of the 'mysterious second personality ... something like an integral subconscious self' that he looked for in actors of Shakespeare's comedies. If Shakespeare understood such a concept, it can only have been intuitively, and, in the creation of virtuoso roles for comic actors, he belonged unashamedly to the theatre of his time.

Shylock

There is no better example than Shylock of Shakespeare's ambivalent approach to comic stereotypes. As either the miser or the gulled heavy father, Shylock's functions in *The Merchant of Venice* have served playwrights since the first formation of a distinct comic drama. If he were a lesser character, or less a character, the play would be a much more attractive prospect for the actors of Bassanio, Antonio, Gratiano, Jessica, Lorenzo and even Portia. As it is now, the sheer weight of Shylock displaces the lovers, turns what is dramaturgically a romantic comedy into a tragicomedy. Even the sketchiest stage history suggests that this was not always the case. We do not know who created the role, but the vigour of the language Shakespeare gave to it suggests that it was written for an actor he admired. Even so, the words can be spoken with conviction by a player who knows that Shylock is an out-and-out villain, and who sees it as his purpose to set him up for an audience-gratifying fall (the kind of reversal that we hope Bartholo will experience in Beaumarchais' *The Barber of Seville*, where Figaro fulfils Portia's function). This is how Thomas Doggett must have played it in Lord Lansdowne's insouciantly anti-Semitic adaptation (1701). It was Charles Macklin's performance of Shylock at Drury Lane in 1741 that radically shifted audience perceptions. Macklin, like all eighteenth-century actors, considered the primary function of serious acting to be the picturesque delineation of the passions. He was more interested than any of his contemporaries in the interaction of 'real' and 'stage' behaviour, but he certainly did not confuse performance and reality. The innovation of his Shylock was its importation into comedy of tragedy's actorly mannerisms, and its effect was ineradicable. It made the role available to tragedians. George Frederick Cooke took it up; so, memorably, did Edmund Kean, who made his sensational 1814 Drury Lane début as Shylock. Cooke had inherited the Garrick tradition of versatility, and was at ease in comedy. Kean, too, quickly became the creature of his own charisma. 'He had no gaiety', wrote G. H. Lewes in a famous essay, 'he could not laugh; he had no playfulness that was not as the playfulness of a panther showing her claws every moment'. For Lewes, Kean's Shylock was of a piece with his Othello, Richard III and Sir Giles Overreach, 'impossible to watch ... without being strangely shaken by the terror, and the pathos, and the passion of a stormy spirit uttering itself in tones of irresistible power'.[6]

There has been a tendency to associate Kean with the Romantic era in literature, but he belongs more truly to the Gothic revival. Between him and Irving, the next great Shylock, audiences had come to demand a theatre of illusion. Irving found common cause with them by grounding the character on the idealised love of a father for his daughter that is so frequent a feature of Victorian fiction. It is only in act 2, scene 5 that Shylock shares the stage alone with Jessica, and then for a mere thirteen lines. Richard Mansfield, who borrowed some of his best tricks from Irving, used to mark her earlier entrance with a tender kiss. Irving added an episode for the Lyceum production of 1879. Act 2, scene 6 was brought to a close, after Jessica and Lorenzo had eloped in a practical gondola, with a street carnival of extras carrying lanterns and dancing. The curtain fell, and then, with the audience still clapping, rose again on a dimly lit empty stage. As silence fell in the auditorium, the distant tapping of a stick was audible. It came closer, and there was Shylock, returning home to his daughter. He crossed the bridge over the canal that has carried Jessica away for ever, paused at the door of his house (a palpable pause) and then knocked. No answer. He knocked again. The curtain fell slowly to signal the interval. Much later, Ellen Terry wrote, 'For absolute pathos, achieved by absolute simplicity of means, I never saw anything in the theatre to compare with it.'[7] It was not Irving's intention to cheat his audience. He played the part as he read it, and he produced the play for an audience that was fixed on character as the key to Shakespeare (fig. 18). The intervention may be illicit, but it is mild compared with much theatrical thinking of the time. Helena Faucit, who had played Portia to Macready's mid-century Shylock, was not untypical in her preparedness to speculate on the fate of Portia and Jessica in the afterlife of the play when she came to write, in her retirement, *On Some of Shakespeare's Female Characters* (1892). Shylock, she anticipates, will be looked after at his end by the kindly Portia, and Jessica, having obtained Portia's permission, will visit her dying father, 'sobbing out her grief and her contrition; and he will remember that he made her "home a hell", and look gently upon her'.[8] There is not much call for *purpose* when *character* is on the theatrical throne.

The Second World War and the Holocaust have impinged on productions of *The Merchant of Venice* around the world. The playing of Shylock requires the declaration of a political attitude from both director and actor. What intrigues me – and this cannot be more than a footnote here – is that the most striking Shylocks I have seen, Laurence Olivier and Antony Sher, have also been the most striking Richard IIIs. The twinning is provocative. Whatever may have been Shakespeare's original intention, Shylock has emerged as a

18 Henry Irving as Shylock, 1879.

tragic role embedded in comedy, and Richard III as a comic role never quite reconciled to tragedy. There are actors – Kean, Irving, Olivier, Sher among them – who operate best between the lines of genre.

Malvolio

It is a mistake that some actors have made to play Malvolio as a near tragic victim. The anonymous reviewer of the bungled Lyceum *Twelfth Night* (1884) tells readers of the *World* that 'I sat next to a gentleman, a total stranger to me, in the stalls; at Mr Irving's last exit we turned to each other and, as if by one impulse, whispered the single word "Shylock".'[9] More conscious than usual of the need to compensate, by his own performance, for the weakness of his bought-in cast of comedians – he later regretted his failure to find three great comic actors for Sir Toby, Sir Andrew and Feste – Irving had built the production around Ellen Terry's Viola and his own Malvolio, whose humiliation in the dungeon was given a full-stage picturesque pathos. Interestingly, though, there was no great tradition of Malvolios on the English stage, nor any familiarity with Molière's monstrous Tartuffe as a plausible theatrical model. *Twelfth Night* had few admirers in either the eighteenth or the nineteenth century, and Samuel Phelps was the first notable actor-manager to elect to play Malvolio (Irving probably saw him in the part at the Gaiety revival in 1876). It was not easy for Phelps or Irving to conceive Malvolio as a comic grotesque of self-regard, properly without place in the festive world to which the comedy aspires. Henry Ainley, who played the part in Granville Barker's revelatory Savoy production of 1912, was praised for his restraint. Almost wherever Ainley is mentioned in theatrical reminiscences, his name is prefaced with the adjectival 'golden-voiced', and he tended to fall back on the nineteenth-century 'grand manner' when not checked. It was clever casting on Granville Barker's part. Ainley's conditioned reaction to the startling stage and costume designs by Norman Wilkinson was built in to his Malvolio: the preserver of time-honoured custom in the newfangled, futurist world Wilkinson had created. What the play invites us to recognise, and what the costume design emphasised, is that Malvolio's change of dress, from sombre black to yellow, is an abandonment of the principles on which he has so far artfully constructed his behaviour. The duper has been decisively duped. If Ainley, who was not a comic actor, had any inclination to usurp the play, Granville Barker denied him the opportunity. Malvolio's is a role without a character. A comic actor will focus on externals, as Nicol Williamson did in the 1974 production at Stratford. How does Malvolio walk? What sort of voice does he have? How does he inhabit his costume? How can he shape his pinched mouth into a smile? Williamson was always remarkable, even when he was least reliable. Like Tarlton's, like that of many of the finest comic actors through history, his humour was not at all amicable. He could make people squirm while they laughed.

Falstaff

Falstaff is the most famous of Shakespeare's 'funny' people. Unusually, the plays in which he appears keep telling us how funny he is. There is not much evidence from stage history, however, that the role is best suited to a comic actor. The reviews of the music-hall comedian George Robey's performance at His Majesty's Theatre in 1935 were generally tolerant but unenthusiastic. That his Falstaff was 'seldom externalised' was, for J. C. Trewin, writing in a 'character' tradition, a merit.[10] But why cast Robey, then? There were eighteenth-century Falstaffs – 'Plump Jack' Harper and Stephen Kemble are the best known – whose claim to fame was their ability to play the part without padding, and James Quin, the finest Falstaff of the pre-Garrick era, had gourmandised himself into grossness by the time he tackled the role. Quin's preferred genre was tragedy, and tragic undertones have been detected in the performances of many subsequently admired Falstaffs. Ralph Richardson at the Old Vic in 1945–6 was, in this respect, exceptional. Kenneth Tynan declared him 'a Falstaff whose principal attribute was not his fatness but his knighthood', whilst insisting that it was 'not a *comic* performance'. 'He had good manners, and also that respect for human dignity which prevented him from openly showing his boredom at the inanities of Shallow and Silence.'[11] It is easier for the actor of Falstaff than for the actor of Shylock or Malvolio to enter into a jocular conspiracy with the audience, and it is necessary for him to do so in his battlefield soliloquies, but he is rarely without an on-stage audience of his own. History has decreed that Falstaff become a 'character' part, played for laughs by a 'serious' actor (see fig. 19).

Double acts

Touchstone's disquisitions on the seven causes (*As You Like It*, 5.4) and Pompey Bum's catalogue of his fellow-prisoners (*Measure for Measure*, 4.3) are almost the last opportunities Shakespeare provided for a 'stand-up' co-median after Will Kemp's defection, but he never abandoned the double act, always a haven for comic actors. There are parts, like Lucio in *Measure for Measure*, which enable the resourceful player to turn every encounter into a double act, however unwilling the accomplice. Lucio is not, in any useful sense, a 'character', though actors have been persuaded to furnish him with one. It is, in performative terms, more helpful to view him as a

19 Ralph Richardson as Falstaff in the Old Vic production of *Henry IV*, 1945.

knave or, in Lesley Soule's terms, as a 'middle-status clown'. Soule's *Actor as Anti-Character* is a brilliantly polemical re-examination of the scope of comic acting before plays were reined in as literature, and her Shakespearean focus is on *As You Like It*. She identifies in the play a range of clowns, from the low (William and Audrey) through the middle status (Touchstone) to the high (Jaques and Rosalind/Ganymede), and enumerates their double acts, concluding: 'The play as a whole is constructed so as to give as many opportunities as possible for players (even those in roles central to the mimetic action) to engage in purely performative clown-like play in order to sustain the fundamentally celebrative purposes of the performance.'[12]

It was, Soule argues, natural for the boy who created the role of Rosalind to play off the discrepancy between actor and character, and the words Shakespeare gave him to speak are subtly addressed to an audience that relished that discrepancy. Twentieth-century all-male productions of *As You Like It* seem to have made it easier for the comparatively underwritten Orlando to persuade audiences that he is worthy of Rosalind.[13] Their same-sex double act revealed hidden humour to many reviewers, and a new level of erotic tension to even more. There are complex reasons for that, and too few fine parts for women in the classic drama to wish this one away. It might be argued, anyway, that Rosalind is a special case. With her fictional character, more than with any other, men have fallen in love. In a telling appendix, Soule cites the frequently acerbic Bernard Levin on Vanessa Redgrave's 1961 Rosalind: 'a creature of fire and light, her voice a golden gate on lapis lazuli hinges, her body a slender reed rippling in the breeze of her love. This is not acting at all but living, being loved.'[14] It has been the fate of even Maggie Smith, perhaps the finest comic actor I have seen, to be sentimentalised by audiences as Rosalind. The part itself, though, is a succession of varying double acts, interspersed with bouts of team-playing. Something of the original may be restored to a post-feminist society.

The comic gusto that characterises many of Shakespeare's heterosexual pairings, from *The Taming of the Shrew* to *Antony and Cleopatra*, is almost actor-proof. The advent of actresses has, in itself, affected the reception of the plays much less than the gradual evolution of a theatre of illusion (which was, of course, advanced by the acceptance of women on the stage). *Much Ado About Nothing* became, in the eighteenth century, the *locus classicus* of harmless marital fantasy, and David Garrick its authoritative promoter. A war of the sexes in which the combatants win by agreeing to surrender has a long comic pedigree, happily guaranteed by the convenient closure of the fiction. (Helena Faucit wisely avoided speculation on the future of Kate and Petruchio, but was confident that Benedick's home would be a happy one, 'all the happier because Beatrice and he have each a strong individuality, with fine spirits and busy brains, which will keep life from stagnating'.[15]) Garrick's particular innovation was to advertise the interrelationship of the play and his own life. When he first played Benedick opposite Hannah Pritchard's Beatrice in November 1748, his own status as a decidedly eligible bachelor was about to change, and the audience that applauded him to the echo was kept well informed of the progress of his courtship. He married Eva Maria

Veigel in June 1749, and the first part he played on his post-honeymoon return to Drury Lane was again Benedick. The actor-manager was sharing with the public his abandonment of bachelor freedoms. Garrick and Pritchard stand at the head of a distinguished list of players of the Beatrice–Benedick double act, not least because *Much Ado* has proved hospitable to the changing sexual mores of the countries in which it has been performed.[16] Advantage has also been taken of the fact that Beatrice and Benedick are not necessarily young. The Royal Shakespeare Company, for example, had a decidedly mature Elizabeth Spriggs and Derek Godfrey in the roles in 1971, and, five years later, Judi Dench and Donald Sinden, well past the marrying age, flavoured the enchantment of late love with an air of astonishment over what had seemed a long-lost opportunity. In the Victorian theatre, Ellen Terry's had been the definitive performance of Beatrice (see fig. 22, p. 165). It was a role that released her to express her own sexuality within acceptable bounds of propriety. George Bernard Shaw was probably right in his conviction that Terry was limited by her long association with Irving, though it made her the most famous English actress of the age; but Shaw was aware, also, of the frustrated clown in Irving that gave his Benedick its bite:

> He was utterly unlike anyone else; he could give importance and a noble melancholy, bound up with an impish humour, which forced the spectator to single him out as a leading figure with an inevitability that I never saw again in any other actor until it rose from Irving's grave in the person of a nameless cinema actor who afterwards became famous as Charlie Chaplin.[17]

We may need to recognise that all the greatest actors through history have been essentially *comic* by virtue of the playful relationship they establish with an audience. They know that we know that this is all an illusion, and they know how to make sure that we know they know it. Ellen Terry wrote this about Ada Rehan, the American actress who charmed English audiences at the end of the nineteenth century: 'She understood, like all great comedians, that you must not pretend to be serious so sincerely that no one in the audience sees through it!'[18]

NOTES

1 For details of rehearsal practices in the Elizabethan theatre, see Tiffany Stern, *Rehearsal from Shakespeare to Sheridan* (Oxford: Clarendon Press, 2000).
2 Quoted in Mrs Clement Parsons, *Garrick and his Circle* (London: Methuen, 1906), 78.
3 David Wiles, *Shakespeare's Clown* (Cambridge: Cambridge University Press, 1987), 116–35.
4 Quoted in Stanley Wells (ed.), *Shakespeare in the Theatre* (Oxford: Clarendon Press, 1997), 191.

5 See Eric Salmon, *Granville Barker: a Secret Life* (London: Heinemann, 1983), 111–13, where the quoted passages form part of a treatment of Barker's attitude to actors.

6 Lewes's essay is on pp.1–11 of his *On Actors and the Art of Acting* (London: Smith, Elder & Co., 1875).

7 Ellen Terry, *The Story of My Life* (London: Hutchinson, 1908), 186.

8 Helena Faucit, *On Some of Shakespeare's Female Characters* (Edinburgh and London: William Blackwood & Sons, 1892), 42.

9 Quoted in Alan Hughes, *Henry Irving, Shakespearean* (Cambridge: Cambridge University Press, 1981), 202.

10 J. C. Trewin, *Shakespeare on the English Stage, 1900–1964* (London: Barrie & Rockliff, 1964), 151.

11 Kenneth Tynan, *He That Plays the King* (London: Longmans, Green & Co., 1950), 48–9.

12 Lesley Soule, *Actor as Anti-Character: Dionysus, the Devil and the Boy Rosalind* (Westport, CT and London: Greenwood Press, 2000), 143.

13 The National Theatre's 1967 production, with Ronald Pickup as Rosalind, and Cheek by Jowl's 1991 production, with the black actor Adrian Lester as Rosalind, were both unusually widely reviewed.

14 Soule, *Actor as Anti-Character*, 186.

15 Faucit, *On Some of Shakespeare's Female Characters*, 326.

16 For an informed stage history of *Much Ado about Nothing*, see John F. Cox's edition in the Shakespeare in Production series (Cambridge: Cambridge University Press, 1997).

17 Christopher St John (ed.), *Ellen Terry and Bernard Shaw: a Correspondence* (London: Reinhardt & Evans, 1949), xxv.

18 Terry, *Story of My Life*, 293.

9

PENNY GAY

Women and Shakespearean performance

The Elizabethan and Jacobean stage

> I shall see
> Some squeaking Cleopatra boy my greatness
> I'th'posture of a whore.
>
> (*Antony*, 5.2.218–20)

Cleopatra, Juliet, Lady Macbeth, Rosalind, Viola and Olivia, and all the rest of the approximately 140 named female roles in Shakespeare, were written as roles for boys or young men.[1] We do not know what the considerable number of women in the audience felt about their exclusion from the stage, either as actors or as writers. On the one hand, they were 'represented' by a male writer's concept and a male performer's body; on the other hand, the many speeches throughout Shakespeare's plays that refer to this fact create a unique bond of sophisticated complicity between actor and audience. It would, after all, have been a 'squeaking boy' who first uttered these words on the stage of the Globe,[2] as his performance moved towards the climax of Cleopatra's great threnody. Shakespeare seems to have written in the confidence that the young actor would perform the role with far greater expertise than his character's derogatory comment suggests.

The age of puberty for males in the early seventeenth century was probably later than it is today; and the adolescent boy can often seem androgynous, his voice not fully broken, his body slim and childish. 'Nay, faith', says Flute in *A Midsummer Night's Dream*, panicking about his gender identity, 'let not me play a woman: I have a beard coming' (1.2.39). Shakespeare's boy actors could have been as old as eighteen, quite able to comprehend and embody the emotional complexities of an Isabella, a Juliet, a Rosalind, a Cleopatra. On the other hand, Viola in *Twelfth Night* – one of the most emotionally challenging of Shakespeare's female roles – has a voice 'as the maiden's organ, shrill and sound, / And all is semblative a woman's part' (1.4.32–3): clearly she was played by a younger boy. Similarly, the lack of height of Maria (*Twelfth Night*), Celia (*As You Like It*), Hermia (*Midsummer Night's Dream*), and others, is commented on; and when Desdemona sings the Willow Song or Ophelia her mad songs of despair, we are obviously not listening to a manly baritone or mellifluous tenor.[3]

But consider also Cleopatra's further denigration of her character and/or the actor playing her: 'i'th'posture of a whore'. 'She' may mean that the historic personage within the play's narrative will be depicted as a whore by the triumphant Romans. It is difficult, however, to avoid the resonances of the syntactic ambiguity here: the nonce verb '*boy* . . . i'th'posture of a whore' reflects early seventeenth-century anxieties about the sexual energies set in play by the spectacle of boys playing women. Much recent scholarship has attempted to tease out, through the reading of other contemporary documents, just what were the erotic and sexual politics of this experience for that original audience.[4] Was it a homoerotic stage? That is, was the pleasure of the audience in watching, for example, the representation of heterosexual lovemaking in fact a much more subversive pleasure in watching a man and a boy make love? Undoubtedly, in *As You Like It* the audience was aware of the *double entendre* in Rosalind's decision to take as her male name 'no worse a name than Jove's own page, / And therefore look you call me "Ganymede"' (1.3.114–15), since 'Ganymede' was a slang term for a young male homosexual. But, as Stephen Orgel argues, 'there is no indication whatever that Shakespeare is doing something sexually daring there, skating on thin ice'.[5] The love of Elizabethan men for boys was often thought of as less dangerous than love for women, whose sexuality was considered to be voraciously overwhelming, making men effeminate. Although the increasingly powerful Puritan element in society fulminated against the theatre in general, the potential for homosexual behaviour was only one aspect of their larger phobia.[6] It was basically 'the universal sexuality evoked by theatre, a lust not distinguished by the gender of its object', Orgel argues (*Impersonations*, 28), which was unacceptable to them.[7]

But for those non-puritanical people, both male and female, who enthusiastically attended the public theatres of Shakespeare's day, at base there can have been no lasting anxiety about the boys and young men who played the women's parts. Within a shared social hierarchy of gender between stage and audience, the roles which the boys performed were unambiguously narratives of women's lives. What might well also have been shared is an underlying, even unconscious (but nevertheless powerful) recognition of the artificiality of such apparently immutable concepts as femininity and masculinity, if they can be put on with a costume and a wink to the audience.

The Restoration and the eighteenth century

The Puritans did succeed in closing down the sexually and politically disruptive theatres in 1642; when they reopened in 1660 on the restoration of Charles II, women began to take the female roles, just as they had done in the performances seen by the court during its exile on the Continent. The earliest public performance by a woman in a Shakespeare role was given, probably, on 8 December 1660, when an unnamed actress played Desdemona in a production of *Othello*. The King's Patent issued in 1662 soon made the new practice obligatory, since such spectacles (i.e. women) provided 'not only harmless delight, but useful and instructive representations of human life'.[8]

English society had changed radically; so must the theatre which represented it to itself. Shakespeare was an 'old' playwright, a writer of the late Middle Ages rather than of the new scientific age. His plays were among those considered worth reviving as crowd-pleasers; but they had to be 'reform[ed] and made fitt'[9] for the post-civil war audience. So, for example, William Davenant revamped *Macbeth*, expanding the character of Lady Macduff to make her a virtuous counter to Shakespeare's 'fiend-like queen'. Throughout the play (until her death off stage) she is a model of wifely decorum, even warning her husband against the temptation of ambition.

Nahum Tate, revising *King Lear* in 1681, declared that he had lighted on an 'expedient to rectify what was wanting in the regularity and probability of the tale, which was to run through the whole a love betwixt Edgar and Cordelia, that never changed word with each other in the original'.[10] Cordelia's part is greatly expanded by this romantic motivation. Keeping her in England allows her to wander on the heath, accompanied by her confidante (necessary in the fashionable French classical model of drama) so that she can be attacked by ruffians sent by Edmund (who plans a rape), and rescued, of course, by Edgar. Cordelia and Lear are arrested, but principles of poetic justice will not let the virtuous heroine die. Cordelia becomes queen, married to the noble Edgar, and 'truth and virtue ... at last succeed'. Goneril and Regan meet their ends by mutual poisoning. So satisfying was all this to the audience that Tate's was the version of *King Lear* performed in England for the next 150 years. Much of its success must be ascribed to its normalising of the role of Cordelia into a romantic heroine who survives, rather than a disturbingly tactless young woman who is almost accidentally killed off stage.

Dryden, the Poet Laureate, wrote his own version of *Antony and Cleopatra*, *All for Love* (1678), which remained the more popular play for 150 years not only because it was more elegantly structured but because his Cleopatra is never so indecorous as she is in Shakespeare; she becomes a more conventionally passionate tragic heroine. In Dryden and Davenant's extravagant expansion of *The Tempest* (1667), Miranda has a sister, Dorinda, thus enabling a good deal of salacious talk about the facts of life between the two naïve young women. Some plays remained relatively unaltered, however: *Othello* and *Hamlet*, with their victimised women, needed no alteration to seem playable. Of Shakespeare's great comic roles, little or nothing was seen of Beatrice, Rosalind or Viola until the 1740s; Congreve, Etherege, Dryden and Farquhar were supplying contemporary witty roles for the actresses.

The names of these first women to act Shakespeare's roles – Elizabeth Barry, Mary Betterton, Anne Bracegirdle – mean little to us today. They played Shakespeare as they played the many new roles written for them, and in so doing, established models of femininity that remained dominant for the next century: the tragedy queen, the virtuous heroine of sentimental drama and the witty heroine.[11] Since the actresses usually came from the impecunious middle class, they had to be trained to act convincingly as members of the leisured gentry: they learnt singing, dancing, walking, wearing the elaborate and impractical clothing of an upper-class lady (the plays were always done in contemporary costume), either in the theatres' 'nurseries' or simply by observation and imitation. That is to say, Shakespeare's women as mediated by the Restoration stage – played by actresses, in rewritten texts – were no more 'real women' than the boys who first performed the roles. They added the potential for the display of 'real' sexuality (bare-breasted women appear in illustrations to Shakespeare texts such as *Othello*); but this fact ultimately only contributed to the lubriciousness of a stage that was set up primarily as a spectacle for the male (even regal) gaze; hence, particularly, the addition of rape or near-rape scenes to Shakespeare texts such as *King Lear*.

The first attempt to restore the Shakespeare text to what was originally played was made by the actor-manager David Garrick in the 1740s. His co-star was Hannah Pritchard, their most notable pairing *Macbeth* (see also chapter 7). Pritchard's performance is the first we read of in which Lady Macbeth as a character is significantly noticed: no doubt this is in some measure due to the cleaning up of the text, so that irrelevant moralising contrasts with Lady Macduff are removed. Instead of a monolithic 'ambitious couple', the audience of 1748 saw a couple locked in profound psychological conflict. They saw, under the rubric of the new aesthetic of sensibility, actors creating the illusion of characters with an inner life, instantly recognisable as 'natural' despite the highly crafted fiction of the situation:

> The beginning of the scene after the murder was conducted in terrifying whispers. Their looks and action supplied the place of words. You heard what they spoke, but you learned more from the agitation of mind displayed in their action and deportment ... [In the Banquet scene] when, at last, as if unable

to support her feelings any longer, she rose from her seat, and seized his arm, and, with a half-whisper of terror, said, '*Are you a man*!' she assumed a look of such anger, indignation, and contempt, as cannot be surpassed.[12]

Pritchard and Garrick's work prepared the way for the achievements of the most famous Lady Macbeth of all, Sarah Siddons, from 1775 onwards. Siddons made her name as a great tragedienne (Sir Joshua Reynolds painted her as the Muse of Tragedy in 1784): as well as playing many contemporary tragic roles, she also shone as Constance in *King John*, Volumnia in *Coriolanus*, Queen Katherine in *Henry VIII*, and Hermione in *The Winter's Tale*. In her 'Remarks on the Character of Lady Macbeth',[13] she demonstrated the study she devoted to creating a character. Lady Macbeth's 'ruling passion', wrote Siddons, is ambition, and she forcefully dominates her husband in the first two acts. Then with the failure to gain content, 'smothering her sufferings in the deepest recess of her own wretched bosom ... she devotes herself entirely to the effort of supporting him'. Siddons's sleepwalking scene reached new heights of expressiveness, coinciding with (and probably helping to form) the late eighteenth-century development of Romantic subjectivity. Hazlitt, remembering her greatest days, wrote of her sleepwalking scene: 'her eyes were open, but the sense was shut. She was like a person bewildered, and unconscious of what she did. She moved her lips involuntarily; all her gestures were involuntary and mechanical ... She glided on and off the stage almost like an apparition'[14] (see fig. 20). Siddons pioneered a simple style of 'timeless' classical costume for women in tragedy, thus relieving the actress of the artificial and stilted action enforced by hoop and headdress. It should come as no surprise, then, that she also played Hamlet (though not in London), the first woman noted as doing so. After her retirement from the stage she continued to give private readings of Shakespeare, in which she would read all the parts, male and female, with thrilling effect (this practice was continued by her niece, Fanny Kemble, and others in the Victorian era).

Siddons was no comedienne, but from the time of Garrick onwards Shakespeare's major comedies, which had languished throughout the previous century and a half, were successful vehicles for a succession of actresses who also flourished as the witty young women of contemporary comedy. Dorothy Jordan, the most famous of them, between 1785 and 1809 played Viola, Rosalind, Imogen, Helena (*All's Well*), Juliet, Ophelia, Beatrice, and Dorinda in Dryden's expanded *Tempest*. She particularly shone in 'breeches' roles – she was trim and athletic on stage – and critics commented on her boundless energy, her ability to touch the heart with pathos (as Viola and Ophelia in particular), her fine singing, and her infectious and natural

20 Sarah Siddons as Lady Macbeth in the sleepwalking scene: 'her eyes were open, but their sense was shut'. Her not holding the candle during this scene was considered revolutionary.

laugh. Rosalind was the most admired of her many roles, and she played it for twenty-seven years. In method and effects the absolute opposite of her colleague Siddons, Jordan appeared to her public as the charismatic embodiment of a new style of young woman, bringing contemporary life to Shakespeare's underestimated comic heroines.

The nineteenth century

The Victorians, however, took their Shakespeare very seriously: his works were to provide moral and spiritual education and inspiration. Playing the women's roles in this atmosphere presented peculiar challenges, although there were gains too. The plays were shorn of their Tate/Cibber/Dryden accretions and alterations, and restored to their pre-Restoration form – albeit abbreviated, rearranged, and shorn of lines that might bring a blush to the cheek of the young person. Consistent efforts were made to present the plays with 'historical' costumes and sets, thereby adding to the educational value of the experience of going to the theatre (see chapter 4 above).

The first Victorian leading lady, and indeed the embodiment of mid-nineteenth-century notions of femininity, was Helen Faucit. Her early work was with Macready – particularly as Cordelia (no longer Edgar's love interest) in the 1838 revival. Carried on stage, dead, in Lear's arms, she defined one of the most iconic of Victorian images, the father weeping over his dead daughter. Her gentle good looks provided the model of young woman-hood for the period: 'with expressive and pleasing features, and in her bearing that somewhat affected English grace of the "Keepsakes" and "Books of Beauty" … the pensive smile, the liquid eyes, the dishevelled hair, the curving shoulders, the satin-like texture of the skin'. Critics raved about her Rosalind (1845), 'the simplicity, the delicacy, the purity of the delineation … the caprice of the part never more ethereally embodied'. In general, Faucit's acting was considered 'the perfection of pathos. She has the art of giving to simple words and sentences a world of meaning, – of appealing directly to the heart, – of opening the deepest depths of feeling.'[15] Despite these comments, she was a woman of striking presence and fine intellect. But when she attempted Lady Macbeth (1864) it was considered a relative failure – not because she was ineffectual or unvaried, or ignored Lady Macbeth's coarser aspects, but because she *did* attempt them, thereby denying her public image of essential and instinctive femininity and substituting for it the 'studied' attitudes of realistic mimesis. John Morley complained, tellingly, that '"I have given suck", etc. is poured out by Miss Faucit in a way that, by tones and gestures, vividly recalls a common spectacle of passion in our London streets – the scold at the door of the gin-shop' (cited Mullin, *Actors and*

Actresses, 183). Faucit (like Lady Macbeth) had become a class and gender traitor in pursuing her professional ambition.

In contrast to the high seriousness of Shakespeare productions in companies run by men, the actress-manager Mme (Eliza) Vestris, whose forte was light comedy and operetta, revived *Love's Labour's Lost* (1839), *The Merry Wives of Windsor* (1839) and *A Midsummer Night's Dream* (1840). Vestris's warmth, wit and sexiness were a welcome change from the image of women that dominated mid-century Shakespeare production, and it is a pity that she did not choose to undertake more of the plays. Her acting was 'full of archness, dash, and piquancy', but, to Victorian critics' eyes, she lacked 'passion or pathos', 'sympathy, tenderness, and strength'.[16] Not a truly womanly woman, in short, but a hugely successful businesswoman in her chosen field.

In 1845, after beginning their careers in their native America, sisters Charlotte and Susan Cushman played Romeo and Juliet, Viola and Olivia, and Rosalind and Celia in London. It was Charlotte, an actress of extraordinary intensity, high intelligence and physical electricity, who burst starlike upon the somewhat moribund traditions of female performance in England. Said the *London Sun*, 'True, we have very lady-like, accomplished, finished artists, but there is a wide and impassible gulf between them and Miss Cushman' (Mullin, *Actors and Actresses*, 143). Her Romeo, for which she became most famous, struck critics with the 'reality' of its embodiment: 'There is no trick in Miss Cushman's performance; no thought, no interest, no feeling, seems to actuate her, except what might be looked for in Romeo himself' (James Sheridan Knowles, in Mullin, *Actors and Actresses*, 144). Notably, she insisted on playing the role as written by Shakespeare, not Garrick's alteration. It was heavily cut for reasons of decency and focus on the star (herself), but questions about the propriety of cross-gender playing of a love story seem not to have arisen. Conventions of gestural decorum on stage would anyway have limited the physical expression of passion between Romeo and Juliet; the most remarked upon scenes were the balcony scene, Cushman's excellent sword-fighting in the death of Tybalt, her passionate anguish in the 'banished' scene with Friar Lawrence, and the final scene. The *Times* reviewer simply wrote, 'For a long time Romeo has been a convention. Miss Cushman's Romeo is a creative, a living, breathing, animated, ardent, human being.'[17] She continued to play the role throughout her career – altogether for twenty-three years (fig. 21). Cushman was also an admired Lady Macbeth and Queen Constance, and a remarkable Emilia in *Othello*, one of the first to be elevated to tragic status.

The most famous home-grown productions of Shakespeare were the seasons undertaken by Charles Kean at the Princess's Theatre in London

21 Charlotte Cushman as Romeo, with her sister Susan as Juliet, 1858.

(1850–9; see chapter 4 above). Ellen Tree was Charles Kean's leading lady
(and wife), taking her place in heavily pictorial productions in which a lesser
actress might well have been upstaged by the scenery. Like Helen Faucit, she
was admired for her 'womanliness'; lacking Faucit's ethereal elegance, she
made up for it by a wider range. She was a charmingly humorous Rosalind
and Beatrice, a touching Viola; she had also essayed Romeo earlier in her
career. Her physical energy provided a base for passionate acting, which
made her an admired Lady Macbeth, and she was able to create a sense of the

character's suppressed inner life: 'The countenance which she assumed ...
when luring on Macbeth in his course of crime, was actually appalling in
intensity, as if it denoted a hunger after guilt' (*Times*, 14 June 1853).

Improvements in transport had made it easier for actresses and actors acknowledged as stars in their own country to attempt to take England by storm
with their Shakespeare; Charlotte Cushman was an early example. Adelaide
Ristori, the great Italian actress, among other non-Shakespeare roles brought
her Lady Macbeth to the London stage, first in Italian translation in 1863,
and after 1873 in English. The play was cut drastically so that it became
predominantly Lady Macbeth's tragedy. Ristori impressed particularly with
the naturalism of her sleepwalking scene: several observers noted that she
breathed so deeply in this that she actually snored. Decorum – acceptable
behaviour for a lady on stage – and 'correctness' – the conventional parameters of Shakespearean interpretation – still constrained English actresses'
performances. The visits of strong performers not thus restricted, limited
though their grasp of the rules of Shakespearean verse might be, served to
loosen up audience expectations and younger actresses' ideas.

One of the most notable of these visitors was the great French actress
Sarah Bernhardt, who in 1899 brought to London her production of *Hamlet*
(in French prose translation), with herself as the prince. Although the production was dismissed by critics as too 'Gallic', the public and members
of the acting profession loved it. This was largely due to the actress's personal magnetism (there had after all been numerous English female Hamlets
since Siddons first played it), but it is also worth noting that Bernhardt was
determined to move the play beyond romantic clichés, to show the prince
not as 'a feminized, hesitating, bemused creature. What I see', she wrote,
'is a person who is manly and resolute, but nonetheless thoughtful ... [he]
thinks before he acts, a trait indicative of great strength and great spiritual
power.'[18]

Another visitor at this time was the American actress Ada Rehan; after
her début in New York in 1882 she brought her Rosalind and Katherina
to London in 1890 and again in 1893–5 and 1897, adding Viola and Julia
(*Two Gentlemen*) to her repertoire of buoyant, arch, cross-dressing heroines.
There was a New World boldness and freedom about Rehan: her ease, her
energy, her spontaneity, her sense of fun – all, complemented by her beautiful
musical voice, were a revelation to Londoners, who had not seen such a
Rosalind for many decades.

They had not been allowed to. Although all her professional life she
longed to play Rosalind, and studied the part obsessively, Ellen Terry, who
dominated the British stage in the last quarter of the century, was quite
simply never given the opportunity. This was largely because most of her

22 Ellen Terry as Beatrice in *Much Ado About Nothing*, Lyceum Theatre, 1882.

professional career – including all her major Shakespeare roles – was spent as stage partner to the actor-manager Henry Irving. Irving mounted productions in which his was the star role – *Hamlet, The Merchant of Venice, Othello, Romeo and Juliet, Much Ado About Nothing, Twelfth Night, Macbeth, Henry VIII, King Lear, Cymbeline* and *Coriolanus*, between 1878 and 1902. There was, he claimed, no part suitable for him in *As You Like It* (yet clearly he would have made an interesting Jaques), and so it was never programmed. Terry's disappointment was keen, so much so that she frequently commented on it in her later career as a lecturer on Shakespeare: 'I have been Beatrice! would that I could say "I have been Rosalind."' Critics and audiences wished it for her (and themselves) too: when she played Imogen in 1896 (though she was already forty-nine years old), Clement Scott noted, 'There was only one remark in the house, "Oh what a Rosalind she would have made!" And many added, "and ought to make".' As Nina Auerbach acutely comments, 'Her own tormenting, superfluous energy seems to have summoned Rosalind to a stage where no Rosalind was allowed: as if by magic, the tearful Imogen/Fidele aroused in receptive spectators visions of the laughing Rosalind/Ganymede.'[19]

Imogen, Terry claimed, was her favourite part, since it enabled her to play the loving and faithful wife, passionate in rejection and courageous in her attempts to reclaim her husband. Throughout her career, Terry preferred roles with which she could identify, women in whom she could find her own ideal characteristics. To 'adapt the part to [her] own personality' was her way of approaching a character, 'make its thoughts her thoughts, its words her words'.[20] It was her own beauty, charm and grace that she infused into her characterisations of Portia, Desdemona and Beatrice. Terry was not, however, an untechnical actress. She prepared intensively for her roles, reading commentaries and studying the lines so as to discover the particular 'womanliness' that informed each one. In the process she reinvented several roles – rather than reproducing or slightly varying traditional interpretations. Her début as Portia in 1874 provoked comments that it was 'like no other Portia ever seen by Shakespearean students … No traces of the stage were there, no renewal of old business, no suggestion of immemorial traditions' (Clement Scott, in Mullin, *Actors and Actresses*, 438). Most significantly, critics noted that 'probably for the first time, the loves of Portia and Bassanio became of more importance and interest than the scenes in which Shylock appears' (Dutton Cook, in Mullin, *Actors and Actresses*, 438); they also noted that in the trial scene she showed sympathy to Shylock, attempting to save him from the consequences of his vengeful resolution. When Terry performed in Irving's production of *Merchant*, she had to play the trial scene to accommodate his conception: she had wanted to be 'quiet', but Irving's Shylock 'was so quiet, I had to give it up. His heroic saint was splendid, but it wasn't good for Portia' (Booth, *Terry*, 114).

Terry's Ophelia (1880) was, according to Henry James, again 'of a type altogether different … In Miss Terry's hands the bewildered daughter of Polonius becomes a somewhat angular maiden of the Gothic ages, with her hair cropped short, like a boy's, and a straight and clinging robe' (Mullin, *Actors and Actresses*, 441). Michael Booth argues that 'from the beginning of her career she was an artistic creation as well as an actress', embodying the age's aesthetic ideals (Booth, *Terry*, 76). She was often painted, and in preparing a role she would plan her look and costume according to the art of the appropriate historical period. Most memorable is the portrait of her as Lady Macbeth, painted by John Singer Sargent in 1888. The blue-green dress, covered with glinting beetles' wings, and the pose (drawn not from the play but from the artist's and actress's imaginations), in which she triumphantly crowns herself, create an image which, Terry said, 'is all that I meant to do' in the part. But her portrayal was not successful with the public, for whom a century of Siddons imitations had created a powerful stereotype. Trying to adapt the role to her own personality and ideas, Terry wrote, 'Everyone seems to think Mrs McB is a *Monstrousness* & I can only see she's a *woman* – a mistaken woman – & *weak* – not a Dove – of course not – *but first of all a wife*'.[21] The upshot, despite the magnificent costume and all that it said about her desire for power, was a performance of pathos rather than anything the public could recognise as tragedy (see also chapter 7). As Michael Booth comments, 'she was ... trapped in the Victorian ideal she had done so much to disseminate in performance' (*Terry*, 108).

The twentieth century

The aftermath of the First World War saw women's demands for equality and the vote begin to take effect and change the face of gender relations. Although it took the best part of the century to dismantle the rhetoric of 'womanliness', at least the constraining preconceptions of the right way to play a role or the right 'look' for the role, which have always been more oppressively applied to actresses (involving, as they do, discursive assumptions about female beauty as well as about gender performance), were severely shaken. This change was assisted by a move towards simpler non-pictorial productions and, more radically, modern dress; for example a *Macbeth* in 1928, in which Lady Macbeth's social ambition was easily readable in her fashionable evening dress – and her cocktail-swigging habit.

The disappearance of assumptions about the necessity of typecasting is illustrated perhaps most comprehensively in the career of Peggy Ashcroft. Her long list of Shakespeare roles included the ingénues (Juliet, Desdemona, Cordelia) and romantic heroines (Viola, Portia, Beatrice, Rosalind, Imogen), but also, defying all received wisdom, a mould-breaking Cleopatra, a psychologically complex Katherina, and a Margaret of Anjou in *The Wars of the Roses*[22] that presented over the course of three plays a kaleidoscope of embodiment not of the 'feminine' but of a multifaceted and complex woman from youthful beauty to raving old age.

Ashcroft, who is the first actress in this narrative to have attended drama school (a belated recognition of the professional status of acting), was frequently likened to Ellen Terry in her early performances. John Gielgud spoke of 'the same kind of shimmering radiance and iridescence and a kind of forthright, trusting quality ... She has a fighting spirit without any pugnaciousness'.[23] Like Terry, she was particularly good at representing the intense ardour of youthful love: it made her Juliet one of the legends of twentieth-century acting, in a 1935 production also starring John Gielgud and Laurence Olivier. Critics spoke of her combination of childlike impetuosity and heart-searing tragedy, the poetry of the great speeches sounding absolutely spontaneous. Of her first Portia, in 1932, a critic wrote that she avoided the mechanical 'Shakespeare voice' (an overly musical utterance that can be heard on old recordings): the 'quality of mercy' speech was spoken 'quite naturally with her hands behind her back and not attempting to orate' (Trewin, cited in Billington, *Ashcroft*, 63).

Ashcroft was not content to remain within the limits decreed by her natural charm. When she was cast as Cleopatra in 1953 it was to take on a role that had had very mixed success in the theatre even after Dryden's *All for Love* was displaced in the nineteenth century. Playing not the statuesque queen so much as the gypsy, she was an athletic figure in a red pony-tailed wig, 'a creation of earth and air and fire which is all happy and unhappy women rolled into one' (Alan Dent, cited in Billington, *Ashcroft*, 149). Too 'English' for some critics in her refusal to use clichés of theatrical sensuality, Ashcroft nevertheless presented a fascinating performance. Actresses since then have tackled the role as of right, unfazed by its contrariety; they have also been aided by a twentieth-century culture that sees nothing reprehensible in women expressing their sexuality.

The twentieth century's other great contribution to the art of acting has been the science of psychoanalysis. In various forms, the legacy of Stanislavsky's ideas about preparing to act a character has encouraged actors to look for complex psychological (i.e. individual, rather than socially determined) motivations for their characters' actions. Ashcroft's Katherina in *The Taming of the Shrew* (1960) was an example of this. First angry at her father's treatment of her, then recognising in Petruchio a clever and unpredictable mate, 'in the final scene she was not so much cowed and acquiescent as liberated from the demon that had first possessed her' (Billington, *Ashcroft*, 185). This 'liberation', based on an assumption that Kate needs a therapist, has been questioned in more recent productions of the play (e.g. Michael Bogdanov in 1978 and Gale Edwards in 1995), productions which recognise the viciousness of the patriarchal system in which Katherina is a commodity; but as a way of complicating the stock 'virago' figure of Kate into a more interesting character, Ashcroft's performance was extremely influential.

Ashcroft's last Shakespearean appearance was as the Countess of Rousillon in *All's Well That Ends Well* (1982), a dignified, warm and witty performance that humanised yet another role that could too easily be played as a stock 'old lady'. By the time she appeared in this, several generations of actresses had followed in her footsteps. Few theatre-goers would disagree that, among them, Judi Dench is the finest British Shakespearean actress of the last half-century. Beginning her career at the Old Vic in 1957, she has in the course of it played Ophelia, Maria (*Twelfth Night*), Katherine (*Henry V*), Phebe (*As You Like It*), Anne Page, Juliet, Hermia, Isabella, Titania, Lady Macbeth, Viola, Hermione and Perdita (doubling the roles), Portia, Beatrice, Adriana (*Comedy of Errors*), Regan, Imogen, Cleopatra, Gertrude, Volumnia and Mistress Quickly – as well as numerous non-Shakespeare roles. A natural comedienne with wonderful comic timing and physical wit, Dench also has a unique voice, musical and husky with a catch in it. It adds to the impression of sadness that underlies some of her finest comic roles (Viola, Beatrice), and its plangency was most telling in the great tragedy roles that she made her own despite the expectations of critics – Lady Macbeth (1976–8) and Cleopatra (1987).

Macbeth was played in an intimate space on a virtually bare set, with Ian McKellen as Macbeth (see chapter 7 above); they were a relatively young couple, physically passionate. Michael Billington's review best sums up the extraordinary effect of this claustrophobic production: 'these are not monsters but recognisable human beings willing themselves to evil and disintegrating in the process'.[24] That disintegration was mapped by Dench in a sleepwalking scene full of strange, heart-rending cries and wails.[25]

By contrast, *Antony and Cleopatra*, with Anthony Hopkins as Antony, was played in the huge space of the Olivier theatre at London's National Theatre. Dench's fabled speed and her physical audacity were of the essence here, as she ran around the vast stage, rolled on the floor with Antony, whipped the hapless messenger with astonishing fury. She was also funny, mockingly witty, sensual, and pathetically touching when momentarily recognising her middle age; finally there was a sort of grand resignation in her death. For those who were lucky enough to see it, in a long run of sold-out performances, this was indisputably great acting (see fig. 23).

Dench's career illustrates a pattern that was new for the enfranchised and independent women of the twentieth-century theatre. Along with the freedom to play any role that interests them, unlimited by physical typecasting or received ideas of how the role should be played, women now have a different relation to the Shakespeare repertoire. Unlike actresses in the previous two and a half centuries, they rarely return to a role – they do not turn up year after year performing 'their' Rosalind or 'their' Lady Macbeth – but play in limited-run seasons and then move on, waiting to be offered a new role by a company director. This presents constant challenges and the potential for artistic growth – a stretching of the artist in directions she or the public might never have imagined her going.

23 Judi Dench as Cleopatra with Miranda Foster as Charmian,
National Theatre, 1987.

A most remarkable example of this was *As You Like It* directed by Adrian
Noble for the Royal Shakespeare Company in 1985. This production, a
modern-dress exploration of a Jungian forest-within-the-mind, was dominated by the pairing of Juliet Stevenson and Fiona Shaw as Rosalind and
Celia. Their friendship was important – not to the exclusion of heterosexual
love, but as a bulwark against the oppression of patriarchal structures.
Stevenson later wrote of her arguments with the director about the staging
of the ending as an uncomplicated celebration; and ultimately 'the dance culminated in a moment of still suspension, as the characters took in an Arden
they were about to leave, and absorbed the *consequences* of the return to
the ordered world'.[26] The play, said Stevenson, 'isn't about confirming cosy
opinions or settled stereotypes. It isn't about a woman in search of romantic
love. The search is for knowledge and faith, and in that search Rosalind

24 Juliet Stevenson as Rosalind and Fiona Shaw as Celia in *As You Like It*, Royal Shakespeare Theatre, 1985.

is clamorous.'[27] Stevenson's rethought Rosalind was both 'bright, buoyant and sexy', and at times 'marvellously grave, melancholy and sombre too'.[28]

Stevenson is one of a number of contemporary actresses who bring a highly honed intellect to classic Shakespeare roles, questioning in particular received notions of gender. Fiona Shaw played an androgynous Richard II in 1995; the asexual role of Lear's Fool was taken by Judy Davis (Sydney, 1986, doubling Cordelia) and Emma Thompson (London, 1990). More radically, actresses have tackled King Lear to great acclaim: Marianne Hoppe (Frankfurt, 1990), Kathryn Hunter (Leicester and London, 1996–7). The German actress Angela Winkler took up the perennial challenge of Hamlet in a production by Peter Zadek that toured to the Edinburgh Festival in 2000. All these actresses (and their directors) insisted that they were doing these roles because the texts challenged and excited them as professional performers, rather than because they sought the 'feminine' in them. Women actors need not only act Shakespeare's women.

A symbolic point at which to pause this narrative is a performance of *The Tempest* in 2000, on the stage of the Bankside Globe. Where once a young boy played Miranda, now an adult woman, Vanessa Redgrave, played Prospero, in a performance of great authority, humanity and humour. Tall and lithe, dressed in trousers and boots and a long leather coat, Redgrave appeared to inhabit the role as naturally as she had done the great cross-dressing role of Rosalind in 1961.[29] This Prospero was neither 'masculine' nor 'feminine', artist or magus, but rather a watchful parent to both Miranda and Ariel (also played by a woman). The performance offered a hopeful image for the new millennium: a concept of gender that no longer confines men or women to predetermined roles, either in life or on the stage.

NOTES

1 There are some arguments (though no evidence) to suggest that some of the older women's roles, e.g. the Nurse in *Romeo*, or Mistress Quickly, were played by adult men. Either way, women were absolutely excluded from acting on the public stage.

2 There is actually no record of any performance of *Antony and Cleopatra* during Shakespeare's lifetime. See Juliet Dusinberre, 'Squeaking Cleopatras: Gender and Performance in *Antony and Cleopatra*' in James C. Bulman (ed.), *Shakespeare, Theory, and Performance* (London and New York: Routledge, 1996), 46–67, for a stimulating discussion of the performance history of Cleopatra.

3 For contemporary evidence about the age of boy players, see Michael Shapiro, *Gender in Play on the Shakespearean Stage* (Ann Arbor: University of Michigan Press, 1994), 34–6, and 245, notes 14 and 15; T. J. King, *Casting Shakespeare's Plays* (Cambridge: Cambridge University Press, 1993), 19, 48.

4 These debates are summarised in Shapiro's introduction to *Gender in Play*, and Jean Howard, *The Stage and Social Struggle in Early Modern England* (London: Routledge, 1994), 159–60. Howard also has a stimulating discussion of women as audience members in the Elizabethan theatre, 76–79.

5 Stephen Orgel, *Impersonations: the Performance of Gender in Shakespeare's England* (Cambridge: Cambridge University Press, 1996), 43.

6 See Shapiro, *Gender in Play*, 38–9, and notes.

7 Shapiro points out that audiences in western Europe 'did not see female actresses in professional companies until *commedia dell'arte* companies introduced the practice' in the late sixteenth century. 'Sexual attitudes may have less to do with the late introduction of actresses to the English stage than the fact that the *commedia dell'arte*, for political, linguistic, and geographical reasons, exerted more influence on the continent.' (ibid., 32–3.)

8 Royal Patent delivered to Thomas Killigrew, 15 April 1662, cited in David Thomas (ed.), *Restoration and Georgian England, 1660–1788* (Cambridge: Cambridge University Press, 1989), 17–18.

9 Lord Chamberlain's records, cited in George Odell, *Shakespeare from Betterton to Irving* (New York: Scribner, 1920), I, 24.

10 Nahum Tate, *The History of King Lear*, ed. James Black (London: Edward Arnold, 1975).

11 Maids, nurses, countrywomen, etc., do not come into this category of influential models of femininity; they are class-based 'character' roles.

12 Thomas Davies, *Dramatic Miscellanies*, quoted in Gāmini Salgādo, *Eye-Witnesses of Shakespeare* (London: Sussex University Press, 1975), 295–6.

13 Undated; pre-1816. Included in Thomas Campbell's *Life of Mrs Siddons* (London, 1839; New York: Benjamin Blom, 1972), 170–84.

14 William Hazlitt, 'Mrs Siddons' in *A View of the English Stage*, ed. Duncan Wu (London: Pickering & Chatto, 1998), 145. Michael Booth summarises audience perceptions of Siddons's Lady Macbeth in Michael Booth, John Stokes and Susan Bassnett, *Three Tragic Actresses: Siddons, Rachel, Duse* (Cambridge: Cambridge University Press, 1996), 43–5.

15 Contemporary comments by Théophile Gautier, and anon., *Athenaeum*, *Tallis's Dramatic Magazine*, quoted in Donald Mullin (ed.), *Victorian Actors and Actresses in Review* (Westport, CT: Greenwood Press, 1983), 182–3.

16 Comments by Robert Lowe, Westland Marston and John Coleman, ibid., 476.

17 *The Times*, 30 December 1845, cited in Jill L. Levenson, *Shakespeare in Performance: Romeo and Juliet* (Manchester: Manchester University Press, 1987), 38.

18 Sarah Bernhardt, letter to the London *Daily Telegraph*, quoted in Gerda Taranow, *The Bernhardt Hamlet: Culture and Context* (New York: Peter Lang, 1996), 68.

19 Quotations in this paragraph are from Nina Auerbach, *Ellen Terry, Player in her Time* (London: J. M. Dent & Sons, 1987), 230–2.

20 Ellen Terry, quoted in John Stokes, Michael R. Booth, Susan Bassnett, *Bernhardt, Terry, Duse: the Actress in her Time* (Cambridge: Cambridge University Press, 1988), 88.

21 Ellen Terry, letter to the American critic William Winter, quoted in Auerbach, *Terry*, 259.

22 This consisted of a conflation by John Barton (with some rewriting) of the three parts of *Henry VI* into two plays, followed by *Richard III*.

23 John Gielgud, quoted in Michael Billington, *Peggy Ashcroft* (London: John Murray, 1988), 7–8.

24 Michael Billington quoted in John Miller, *Judi Dench* (London: Weidenfeld & Nicolson, 1998), 149.

25 The production was recorded for television and is available on video.

26 Fiona Shaw and Juliet Stevenson, 'Celia and Rosalind in *As You Like It*' in Russell Jackson and Robert Smallwood (eds.), *Players of Shakespeare 2* (Cambridge: Cambridge University Press, 1988), 119–20.

27 Juliet Stevenson in Carol Rutter, *Clamorous Voices: Shakespeare's Women Today* (London: Women's Press, 1988), 121.

28 Benedict Nightingale, *Listener* (25 April 1985).

29 Redgrave also played Cleopatra in a number of productions in the previous two decades, often appearing in male dress in her opening scenes. Her performances were characterised by a 'gauche, boyish, bony Englishness' (John Peter, *Sunday Times*, 1 June 1986).

IO

ANTHONY B. DAWSON

International Shakespeare

Appropriation anxieties

In 1981 at the Théâtre du Soleil in Paris, Ariane Mnouchkine directed a production of *Richard II* using her own French translation. Inspired partly by Antonin Artaud's dictum that 'the theatre is oriental', she told an interviewer: 'When we decided to perform Shakespeare, a recourse to Asia became a necessity.'[1] She spoke of trying to find an antidote to the 'psychological venom'[2] which infects western acting; wanting to break from the realistic tradition, she relied on a combination of Shakespeare's text and Asian form. Accordingly, she ignored the play's specifically English, *national*, resonance, instead importing movement, costumes and a hieratic style borrowed from Japanese *Kabuki* and *Noh*, interlaced with Balinese and *Kathakali* influences plus various styles of Asian music. The result was a blend designed to reveal the play's 'sacred and ritualistic aspects'[3] and the chief means were the disciplined bodies of the actors and the words. Colette Godard describes the effect: the actors face the audience, 'knees flexed...hands ceremoniously spread. With their heads held erect, almost never looking at each other...they project their lines directly at the audience'. The words 'come across with incredible clarity...It's as if these weren't characters, but bodies traversed by a single voice'. But the temperature is not uniformly cool: at the end, Bolingbroke 'dares [to] kiss the lips of the murdered king, before laying himself out...tiny and fragile at the centre of an enormous bare carpet'.[4] The formal production values '[gave] the text an autonomy'[5] and allowed the actors to express the 'states' of the various characters.[6] Mnouchkine was seeking theatrical means that would answer to Shakespeare's 'extraordinary ability' to 'transpose everything into poetry' and at the same time 'to speak in the voice of a character'.[7] In such a laboratory, the theatrical traditions of Japan become a research source and an inspiration, but the production itself does not pretend to be authentically Japanese.

I choose this production from many possible ones to introduce 'international' Shakespeare. *Richard II* began life as a play with strong national roots: it famously celebrates the 'sceptred isle'; its relevance to contemporary politics was noted, in their different ways, both by Queen Elizabeth and by her favourite-turned-rival, the Earl of Essex; it spoke ambiguously of the Irish question that haunted Elizabethan policy and ruined the Earl's career. And it was instrumental, along with so many of Shakespeare's plays, in helping to construct the idea of the English nation, at its point of origin and subsequently.[8] Mnouchkine translates not only the text but the history and the politics of the play; her choice of Asian form distances it from its roots and universalises it.

Needless to say, such 'interculturalism' has not gone uncriticised. Citing Edward Said, Dennis Kennedy attacks Mnouchkine's 'orientalism' as 'a process of commodifying the Other, of . . . maintain[ing] alterity for the sake of controlling it'.[9] Mnouchkine's Parisian colleague, and celebrated Shakespeare director, Peter Brook, has been the target of similar, though more widespread and searching criticism. Was he, his opponents ask, justified in adapting a Sanskrit classic, the *Mahabharata*, using a collage of Indian and western theatrical conventions and a deliberately multicultural cast, all in the interests of a universalising, 'transcultural' vision of a singular human essence – a vision that suppresses the uniqueness and historical reality of the source culture?[10] Of course the simple answer is yes – a theatre artist can do what she or he wants. But critics like Kennedy are wary. Noting its scenographic and conceptual resemblances to the *Mahabharata*, he denounces Brook's *Tempest* (1990) because Brook 'was blind to imperialist issues, and actually took trouble to upset [the colonialist] reading'.[11] Kennedy seems to assume that post-colonial discourse offers the only valid way of interpreting the play, and he reads Brook's ideological failure as complicit with the 'message . . . of global capitalism'.[12] Thus do debates rage about the ideological implications of western intercultural practice, and theatre artists who believe in something like a universal human core are taken to task by 'slit-eyed' (the phrase is Harry Berger's) critics of a materialist bent who see cultures as fundamentally incommensurate, deny the existence of human universals, and are wary of the power relations they think are lurking behind the supposedly naïve essentialist claims of artists like Brook or Mnouchkine.

The materialist, post-colonial critique depends on an idea of the value of cultural and national sovereignty, and the related ethical suspicion of cultural appropriation. These ideas are themselves the product of the long history of nationalist aspiration, one ironically linked to, among other things, the history of Shakespeare's international presence. As I shall show, Shakespeare has often been associated with the national hopes and ambitions of certain cultural or linguistic groups – starting of course with the English, but spreading far beyond the British Isles. His international presence has shaped both aspirations of sovereignty and ideological suspicion. Thus the intercultural impulse and the critique of it have, one could say, a common source. The process began in the early modern period, when the supranational (broadly European) culture identified with Latin and classical civilisation began to give way to vernacular cultures, a move that eventually led to the dominance of the nation-state. Shakespeare played a role in that shift.

From the beginning, Shakespeare has occupied an international space. If we exclude the histories, almost all his plays are set beyond the borders of England – all but one comedy, *The Merry Wives of Windsor*, one tragedy, *King Lear*, and one romance, *Cymbeline*. And in all three of these, as indeed in the histories and in *Macbeth* (Shakespeare's other 'British' tragedy), national and extranational loyalties encounter each other.[13] The models and sources he drew on were frequently European rather than British, part of an international literary and dramatic heritage. Moreover, performances began migrating shortly after they originated on London stages, with touring companies taking versions of the plays to foreign shores. Aside from the celebrated performances of *Hamlet* on board the good ship *Dragon* off the coast of Sierra Leone in 1607–8 (not strictly speaking international in that they were performed primarily for the entertainment of the English crew),[14] there are records of continental performances on the part of 'English comedians' from as early as 1585, when a troupe of English players performed at, of all places, Elsinore. By 1604, when a version of *Romeo and Juliet* was played at Nördlingen, some of Shakespeare's plays (simplified and foreshortened) had begun to make their appearance in Germany and eastern Europe. Both *Titus Andronicus* and *Hamlet* were in the repertory before 1620, when a version of the former was published in German. An adaptation of *Hamlet*, *Der bestrafte Brudermord*, known from an early eighteenth-century manuscript, no doubt has its roots in the kinds of translations that resulted from these early English troupes.[15] Following the publication of the First Folio in 1623, there are records of performances of *King Lear*, *Julius Caesar* and possibly some of the comedies.

Not surprisingly, *Richard II* and the other history plays do not turn up in these records of early international performance. And in that fact we can perhaps detect the important dialectic between Shakespeare as a 'national' playwright ideologically implicated (for better or for worse) in a nation-building project inextricably linked to the ambitions of (British) empire, and Shakespeare as a writer who belongs to the world and who has been appropriated by nations such as Russia, Japan and especially Germany as uniquely their own. The view now fashionably current in Anglo-American academic circles, that Shakespeare's texts are in one way or another complicit with colonialism and other forms of domination, needs to be understood in the light of this story of Shakespearean migration. We can perhaps more usefully think of Shakespeare as a kind of engine of cultural appropriation. *Titus Andronicus* was one of the earliest plays to make the journey from England to Germany, from exotic English to vernacular German. This is a play about the Roman conquest of 'Germany' (the barbaric Goths) that features a black African 'Moor' in a spectacularly villainous role. The fact that it enacts variations on the theme of 'otherness' makes it ripe for intercultural exchange. My larger point is that such exchanges facilitate developing nationalisms, ultimately enabling the very ideas of cultural sovereignty that underwrite the critique of appropriation.

Even nations such as France and Italy, which did not go so far as to link national aspirations to Shakespeare, did, under the impetus of Romanticism, embrace his 'savage genius' (to adopt Voltaire's ambivalent phrase). French theatrical tradition, though deeply embedded in national style and idiom (with the dominance of the *Comédie Française*), came eventually to place Shakespeare at or near the centre. In 1934 a performance of *Coriolanus* at the Comédie Française 'was used as a signal for the abortive fascist coup'[16] and sparked riots among partisans of both the left and right. By the time of the post-war years, one French critic could write that, with 'the very foundations of our civilization shattered', Shakespeare had taken on an extra importance in his depiction of familiar situations and his answers to 'those problems that torment us'.[17] In Italy, Shakespeare made his mark on the great romantic playwright Alessandro Manzoni, who, working from a French translation, defended and imitated Shakespeare's conscious artistry, and of course on Verdi; in the work of twentieth-century directors such as Giorgio Strehler and Leo de Berardinis, Shakespeare has been as crucial as he is to Mnouchkine or Brook working in France.

While recent cultural critics have interpreted the export of Shakespeare as part of the strategy as well as the burden of empire, theatres in diverse parts of the globe have embraced his work as deeply relevant to their own diverse cultural situations, even at times as liberatory. Still, various questions arise. What role has the export of Shakespeare played in places like India? Has it served the interests of British domination, provided a way to imagine freeing people from such domination, or neither? Are the liberating effects clearly associated with certain performances of Shakespeare in Berlin, Prague or Moscow simply a result of the political context of such productions or are they traceable to a deep and embodied comprehension, evident in the texts, of the struggles of individuals in the face of power? What sort of difference has Shakespeare, brought to Paris, Delhi, Tokyo, Johannesburg, or even the remote Indian province of Mizoram,[18] actually made? What is the most appropriate relation of 'Shakespeare' to indigenous performance traditions? Such questions are important, though they may also seem beside the point, since theatrical producers, as they have always done (witness the 'English comedians'), will raid the available archive for whatever they can use. And Shakespeare is both eminently available and useable.

Let us consider an example even more complex than Mnouchkine's *Richard II*. How might we situate and respond to the deeply 'hybrid' production of the *Kathakali King Lear*? The production was first performed in 1989, in Kerala, the home state of *Kathakali*, a mode of performance that originally developed around 1600 (just when Shakespeare was writing plays for the Globe) as itself a blend of indigenous art forms. The *Kathakali Lear* opened in a Victorian hall with a proscenium stage, a vestige of the British colonial presence. The show subsequently travelled to different parts of Asia and to continental Europe as well as to the Edinburgh Festival. In the summer of 2000 it played at the Bankside Globe in London, completing a kind of symbolic circle (when Shakespeare's colleagues named their theatre the Globe, they were no doubt thinking of the ancient connection between the world and the stage, but the name now registers more complex dynamics). The text was originally adapted by Australian writer-director David McRuvie, translated into Malayalam by Kerala poet Iyyamkode Sreedharan, and then staged by McRuvie and a French dancer, Annette Leday, in collaboration with a group of established *Kathakali* actors.[19] The play was reduced to nine crucial scenes, the cast to eight characters; the performance exploited the tradition of elaborate and colourful costumes and masks, each representing a traditional type, and was marked by a rich musical score, singing and gestural, mimetic dance. The fool, for whom there was no parallel in *Kathakali*, was adapted from Sanskrit drama. The process, as Ania Loomba remarks about a similar adaptation of *Othello* into *Kathakali*, was not just about adapting Shakespeare but also about how a traditional performing art 'can negotiate its own future'.[20] In other words, as an experiment in interculturalism, as a 're-elaboration' of Shakespeare,[21] the *Kathakali Lear* was as much about what Shakespeare can do to and for *Kathakali* as it was about what happens to Shakespeare when, like Bottom, he is translated into something quite different but still recognisable.

The new global economy, the technological bridging of cultural boundaries, international tourism, the commodification of 'foreign' cultures, the growing awareness of cultural hybridity – all these and other globalising features of the postmodern world have enabled, indeed made inevitable, the kinds of mixes I have described. The issue now is not just internationalism but interculturalism. And one question for a discussion of 'international'

Shakespeare in a Companion volume on performance, published by a major academic press with worldwide distribution, is therefore not simply what has happened to Shakespeare on the international stage, but what kind of intercultural dilemmas does the internationalisation of Shakespeare pose in the theatre, which is after all, or was until very recently, an institution of deep cultural specificity and locatedness.

There are, as I have already mentioned, critics who get angry at the presumptions of intercultural theatre, especially when the apparent exchange is interpreted as a repetition, in a seemingly benign vein, of the depredations of imperialism. Against what he sees as the facile universalism of Peter Brook, or the naïve homogenising of 'oriental theatre' in the writings of Antonin Artaud, or especially the unacknowledged ethnocentrism of Richard Schechner's essays on, and practice of, ritual theatre, Rustom Bharucha poses what he calls an 'ethics of representation'.[22] Bharucha's critique of what Schechner sees as 'a world of colliding cultures no longer dominated by Europeans and Americans, no longer dominable by anyone'[23] is rooted in his sense that western money and power inevitably distort any such potential for equal exchange. Cultural tourism only goes one way. Bharucha is angry too at the failure of practitioners like Brook, Schechner and Eugenio Barba to *historicise* the rituals and traditions they adopt and adapt. This is the nub of his critique. In lifting rituals or traditions from their local context, internationalist western directors mystify them, recruiting them into a universalist project that strips them of their rootedness and hence their value. Paradoxically it is the particular, local meanings, the specific histories, that give such ritual practices any 'universal' meaning they can lay claim to.

Against this cogent attack, Patrice Pavis, a cautious defender of intercultural theatre, has responded: 'the danger [of a "stealthy imperialism"] certainly exists, but isn't there something a little ridiculous and demagogic in the concern of someone like Bharucha ... who warns intercultural directors not to exploit "donor" countries by appropriating their substance ... when these artists make the effort not to reduce one culture to another, while assembling the theoretical and meta-cultural bridges that allow us to observe a give-and-take between them' – especially in a global context wherein 'Japanese and Indian culture have abundantly drawn from western technology'.[24] Later in his book, Pavis situates interculturalism dialectically, noting the potential for both 'whitewashing' and genuine exchange. In any case, he suggests, it is futile to rail against the inevitable, since the turn to interculturalism is part of the theatre's need for *mise-en-scène* and reliance on cultural tourism (again, we may note a continuity with early Shakespearean migrations).

The cross-cultural currents do not flow only from west to east, especially where Shakespeare is concerned. In 1988 and again in 1992, Yukio

Ninagawa brought his production of *The Tempest* to Great Britain where it was enthusiastically received (as were his earlier *Macbeth* (1985) and later *Hamlet* (1998)). Staged as a rehearsal of a *Noh* version of Shakespeare's play, the production featured a raised *Noh* theatre towards the back of the stage, on which some, though not all, of the action took place. As Tetsuo Kishi argues,[25] some of the effects (such as the spectacular opening storm) were produced using conventions completely different from, indeed at odds with, *Noh* drama. At other times, elements derived from *Noh* were used out of context, distorting the meanings they traditionally evoke, merely gesturing towards an indigenous tradition while being folded into a different set of international conventions.[26] English reviewers generally hailed such effects as not only wonderful in themselves, but consistent with the style of *Noh* or even the direct result of it. Kishi shows plainly that the reviewers lacked any real knowledge of *Noh* and were responding to a vaguely 'Japanese' feel, or rather a mélange of elements common to a broadly international style, arranged within a frame derived from and dependent on Japanese tradition. Here was a Japanese director raiding and perhaps 'whitewashing' his own tradition in the interests of (to recall the contradictions outlined by Pavis) experimental postmodern *mise-en-scène*, truth to 'Shakespeare', and international recognition. But at the same time, and paradoxically, Ninagawa was trying to reach his local, Japanese audience. He told an interviewer that he chose 'Japanising visual elements' in an attempt to find a visual equivalent to Shakespeare's language whose 'meanings' are too difficult to convey in such a different language.[27] Kishi criticises Ninagawa for not finding a style compatible with both Japanese tradition and Shakespearean dramaturgy – hence using, for example, the open stage with its built-in consciousness of the audience.[28] While this critique relies on a fairly conservative attitude towards Shakespearean performance – that it should as far as possible reproduce or find a modern equivalent for the original performance conditions – Kishi's point offers one way of approaching the appropriative dilemmas of intercultural theatre. One should seek in one's own culture the most precise equivalences to the features of the source culture; substituting spectacle for the nuances of language may be tempting, but it falsifies meanings in both directions. Shakespeare requires an attentiveness to language, even in translation, because his was a verbal theatre, low on spectacle and high on rhetoric. In appropriating Shakespeare as he does, Kishi implies, Ninagawa is guilty of a presumption analogous to that of western interpreters who import various 'oriental' practices into their productions, decontextualising and therefore deracinating them.

Such a view, while it reminds us that authentic translation is worth striving for and not impossible, ignores the historical and political inequalities emphasised by Bharucha. Perhaps, too, it underestimates the power of the individual *auteur* in modern theatre, where cultural tourism facilitates not only the quick assimilation of foreign practices but also the lionisation of certain directors whose sophisticated recombination of diverse cultural elements is an important part of their appeal. Indeed, directors such as Ninagawa, Brook, and Mnouchkine have attracted cultural tourists precisely because they have consciously developed their own uniquely eclectic style. And a problem in discussing intercultural Shakespeare is that one often winds up discussing the *auteur*, the major artist, postmodern and inevitably global in outlook, who, as theatre artists have always done, raids the archive in order to dig out whatever elements will work to convey his or her unique vision. For this reason it might be revealing to look at less spectacular examples of intercultural exchange.

In 1992, Minoru Fujita planned and oversaw an adaptation of *The Tempest* for *Bunraku* performance, presented first in Osaka and later at the Tokyo Globe. The differences in style are enormous. *Bunraku* uses hand-held puppets about half human size, usually manipulated by three silent puppeteers, one (who handles the head and right arm) ceremoniously robed, the other two in black with hoods covering their faces. The text is chanted by a single chanter to the accompaniment of specially composed *shamisen* music. But at the same time, the evident artifice of *Bunraku*, along with its ability to call up deep and precise emotions, is analogous with the theatricality of Shakespeare's romances where artifice and deep feeling are compellingly linked (as for example in the final scene of *Winter's Tale*). By relying on the banishment theme prominent in Shakespeare's play as well as in both *Bunraku* and *Kabuki*, Fujita and his colleagues were able to forge another link. This meant certain losses (the magic of the original was downplayed; Caliban, for whom no Japanese analogue exists, lost much of his resonance) but it also entailed a gain in tragic consistency deriving from 'its impassioned recreation in the mould of the classical Japanese drama of rage and renunciation'.[29] There was another interesting gain – this time for *Bunraku* itself: though Japanese drama contains nothing corresponding to Ariel, the musician and chanter managed to find a melody that 'inspired the puppeteers to manoeuvre the puppet of the kimono-clad Ariel to look lingering and air-supported within the stage space. This freedom from gravitation in Ariel was indeed a theatrical innovation, which will ... develop into an asset in *Bunraku* performance.'[30] Hence, in this instance, the importation of Shakespeare into a traditional Japanese form (as with the *Kathakali* experiments discussed above) provides a model for a genuine two-way exchange; Shakespeare is reconfigured and so is the form into which he has been inserted. Ideological anguish recedes, indeed is non-existent, in this kind of interculturalism. And yet it looks quite similar to the kinds of projects set in motion by a Brook or a Barba, where the practices of one tradition are assimilated to those of another and both are, to a greater or lesser degree, transformed.

A startling production of *A Midsummer Night's Dream* directed by the young German sensation Karin Beier in 1995 provides a quite different example of the reach of international, or intercultural, Shakespeare. The 28-year-old Beier, who has said that Shakespeare is '*the* man' in her life, gathered a team of fourteen actors from nine countries and had them all speak in their own languages. The confusion in the woods became a linguistic cacophony, a UN meeting without simultaneous translation. That this created as many problems for the play as it solved, at least in terms of production values and the effect on the audience, is less important than what it suggests about the broader picture. The production highlighted differences in national style as well as language, and foregrounded them metatheatrically. This strategy of course picked up on the play's highly self-conscious reflexivity. In the mechanicals' argument about the best approach to mounting their production of 'Pyramus and Thisbe', the characters demonstrated their native traditions and were simultaneously mocked by the others – 'an Italian *commedia dell'arte* activist ... vainly [tried] to impress a Stanislavski trained Russian actress playing Starveling and almost [came] to blows with the Polish Bottom and defender of Grotowski'.[31]

This production foregrounded the problem of translation, which is always there in 'foreign' Shakespeare and which is fundamental to the processes of exchange begun with the early English troupes and still going on. Dennis Kennedy uses the phrase 'Shakespeare without his language' to indicate what can be lost but also to suggest what can be gained by translation. Especially when it uses a contemporary idiom, Shakespeare in translation can, Kennedy suggests, provide 'a more direct access to the power of the plays',[32] though he skirts the question of what exactly that power may consist in. J. R. Brown likewise proposes that translation can 'bring new sightings of the imaginative vision that created the plays'.[33] It does so by bringing home with immediacy what in our familiarity with the English text can be easily glossed over as well known, ignored as archaic, or appreciated as 'poetic' without being fully felt or understood. Beier of course was not intent on offering direct access to the power of the play, but rather drawing metatheatrical attention to the linguistic surface through which one must peer in order to trace that 'imaginative vision'.

What her ambivalent romance with Shakespeare brought out was precisely the old man's promiscuity, his willingness to dance with many partners and speak in many tongues. Her *Midsummer Night's Dream* not only showed her awareness of her man's international reputation, but wove it into the fabric of the show, foregrounding the difficulties it poses and the new opportunities it provides. Languages and national styles coalesce around Shakespeare.[34] But they also diverge from and remake their source of inspiration. The mechanicals' insistence on the importance of their theatrical project was both mirrored and reconfigured by each actor's comic insistence on the value of his/her national style. Shakespeare's play, that is, in its original 'local habitation', imagines and enacts a temporary harmony constructed by and in theatre; the polyglot habitation accorded it in Beier's production speaks of the theatre's new global situation and the seriocomic attempts to cross lines of division without giving up the deeply felt values of the local. While Beier's experiment was more European than truly global, nevertheless, the besetting problems of a Europe bent on unity but richly anchored in a thousand local divisions can be seen as an instance of the larger problems of disharmony and unity as they affect the globe as a whole.

Paradoxes of the national — the case of Germany

Wilhelm Hortmann sees Beier's experiments as signalling 'the end of a paradigm that had governed Shakespeare productions on the German stage' for more than a century: what 'had begun as a distinctly nationalistic appropriation of the poet as a German author ... now showed signs of being dissolved in ... internationalism'.[35] The point is crucial, because of all transmutations of Shakespeare, his remake into *the* paradigmatic German writer has been the most long-lived and the most profound. In 1915, with young Germans and Englishmen facing each other in trenches dug out of the Flanders mud, the playwright Gerhart Hauptmann wrote that Shakespeare's 'soul has become one with ours: and though he was born and buried in England it is in Germany that he is truly alive'[36]; the next year, another dramatist, Ludwig Fulda, using the famous battle-cry '*unser Shakespeare*', proclaimed that Shakespeare had been born in England by mistake: 'we may call him [ours] by right of spiritual conquest. And should we succeed in vanquishing England in the field we should ... insert a clause into the peace treaty stipulating the formal surrender of William Shakespeare to Germany'.[37]

Indeed, the sense of national self-consciousness that led to the development of Germany into a major European power is traceable partly to the cultural currents flowing from and around Shakespeare's plays. The impetus began in the late eighteenth century with the move to translate the plays, a process that culminated in the great Schlegel-Tieck translations, published over a number of years from 1797 to 1840. Still in use today, this translation, along with the works of Goethe and Schiller, demonstrated 'that German could achieve a range and expressiveness equal to Shakespeare's English'.[38] It thereby contributed to the growing sense that German language and culture, embodied in a national theatre of the sort that Goethe and Schiller imagined and began to put into practice in Weimar around the turn of the nineteenth century, could lead to the kind of social cohesion necessary for genuine nation-building. Translation, as it has in many places since, made Shakespeare indigenous rather than foreign. Germany thus stands as the most salient instance of transformation through vernacular appropriation; it occupies the dominant position in the story of Shakespearean internationalism and the connection of Shakespeare to the rise of cultural sovereignty in different parts of the globe. When in 1844 Ferdinand Freiligrath drew his famous parallel between German political pusillanimity and the romantic Hamlet's delicate recoil from his daunting task ('Germany is Hamlet'), he was drawing on, and politicising, the appropriation of Shakespeare for matters German that was already well established by mid-century, and that underlay, though no doubt at some remove, the subsequent drive for liberty and eventual unification.[39]

Germany's love affair with Shakespeare began inauspiciously. Frederick the Great, under the influence of Voltaire and French neoclassicism, dismissed the plays as 'laughable farces, worthy only of being played in the wilds of Canada'.[40] While his remark inadvertently foreshadows Shakespeare's international potential (and the establishment in 1953 of the first modern 'Shakespearean' theatre at Stratford, Ontario), it points more directly to the lack of fit between the plays and the canons of eighteenth-century theatre, something that was felt by more sympathetic readers as well. Johann Gottfried Herder, in a famous essay of 1773, recognised the interweaving, fluid style of the plays, but could not imagine how their kaleidoscopic effects could be staged. Like so many English writers of the same era, he concluded that they had to be radically adapted to suit the neoclassical stage, so that in the theatre one saw only the 'ruins of a colossus'. Thus German intellectuals formulated a similar opposition as in England between an élite Shakespeare to be savoured by the literary man in his study and a popular Shakespeare vulgarised by his exposure in the theatres. Nevertheless, as Simon Williams shows, during the course of the nineteenth century an array of actors and directors began to find ways to make 'the vision of Shakespeare initiated by the writings of *Sturm und Drang* [such as those of the young Goethe] into a reality on stage'.[41]

German Shakespeare in the twentieth century shows some of the tensions of its history. Goethe's aesthetic vs. Freiligrath's political, for example, is visible in the opposition between Max Reinhardt and Leopold Jessner in the first third of the century. Reinhardt was devoted to magic and festive vitality, seeing 'theatre as a community ritual',[42] while Jessner wanted to speak to his time and place, and adopted expressionist techniques to do so. Bertold Brecht extended the political, anti-aesthetic critique, emphasising distance as an antidote to what he scorned as the theatre's desire to hypnotise its audiences. Despite Brechtian suspicions and the expressionist move to externalise personhood, the humanist interest in character remained at the centre of German Shakespeare until the 1960s, when a new generation of directors, including Peter Zadek, Hansgünter Heyme, Heiner Müller and Peter Stein rejected psychological nuance and character consistency. They embraced the disassembling advocated by Brecht, together with radically inventive scenography and a distaste for heroism of any stripe; their productions displayed a distrust of politics and political authority, a talent for the sensational, an almost desperate insistence on overtly erotic displays of sexuality, and a humorous delight in undoing the pieties of bourgeois society; experimental and often dazzling, their work was also one-sided.

Over the past 200 years, then, German Shakespeare has succeeded in domesticating the 'foreign', denying the fundamental Englishness of Shakespeare, the very quality that has been the preoccupation of both English imperialists since the eighteenth century and those recent materialist critics who have sought to expose the link between Shakespeare and empire and trace its ideological and historical trajectory. More than any other national appropriation, the German example illustrates the usefulness of Shakespeare in the process of constructing the idea of cultural sovereignty and, ultimately, of deconstructing it. Recent German theatrical production has both acknowledged the cultural centrality of Shakespeare and targeted his complicity with the various dangerous and destructive dead-ends that the German nation has experienced in its relatively short life.[43] But the cultural critique would not be possible without the original embrace. In absorbing Shakespeare, the German nation opened up the possibility of his being used against it. Such doing and undoing is an integral part of the dynamics of the national–international dialectic.

Hamlet and opposition in Eastern Europe

As the connection between Shakespeare and German nationhood developed, it also spread, through translation and geographical proximity, to contiguous spheres – most obviously to Eastern Europe, territory familiar to the early English 'comedians' and home to competing nationalisms, many of which have at some time or another adopted and adapted Shakespeare for political purposes. In 1748 the Russian nobleman, Alexander Sumarokov, published a translation/adaptation of *Hamlet* that focused almost exclusively on the prince's duty to set the citizens free of the tyranny visited on them by Claudius and his scheming henchman (the real instigator of the crimes), Polonius. Even the 'To be' soliloquy was shifted from metaphysical puzzlement to a concern with the common people and culminated in Hamlet's decision to free them.[44] The same kind of feeling underlay the brilliant performance of Pavel Mochalov as the prince almost a century later (1837), when a famous interpolated line sounded the dominant note: 'Afraid, I am afraid for man.'[45] He roused the souls of those who had 'become silent under the yoke of Nikolaevan despotism' and 'reflected the spirit of resistance ... among the Russian intelligentsia after the suppression of the Decembrist insurrection, as the growth of radically democratic ideas ... led to the revolutions' of 1848 all over central Europe.[46] During the same period (c. 1750–1850), the liberatory potential of Shakespeare in central Europe was linked to national movements and especially to translation into local languages such as Polish, Czech and Hungarian. In 1790, for example, Ferenc Kazinczy's Hungarian version of *Hamlet* included numerous topical references and a preface in which Kazinczy wrote: 'Who would not cry with joy when our destroyed, trampled-on nation raises its head from the dust once more?';[47] as illustration of this noble aim, Hamlet succeeded in killing the tyrant and survived to mount the throne and rule justly.

After the Russian revolution, *Hamlet* continued to needle the authorities, and not just in the Soviet Union. There were politically provocative versions by Sergei Kirov (1932), Grigori Kozintsev (1954) and Yuri Lyubimov (1971) in Russia; in Poland, Czechoslovakia and other parts of Eastern Europe theatrical opposition was even more overt. In 1956 in Cracow, in Prague in 1978 (where the First Quarto was used), and again in Bucharest in 1989, the bitterness of and opposition to totalitarian oppression found expression in trenchantly allusive *Hamlet*s that emphasised the ubiquity of surveillance and interrogation, and even the grotesque possibilities of mass death.[48] Since the break-up of the Soviet empire, such politicised Shakespeare has of course been less in evidence, but in places like the Balkans, where internecine strife has been particularly deadly, producers have turned to Shakespeare to illuminate dark corners of the conflict. One example, not a *Hamlet* this time, will have to suffice: the Romany company, Pralipe, and their *Romeo and Juliet*. Based in Macedonia, the company was forced, as the Romany people have so often had to do, to leave their home for political asylum in Germany. Their *Romeo* was set in Bosnia, Juliet a Muslim and Romeo a Christian; the bombed-out ancient bridge at Mostar was used as a twisted balcony for Juliet, who spoke to Romeo over the gorge. There was no reconciliation at the end, no peace, but only bursts of machine-gun fire.[49] The tragedy of exile, displacement and ethnic conflict, together with the

impossible promise of intercultural communication, marked both the circumstances of the production and the interpretation of the play, showing
once again the extraordinary range of appeal and potential application that
producers worldwide and over the centuries have found in Shakespeare's
texts.

It's not cricket (and yet it is)

Like Shakespeare, cricket is a British export. A 1970s documentary film
called *Trobriand Cricket: an Ingenious Response to Colonialism*, demonstrates how Trobriand islanders took over the game introduced by British
missionaries and utterly transformed it in order to bring it into line with
their traditions. The game becomes an instance of *kayasa*, or ritualised
competition traditionally associated with war. Teams come from different
villages and can have fifty or sixty men decked out in the paraphernalia of
warfare; 'bowling' is aligned with traditional spear-throwing; there are elaborate chants after every 'out' (many of which reconfigure recent colonial and
post-colonial history); and magic is rife. What is at stake is not winning (the
host village always formally wins, but not by too much so that the visitors
are not disgraced), but political positioning founded on exchanges of gifts
and food. And yet the game is clearly cricket, with wickets, batsmen, run-
scoring, etc. It is a telling example of how cultural exports that a dominant
culture brings as part of a 'civilising' project are absorbed and refashioned,
contributing to a new and unique cultural phenomenon that cannot be explained in terms of a simple model of ruler and ruled. As with cricket, so
with Shakespeare, especially in those areas of former British rule where, it is
sometimes argued, Shakespeare has been deployed as an instrument of mas-
tery. Deformations and re-elaborations of cultural exports cast some doubt
on the claims made by materialist critics of various persuasions that, for
example, '*The Tempest* is not only complicit in the history of its successive
misreadings [as they have abetted imperialism], but responsible in some measure for the development of the ways in which it is read [i.e. ways supportive
of colonialist ideology]'; or again, that Shakespeare is 'the greatest weapon
in the arsenal of British high culture'; or that 'cultural exchange' only goes
one way – 'nothing is returned to the cultures whose forms are appropriated
for Western art' primarily because of 'the superior economic power of the
colonizing metropolis'.[50] The situation is more complicated than the polar-
ities of margin–centre, West–East, coloniser–colonised, international–local,
often deployed by such critics, might suggest.

Let us briefly return to the question of Indian Shakespeare. As Jyotsna
Singh and Ania Loomba have shown, the history of Indian Shakespeare is not

a simple matter of the coloniser imposing his culture on the colonised – and with it an implicit standard of moral value – as an adjunct to rule.[51] Loomba provides an account of how, after about 1850, the already heterogeneous Parsi theatre, in combination with other local theatrical traditions, transformed Shakespeare into folk performances (often with dozens of songs added, even for *Hamlet*!) that were largely indigenous in character. Then, in the early decades of the twentieth century, Parsi theatre fed directly into the emerging Bombay film industry, taking the refashioned Shakespeare with it – sometimes directly as with a film of *Hamlet* in 1935, but more often indirectly, in terms of style. Hence the opposition that forms the cornerstone of the Merchant Ivory film, *Shakespeare Wallah*, between Shakespeare and Indian film, high and low culture, is not nearly so sharply demarcated as might at first appear.[52] Given divergent cultural conditions, Shakespeare, like cricket, can emerge as quite a different game from what he originally was.

Loomba argues persuasively that such examples of mixture and interpenetrating influence cannot be adequately explained by deploying the familiar binaries of post-colonial theory, especially the view that pits emergent nationalism against colonial oppression. Citing L. Lal, she concentrates on the contradictions and blurred distinctions that such mixing generated: colonial rule sparked 'modernising' changes in class relations and urban growth; this in turn led to the development of institutions such as the Parsi theatre and the Bombay film industry, which themselves had a nationalist appeal through their re-elaborations of cultural heritage and their reminiscence of a pre-colonial past. At the same time, colonial rule also in some ways encouraged a nostalgic look backwards, and the desire for the new and 'foreign' was partly the result of forward-looking nationalist aspiration.[53] As a crossing point for these multiple influences and discourses, Parsi Shakespeare testifies to the complexity of cultural borrowing.

We might then be able to conclude that global narratives concerning the export and import of Shakespeare need to be reconfigured as series of linked and contextualised local ones. They are what Natalie Davis has recently called 'braided histories'.[54] Even something like the Zulu *Macbeth/Umabatha*, which Kate McLuskie has very astutely described in relation to competing ideologies of art vs. commerce, indigenous vs. colonial, local/historical vs. universal, might usefully be liberated from the constrictions of this kind of analysis.[55] That is because, as a reconfiguration of Shakespeare and Zulu culture, it braids together elements that would not be available without the colonial history behind them but that at the same time are not explicable only in terms of that history. As an engine of cultural appropriation and sovereignty, Shakespeare works two ways. Perhaps Nelson Mandela recognised this when he 'praised the production for its dramatization of "the universality of ambition, greed and fear"'.[56] McLuskie clearly considers such claims naïve, and dependent on 'the discourse of the universality of Shakespeare' that is tied, she asserts, quoting Richard Halpern, to the values and power of 'the empire on which the sun never sets'.[57] But I think it worth taking the recourse to universality seriously, linked as it is to the work of directors like Brook who seek in the theatrical traditions of other cultures a way of tapping those universal human elements.[58] McLuskie and Kennedy regard this kind of move as an unjustified, even falsifying substitution of 'an aesthetic experience for a social one'.[59] But this assumes that the social is necessarily paramount, or indeed that the two kinds of experience are actually extricable. While it is certainly true that a production like *Umabatha* provides 'a particular insight into modern institutions of the cultural reproduction of Shakespeare',[60] narratives of cultural politics and theatrical commodification are not the only, and may not be the best, way to approach the phenomenon. At least they have to be qualified by an approach that asserts the complex reciprocities involved.

Given the way our postmodern world seems to incorporate and perhaps even homogenise 'other' cultures, making what were formerly local cultural institutions and memories into something widely accessible, are we in danger of producing a single 'universal' culture that would obliterate 'otherness' altogether? Some of those who are worried about the dominance of 'universal' Shakespeare might say yes, regarding 'otherness' as a kind of ruse, a mere mirror for our sense of our own cultural identity, but other theorists have taken a different view. Aleida Assmann, for example, has suggested that 'the other', formerly a 'menacing, anxiety-provoking term...has become the central value of postmodern culture'. Her assessment is that '"difference" has assumed a new meaning. It is no longer...judged from the point of view of unity...[but] recognized as a basic human need'. One does not have to rely on an outmoded universalism, she argues, to retain the value of 'the concept of humanity', recognised as a construct but one that nevertheless has 'vital functions'.[61] No longer enlisted as a way of 'legitimizing hegemonic claims', notions of universality, such as those invoked by producers of Shakespeare all over the globe, serve to underwrite and protect difference. Assmann adopts Austrian poet and dramatist Hugo von Hofmannsthal's praise of erotic 'encounter', which preserves difference (in contrast with 'embrace', which does not), as a metaphor for intercultural 'translatability'. While locally founded cultural memory will continue to sustain theatrical performance, we might then say, its being absorbed into the memory of others need not obliterate it. It changes it in all kinds of unforeseen ways, but theatrical history, like history generally, is a chronicle of change.

Looking back to the early days of international Shakespeare, we can recognise in the encounters he chronicles – with Wales, Scotland, and Ireland, with the Mediterranean Renaissance world, with Greece, Rome and Russia, with Africa and, tentatively and elusively, with America – something of that need for otherness, not simply as a way of defining self or effacing difference, but as a means of braiding the local and the foreign in order to acknowledge their inseparability. The result is what has from the very beginning been celebrated as a mirror that reflects the universal face of humanity;[62] though that vision has been contested in recent days as itself hegemonic and oppressive, such a response seems inadequate to explain the intensity and extensiveness of the encounters between Shakespeare and the world. The strange, eventful history of international, now intercultural, Shakespeare shows how the historically and geographically particular, given also the elusive and indefinable ingredient of genius, can be reconfigured as the universal in a thousand different locations.

NOTES

1 Patrice Pavis (ed.), *The Intercultural Performance Reader* (London: Routledge, 1996), 95. On Shakespeare and different Asian traditions of performance, see also chapter 14 below.
2 David Williams, *Collaborative Theatre: the Théâtre du Soleil Sourcebook* (London: Routledge, 1999), 94.
3 Pavis, *Intercultural Performance Reader*, 96.
4 *Le Monde*, 15 December 1981, cited in Williams, *Collaborative Theatre*, 91–2.
5 Williams, *Collaborative Theatre*, 95.
6 The term *state* refers to an inner passion, not psychologised but expressed outwardly through actorly discipline and form; Mnouchkine emphasises the succession of states in discontinuity, each played to the hilt.
7 Mnouchkine, quoted in Williams, *Collaborative Theatre*, 94.
8 Recent scholarship has underlined the nationalist implications of Shakespeare's work, both in its original setting (see Richard Helgerson, *Forms of Nationhood: the Elizabethan Writing of England* (Chicago: University of Chicago Press, 1992)) and later during the eighteenth and nineteenth centuries, when Shakespeare was being constructed as the quintessentially English writer (see Michael Dobson, *The Making of the National Poet: Shakespeare, Adaptation and Authorship, 1660–1769* (Oxford: Oxford University Press, 1992) and Margreta De Grazia, *Shakespeare Verbatim: the Reproduction of Authenticity and the 1790 Apparatus* (Oxford: Oxford University Press, 1991)).
9 Dennis Kennedy, 'Shakespeare and the Global Spectator', *Shakespeare-Jahrbuch* 131 (1995), 54.
10 Brook himself has said of the *Mahabharata* (and his remark applies to his other intercultural projects), 'We returned from India knowing that our work was not to imitate but to suggest...without pretending to be what we are not' (Peter Brook, *The Shifting Point, 1946–1987* (New York: Harper & Row, 1987), 162).

11 Kennedy, 'Global Spectator', 58.

12 ibid., 59.

13 For an interesting argument that Shakespeare needs to be viewed as a British and not an English writer, and hence always already inter-national, see Willy Maley, '"This Sceptred Isle": Shakespeare and the British Problem' in *Shakespeare and National Culture*, ed. John Joughin (Manchester: Manchester University Press, 1997), 83–108.

14 See E. K. Chambers, *William Shakespeare: a Study of Facts and Problems* (Oxford: Clarendon Press, 1930), I, 334. Two performances of *Hamlet* and one of *Richard II* were offered, mainly to offset the dangers of 'idleness and un-lawful games', though some foreign guests were present for at least one of them.

15 For a fuller discussion see Simon Williams, *Shakespeare on the German Stage, 1586–1914* (Cambridge: Cambridge University Press, 1990), 35–9 and chapter 12 below.

16 A. José Axelrad, 'Shakespeare's Impact Today in France', *Shakespeare Survey* 16 (1963), 56.

17 Jean Jacquot, quoted ibid.

18 See Ania Loomba, '*Hamlet* in Mizoram' in *Cross Cultural Performances: Differences in Women's Re-visions of Shakespeare*, ed. Marianne Novy (Urbana: University of Illinois Press, 1993), 227–50 for a full discussion of the peculiar effects that *Hamlet* performance has had on the population of Mizoram.

19 I have relied on Phillip Zarilli for my information about this production: 'For Whom is the King a King? Issues of Intercultural Production, Perception and Reception in a *Kathakali King Lear*' in *Critical Theory and Performance*, ed. Janelle Reinelt and Joseph Roach (Ann Arbor: University of Michigan Press, 1992), 16–40.

20 Ania Loomba, '"Local-Manufacture Made-in-India Othello Fellows": Issues of Race, Hybridity and Location in Post-Colonial Shakespeares' in *Post-Colonial Shakespeares*, ed. Ania Loomba and Martin Orkin (London: Routledge, 1998), 163.

21 Zarilli ('For Whom?' 19) adopts the term 're-elaboration' from Pavis, who uses it to describe the intercultural dynamics of *mise-en-scène*.

22 Rustom Bharucha, *Theatre and the World: Essays on Performance and Politics of Culture* (New Delhi: Manohar, 1990), 40.

23 Quoted ibid., 46; see also Richard Schechner, 'From Ritual to Theatre and Back: the Structure/Process of the Efficacy-Entertainment Dyad', *Educational Theatre Journal* 26 (1974), 455–81, and 'A Reply to Rustom Barucha', *Asian Theatre Journal* 1:2 (1984), 245–53.

24 Patrice Pavis, *Theatre at the Crossroads of Culture* (London: Routledge, 1992), 179.

25 Tetsuo Kishi, 'Japanese Shakespeare and English Reviewers' in *Shakespeare and the Japanese Stage*, ed. Takashi Sasayama *et al.* (Cambridge: Cambridge University Press, 1998), 110–14.

26 See Kennedy, 'Global Spectator', 60–3 for an ideological critique of this production's eclecticism, the failure of its cultural blending to evince 'political or social concern'.

27 Kishi, 'Japanese Shakespeare', 116.

28 ibid. 118–20.
29 Minoru Fujita, 'Tradition and the Bunraku Adaptation of *The Tempest*', *Shakespeare and the Japanese Stage*, ed. Takashi Sasayama *et al.* (Cambridge: Cambridge University Press, 1998), 191.
30 ibid., 191.
31 Wilhelm Hortmann, *Shakespeare on the German Stage: the Twentieth Century* (Cambridge: Cambridge University Press, 1998), 474.
32 Dennis Kennedy (ed.), *Foreign Shakespeare: Contemporary Performance* (Cambridge: Cambridge University Press, 1993), 5.
33 J. R. Brown, 'Foreign Shakespeare and English-Speaking Audiences' in *Foreign Shakespeare*, ed. Kennedy, 34.
34 An issue of *The New Yorker* (18 Dec. 2000) carried three articles that further illustrate this point. In one, the president of the University of Michigan quotes Shakespeare in support of his views on affirmative action (46); in another, Robert Sturua, probably the best-known Georgian director, remarks that 'This is a Shakespearean sort of country ... and our leader [Edward Shevarnadze] is the most Shakespearean among us, with all his flaws and all the gifts' (55); the third was a review of Peter Brook's production of *Hamlet*, staged at his home theatre in north Paris, performed in English with a multicultural cast and Asian music (100–1).
35 Hortmann, *Shakespeare on the German Stage*, 475. See also chapter 12 in this book.
36 *Shakespeare-Jahrbuch* 51 (1915) vii, quoted in Hortmann, *Shakespeare on the German Stage*, 3.
37 Quoted in Hortmann, *Shakespeare on the German Stage*, 4.
38 Williams, *Shakespeare on the German Stage*, 151.
39 German performances of *Hamlet* until well into the twentieth century, however, tended not to follow Freiligrath's implicit call for a more active and political Hamlet, preferring for the most part to replay variations on Goethe's conception of the prince's exquisite but tragically inadequate sensibility, the noble soul who sinks beneath the burden he can neither bear nor cast away.
40 Quoted in Williams, *Shakespeare on the German Stage*, 24. Voltaire had previously written that, though Shakespeare occasionally dropped pearls amidst the vast dung-heap of his works ('quelques perles ... dans son immense fumier'), his plays could scarcely please except 'in London and in Canada'. See Frances Wilkshire, 'Garrick's Role in the Shakespeare Controversy in France' in *The Age of Theatre in France*, ed. David Trott and Nicole Boursier (Edmonton: Academic Press, 1988), 219–20.
41 Williams, *Shakespeare on the German Stage*, 26.
42 Hortmann, *Shakespeare on the German Stage*, 36.
43 A brilliant and important example is Heiner Müller's *Hamletmaschine* of 1989/90, discussed by Wilhelm Hortmann in chapter 12 below.
44 Zdeněk Stříbrný, *Shakespeare and Eastern Europe* (Oxford: Oxford University Press, 2000) 27–9.
45 Eleanor Rowe, *Hamlet: a Window on Russia* (New York: New York University Press, 1976), 43.
46 Y. Dmitriev, quoted ibid., 45; and Stříbrný, *Shakespeare and Eastern Europe*, 45.
47 Stříbrný, *Shakespeare and Eastern Europe*, 46.

48 For a more extended discussion of these and other twentieth-century Eastern European performances, see chapter 12 below.

49 Stříbrný, *Shakespeare and Eastern Europe*, 141–2.

50 Quotations are from Thomas Cartelli, *Repositioning Shakespeare: National Formations, Postcolonial Appropriations* (London: Routledge, 1999), 104; Kennedy, 'Global Spectator', 53; and Kate McLuskie, '*Macbeth/Umabatha*: Global Shakespeare in a Post-Colonial Market', *Shakespeare Survey* 52 (1999), 163. I deliberately cite perceptive critics who, despite their alertness to the complexities of intercultural exchange, nevertheless read it in strictly political and ultimately polarised terms.

51 See Jyotsna Singh, 'Different Shakespeares: the Bard in Colonial/Postcolonial India', *Theatre Journal* 41:4 (1989), 445–58, and Ania Loomba, 'Shakespearean Transformations' in *Shakespeare and National Culture*, ed. John Joughin (Manchester: Manchester University Press, 1997), 109–41. See also chapter 14 below.

52 Loomba, 'Transformations,' 128–9.

53 ibid., 130.

54 Professor Davis used the term in a series of lectures given at the University of British Columbia in January–February 2001. The lectures form part of her new book on the complexities of cultural mixture.

55 The production, which continues to tour, played at Shakespeare's Globe in the spring of 2001.

56 McLuskie, '*Macbeth/Umabatha*', 155. Anthony Sampson has recently written about the importance of Shakespeare, especially plays such as *Julius Caesar*, for the South African liberation movement and notes the irony of certain groups in present-day South Africa seeking to ban precisely those plays that loomed large in the imaginations of figures like Mandela. *Observer*, 22 April 2001, 27.

57 McLuskie, '*Macbeth/Umabatha*', 158, 161.

58 'The signs and signals from different cultures are not what matters; it is what lies behind the signs that gives them meaning . . . The theatre . . . exists to open us to a wider vision' (Peter Brook, *Threads of Time: a Memoir* (London: Methuen Drama, 1998), 144).

59 Kennedy, 'Global Spectator', 55, quoted in McLuskie, '*Macbeth/Umabatha*', 162n.

60 McLuskie, '*Macbeth/Umabatha*', 164–5.

61 Aleida Assmann, 'The Curse and Blessing of Babel; or, Looking Back in Universalisms' in *The Translatability of Cultures*, ed. Sandford Budick and Wolfgang Iser (Stanford: Stanford University Press, 1996), 99.

62 The idea was already current when Ben Jonson wrote in the Folio of 1623 that his rival was not for an age but for all time.

II

PETER HOLLAND

Touring Shakespeare

'The actors are come hither my lord.'
(*Hamlet* 2.2.359)

All spectators at the theatre are tourists, taken from their everyday world into the strange other country they visit for the duration of the theatre performance, a mixture of a fictive world where the events of the drama unfold and a fantastical space where actors and crew collaborate to create the fiction through the physical skills of their performance techniques. But theatre companies too are often tourists, displaced from their home-base, taking their work to places that may be like their origins or completely alien, playing to audiences that may not understand a single word spoken on-stage or to people who know the text as well as the actors themselves. They may act in a local theatre or bring their theatre with them. Their visit may be part of a regular tour, an expected arrival for the local theatre-goers, or it may be an unprecedented event, something that transforms irrevocably the local culture into which the particular otherness of the plays or production techniques has intruded.

Touring Shakespeare's plays in England and abroad has been a substantial factor in the economy of the theatre and in the culture of performance since the 1590s, and yet it passes, for students of theatre, largely unnoticed. There is almost too much of it to account for: almost every country has its own examples of touring theatre companies and almost all of them include companies touring with Shakespeare in their repertory. The companies may be major international groups like the Royal Shakespeare Company, or small-scale local amateur troupes; they may have travelled thousands of miles or from the next town; there may be a 100 actors or only 5; the plays may be performed uncut or heavily adapted, in the local language or a foreign one; there may be elaborate sets or a bare acting space; there may be extensive notices in local and national newspapers or, more often, almost none.

For all its plenitude, there is no history of touring Shakespeare. Instead there are local examples, pieces of the narrative, some of which I have juxtaposed in this chapter to suggest something of the range of significance that touring has for the history of Shakespeare in performance and practice of theatre in widely differing contexts.

Between October 2000 and June 2001 the Royal Shakespeare Company toured a new production of *The Tempest*: '[It] marks the 21st anniversary of the RSC mobile theatre tour, which will see leisure centres and sports halls throughout the UK transformed into state-of-the-art theatre auditoriums. Five articulated lorries will travel the length and breadth of the country . . . carrying over 50 tonnes of equipment, including auditorium seating, washing machines and even the tea urn!'[1] The production opened at the RSC's London home, moved to Budapest for the European Union of Theatres Festival, then to Stratford-upon-Avon before touring to thirteen towns in the UK, interrupted by ten days in Portugal and ending with an arts festival in Virginia and two weeks at the Globe Theatre in Tokyo.[2] This long and exhausting schedule is a significant part of the RSC's work. *The Tempest*'s UK travels took the production primarily to towns without a permanent theatre, while its international tour involved participation in two international arts events. The former is part of the RSC's commitment to reaching a national audience – 80 per cent of the population of the UK were, at some point in the year 2000, within one hour's drive of an RSC production; the latter is part of the network of globalised culture in which the RSC also participates. The audiences thus ranged from UK spectators with no regular experience of Shakespeare in the theatre to the cosmopolitan sophistication of cultured arts audiences often with little English.

The broadly nineteenth-century costuming and fairly conventional approach to *The Tempest* in this production – here a drama of the family – coupled with music for the actors' unaccompanied voices or played by the actors themselves, made the production likely to be as effective in a small English town as in Tokyo. With film sequences played onto a simple structural white set of waves, the production's design demonstrated the necessary adaptability of touring productions, even when the UK tour included seating and lighting as well as set and costumes, though this comparatively small-scale production found that its set needed further abbreviation when the production played in the RSC's own theatre, The Other Place in Stratford, the smallest venue on the tour. Design for such touring productions has to confront playing spaces of wide variation, just as the actors may be playing in theatres with a maximum capacity of 150 or 1,500, needing to adjust and rethink the scale of every aspect of their performances as a result. Accessible in theatrical technique, unexceptionable in interpretation, strongly cast and visually effective, this production of *The Tempest* epitomises the possibility in England of major touring productions by important companies with strong casts and a fine production team in spite of the considerable cost and the difficulty of finding sponsorship: conventional Shakespeare productions need casts of at least fourteen, and salaries, with their associated touring allowances, make up by far the largest part of the budget for professional tours.[3] Touring Shakespeare becomes, in such a guise, a thoroughly unprofitable activity, with UK ticket prices kept as low as is practicable, so that it is associated with a kind of missionary zeal: spreading the word that Shakespeare in the theatre can be pleasurable and popular without needing to 'dumb down' for a broad audience.

Elizabethan touring

The touring by the RSC of its latest production of *The Tempest* outside England has a long history of antecedents. As early as the 1590s small companies of actors from England, soon known as the English Comedians, were touring in Germany, playing in courts under aristocratic patronage and in civic spaces like marketplaces, inn-yards and fencing-schools. Driven to find new audiences by the intense competition in provincial English touring, Robert Browne's company arrived in 1592 to provide court entertainment for Duke Heinrich Julius of Brunswick; Browne led a variety of groups across Germany for the next thirty years. For an English traveller who saw them at a fair in Frankfurt in 1592, there was something contemptible about both the quality of production and their rapturous reception:

> I remember that when some of our cast and despised stage-players came out of England into Germany, and played at Frankfurt at the time of the mart, having neither a complete number of actors nor any good apparel nor any ornament of the stage, yet the Germans, not understanding a word they said, both men and women, flocked wonderfully to see their gesture and action rather than hear them, speaking English which they understood not, and pronouncing pieces and patches of English plays, which myself and some Englishmen there present could not hear without great wearisomeness.[4]

By 1618 there were four or five established companies of English comedians touring Germany and by then the companies included German actors as well as English, performing a repertory that extended far beyond that of the London stage and playing in German as well as (or instead of) English. Morison's cynical judgement that it was only the worst actors that toured may have been unfair, for the actors had to adapt to very different playing conditions: there were no permanent theatres and, as Morison noted, they had little by way of stock of costumes or props. If their repertory was initially the latest English plays, the English Comedians had to make massive adjustments. In a context where the plays' language was almost irrelevant, reports often praised the music, the dancing and the acrobatics. The clown became the most important acting member of the company: one of the companies' most significant contributions to German theatre was the clown-figure Pickelherring, who appeared in dozens of plays in their repertories. The companies varied substantially in size: John Spencer's troupe at one point numbered as many as twenty-four members, many of whom were musicians.[5]

The plays themselves were transformed. Texts were brutally cut and adapted (and later, of course, translated). Shakespeare's plays became a resource of narratives and fragments of his plots, heavily reworked, were used by German dramatists throughout the seventeenth century writing for other kinds of companies. But if these adaptations retained barely a line of Shakespeare, other examples of the influence of particular plays show complex metamorphoses. The troupe led by John Green, once the principal clown of Robert Browne's company, performed a *Hamlet* play in Dresden in 1626, though there is no evidence whether this was Shakespeare's play or some other version. By the later seventeenth century a German company was playing a version of *Hamlet* called *Der Bestrafte Brudermord* (*Fratricide Punished*), about one-fifth the length of Shakespeare's, with the complexities of action, language and thought ironed flat into a linear, exciting, moral drama.[6] There were versions of *Titus Andronicus* (published in German in 1620), *A Midsummer Night's Dream* (written *c.* 1657), *The Merchant of Venice* (perhaps as early as 1611) and others. The English Comedians had a profound effect on German theatre, in some respects creating a theatre culture where there had been none, and their repertory influenced the development of a vernacular drama. Yet the changes necessary to play to non-anglophone audiences resulted in a performance mode that initially had little and progressively had less to do with the original repertory and its manner of performance.

Touring in Britain and America

The English Comedians had to develop a performance style to suit their own limitations and the particular requirements of their audience. A latter-day example might be the group Actors From the London Stage, who for twenty-five years have toured US campuses playing Shakespeare with casts of five.[7] Where the RSC's *The Tempest* needed five articulated lorries for its materials, Actors From the London Stage are restricted to touring with whatever costumes and props will fit into a single large suitcase. Each week's residency includes three performances of a Shakespeare play, performed relatively uncut but with the rapid changes inevitable with such a small cast and with duologues often having to be performed by an actor speaking to him or herself. Where, in the case of Cambridge Experimental Theatre, which toured Europe in the 1970s and 1980s performing Shakespeare with casts as small as two, the small size became part of an interpretative model (so that, for instance, *Macbeth* became a play about evil possession, performed only by Macbeth and a witch, while their four-actor *Hamlet* was a study in the dissolution of the concept of the essentialist character[8]), for Actors From the London Stage the small size is an economic necessity turned to purely theatrical effect, displaying great skills but not seeking to turn the consequence of necessity to analytic ends.

The company's aim is explicitly educational, the performances constituting the most visible part of their stay but being intended to be less significant than their classroom presence. At a university level they represent an example of Shakespeare's presence in 'TiE', Theatre in Education, as it is known in Britain, where the performance of the play is often the culmination of a sustained investigation of the processes of not only theatre-making but also the interpretative procedures of working with Shakespeare. Performance in this model of touring becomes the visible end-product of a process revealed and analysed in discussion, with the actors teaching how theatre is made.

Actors From the London Stage make virtues of theatrical necessity, but a comparable American company, the Shenandoah Shakespeare Express (known as SSE), founded in 1988, argue for their style as a modern replication of early modern theatre practice. Rather than the quasi-authenticity associated with Shakespeare's Globe the SSE, by following 'the basic principles of theatrical production in Shakespeare's time... attempts to give its audiences some of the pleasures that an Elizabethan playgoer would have enjoyed'.[9] Hence they choose to double extensively, because, by '[w]atching actors play more than one role, an audience can experience another aspect of Elizabethan playgoing: the delight of watching a favorite actor assume multiple roles'. They use cross-gender casting: 'the SSE is not an all-male company, but we try to re-create some of the fun of gender confusions by casting women as men and men as women'. They play in natural light because 'Shakespeare's actors could see their audience' and therefore 'SSE actors can see you'. Their costumes reflect early modern practice by being colourful, helping doubling and identifying social position. Above all their style of performance is epitomised by their commitment to a brisk speed, trying to keep the 'promise' of the Chorus in *Romeo and Juliet* in 'the two-hours' traffic of our stage' (Prol. 12) 'through brisk pacing, no intermission, and a continuous flow of dramatic action'. Reviewers respond to this translation of early modern forms by seeing it as 'pure' Shakespeare: 'Stripped of frippery and frilly accents, but also unencumbered by "modernising" conceits – Hamlet in a helicopter! Macbeth on wheels! – Shenandoah's Shakespeare is, simply, fresh, fine theater. Its combination of intelligence, spirit and sheer kinetic energy is profoundly exciting. This is pure Shakespeare, richly alive.' The reviewer of this 1993 production of *Romeo and Juliet* went on to praise the costuming, in which 'everyone wears black jeans, white lace-up "poet's" blouses and black sneakers, but the Montagues get blue scarves and the Capulets red': 'The simple, inventive use of these minimal elements is typical of the Shenandoah approach: stripped-down, expressive, carefully thought out, supporting the words without ever distracting from them. In a word, uncluttered.'[10] The logistics of touring and a theory about how to recreate early modern practice for a contemporary audience have here converged into a theatre style for Shakespeare that is clearly extremely effective for its intended audiences. Its purity is in the eye of the beholder, but the effect is energising, driven on by the enthusiasm of their usually young casts.

Actors From the London Stage and the Shenandoah Shakespeare Express expect their audiences to be largely unused to theatre performance and their mode of theatre accommodates them. But touring can often have to negotiate with local modes of watching that seem intractable. This is not necessarily the result of actors and audiences not sharing a common language. In 1965 Joe Papp took *A Midsummer Night's Dream* away from the security of his Shakespeare theatre in Central Park in New York's Manhattan for free performances in poor suburbs of New York, like Brooklyn and Queens. With a mobile stage and auditorium strikingly like that used for the RSC's small-scale touring, the company set up in school playgrounds. There were no tickets and no reserved seats; publicity was by word of mouth, posters and announcements by loudspeaker vans touring the area. In all some 70,000 people attended the performances. There were problems: some performances were abandoned when local gangs caused trouble over this invasion of playgrounds that they regarded as their territory.

An audience study by a team from Columbia University included interviews with play-goers, asking them about the plot of the play and audiences' reactions.[11] The report offers detailed accounts of how little of Shakespeare's language or even of the plot was understood. But interviewees spoke about audience noisiness: one said apologetically, 'No one really did it on purpose. The people had to do something during the play' (41). The researchers' response was to suggest that for future productions '"social controllers" [be] strategically *seated* in various parts of the house [to] reinforce the norm of quiet. They can act as professional "shooshers"' (44). For these researchers, Shakespeare represents the epitome of high culture, even though popular with these audiences. Unwilling to reinvestigate their own categories, the researchers want the play-goers to fit their paradigm of theatre etiquette, just as the actors, disturbed by the audiences' refusal to watch the production traditionally, were unable to alter their work to suit this different mode of response. Touring Shakespeare in these circumstances has as much to do with cultural clashes as with acts of inter-cultural (or here '*intra*cultural') communication. The assumption that an audience must be taught to be quiet because that indicates attention, conflicts with the fact that the audiences plainly did enjoy the performances and expressed that enjoyment in part by not being silent. But the report also eloquently indicates that the distance from Manhattan to Queens charted an immense cultural gulf.

Nineteenth-century tours

Where Actors From the London Stage, as the English Comedians in Germany, redefine their work so that communication happens immediately and effectively, Papp's company saw their high-cultural production as a fixed entity. In a global culture in which some theatre productions are legally obliged to be reproductions of an original (as in the case of, say, *Cats* or *Les Misérables*), the roots for such a theory of reproduction lie in the transport of an entire metropolitan production out on tour. In the nineteenth century touring rarely involved moving more than the stars and a few senior actors. When Charles Kean was planning to tour to Australia in 1864, James Cathcart, an actor who had worked with him in England, wrote anxiously, 'I have within the last few days received a letter from my sister in Australia, in which she speaks of the wretched inefficiency of the Actors there, which makes me think you will miss the assistance you have been so long accustomed to.'[12] Cathcart was seeking employment in Kean's touring company (and was successful), but there were often surprises among the actors who were recruited locally: Kean noted that at one performance in Australia an actor who had to double the Ghost 'with the last two acts of Laertes ... had been a convict'.[13]

While such *ad hoc* casting from the local talent pool was standard, it was also increasingly viewed as unsatisfactory. But the difficulties of doing more were widely understood. Henry Irving's decision to tour America in 1883 with the full Lyceum company from London together with its sets and costumes, posed enormous problems of logistics. After performing in Philadelphia, Irving agreed to send much of the material back to New York, including 'twenty-seven cloths, eighty flats, sixty wings, ninety set-pieces, and twelve framed cloths', since even if 'we could have carried them conveniently, we would not have got them into many of the theatres'; but what was left filled 'two sixty-two-feet cars, and one huge gondola-car' for their special trains; the costumes alone filled '120 great baskets, the properties being packed in thirty baskets making a total of 150'.[14]

The greatest impact of Irving's productions lay in the detailed archaeological realism of the scenery. The set for the trial scene showed 'the frescoed interior of the hall of justice . . . a complete reproduction of the period'. But it was almost too realistic: 'I understand some people thought it worn, mistaking the tone for dirt.'[15] In order to ease the problems of moving such enormous sets, Irving had some sets reproduced by local scene painters before the company arrived: 'Indeed, the companies following us will find portions of the cathedral of Messina [for *Much Ado About Nothing*] around the walls of many an American theatre.'[16] Irving's *The Merchant of Venice* seemed to one reviewer to represent not only 'everything as it might have happened in Venice', but also 'as it did appear in Shakespeare's imagination'.[17]

Irving did not perform *Hamlet* in New York, in order to avoid the possibly disadvantageous comparison with the brilliant performance by Edwin Booth, especially after three New York reviewers came to Philadelphia and found his Hamlet mannered. He was, however, prepared to confront Booth's success as Shylock. But what reviewers singled out for praise was the effectiveness of his *mise-en-scène*, particularly in *Macbeth*, which Irving brought to America on a subsequent tour. 'It is', wrote one reviewer, 'like reading Dante's *Inferno* again – by turning over Doré's pictures.'[18]

In all Irving toured America on eight occasions in eighteen years, each trip taking up much of a year. It was highly profitable: Irving took over $500,000. But it was also something that affected American Shakespeare production, with others trying to imitate the kind of visual effects that Irving had demonstrated, as they had done in imitation of Charles Kean's spectacular stagings in the 1840s.[19]

For Kean and Irving, their acting was disliked and their sets praised. This is indicative of another outcome of the intercultural effect of touring: the surprising discrepancies of praise and blame. As Robert Speaight commented,

> Methods proper to a particular national tradition have often surprised the foreigner. When the Old Vic came to Paris after the war with *Lear* and *Richard III*, the French were stunned by Olivier's performances, but they found the productions old-fashioned. Those who remembered Mounet-Sully [a great nineteenth-century French Hamlet] made their comparisons; there were no comparisons to be made with [the productions by] Copeau and Antoine.[20]

The strengths of Olivier's acting could not cover up the lack of a radical and experimental theatrical style of the kind that French theatre culture looked for and admired. Tradition in Shakespeare production – unlike in Racine – was not admirable in itself. The confrontation of two theatre cultures can be intensely disappointing: as Speaight suggests in English theatre companies' encounters in Soviet Russia, where 'they have been astonished to find Shakespeare hamstrung by realist productions which, in Britain, had been buried with Beerbohm Tree. Prepared for socialist realism, they found capitalist realism instead' (*Shakespeare on the Stage*, 251).

These are modes of theatrical encounter, but they can burgeon into a different order of opposition. Edwin Forrest's tour to London in 1845 attracted a series of hostile newspaper reviews by John Forster, a friend of Forrest's English rival, Macready. Forrest, furious and blaming Macready, hissed Macready's performance in Edinburgh in March 1846. Forrest, returning to America, accused his London critics of 'that narrow, exclusive, prejudiced, and I may add, anti-American feeling which prescribes geographical limits to the growth of genius and talent'.[21] When Macready toured America for the third time in 1848/9, the result was a clash of culture, class and nationalism. After considerable success in overcoming the opposition in Philadelphia, Macready's performances in New York in May 1849 led to a public demonstration outside, where, in handbills, 'workers' were encouraged to 'express their opinion this night at the English Aristocratic Opera House', the renaming of the theatre carefully drawing attention to its class bias and attributing to it foreign power. Charged by cavalry, thirty-one rioters died. Shakespeare and a disagreement about who might be seen as the greatest Shakespearean actor of the period led to a clash that defined not only Anglo-American relations, but also the place of the theatre in the structure of American society, given that Macready had been encouraged to stay by many prominent members of New York 'society'. Touring brought a particular immediacy of presence that made possible the explosive response, far in excess of anything Forrest's hurt pride required.[22]

In such a context, the crucial factor is competition between actors playing to an audience that is familiar with the play. But some international touring is necessarily a moment of cultural encounter, the introduction of Shakespeare to an audience that has never seen his work. The visit by the company run by George Crichton Miln to the Gaiety Theatre in Yokohama in Japan in 1891 constituted the first complete Shakespeare productions performed in Japan.[23] Miln had toured forty American cities in two months in 1882. After subsequent and more elaborate tours of America had proved successful, Miln took his company to Australia in 1888, where he was praised for the novelty of his productions, staging *Hamlet*, as a reviewer commented, 'as it has never before been staged in the colonies'.[24] It was his cutting of the text that impressed the local audiences (omitting, for instance, Claudius at prayer) but also some stage effects: in the closet scene, the ghost did not appear but light flashed across the stage at his 'entrance'. Again, like Charles

Kean and Irving in America, it was the stage images and the production's approach to the play that impressed the knowledgeable audience far more than the work of the star actor. After a second tour of Australia finished in 1890, Miln took his company on to Asia, visiting Calcutta, Rangoon, Singapore, Shanghai and Hong Kong before arriving in Japan, where they played *Julius Caesar* in Tokyo before their one-week season in Yokohama. Presenting seven Shakespeare plays in the week, including *Hamlet*, *The Merchant of Venice*, *Romeo and Juliet* and *Othello*, Miln's work provided the first significant encounter with Shakespeare in performance for a number of Japanese intellectuals, offering a vision of a kind of drama profoundly alien to Japanese forms. In part Miln's own acting could be praised in Japan because of its rhetorical style, which, though it had led Australian critics to record severe doubts, enabled Japanese audiences to admire a manner that was reminiscent of *Kabuki* and hence less strange. But, whatever the aesthetic worth of the productions, the mere fact of Miln's making it possible to see Shakespeare in performance proved strongly influential on the developing Japanese fascination with Shakespeare.

The work of companies like Miln's, spreading professional theatre and particularly Shakespeare initially through the Empire and then beyond, was crucial in the dissemination of Shakespeare as performance text. W. J. Holloway, whose company toured the Empire in the 1890s with eleven Shakespeare plays in their repertory, commented in his farewell speech in Cape Town, South Africa, in 1901 at the end of one tour: 'When he had first come to Africa some six years before he was told that if he played Shakespeare's works it would mean his financial ruin, but through the generosity of play-goers on that occasion here and at other places where he had had the honour to present the works of the great bard, that had been entirely disproved.'[25] The rhetoric of bardolatry is here combined with an awareness of the financial risk involved in playing Shakespeare rather than the popular melodrama that audiences might be assumed to prefer. There is a kind of missionary zeal as well as a profit motive in such touring, an acceptance of a cultural responsibility to educate audiences in drama that the actor-manager perceives as civilising.

Perhaps the most remarkable of such cross-cultural encounters was the tour to Paris of an English company, led by Charles Kemble, in 1827. An earlier tour in 1822 by a different company had been disastrous. The combination of French suspicion of the barbaric drama of Shakespeare and the too recent ending of the war in 1815 created a near riot at a performance of *Othello*. Audience shock at the sight of Desdemona smothered by Othello was reinforced by cries of 'Down with Shakespeare! He's Wellington's lieutenant.'[26] French audiences had so far only encountered Shakespeare in the adaptations by Jean-François Ducis and others, where the unacceptable wildness of Shakespeare had been tamed to the rules of French neo-classicism.[27] But, even five years later, the passionate drive to create French Romanticism had been given great impetus by Stendhal's *Racine and Shakespeare* (1823). France's growing fascination with all things English (from Byron to Windsor soap) led Emile Laurent to engage a company drawn from three London theatres (Covent Garden, Drury Lane and Haymarket) as well as some provincial actors. Before the first performance, Sheridan's *The Rivals*, William Abbott, the company's manager, spoke to the audience of the company's nervousness in presenting 'the masterpieces of our dramatic literature before an enlightened people whose own theatre possesses so large a number of excellent works ... The English poets have in no sense obeyed those established laws recognised by authors which France considers to be arbiters of taste.'[28]

Reasonably successful though *The Rivals* was, it was the performance of *Hamlet* on 11 September 1827 that would be crucial. Traditionalist newspapers had already advised the company to cross the Channel back to England while others, more radical in leaning, had been prepared to suggest that Shakespearean drama, its failure to respect the unities notwithstanding, could provide a useful model for French historical drama. In the audience were all the crucial figures in the French romantic movement: Victor Hugo, Alfred de Vigny, Eugène Delacroix, Théophile Gautier and Alexandre Dumas.

The result was triumphant. Kemble's acting, especially in the play scene, was enthusiastically applauded. While the audience had little tolerance for the closet scene, with its denial of decorum in the murder of Polonius, they were overwhelmed by Harriet Smithson's Ophelia in the mad scenes. The combination of traditional stage business with her brand of vivid realism produced an emotional power that the French theatre had not generated. Smithson, not till then a particularly distinguished actor, ended the night's performance as a star. As Juliet later in the season, she was equally successful and it was Smithson, as much as Shakespeare, who became the rallying point for Romanticism. As Raby argues, 'while Shakespeare ... became a catalyst for the French Romantics, Harriet as Ophelia and as Juliet became for a while their figurehead and symbol'.

Shakespeare's drama enabled the release of a kind of performance – realist, emotionally daring, vulnerable, mad, emphatic – that in its alienness from the forms of French classical drama made possible a wholly new form. The development in subsequent years of French drama, through the violent première of Hugo's *Hernani* and the plays of many of the others present at that performance of *Hamlet*, was entirely dependent on an acceptance of Shakespeare as a new icon, no longer a foreign barbarity but now a liberating power of emotional possibility. As Dumas wrote later of the experience, defining it as the moment that turned him into a playwright,

> [The actors] announced Hamlet. I only knew that of Ducis. I was going to see Shakespeare's. Imagine someone blind from birth to whom sight is given, who discovers a whole world of which he had no concept ... and you will have an idea of the enchanted Eden to which that performance opened the door for me ... O Shakespeare, thank you! O Kemble and Smithson, thank you! Thanks to my God! Thanks to my angels of poetry! ... I recognised that, in the world of theatre, everything came from Shakespeare, as, in the real world, everything comes from the sun ... I recognised at last that he was the man who had created most after God.[29]

Touring within Britain

Dumas's rhapsodic response describes the exceptional but, as I indicated at the start of this chapter, much touring is the normative experience of regular visits. In England that might be typified through the late nineteenth and much of the twentieth centuries in the work of Frank Benson and Donald Wolfit, actor-managers whose careers depended on touring their own companies across the entire country, avoiding London where, on the rare occasions they played there, they were often signally unsuccessful.[30] To metropolitan critics their work was old-style barnstorming without any interpretative novelty; Ronald Harwood's subtitle for his biography of Wolfit identifies his work 'in the unfashionable theatre'. But their belief in touring, in a social responsibility to take the emotional power and vision of Shakespeare, as they conceived it, to all parts of the country connects directly with the RSC's current commitment to tours like that of *The Tempest*.

Frank Benson (1858–1939) had begun with Irving at the Lyceum, but by 1883 he had bought the assets of a touring company and renamed it after himself. Benson's company was engaged by Charles Flower to perform at Stratford-upon-Avon in 1886 and they continued to provide the Stratford Festival season for more than thirty years. If Benson's work looks to be in the mould of provincial touring from the eighteenth century onwards, there were striking innovations. He was prepared to experiment with the text, performing a virtually uncut Folio text of *Hamlet* in 1899 by splitting the play between matinée and evening performances. He was also not prepared to restrict his work to the conventional and limited canon of the most popular plays: in the course of his career he produced thirty-five Shakespeare plays. It was appropriate that Benson should have been knighted in the Royal Box at Drury Lane in 1916 as part of the Shakespeare Tercentenary celebrations. If his long career belongs to a past era – he was still playing Hamlet at the age of seventy-three – his style of production was based on principles that seem in advance of his time: training actors in verse-speaking, refusing to adapt the plays to increase the star's dominance of performance, keeping scenery simple and subordinate to the play. The last point may sound like an economic necessity for touring, but it was also an unusual theatrical virtue for the period. Benson's company – or rather companies, since at one point there were four different Benson companies on tour at the same time – was an ensemble, not a star vehicle, and Benson and his wife Constance took their responsibilities for training young actors seriously. Also significant was Benson's wider commitment to education: he put on special matinée performances for schools, not only to increase income but also to ensure that schoolchildren were able to see Shakespeare on stage.

Sir Donald Wolfit (1902–68) began in touring, but his fame as a Shakespearean actor was established at the Old Vic in 1929–30. From 1936 to 1960 he led his touring company across Britain and the USA. What some praised as his bravura acting, others mocked for the same qualities of excess, a Victorian actor half a century too late. But, like Benson, Wolfit was committed to Shakespeare for the broadest possible audience, exemplified by his performances of 'Lunchtime Shakespeare' in London during the air-raids of the Blitz in 1940, as if speaking Shakespeare was an act of national defiance against the threatened bombings.

Benson and Wolfit worked outside the narrow metropolitan world. A later example of such commitment to 'the provinces' is the work of the English Shakespeare Company, run by Michael Bogdanov and Michael Pennington. Where Benson and Wolfit were, in part, anxious about London's critical response to their work, Bogdanov and Pennington were determined to work outside the major theatrical institutions of the RSC and the National Theatre and take Shakespeare's histories to the whole country. As Pennington puts it, 'the tendency to centralise Britain's artistic life in the metropolitan areas ... obviously creates two nations, paying one tax'.[31] The ESC would reach the other nation, playing Shakespeare's two tetralogies of histories (with the three parts of *Henry VI* recut into two plays) in productions that were aggressively modernised not only to make the plays immediately relevant to the audiences, but also to argue for the fundamental connection between the political debates of Shakespeare's history and the politics of late twentieth-century Britain. Most notoriously, Bogdanov staged Henry V's expedition to France with the army as a bunch of English football hooligans chanting ''Ere we go! 'Ere we go!' while unfurling a banner with the slogan 'Fuck the Frogs'. The impact of the moment does not deserve to be separated from the production's sustainedly intelligent investigation of the nature of popular revolt, of the controls exerted by central government and of the development of individual rule. The ESC was proud both that most members of the audiences stood to cheer and that some wrote angry letters to the Arts Council protesting at such an 'indecent and subversive production'.[32] The ESC's challenge to what it saw as the political conservatism of contemporary Shakespeare productions can be paralleled in the exhilarating work of two other touring companies: Cheek by Jowl, whose productions challenge conventional readings of Shakespeare's sexual politics; and Northern Broadsides, whose use of northern voices denied the dominant southern sound of Shakespeare's text.[33]

Foreign tours to London

London reviewers, when they noticed the ESC's work at all, tended to pick holes in the design eclecticism, disdaining it as a kind of provincialism. But the encounter between the same group of critics and foreign styles of Shakespeare productions visiting London reverses the image of provincialism. While my concentration so far has been primarily on English productions on tour, I want to end with three examples of productions touring to London. The first was the visit of Yukio Ninagawa's production of *Macbeth* to London in September 1987. Widely praised by astonished critics, the production was seen as a combination of stylisation and a more conventionally Shakespearean mode of acting emotion.[34] Reviewers found no problem of language but their response was controlled by an orientalist concept of the otherness of Japanese theatre: as Christopher Edwards commented in *The Spectator*, its 'Eastern-seeming formality, stylisation and sense of ritual' could be accepted since they 'create, for the actors, far greater freedom for the expression of poetic emotion than could any tradition of realistic Western theatre'.[35] The success of Ninagawa's production lay in the strangeness of its dramatic mode. Yet reviewers could not understand the precise meaning of Macbeth's gestures or of the much-admired set, dominated by a huge Buddhist altar, or of the petals dropping from the blossoming cherry trees; all were recuperated into a western aesthetics of beauty, so that their meaning in Japanese culture was effectively masked from the critics, who did not even see that they were missing something. Here, touring met with incomprehension and yet extravagant praise.

In 1992 the Canadian director Robert Lepage directed *A Midsummer Night's Dream* for the Royal National Theatre in London. While this was not a touring production, the visit of a fiercely experimental foreign director produced a vehement and near-unanimous chorus of loathing from the reviewers.[36] Lepage's *Dream* was seen or rather heard as a failure to articulate Shakespeare's language, especially by those members of the cast who were non-Anglophone. Angela Laurier as Robin, marvelled at for her acrobatics and physical contortions, was mocked for her pronunciation: 'she negotiates English verse with all the nimbleness of Inspector Clouseau'.[37] The multicultural casting and style produced a xenophobic and colonialist reaction so that, for example, where otherness in Ninagawa's *Macbeth* was praised, here the sound of the gamelan music became 'oriental scratch and jangle'.[38]

Refusing to accept that a French Canadian could justifiably be attempting to connect Shakespeare to a theatrical mode quite alien from the English Shakespeare tradition, the critics adopted a resolute stance of imperious disdain. They offered similar responses to the productions toured to London from America, Japan, Germany, Israel and Georgia for the 'Everybody's Shakespeare' season in London's Barbican Theatre in 1994; Charles Spencer in the *Daily Telegraph* was the most outspoken: 'Although it is stimulating to be exposed to different views of Shakespeare, there is something coals-to-Newcastle-ish about importing foreign-language productions to England: there we sit, following an edited version of the script in surtitles while listening to the performers delivering the matchless poetry in an incomprehensible tongue.'[39] G. H. Lewes, analysing the Shakespeare performances of the French actor Fechter and the Italian Salvini in London in the mid-nineteenth century, recognised that language was not a barrier either to understanding or to judgement:

> The terrible disadvantages of an intonation and pronunciation which play havoc with Shakespeare's lines [have not] prevented Fechter from 'drawing the town' ... It may draw you to the theatre out of curiosity, but it will not stir your emotion when in the theatre ... No sooner are you *moved*, than you forget the foreigner in the emotion. And the proof that it really is what is excellent, and not what is adventitious, which created the triumph of Fechter in Hamlet, is seen in the supreme ineffectiveness of his Othello.[40]

Indeed, Lewes's minute analyses of Fechter's and Salvini's approaches to particular lines never mentions that they were not speaking English. The text is perceived in, rather than behind or in tension with, the actor's performance. Lewes heard in foreign voices precisely what Spencer did not: 'matchless poetry'.

Lewes's openness to the possibility of such actors being successful was in marked contrast to the closed responses of London critics to foreign tourists 120 years later. The director of the 1994 festival, Michael Kustow, responded furiously to the critics' attitude: '"Maidenly" is the word that comes to mind – as if the critics were struggling to keep the notional Shakespearean legs together to repel foreign penetration. Maidens preserving our classical heritage intact, perhaps, but also skinheads warning off trespassers.'[41] But the critics' mockery of productions that involved different kinds of rigour and that were not subservient to the reverential construction of 'Shakespeare' that characterises English productions saw such work as iconoclastic, 'a kind of cultural Stalinism . . . hostile to civilized values' (Alastair Macaulay, *Financial Times,* quoted Kustow, 'Shakespeare's Little England'). Paul Taylor, responding to Kustow, accused the touring productions of 'studied heartlessness',[42] but he could not see that that might be the result of either his response or the productions' intentions. Heartless Shakespeare is not necessarily bad, unless, as for Taylor, heart-warming feeling is seen as necessarily and undeviatingly a part of Shakespeare in performance in every social, political and historical context.

In this particular cultural clash about whose view of Shakespeare should prevail, an English critical orthodoxy or a non-English range of responses that widely differed one from another among themselves, the problems of touring Shakespeare transculturally, become especially visible. The encounter with something distinctly and demandingly other, whether it is Shakespeare's play itself as in Paris in 1827, or a way of approaching the play as in London in 1994, reminds us of the fundamental foreignness that is the experience of watching drama and of the other country which is the theatre.

NOTES

1 The RSC homepage, www.rsc.org.uk, accessed 14 March 2001.
2 As well as *The Tempest*, the RSC also took its production of the three parts of *Henry VI* and *Richard III* for a three-week residency to the University of Michigan in February 2001; the university's funding had made the productions possible. Since the mid-1970s the RSC has transferred all or nearly all its Stratford summer productions to Newcastle for a short season before moving them to London, thereby ensuring that audiences in the north of England are more easily able to see the company's work. I have not included any mention of their extensive touring of non-Shakespearean drama.
3 Another example of UK touring Shakespeare by a major company might be the work of English Touring Theatre (ETT), who toured eight Shakespeare productions in the period 1993–2001. ETT, though based in Crewe until 2001 and thereafter in London, is, as its name implies, a company permanently touring.
4 Fynes Morison, *Itinerary*, quoted in Ernest Brennecke, *Shakespeare in Germany 1590–1700* (Chicago: University of Chicago Press, 1964), 5–6 (my modernisation).
5 See Simon Williams, *Shakespeare on the German Stage*, vol. I, *1586–1914* (Cambridge: Cambridge University Press, 1990), 33.
6 For a translation, see ibid., 253–90.

7 For further details of their history and practice, see their website www.aftls.org

8 The *Hamlet* production was adapted and filmed in 1987. See Graham Holderness, 'Shakespeare Rewound', *Shakespeare Survey* 45 (1993), 63–74 (especially 69–71), and Nigel Wheale, 'Scratched Shakespeare: Video-Teaching the Bard' in Lesley Aers and Nigel Wheale (eds.), *Shakespeare in the Changing Curriculum* (London: Routledge, 1991), 203–21.

9 Quoted from SSE's self-description on www.ishakespeare.com/p-au.htm, accessed 27 March 2001.

10 Review of *Romeo and Juliet*, *Boston Globe*, 17 August 1993 (reprinted on SSE website).

11 See Richard Faust and Charles Kadushin, *Shakespeare in the Neighborhood: Audience Reaction to 'A Midsummer-Night's Dream' as Produced by Joseph Papp for the Delacorte Mobile Theater, a Report* (New York: Twentieth Century Fund, 1965).

12 Quoted in J. M. D. Hardwick (ed.), *Emigrant in Motley* (London: Barrie Rockliff, 1954), 57.

13 ibid., 151.

14 Irving quoted by Joseph Hatton, *Henry Irving's Impressions of America* (London, 1884), II, 264–5.

15 ibid., 265–6.

16 ibid., 266.

17 Quoted by Charles H. Shattuck, *Shakespeare on the American Stage* (Washington: Folger Shakespeare Library, 1976–87), II, 164. I am indebted to Shattuck's work for much of the material on nineteenth-century touring in the United States.

18 ibid., II, 182.

19 Kean's production of *King John* in New York in 1846 involved the making of over 170 costumes and scenery covering 15,000 square feet for the fourteen settings; there were, at one point, over 150 actors on stage. See ibid., I 108.

20 Robert Speaight, *Shakespeare on the Stage* (London: Collins, 1973), 251.

21 Shattuck, *American Stage*, I, 80.

22 For a play based on these events, see Richard Nelson, *Two Shakespearean Actors* (London: Faber, 1990).

23 On the Miln company tours see Kaori Kobayashi, 'Touring in Asia: the Miln Company's Shakespearean Productions in Japan' in Edward J. Esche (ed.), *Shakespeare and his Contemporaries in Performance* (Aldershot, UK: Ashgate, 2000), 53–72. On Miln's tours to India see Kaori Kobayashi, 'Shakespeare Wallah: George C. Miln's Shakespearean Productions in India', *Australasian Drama Studies* 33 (1998), 117–27. Kobayashi's articles provide almost all my information on Miln's work.

24 Quoted ibid., 59.

25 Quoted in David Holloway, *Playing the Empire* (London: Harrap, 1979), 92.

26 See Peter Raby, *'Fair Ophelia': a Life of Harriet Smithson Berlioz* (Cambridge: Cambridge University Press, 1982), 46.

27 See Marion Monaco, *Shakespeare on the French Stage in the Eighteenth Century* (Paris: Didier, 1974).

28 Quoted in Raby, 'Fair Ophelia', 54.

29 Quoted in W. D. Howarth, *Sublime and Grotesque: a Study of French Romantic Drama* (London: Harrap, 1975), 97 (my translation).
30 See J. C. Trewin, *Benson and the Bensonians* (London: Barrie & Rockliff, 1960); Ronald Harwood, *Sir Donald Wolfit CBE* (London: Secker & Warburg, 1971). See also Harwood's play, *The Dresser* (Ambergate: Amber Lane Press, 1980) for a dramatisation of his experiences as Wolfit's dresser.
31 Michael Bogdanov and Michael Pennington, *The English Stage Company: the Story of 'The Wars of the Roses', 1986–1989* (London: Nick Hern, 1990), 4.
32 ibid., p.302
33 See Simon Reade, *Cheek by Jowl: Ten Years of Celebration* (Bath: Absolute Classics, 1991).
34 For a critical response, see John Russell Brown, 'Foreign Shakespeare and English-Speaking Audiences' in Dennis Kennedy (ed.), *Foreign Shakespeare: Contemporary Performance* (Cambridge: Cambridge University Press, 1993), 21–35 (especially 32–4).
35 ibid., 33.
36 See Barbara Hodgdon, 'Looking for Mr Shakespeare After "The Revolution": Robert Lepage's Intercultural *Dream* Machine' in James C. Bulman (ed.), *Shakespeare, Theory, and Performance* (London: Routledge, 1996), 68–91.
37 ibid., 78.
38 ibid., 80.
39 Quoted in Peter Holland, *English Shakespeares: Shakespeare on the English Stage in the 1990s* (Cambridge: Cambridge University Press, 1997), 255.
40 George Henry Lewes, *On Actors and the Art of Acting* (London, 1875), 130.
41 Michael Kustow, 'Shakespeare's Little England', *Independent*, 19 November 1994 (Weekend Arts, 29).
42 Paul Taylor, 'This is the Way to do it', *Independent*, 24 November 1994, 28.

12

WILHELM HORTMANN

Shakespeare on the political stage in the twentieth century

Did Shakespeare have a political agenda? Up until forty years ago most scholars and readers would have affirmed that his reputation rested on exactly the opposite, namely on *not* being partisan, but for *all* time.[1] For centuries his plays were seen as timeless models of human nature; as such they were performed on the stage, as such they were studied, debated, translated into many languages, assimilated into foreign literatures and adapted to widely different media. None of his plays are *drames à thèse*, and yet they have been appropriated by the political stage like no other.

The reason for this is simple. Although the plays are not partisan (unless the general support of the Tudor myth in the histories is counted as such) they deal with material eminently suited to transformation into political theatre. The history plays and the Roman plays for example can be read as so many case histories of the ways of gaining, wielding and losing power, and the protagonists are thoroughly familiar with Machiavelli's lessons in *Realpolitik*. However, the conflicts shown are never played out merely on the surface level of intrigue and counter-intrigue. They are always set within a wide moral frame including questions of legitimacy, of right versus might, and they never lose sight of the metaphysical dimension of order versus chaos. Furthermore, the many soliloquies and dialogues in which these questions are broached represent not only fully fledged theories of politics but – given a critical political situation in a given country at a given time – constitute a serious attack on the ruling class or system. During the last years of the Nazi regime in Germany, performances of the history plays were forbidden; they contained too many examples of cruel power grabbers being brought to rough justice. *Troilus and Cressida* fell out of official favour as well. German audiences who used to thrill to Ulysses' speech on 'degree, priority, and place' (1.3) might have discovered more pertinent matter in the nihilistic railings against authority by the 'deformed and scurrilous Grecian' Thersites than in the grandiloquent heroics of the warriors of both sides. In certain political situations some Shakespeare plays only need to be played straight to be politically subversive. Stalin knew why he did not want Soviet audiences to watch *Hamlet*. Even in Shakespeare's time a performance of *Richard II* parallel to the Essex rebellion gave the play a contemporary political twist that might well have proved fatal to the playwright.

There is political matter even in the comedies. Duke Frederick has usurped the place of the exiled Duke in *As You Like It*; Prospero in *The Tempest*, himself a victim of usurpation, has usurped the island from native Caliban and thus invited scathing post-colonial interpretations; *Measure for Measure* can be regarded as one long disquisition on the right use of authority; after the Holocaust *The Merchant of Venice* is obviously no longer the same play; and feminist readings of practically all the comedies will yield plentiful instances of outspoken or unconscious sexism: politics, in other words, is either explicit or implicit in most of the plays.[3]

It is a matter of directorial decision whether the political potential of a play is realised in performance or not. Productions designed to represent the national heritage and aimed at a general audience seeking first acquaintance with the plays (like the well-known BBC television series of the 1980s) will refrain from projecting political messages. Equally, most stage productions of Shakespeare until well into the 1920s were apolitical: their *raison d'être* was to celebrate great dramatic poetry and identify with the larger-than-life characters, as presented by actors keen on coveted roles for audiences who knew and revered the plays from their schooldays and enjoyed the communal ritual of seeing them enacted in exemplary and largely traditional form. The First World War and its aftermath disrupted this civilised consensus for good. Conditions in several European countries, Germany, Poland, Czechoslovakia, Soviet Russia, were such that for theatre to provide the 'culinary' entertainment (Brecht) of pre-war days was felt to be irresponsible by avant-garde directors. Theatre should respond to the pressures of the age rather than deflect the minds of the viewers from urgent concerns by aesthetic diversions. For Erwin Piscator and to a lesser extent for Bertolt Brecht this meant sociocritical agitation, turning the stage into a political platform and using contemporary plays to provide comments on burning questions like abortion, pacifism, exploitation, or mass unemployment. For Leopold Jessner this meant shaking the classics out of their museum-like torpor and giving them a topical edge, by a variety of means. Both strands have persisted: each year there is a tremendous output of sociopolitical plays on every conceivable subject, just as the movement to reshape the classics into political commentary begun with Jessner shows little signs of abating. It is this latter phenomenon that the rest of this chapter will discuss.

For the political potential of Shakespeare's plays to be released, three things must come together: a political or social situation crying out for critical comment; a director and ensemble willing, able (and also ruthless enough) to use the plays for this purpose; and audiences alive to the sociopolitical climate and therefore primed to catch allusions. The combination of these three requisites during the twelve years of Nazi rule in Germany, in West Germany during the 1960s and 1970s, and in East Germany for the period from 1945 to 1989, makes the German example the most indicative. There are, however, many other cases in point; especially in Eastern Europe, where Stalinist dictatorships in countries locked behind the Iron Curtain and waves of rigorous suppression drove theatre people to protest against the prevailing inhumanity, in particular by means of Shakespeare. (See also chapter 10 above.)

Leopold Jessner, directing *Richard III* at the Staatstheater in Berlin (1920), set the pattern for the more pointedly politicised performances of the future. Attention was no longer to be focused on the clash of heroic individuals; instead, the production should illustrate an overarching concept in order to bring out the 'essence' of the play. After four years of mass slaughter in Flanders fields, the time for admiring traditional heroes was past. For a generation formed 'under the hydraulic pressure of events', proclaimed the shell-shocked Piscator, it was necessary 'to formulate the insights tested under the thunder of the guns'. Or, in the words of Leopold Jessner: 'The face of the age had changed, and so . . . of necessity, had the theatre.' Fritz Kortner as Richard was too powerful an actor to allow himself to be contained in a formula, but his expressionist acting was distinctly shaped to highlight the 'career of power based on violence and murder' that Jessner felt the play exemplified (fig. 25). Six years later he directed *Hamlet* as a denunciation of the corrupt and fawning imperial court surrounding the kaiser, who had been forced to abdicate after the war. *Hamlet*, to Jessner, was a political play even if Berlin audiences were not yet prepared to see it as such. 'What possible interest . . . could the psychology of the Hamlet-figure have for a contemporary audience? The gramophone record of "To be, or not to be" is worn out.'[4]

Hitler's assumption of power and the ensuing strict surveillance of the theatres reduced the chances of making a classical play comment on the present state of Germany and the pernicious character of its leaders. There was one exception, *Richard III* directed by Jürgen Fehling at the Staatstheater in Berlin in 1937. Richard (Werner Krauss) cultivated an exaggerated limp (putting everyone in mind of Joseph Goebbels, the deformed and deadly Minister of Propaganda), his bodyguards wore black SS-type uniforms, the costumes of the murderers of the princes suggested the outfit of other Nazi ruffians, and the Scrivener spoke his revealing lines directly at the audience. The production caused great offence in official quarters, but the allusions,

25 *Richard III*, directed by Leopold Jessner at the Staatstheater, Berlin, 1920, with Fritz Kortner as Richard and Rudolf Forster as Buckingham.

though perfectly comprehensible to those who wanted to see, were ambivalent enough to prevent the director from having to suffer serious consequences.

Across the border, in neutral Switzerland, there was no need for guarded suggestion. At the Zurich Schauspielhaus a group of Jewish and left-wing actors and directors who had fled the Nazi terror were determined to use the stage as a platform and to sharpen the political awareness of their audience. In their first Shakespeare production, *Measure for Measure* (1933), the director Gustav Hartung took pains to work out the analogies between Angelo and Hitler; in later productions of politically relevant plays such pointed reference was no longer necessary. The Swiss spectators had no illusions any more about the dangerous clique ruling Germany. They realised that Shakespeare was indeed a contemporary author: his presentation of pre-Tudor power struggles reflected their immediate experience. Under the shadow of war, *Troilus and Cressida* (1 September 1938) held a special lesson for the Swiss nation: Hector (who does not want the war) is killed the very moment he has laid down his arms. The Swiss heeded the warning. Theirs was to be an armed neutrality. A year and a day later they ordered general mobilisation.

It does not need a general catastrophe of the Hitler type to give Shakespeare plays a topical edge. For a racially segregated society *Othello* deals with a burning concern, even if Othello is only played by a white man painted black. If, however, he is a black man wooing, winning and murdering a white Desdemona, the whole issue of miscegenation is invoked and likely to divide audiences. In South Africa under apartheid conditions Janet Suzman's 1987 production of the play at the Market Theatre in Johannesburg ran into further difficulties: the black actor, John Kani, who had to pass through several road blocks and was himself frisked by white policemen in an in-sulting manner before reaching rehearsals, found it increasingly difficult to achieve the emotional equilibrium that would allow him to bow to the 'Most potent, grave, and reverent signiors, / My very noble and approved good masters' (1.3.76 f.) and to indulge in glorying reminiscence of how he won fair Desdemona's consent.[5]

Unpredictable extraneous events and conditions like those described above can suddenly charge plays with contemporary meaning. In such cases it is not even necessary to alter the text; it is the act of performing a particular play at a particular historical juncture that constitutes the political significance. The case is different when directors and ensembles deliberately decide to turn performance into politics. At this point they enter the wide area of conscious reinterpretation and adaptation, to put across preconceived messages. Again, the developments in German theatre, East and West, are indicative.

Brainwashed and dissected: political Shakespeare in Germany, 1964–1990

Early in his career Brecht attacked the traditional veneration of the classics, Shakespeare included, as a form of cultured self-hypnosis. They were valu-able only as 'Material' (i.e., the reworkable substance of a play), and needed reshaping from a clear ideological standpoint to give them contemporary relevance. His adaptation of *Coriolanus*, first staged in 1964 by the Berliner Ensemble eight years after his death, showed textual alterations designed to undermine the legitimacy of senatorial rule by giving the citizens recognis-able characters and interests, turning the tribunes into politically conscious people's representatives, and making Volumnia in the end side with Rome and the people reject her son.[6] Compared with the subsequent mutilations of Shakespeare's texts by younger directors, Brecht's handling was conservative. Its impact derived from its undeflected political focus – and from its exemplary *mise-en-scène* as non-identificatory, presentative theatre.

In the 1960s and 1970s Brecht's disciples in East and West Germany subjected the history plays to similar, though far more abrasive ideological questioning. In this they followed the lead of Jan Kott, the Polish director and Shakespeare scholar, whose merciless analysis of the plays in *Shakespeare our Contemporary* (1965) reduced the dynastic power struggles to a 'Grand Mechanism'. He revealed the efforts of the agents involved to claim legal or moral motives for their destructive actions as so much 'ideology', that is, as an either conscious or unconscious concealment of selfish urges behind acceptable discourses. The three parts of *Henry VI* and *Richard III* provided welcome copy for debunking and critique. Of the three productions – John Barton and Peter Hall's *The Wars of the Roses* (Stratford, 1964), Giorgio Strehler's *Il gioco dei potenti* (Milan, 1965) and Peter Palitzsch's *Der Krieg der Rosen* (Stuttgart, 1967) – the latter was the most uncompromising, a stark denunciation of the power game that underlined the message by the dramaturgic and visual means of expository theatre. Scenes were reshuffled to bring out blatant contrasts and contradictions. A narrow frieze above the whole width of the stage displaying broken weaponry, severed limbs and skeletons as emblems of war and destruction, served as a constant reminder of the human cost of the power game (fig. 26). In 1968 the Swiss dramatist Friedrich Dürrenmatt brought out his adaptation of *King John*, which premiered at Basle and was widely performed during the next two years. In this adaptation King John and Philip of France are absolutely amoral, war to them is a sport, contracts are there to be broken, their citizens, mere 'scum', pay the cost, and Cardinal Pandulpho, risen from the gutter, understands and absolves it all. Only the Bastard, ineffectual spokesman of reason and humanity, is a figure of faint hope.

In the view of Jan Kott and the new generation of directors that followed in his footsteps, history was a nightmare. Existence under the shadow of 'the Bomb' had become a philosophical absurdity. The threat of nuclear annihilation and its deterrent involved such baffling contradictions that the intellectual's response could only be to work towards a radical critique of the ideology that had led to this impasse. No means were to be spared to expose its underlying absurdity and inhumanity, and the theatre would have to play its part. It was impossible that in a world gone insane the classics should remain inviolate loci of meaning. They had long been treated as icons of ultimate reconciliation, but the order and harmony traditionally regained in the fifth acts were now felt to be fraudulent shams. It was this mood of profound disaffection that produced the impulse to wrench

26 Peter Palitzsch's *Der Krieg der Rosen*, Stuttgart, 1967.

the classics from their moorings. Look beneath *King Lear* and find Beckett's *Endgame*, as Kott suggested. Look beneath *Macbeth* and find a meaningless succession of treachery and slaughter, was the lesson to be learnt from Eugène Ionesco's *Macbett*. The adaptations and recastings of Joseph Papp, Charles Marowitz, Edward Bond, Tom Stoppard and many others were similarly radical transvaluations that reflected the progressive schizoidism in the world-view of western man.

Whether such adaptations should count as *bona fide* political theatre is a moot point. They were certainly part of the great cultural revolution of the 1960s and 1970s in which traditional institutions and figures of authority were dismantled. In Germany this cause was taken up with greater insistence than elsewhere because the theatrical avant-garde were bent on finding *their* answer to the question of all questions: 'What had made the Holocaust possible?' Were the classics really innocent of complicity with the forces that had led to this abyss? Adolf Dresen, an East German director rehearsing *Hamlet* in the harbour town of Greifswald on the Baltic in 1964, summed up the dilemma in the succinct phrase 'Buchenwald is near Weimar', that is, the proximity in Germany of the worst (the infamous concentration camp) and the best (Weimar, home of Goethe and Schiller, seat of the muses) is no coincidence. This conviction spurred German theatre people to subject the classics to a painful questioning in order to discover hidden pockets of 'ideology'. Shakespeare, in this process, was psychoanalysed, politicised and brutalised in order to strip his plays of an imputed tendency towards affirmation and to rescue them from what Peter Brook called 'deadly theatre'. To recoup their original explosive power and make them reveal their inner material contradictions, they were inserted into radically contemporary contexts.

From 1964 to the early 1980s, West German theatres underwent a veritable revolution with productions out-Kotting Kott in the service of revealing hidden power structures and unmasking their exploiters to effect the ideological transformation of their audiences. In the critical political discourse of the time, state power was execrated. Marxist or left-wing directors could be relied on to show the acquisition and wielding of power as acts of unmitigated selfishness, treachery and cruelty. For example, Duke Vincentio in *Measure for Measure* was progressively turned into a villain after having been revered as a basically benign, if occasionally odd patriarchal ruler. Other figures of authority also lost their aura. The means to this end were heavy alterations of the text, drastic cuts and deliberate presentations against the grain. Audiences felt they were being brainwashed and intentionally deprived of treasured cultural experiences. But in cases where such innovative productions were indeed the result of plausible new readings, and furthermore accompanied by appropriate visuals, the departure from tradition was compensated for by opening up a thrilling new aesthetic, albeit of disjunction, shocks, *non sequiturs*, but also of unprecedented penetration into the deep core of the texts. Hansgünther Heyme, Hans Hollmann, Claus Peymann, Peter Stein, George Tabori and Peter Zadek were among the foremost directors to have effected this change.

East Germany

The situation in East Germany was different. Theatre was expected to contribute to the establishment of a socialist culture based on a militant and optimistic, that is socialist, humanism. Charged with this agenda, and under fairly strict control by Party ideologues, there was no room for an art free from politics, neither in principle nor in practice. The authorities favoured an art of affirmation, not of criticism. But at the height of the Cold War in the 1960s the artists who at first had trustingly supported the guidelines laid down by the authorities began to chafe under the discrepancy between their own (critical) view of socialist reality and the confident and roseate representations they were expected to produce. Shakespeare was part of the official GDR culture and he was proclaimed as a precursor of socialist humanism during the state celebrations on the occasion of the quatercentenary in 1964. In the light of such elevated endorsement it is not surprising that deviations from normative stagings were treated as wilful attacks on the 'Heritage'. To theatre artists with a knowledge of the exciting work done in their field elsewhere, this constituted a suffocating restriction. Yet opposition could never express itself in total negation or rejection, as in the West; it had to operate by subterfuge.

In this process critically minded theatre people received unexpected support through Robert Weimann's *Shakespeare and the Popular Tradition*, a study of the plebeian elements in early English drama and their reflection in the work of Shakespeare. This profound and scholarly investigation had extraordinary consequences for theatrical practice. At the same time as Mikhail Bakhtin's exposition of the medieval carnivalesque counter-culture in the works of Rabelais became known in the West, Robert Weimann unfolded the spectrum of popular (and subversive) characters, attitudes and qualities to be found in the dramatic traditions since antiquity and their re-emergence in Shakespeare's plays. Of immediate relevance was the linking of the Vice-figure to Richard III and Iago. Vice-type Richards soon abounded in East and West Germany, but for a villain to jump down into the stalls, harangue spectators at close quarters and thus enmesh them in a complicity of evil was a new experience for East German audiences used to being kept at Brechtian distance (*Richard III*, directed by Manfred Wekwerth, Berlin, 1972). Weimann also pointed out the great subversive potential inherent in performance itself, a danger well known to the Puritan enemies of the theatre in Shakespeare's time. East German Shakespeare directors welcomed the scholarly support of their desire to brush the plays the wrong way. It was also in the staging of the comedies that contemporary attitudes not provided for in the Party programme found expression.

In the 1970s most performances of *A Midsummer Night's Dream* on East German stages departed from the Reinhardtian model with a vengeance. Hippolytas were brutally subjugated, little love was lost between the young couples, and their release in the forest near Athens took on extreme forms of aggressiveness and sexual directness. This was not only an imitation of western examples and a reflection of changed relations between the sexes, even under socialism, but also signalled profound disaffection and an unsolvable dilemma. The three worlds of the *Dream* invited experiments with class differences and social contradictions. Some directors managed a qualified final harmony in the fifth act, for example Christoph Schroth in his production at Halle in 1971; Alexander Lang (Berlin, Deutsches Theater, 1980), however, so drove his ensemble to explore the disjunctive potential of the play that no return to a socially viable community was indicated.

More direct protests could be registered with *Hamlet*. The prince could be presented as an angry young man and dangerous outsider, and above all the analogy between the GDR, fenced in behind death-strips and barbed wire, and 'Denmark is a prison' was too obvious and inviting not to be touched upon. Laertes waving his blue passport, the coveted document allowing trips to Paris, only raised an understanding laugh; but forcing spectators past barbed wire on their way to the ticket office, with a machine gun mounted on the theatre roof (Potsdam, 1983, directed by Piet Drescher), took the joke too far: the machine gun was forbidden. It was left to Heiner Müller, an author of unusual poetic power and famous for abrasive plays about life and work in the GDR, to use Shakespeare for a final showdown. Inspired by a grim vision of history that had informed his translations/adaptations of Shakespeare and Greek plays, Müller linked *Hamlet* and his own incredibly brutal ten-page scenario entitled *Hamletmaschine* to form an oppressive and imposing amalgam. It constituted an ultimate reckoning, taking in human history from ice age to heat death and presenting an irredeemable world at the end of reason, culture and time. It was a dirge for the state that went out of business when the production was prepared and a gloomy comment on the globalised world that took over (Berlin, 1989/90; fig. 27).

27 Heiner Müller's *Hamlet*, 1989/90.

Political Shakespeare in Eastern Europe

The reception of Shakespeare in Eastern Europe owed a great deal to the German example. The Schlegel-Tieck translation (1797–1840), which turned Shakespeare into the 'third German classic' next to Goethe and Schiller, often served as a bridge for Czech, Hungarian, Polish and Russian translators. Shakespeare in Eastern Europe came to be closely linked to intellectual movements striving for greater national and cultural independence. His characters were familiar figures to the reading public, above all Hamlet; his dilemma caught the imagination of countless young idealists: 'Hamletism' denoting indecision, political ineffectualness, dreamy self-absorption, was a recognised condition of the soul among Russian intellectuals in the mid-nineteenth century.

Polish writers and theatre artists interpreted 'To be, or not to be' as the ultimate question that their compatriots (till well into the twentieth century) would have to answer in order to achieve (or regain) national independence or civil liberty. 'To fight, or not to fight' was the question that marked the Polish dilemma. In periods of political unrest in Poland after the Second World War (1956, 1968, 1970, 1981) there was a significant rise in *Hamlet* productions.[7] The play could easily be made to comment on the actual political situation dealing, as it does, with undiscovered but suspected crimes, usurpations, military coups, surveillance and international imbroglios, aspects that Polish audiences felt immediately related to contemporary politics in their country. After the proclamation of martial law in Poland in 1981, the 1982 *Hamlet* directed by Andrzej Wajda had a Fortinbras in the uniform of the hated Polish Security Forces, and Hamlet's lines 'Forgive me this my virtue, / For in the fatness of these pursy times / Virtue itself of vice must pardon beg' (3.4.153–5) earned standing ovations.[8] Similarly, the *Hamlet* produced in Cracow (1956), two years after the 20th Congress of the Communist Party of the Soviet Union in which Khrushchev had disclosed the extent of Stalinist crimes, vibrated with political immediacy.

The appropriation of Shakespeare in Eastern Europe was intimately connected with the national revivals in most Slavonic literatures, translation of his works into Hungarian, Czech, Slovakian, Slovene, Serbian for example helping to raise the status of the vernacular languages in relation to German, the official and literary language of the Habsburg Empire. Russia had its own Shakespeare tradition. His literary influence was immense, all the major authors (Pushkin, Lermontov, Turgenev, Dostoevsky, Tolstoy) succumbing to his spell or battling with his mighty shadow, but stage productions were hampered by censorship.

Censorship continued to dog theatrical performances after the Bolshevik revolution of 1917. 'Political' Shakespeare in the sense of making the plays comment critically on government decrees or Party policies was out of the question. Only a few directors would risk topical allusions, least of all with *Hamlet* (later to be forbidden altogether by Stalin), which had such obvious applicability to political practice in dictatorships. Director Nikolai Akimov was the exception. His 'entirely iconoclastic, grotesque' *Hamlet* of 1932 at Moscow's Vakhtangov Theatre became really topical only two years later when Stalin travelled to Leningrad 'to kiss dear comrade Kirov in the coffin', the popular Leningrad Party secretary suspected of having been murdered at Stalin's instigation. Shades of Claudius hypocritically mourning his 'dear brother's death'.[9] Though deprived from turning Shakespeare into politics, Soviet theatre enjoyed striking innovations in staging inspired by Russian constructivism, a movement that influenced set design in the rest of Europe until well into the 1930s. Theodore Komisarjevsky mounted a much debated 'aluminium' *Macbeth* at the Stratford Memorial Theatre in 1933. Other emigrés took the style to the Continent and even the United States. The Russian enthusiasm for *Hamlet* was reinforced by Boris Pasternak's idiomatic translation of 1939 and its production at the Taganka Theatre in Moscow by Yury Lyubimov with the poet and protest singer Vladimir Vysotsky in the title role. In its long run of 217 performances between 1971 and 1980 Moscow audiences came to identify Vysotsky with Hamlet, and 'the Prince in a metaphorical Soviet gulag' with their own situation 'of a spiritually deprived living death', in protest against which Vysotsky 'declaimed, to the accompaniment of his guitar, Pasternak's once forbidden poem "Hamlet"' at the beginning of each performance.[10] Although the production was a radical departure from the traditional manner of presenting the play, there was no attempt to deconstruct the Hamlet figure. Nor were the political implications foregrounded to the extent of obscuring the philosophical and psychological dilemmas Hamlet has to face. A similar balance can be observed in the famous *Hamlet* film directed by Grigori Kozintsev of 1964. A single, silent scene introduced by the director sufficed to transmit the 'political' lesson: Ophelia is being encased in tight courtly costume and taught to dance, smile and be a subservient doll in the hands of her manipulators: the young are doomed from the start.

The Czech appropriation of Shakespeare was at first less dominated by the desire for political independence than the desire for cultural independence. In the 1920s and 1930s the Czech National Theatre in Prague won international fame for its daring staging with expressionist sets and abstract stage constructions in the manner of the Soviet avant-garde, but it was only when the country was occupied again, first by German troops (1938–45) and then as a Soviet satellite in 1948, that pressing occasions for 'political' Shakespeare arose. The 1941 production of *Hamlet* in the Vinohrady Theatre in Prague is said to have 'emphasised, with due caution, the helpless situation of an intellectual attempting to endure in a ruthless environment'.[11] Twenty-three years later director Otomar Krejča and stage designer Josef Svoboda, both with outstanding international careers before them, collaborated in a rousing presentation of *Romeo and Juliet,* which caught the mutinous restlessness of Czech youth trapped in the stifling Cold War atmosphere. After the crushing of the Prague Spring by the Soviet-led invasion of Czechoslovakia in 1968, theatres were once again thrown back on guarded allusion and insinuation. It took ten years before another *Hamlet* production expressed the feelings of the young generation. Directed by Evald Schorm at the small Balustrade Theatre in Prague, this 'raw, underdone *Hamlet,* with blood dripping from wide-gaping wounds in both bodies and souls' was a tragical farce in which the presumptions of the high and mighty were shown in all their futile absurdity. The grave-diggers were clowns who took over the end of the play, pulled a camouflage net over the corpses and dusted the heap with disinfectant. According to the testimony of Zdeněk Stříbrný, spectators felt shattered but also 'a peculiar relief, a kind of modern absurd catharsis'.[12]

Colonial and post-colonial Shakespeares: *The Tempest*

The examples discussed so far sketch national appropriations inside Europe that derive from similar motivations and follow similar patterns. Cultural exchange here was between equals sharing in a common European heritage. Shakespeare in the colonies and in commonwealth countries was a different matter, although politically unproblematic as long as his works were unchallenged items in school or college curricula, where the study of this unparalleled genius was said to bring the choicest fruit of western culture (second only to the Bible) to the knowledge of less fortunate or even totally untutored races. Canon-building and empire-building went hand in hand; native cultures were marginalised by the hegemony of the 'mother' country. It was only when the freedom movements in Africa and Asia achieved independence for their countries in the 1950s and 1960s, and a new generation of indigenous intellectuals supported by sympathetic activists from abroad contested the legitimacy of colonial domination, that the questions at issue could be properly focused. (See also chapters 14 and 15 below.)

The appropriation of Shakespeare is paradigmatic for the problems emergent nations face in establishing cultural identity as a compromise between imitation, rejection and assimilation. A Mozart symphony, leaving aside pop versions and arbitrary rearrangements, has to be played the same everywhere. *The Tempest*, to be stageable at all, has to be translated into the vernacular or literary language of the region concerned, and assimilated to indigenous theatre traditions. Performing the play in imitation of western models is no longer enough. Awareness of one's cultural independence forbids such 'mimicry' and demands that the alien play be rewritten according to the nation's own cultural/ideological code. Viewed from a post-colonial stand-point, Caliban's abject serfdom and his clear insight into the process by which the colonising Prospero has taken possession of the isle provides such obvious parallels to the fate of formerly colonised nations that fundamental revisions are *de rigeur*. Prospero's legitimation of his rule rests on a single point, namely the assertion that Caliban's debased nature is impervious to nurture, 'Being capable of all ill!', as proof of which he points to Caliban's attempted rape of Miranda. This, for centuries, has clinched the argument, and post-colonial interpretations have had to find a way around it. By de-constructing the relevant passages it is easy to show that Shakespeare was voicing commonplace contemporary assumptions: for example, about native languages as so much 'gabble', about the natives' ignorance of good and evil, their general intractability and their uncontrolled sexual passions. These are now recognised as items in the colonial ideology of the time and are firmly rejected. Caliban is rehabilitated, Prospero made to stand in the dock.

Directors following this altered view of the play on the stage have turned Prospero into a morose and spiteful authoritarian and raised Caliban's com-plaint to the level of a forceful and justified demand for freedom. The stum-bling block of the attempted rape remains and they have gone to some length to clear it out of the way: for example, by casting an attractive young man for the role, allowing Miranda to flirt with Caliban when the old man is not looking, and generally downplaying both Miranda's aversion and the sig-nificance of the long-past criminal attempt. Only Peter Brook in his widely travelled multiracial production (Zurich, 1990) managed to alter the emo-tional geometry of the play in such a manner that even this scene, for a few performances at least, became an asset. His black Prospero, a wise and gen-tle African magician, made the issue of white domination and colonisation irrelevant; Miranda was a beautiful Indian princess and the understudy for Caliban a blond, handsome, serious youth. His answer to Prospero's accu-sation 'till thou didst seek / To violate the honour of my child' was a joyous exclamation

> O ho! O ho! would't had been done!
> Thou didst prevent me; I had peopled else
> This isle with Calibans.

The moment's pause that followed gave the audience time to realise that these two beautiful creatures would indeed have been ideal progenitors of a happy race of islanders, and spectators experienced, with Caliban, the fleeting vision of a utopian state of beauty and bliss.

Brook's *Tempest* dissolved the political contradictions that other directors, committed to militant anti-colonial agendas, deliberately seek out and bring to the fore. The Caliban syndrome of having to use the oppressor's language to find one's voice has stimulated writers in Anglophone (and even Francophone) ex-colonies to thorough rewritings of *The Tempest* in the course of which they have changed historical perspective, colour, gender, *dramatis personae*, focus and action. A significant adaptation was conceived by Aimé Césaire, the scholar, politician and dramatist. Born in Martinique, Césaire, together with Léopold Senghor and Léon Damas, founded the anti-colonial négritude movement, whose members consciously embraced Africanness without rejecting European influences. He turned Caliban into a radical revolutionary and Ariel into the reformist agent of power, introduced two gods from the West African Yoruba pantheon who disturb Prospero's theatricals but allow him, an enlightened thinker and a fugitive from the Inquisition, to remain on the island (*Une Tempête*, Paris, 1969).[13] The Caribbean essayist and novelist George Lamming (*Water With Berries*, 1972) sees *The Tempest* as a key scenario for unfolding the identity quests of artists and intellectuals under post-colonial conditions. African appropriations of Shakespeare have been more preoccupied with rectifying a historical misrepresentation and injustice; the attitudes range from total rejection (Ngũgĩ's *Decolonising the Mind*, 1986) and protest against the 'Othello complex' of uncritical cultural assimilation (in *Ballads of Under-Development* by the Ugandan poet Taban Lo Liyong, 1976) to politically subversive adaptations in Afrikaans in South Africa under apartheid conditions by authors such as André Brink and Uys Krige. Not surprisingly, feminist writers have discovered Miranda as the object of patriarchal domination. In Anglo-Canadian literature her submission to Prospero's order has even come to symbolise the country's former relation to imperial Britain, a state from which both have to liberate themselves to achieve selfhood. Audrey Thomas, Margaret Laurence and Sarah Murphy are among the authors who explore this twofold orientation.[14]

With the passing of the decolonising phase of the 1960s into history and the gradual fading of the cultural anguish caused by colonial constellations there is less cause for political Shakespeare theatre than before. Embattled confrontations still occur on the theoretical plane in the field of post-colonial studies. On the stage, intercultural Shakespeare has produced a new order of primarily aesthetic appropriations, highly poetic refashionings of the plays in non-European theatre traditions. They are contested. The accusations are that intercultural Shakespeare panders to global consumerism, debilitates through wanton eclecticism and despoils native traditions.[15] Truly decolonised interculturalism apparently is difficult to achieve.

NOTES

1 Post-structuralists would disagree. The analytical methods of New Historicism and cultural materialism are designed to reveal substrata of 'ideology' in overtly clear texts. Cf. Stephen Greenblatt, *Renaissance Self-Fashioning: From More to Shakespeare* (Chicago: University of Chicago Press, 1980); Jonathan Dollimore and Alan Sinfield (eds.), *Political Shakespeare: New Essays in Cultural Materialism* (Manchester: Manchester University Press, 1985); and John Drakakis (ed.), *Alternative Shakespeares* (London: Routledge, 1985).

2 Little wonder that their author has been credited with the 'invention of the human'. See Harold Bloom's monumental tribute to the Bard in *Shakespeare. The Invention of the Human* (London: Fourth Estate, 1998).

3 See Philip C. Kolin, *Shakespeare and Feminist Criticism: an Annotated Bibliography and Commentary* (New York and London: Garland, 1991).

4 See Wilhelm Hortmann, *Shakespeare on the German Stage: the Twentieth Century*, with a section on Shakespeare on stage in the German Democratic Republic by Maik Hamburger (Cambridge: Cambridge University Press, 1998), 80, 56, and 58.

5 Janet Suzman writes about the production in *Shakespeare in the Twentieth Century: Proceedings of the Sixth World Shakespeare Congress, Los Angeles, 1996*, ed. Jonathan Bate, Jill L. Levenson and Dieter Mehl (Newark: University of Delaware Press and London: Associated University Presses, 1998), 23–40.

6 See Maik Hamburger's description in Hortmann, *Shakespeare on the German Stage*, 379–82.

7 See Krystyna Kujawińska-Courtney, 'Der polnische Prinz: Rezeption und Appropriation des *Hamlet* in Polen' in *Shakespeare-Jahrbuch* (1995), 82–92.

8 *ibid.*, 90.

9 See Zdeněk Stříbrný, *Shakespeare and Eastern Europe* (Oxford: Oxford University Press, 2000), 83 and 85.

10 See Spencer Golub, 'Between the Curtain and the Grave: the Taganka in the *Hamlet* Gulag' in Dennis Kennedy (ed.), *Foreign Shakespeare. Contemporary Performance* (Cambridge: Cambridge University Press, 1993), 158–77.

11 See Jarka Burian, '*Hamlet* in Postwar Czech Theatre' in Dennis Kennedy (ed.), *Foreign Shakespeare. Contemporary Performance* (Cambridge: Cambridge University Press, 1993), 195–210.

12 See Stříbrný, *Shakespeare and Eastern Europe*, 119.

13 For the more recent theatre situation in Africa, especially Nigeria, with Ola Rotimi and Wole Soyinka as chief exponents, and the sheer language problems they face in establishing an indigenous theatre in a nation where dozens of major languages are in use, see the various studies by Martin Banham, including chapter 15 below.

14 A. Thomas, *Prospero on the Island* (1971), M. Laurence, *The Diviners* (1974), S. Murphy, *The Measure of Miranda* (1987). For a multifaceted combination of

feminist and post-colonial readings of *The Tempest,* see Marina Warner's novel *Indigo* (1992) and the Jamaican Michelle Cliff's *No Telephone to Heaven* (1987).

15 See the debate in *The Intercultural Performance Reader,* ed. Patrice Pavis (London: Routledge, 1996), especially the contributions by Erika Fischer-Lichte, Biodun Jeyifo, Martin Banham, Rustom Bharucha and others. John Russell Brown, however, in *New Sites for Shakespeare* (London and New York: Routledge, 1999) sees chances for mutual enrichment in intercultural contact.

13

MICHAEL A. MORRISON

Shakespeare in North America

On 2 June 1752 the *Charming Sally* arrived in the harbour near Yorktown, Virginia, carrying among its passengers twelve adult actors and three of their children. Organised in London by William Hallam, the erstwhile proprietor of a minor London theatre, the New Wells, and led by his brother Lewis, the company was drawn in the main from the ranks of metropolitan and provincial players of modest accomplishment. After an interval of three months, during the course of which the company awaited official permission to perform and worked to refurbish the primitive playhouse in nearby Williamsburg, they commenced their season with *The Merchant of Venice* on 15 September – an event generally considered to be the first significant professional staging of Shakespeare in America.[1]

For a number of years after the arrival of the Hallams, theatre in America, and the smaller world of the Shakespeare theatre within, was a distant colonial extension of English culture. The actors who came were largely those whose opportunities for advancement were limited in their homeland; for the first half-century of American Shakespeare performance and beyond, sophisticated observers in London would likely have viewed the theatrical emigrés who journeyed to America's shores as being no less marooned than Prospero on his distant isle. 'As an actor, you would be extinct', Thomas Holcroft warned his protégé Thomas Abthorpe Cooper prior to his westward voyage in 1796, 'and the very season of energy and improvement would be for ever passed'.[2] In years to come, however, the New World would become a requisite journey for major English and continental Shakespearean stars seeking to fill up their coffers and add to their laurels; and in time America would produce outstanding performers of its own, actors and actresses who would invite favourable comparison with the best the motherland had to offer. From relatively modest beginnings, when it might fairly have been called a provincial shadow of the great English tradition from which it emerged, the Shakespeare theatre in North America, particularly in the United States, grew to assume its own unique cultural identity.

Early stages: beginnings to 1810

Shakespeare was acted on the American stage before the arrival of the Hallams, but we know little of the performers and performances. On 23 March 1730, one Joachimus Bertrand, a whimsical New York physician, advertised in the *Gazette* to promote a forthcoming amateur production of *Romeo and Juliet*, in which he was to play the Apothecary. On 5 March 1750 a company led by Walter Murray and Thomas Kean – 'stage-struck tradesmen and their wives', as one historian called them – presented the Colley Cibber version of *Richard III* at a makeshift theatre in New York; the troupe acted there for sixteen months before departing for Virginia and Maryland, where they acted sporadically for a year, then disbanded. On 26 December 1751, Robert Upton, sent to New York as William Hallam's advance man, performed Othello at the theatre on Nassau Street that Murray and Kean had abandoned. A month later he acted Richard III, and soon afterwards he returned to England. Lewis Hallam dismissed Murray and Kean as 'that sett of pretenders', and William Dunlap, the first historian of the American stage, called them 'idle young men perpetrating the murder of sundry plays'. It is likely that these assessments are unduly harsh, but given the short-lived, peripatetic nature of these early troupes, and the Hallams' superiority in terms of organisation and personnel, we might consider the Hallam *Merchant of Venice* as the first noteworthy American staging.[3]

In 1753 the Hallam company moved to New York; the following year they played engagements in Philadelphia and Charleston, South Carolina; and in 1755, they journeyed to the West Indies, where they merged with a company led by the English actor-manager David Douglass, who married Lewis Hallam's widow after Hallam's death that year. Three years later the company returned to the mainland, where it soon became known as the American Company, and eighteen-year-old Lewis Hallam Jr. assumed leading roles with Douglass. The younger Hallam became America's first Hamlet in Philadelphia on 27 July 1759; within a few years he emerged as America's leading Shakespearean interpreter. Accounts of Hallam's performances suggest that his style owed more to the declamatory school of James Quin than the more natural style of Garrick. In tragedy he was at times accused of mouthing and rant; yet he was highly regarded by his contemporaries. Alexander Graydon, a Pennsylvania attorney and soldier who saw him in his prime, recalled that he 'had merit in a number of characters ... No one could tread the stage with more ease ... He was ... at Philadelphia, as much the soul of the Southwark Theatre, as ever Garrick was of Drury Lane'. Douglass, too, possessed limited abilities – 'rather a decent than shining actor' in Graydon's estimation – yet he was a capable manager and gave America its first Falstaff and King John.[4]

During its early years, the American Company was often forced to contend with religious objections to theatre in general, particularly in Quaker Pennsylvania and Puritan New England; in Rhode Island in 1761 it was necessary to present *Othello* disguised as a series of 'Moral Dialogues'. In 1774 the Continental Congress, anticipating the revolution, prohibited theatre altogether, and the troupe settled in Jamaica. By that time, according to Hugh F. Rankin's calculation, fourteen of Shakespeare's plays had been performed in America at least 180 times, and he speculated that 500 might be a more reasonable estimate.[5] Of these, *Hamlet, Richard III, Macbeth, The Merchant of Venice, Romeo and Juliet, Othello* and *King Lear* were given a disproportionate number of performances. *Cymbeline*, a popular vehicle for the actresses Margaret Cheer and Nancy Hallam, was performed occasionally, as were *King John, Henry IV* and several more; but the repertory would remain limited well into the next century.

After the peace of 1783 what remained of the company established a base in New York with Lewis Hallam Jr as leading actor and John Henry as co-manager. By the mid-1790s permanent companies, which also featured Shakespeare at the heart of their repertories, had been organised in Philadelphia, Boston, Charleston and Providence. By that time, too, a number of star actors, emigrants from the motherland, had established themselves as popular bravura interpreters who found favour with the American public. None were of the calibre of England's reigning favourites, John Philip Kemble and Sarah Siddons; yet unlike the actors of the Hallam troupe forty years earlier, most had experience at leading London and provincial theatres. The early nineties saw the arrival of John Hodgkinson, a gifted veteran of the provinces, Charlotte Melmoth, who had performed leading roles at the patent houses, and the peripatetic Covent Garden veteran James Fennell; Elizabeth Kemble Whitlock, the younger sister of Sarah Siddons, who had occasionally played leading Shakespeare roles at Drury Lane, was recruited by Thomas Wignell for the Chestnut Street Theatre in Philadelphia in 1794 and soon established herself as a rival to Melmoth. Ann Brunton Merry came to America in 1796 after considerable success in the provinces and at Covent Garden; for twelve years, until her death in 1808, she was the new nation's reigning Shakespearean actress.

But by far the most successful Shakespearean performer during the early years of American independence was Thomas Abthorpe Cooper (fig. 28). Cooper was raised in London by William Godwin and schooled for the stage by Thomas Holcroft. After a provincial apprenticeship, he played Hamlet and Macbeth at Covent Garden to mixed reviews, although the consensus

28 Thomas Abthorpe Cooper.

was that he was a young actor of promise. In 1796, at age nineteen, he was recruited along with Anne Merry for the Chestnut Street Theatre, and, despite Holcroft's protestation, embarked for Philadelphia. In his early years in America, in Philadelphia and at the Park Theatre in New York, Cooper made a strong impression upon audiences as Hamlet, Macbeth, Romeo, Richard III, Coriolanus, Othello and several more. Tall, with 'a handsome face and a commanding and an Apollo-like figure', and a voice that was 'full and of considerable compass', he became a national celebrity. Although some critics chided him early in his career for acknowledging acquaintances in the audience and inadequate memorisation of his lines, he was nonetheless viewed as America's unrivalled Shakespearean interpreter. The actor and manager Noah Ludlow, who worked with him a number of times, recalled that Cooper's style 'was founded on the John Kemble school, a little modified, perhaps; rather more impulsive in passionate scenes, but possessing all the towering grandeur of that great English tragedian'.[6]

Cooper remained active through the 1830s. By that time, however, he was past sixty, and his style was considered increasingly old-fashioned. As in England, the more passionate method of the Romantics had swept aside the reigning formalism of the Kemble school, and audiences and critics had begun to feel that he lacked the flash and fire of a Kean, a Booth, or a Forrest. By then regarded as a 'celebrated old veteran', he toured the land with his daughter Priscilla; he retired from the stage in 1840 and ended his career with a political appointment as a New York City customs inspector.

During the 1790s a number of new theatres were built in the major population centres, and there was a general improvement in the quality of Shakespearean scenery and effects. Although the announcement for the initial Hallam season claimed that 'the Scenes ... are all new, extremely rich, and ... being painted by the best Hands in London, are excell'd by none in Beauty and Elegance',[7] it is likely that much of the scenery was refurbished cast-offs from the New Wells. Generalised stock scenery would continue to rule the stage until well into the nineteenth century, but in New York, especially, some productions – Cooper's début as Hamlet, for example – were of original design, and were executed with great care and expense. By the end of the eighteenth century much of the scenery at America's 'finer' theatres was of the same quality as that of London's leading playhouses.

Professional Shakespeare in Canada began with the arrival in Halifax, Nova Scotia, in 1768 of a small company led by Henry Giffard and an actor named Mills; they had performed previously in North Carolina and journeyed northwards through New England. During their ten-week season, in which they performed twice a week, they presented Garrick's *Catherine and Petruchio*. In 1786, Edward Allen, for many years a prominent member of Lewis Hallam Jr's company, brought a troupe that included William Moore and John Bentley to Montreal and presented *Henry IV*, *Richard III*, *Othello* and several more, there and in Quebec City. Allen led a company in Montreal from 1787 until 1790, while Bentley and Moore remained to perform and manage in Quebec City. During the early 1800s the Theatre Royal, Halifax performed *Catherine and Petruchio* and toured it to Saint John, New Brunswick; William H. Prigmore, who had acted in Philadelphia, New York and elsewhere since 1792, started a professional company in Montreal in 1808 ('as deficient in talent as in numbers', according to the Anglo-American actor-manager John Bernard) and performed *The Tempest* and *Othello*; Bernard himself performed Shylock in Quebec City and Montreal; Noble Luke Usher journeyed from Boston to Quebec with Othello, Hamlet, Richard III and Romeo in his repertory. Yashdip S. Bains estimated that from the time of the arrival of Giffard and Mills in Halifax and Edmund Kean's appearances in Montreal and Quebec City in 1826, Canadians witnessed seventeen Shakespeare plays on about 200 occasions. *Catherine and Petruchio* was acted with the greatest frequency, while *Richard III* was performed often, followed by *Othello*, *The Merchant of Venice*, *Romeo and Juliet*, *Macbeth*, *Hamlet* and *King Lear*.[8]

Romanticism and its aftermath: 1810–1860

Between 1810 and 1822 Americans had the opportunity to witness in their own land the skills of three of England's greatest tragedians, George Frederick Cooke, Edmund Kean and Junius Brutus Booth. Although their performances could be famously erratic, they were, at their best, Shakespearean actors of transcendent ability; their impersonations introduced American audiences to the more tempestuous, impulsive Romantic methods of performance.

Cooke was the first to arrive. In 1810, Thomas Cooper, on a visit to England, persuaded Cooke to make the journey to America. His arrival created a furor; Cooke's initial appearance as Richard III at the Park Theatre in New York brought a record $1,820 into the box-office. During his two seasons in America he also played Iago, Shylock, Falstaff in *1 Henry IV* and *The Merry Wives of Windsor*, Lear, Othello, Macbeth, Henry VIII and King John. Cooke played extended engagements in Boston, Philadelphia, Baltimore and Providence and, in doing so, helped to establish the touring star system, in which a leading actor would tour for a season with local stock companies playing in support. Cooper, Anne Merry and other leading actors with resident companies had played elsewhere as visiting stars before his arrival, but it was Cooke, the first great foreign tragedian to appear in the United States, who firmly established a system that would remain the standard until Irving's arrival in the eighties with his Lyceum company. Although he could be notoriously unpredictable – his quixotic personality and bouts with the bottle often affected his performances – he was, at his best, an electrifying performer, an actor whose visceral yet 'natural' style of playing set new standards for American audiences. Cooke died in New York in 1812; although he was much admired, his sojourn was too brief and his skills too idiosyncratic to influence the course of American Shakespeare performance, which would remain grounded in the Kemble school for more than a decade to come.

Edmund Kean came for his first American tour during the season of 1820/1. Though he was greeted with uncertainty by the press, audiences were enthusiastic. His repertory included Richard III, Hamlet, Lear, Othello and Shylock, along with a number of non-Shakespeare roles. Kean's vigorous genius and intense fire and vivacity – 'nature itself uncovered and set free in its deepest intensity and power' in the words of one American observer – created as much of a sensation as Cooke's initial engagement.[9] In May 1821, at the end of his season, Kean refused to play in Boston when greeted by what he considered to be an inadequate house, which led to sharp criticism by the American press. He returned in 1825, in the wake of a sensational London

29 Junius Brutus Booth as Richard III.

trial in which he was sued for damages by a London alderman whose wife had been Kean's mistress; he played successfully in New York, Philadelphia and other cities, though his performances were at times interrupted by catcalls of 'Huzzah for the seducer' and flurries of oranges hurled on stage. His ill-starred reappearance in Boston resulted in the first theatre riot in America on the night scheduled for his opening, the result of his unwillingness to perform for a small audience five years earlier; Kean fled the city without acting.

Except for a brief return journey, Junius Brutus Booth (fig. 29) spent nearly his entire career in America. After establishing himself as a rival to Kean in London during the late 1810s, Booth emigrated to America in 1821, where he sired a theatrical dynasty: his sons Junius II, Edwin and John Wilkes all became actors. Until his death in 1852 he acted regularly and with great success. Cooke and Kean had confined themselves mainly to the larger eastern cities, yet by the late 1820s theatre had expanded to dozens of smaller cities and towns throughout the Great Lakes region and the Ohio and Mississippi valleys. Booth brought great Shakespearean acting to Richmond, New Orleans, Pittsburgh, St Louis, Cincinnati, and many more, and towards the end of his career he became the first great tragedian to act in California. Although Booth, like his Romantic antecedents, could be an inconsistent performer, the result of drink and streaks of aberrant behaviour, which at times verged on madness, Noah Ludlow recalled that 'When in full possession of those great mental and physical powers with which nature had endowed him', he was 'the most finished and complete representative of tragedy ... that ever came within my observation.' He excelled as Richard III, Lear, Iago, Othello, Hamlet and Cassius; Walt Whitman, with whom he was a favourite, wrote that 'The words fire, energy, *abandon*, found in him unprecedented meanings.'[10]

In the late twenties and thirties there came from England, as well, actors whose more 'refined' style contrasted sharply with the tempestuous Romantics. William Charles Macready paid his first visit to the United States in 1826. He was much admired by American audiences and critics and returned during the 1843/4 and 1848/9 seasons; the latter season was marred by the famous Astor Place riot. Charles Kemble and his daughter Fanny came in 1832 and acted in *Hamlet*, *Romeo and Juliet*, *King John* and several more; Fanny, in particular, conquered American audiences with her blend of vivacity and elegance.

None of these performers from abroad, however, made as great an impact as America's first native-born tragedian. Edwin Forrest made his professional début in Philadelphia in 1820. After gaining valuable experience in the heart land, he played second leads to Kean in Albany during the 1825/6 season, including Richmond to Kean's Richard and Iago to his Othello. Kean encouraged Forrest, who was profoundly influenced by the older actor's style. On 23 June 1826, Forrest appeared at a benefit at the Park Theatre in New York in the role of Othello and was an instant success; he subsequently toured as a star, with brief interruptions, for more than forty years. Forrest was a larger, more powerful man than Kean or Booth, muscularly built, athletic, with a voice 'like the falls of Niagara' (though he also excelled in quiet, tender passages); in his youth he possessed Byronesque good looks. In addition to Othello, his Shakespearean repertory included Richard III, Lear, Hamlet, Macbeth, Mark Antony and Coriolanus (fig. 30). A writer for the *Albion* (2 September 1848) remarked that 'He has created a school in his art, strictly American, and he stands forth as the very embodiment, as it were, of the *masses* of American character ... His Shakespearean characters are all stamped with the same intense energy of expression, and overwhelming display of physical force.' Lear and Hamlet were 'in his hands frequently like enraged Titans, both in look and manner', while Macbeth was 'the ferocious chief of a barbarous tribe' and Othello, 'with all its many beauties', was nonetheless 'truly the ferocious and "bloody Moor"'. As one biographer

30 Edwin Forrest as Coriolanus.

noted, however, 'He covered the stage with a firm and graceful stride', and his leading ladies 'often insisted that no man ever bowed and kissed a hand more gently'.[11] While critics at times complained of a lack of subtlety in his playing and he was never fully acceptable to the more 'refined' elements of American society, he was acknowledged as an original, an actor of compelling power and magnetism whose portrayals provoked wild enthusiasm.

Forrest acted successfully in England in 1836 and again in 1845, when he performed Macbeth to critical acclaim; one performance during the latter engagement was interrupted by a claque, however, and Forrest, believing Macready's partisans to be responsible, hissed Macready during the English tragedian's performance of Hamlet in Edinburgh soon afterwards. In May 1849 the enmity of Forrest's supporters towards Macready when the tragedians were appearing in rival productions of *Macbeth* in New York resulted in the Astor Place riot in which 31 people were killed and more than 100 were injured. Forrest's reputation was damaged further by a sensational divorce trial in 1851; he retired temporarily in the late fifties, but he emerged in 1860 and continued to perform and give readings until shortly before his death in 1872.

In the years that Forrest was thrilling American play-goers with his robust impersonations, Charlotte Cushman, the first native-born actress to be regarded as first rank both at home and abroad, rose to the status of America's greatest tragedienne. Like Forrest, Cushman spent her early days in the profession outside the sophisticated eastern cities. In 1836 she made her New York début as Lady Macbeth. Within a few years she had exploited the rage for actresses in breeches roles that swept America during the thirties and early forties to establish herself as a much heralded Romeo; she later played Wolsey and Hamlet. In the mid-forties she acted Shakespeare heroines with Macready in New York and London. In the latter city she also appeared as a star, earning praise for her Lady Macbeth, Romeo (the *Times* found her 'far superior to any Romeo that has been seen for years'), Orsino, Queen Katherine and Rosalind. Upon her return to America in 1849 she was greeted as a star of the first magnitude. She continued to perform until 1875, dividing her time between America, England and Europe. Tall and broadly built, with a husky, powerful voice and superb elocution, she projected a bold, majestic quality; her characterisations were informed by subtleties and keen intellectual insights. 'Her best achievements in the illustration of Shakespeare', wrote William Winter, 'were ... of the highest order of art ... [and] filled the imagination with a satisfying sense of completeness, beauty, and power.'[12]

During the age of Forrest and Cushman, America produced a number of gifted native interpreters, who achieved eminence and international renown. The versatile tragedians E. L. Davenport and James E. Murdoch, polished, intellectual performers, were well received in England as well as in America. James H. Hackett was famous primarily for a series of 'Yankee' roles, but was known to audiences for several generations as a superlative Falstaff. Noteworthy as well among American Shakespeareans of the era is the African-American tragedian Ira Aldridge. Aware that the vistas for non-white performers were severely restricted in his native land, he spent his career almost entirely in England and Europe. After a quarter-century in the English provinces, he established a reputation as a masterful Shakespearean in London and other European capitals during the fifties and sixties, with a repertory that included Othello, Shylock, Lear, Macbeth and Aaron in *Titus Andronicus*.

North American scenography throughout the early 1840s essentially retained the values that had served the Hallams nearly a century earlier – generalised stock wing-and-groove scenery in which a generic castle or forest might serve any number of plays remained the standard. However, Charles Kean's arrival for his third American tour during the 1845/6 season with a number of 'archaeologically correct' productions signalled the dawn of a new era. Kean's *Richard III* and *King John*, presented with elaborately pictorial settings at great expense, introduced American audiences to the spectacular Shakespeare that London had known for several decades. In the early and mid-fifties the popular low comedian and manager William E. Burton became the first native practitioner to follow Kean's example when he produced sumptuous revivals of *The Merry Wives of Windsor, A Midsummer Night's Dream, The Tempest* and *The Winter's Tale.*

The growth of Shakespeare theatre in Canada was far slower than in the United States, due to its smaller population and the fact that it had far fewer urban centres. Through the first half of the nineteenth century significant productions were largely confined to Montreal, Quebec City, Halifax and Saint John. In 1816 a resident company in Halifax, led by Addison B. Price, included *Romeo and Juliet, Hamlet, Richard III* and several more in its repertory and toured to Saint John. In 1825 the Theatre Royal opened in Montreal, led by the American tragedian Frederick Brown, an actor of the neoclassical school and Charles Kemble's brother-in-law, who had made a number of Canadian appearances since 1818. Brown's roles during his artistically successful and financially disastrous Theatre Royal season included Richard III, Hamlet, Shylock, Coriolanus (which he staged in the historically accurate style of John Philip Kemble) and Lear. In 1826, Edmund Kean acted extended engagements in Montreal and Quebec City. While in Canada he became an honorary chieftain of the Huron Indians; he was so pleased by the honour that he had a portrait made while wearing Huron ceremonial robes. Charles Kean acted in the same two cities in 1831, as did Charles and Fanny Kemble two years later. Although theatrical standards in general were lower than those in the United States in terms of supporting companies and theatre buildings, major stars came nonetheless, though somewhat sporadically. Thomas Cooper performed Othello with the stock company in Saint John in 1830; Junius Brutus Booth, James H. Hackett and William Charles Macready all made Canadian appearances before 1850. In 1853 the actor-manager John Nickinson took over the Royal Lyceum in Toronto. During his six years of management he presented a number of Shakespeare productions with a Canadian resident company; he became a popular favourite, noted especially for his Dogberry and other comic roles.

The genteel tradition: 1860–1920

The years between 1860 and 1900 were a golden age of American Shakespeare performance, as actors in general began to move away from the robust portrayals of Edwin Forrest towards a more restrained and subtle method. No actor would exemplify the new order better than Edwin Booth. The son of Junius Brutus Booth, Edwin served his apprenticeship in California and

31 Edwin Booth as Hamlet.

in the late fifties began to build a reputation in the sophisticated cities of the east. Booth was a superlative Iago, Othello, Brutus, Lear and Shylock, and an effective Benedick and Petruchio; his Hamlet (fig. 31) became a theatrical legend. To American play-goers of the period between the early 1860s and his retirement in 1891, Booth's Dane, described by William Winter as 'like the dark, mad, dreamy, mysterious hero of a poem', and acted 'in an ideal manner, as far removed as possible from the plane of actual life', was the most renowned Shakespearean impersonation of their time.[13] Booth's purity of elocution was unmatched among his contemporaries; his low, rich, musical voice was almost universally praised for its range and beauty. Booth was gifted with brooding, poetic good looks and expressive eyes and features; his characterisations were illuminated by penetrating intellectual and spiritual insights. A series of personal misfortunes – the death of his wife in 1863, his brother's assassination of Abraham Lincoln in 1865, the loss, in 1873, of Booth's Theatre, his 'great national temple' of dramatic art, due to financial mismanagement – only strengthened his awareness of the nature of tragedy. His 100 consecutive nights of *Hamlet* at the Winter Garden Theatre in New York during the 1864/5 season inaugurated the era of the Shakespeare long-run in America, and he played the role, in cities large and small, for more than thirty years. He also acted in England and Germany, and in 1881 he alternated Othello and Iago with Henry Irving in London.

Play-goers in the age of Booth were also privileged to witness the performances of a number of other accomplished tragedians. The Anglo-French actor Charles Fechter brought his 'colloquial' Hamlet to America in 1870 and offered it regularly until his retirement in 1877. Lawrence Barrett is often mentioned in connection with Booth, and justly so; between 1886 and 1891 he produced and directed Booth's largely triumphant final tours, in three of which he co-starred. A leading tragedian from the sixties onwards, he had a voice of exceptional range and sensitive, ascetic features. As was the case with most actors of his generation, he spent much of his career in Booth's shadow. Critics at times found his acting to be mannered and lacking in warmth; nonetheless he was highly regarded by his contemporaries. His finest impersonation was Cassius, which he played in his last years to Booth's Brutus. Another contemporary tragedian who attained distinction in Shakespeare roles was the Irish-born John McCullough, who early in his career became a protégé of Edwin Forrest. He was, like his mentor, a large, handsome, well-built man with a strong voice and crystalline elocution, though he was far more genial in temperament. A capable Lear, Coriolanus and Othello, he carried a more subtle version of Forrest's heroic style into the seventies and eighties.

During this same period America witnessed the portrayals of a number of gifted Shakespearean actresses, both domestic and foreign. In the late 1860s the 'heavy' tragediennes Fanny Janauschek and Adelaide Ristori came to America and impressed audiences with their powerful impersonations of Lady Macbeth. The actresses whose popularity was greatest, however, tended towards a repertory in which the comedies and romances, along with Juliet, provided their principal roles. The first of these to arrive was the English-born Adelaide Neilson, who came in 1872 and returned three more times before her premature death in 1880, when she was in her mid-thirties. Neilson was esteemed by American audiences for her enchanting Viola and Imogen; but the role in which she conquered America thoroughly was Juliet. William Winter noted that 'there has, in our time, been no Juliet as fascinating and irresistible'.[14]

The Polish-born Helena Modjeska began her American career in 1877 and remained a major presence on the American stage until the early 1900s. Although she never lost her distinct Polish accent, the vivacious, charismatic Modjeska was much admired for her Juliet, Rosalind, Viola and many more; she played Ophelia, Lady Macbeth and other tragic roles capably, and during the 1889/90 season toured with Edwin Booth.

The most highly esteemed native-born actress of the period was the beautiful, red-haired Mary Anderson. Tall and elegant, with an expressive contralto voice, she gave New York her first Juliet at age eighteen. Although she acted other roles occasionally, her Shakespearean repertory was confined mainly to Juliet, Rosalind, and the doubling of Hermione and Perdita, all of which she performed in England as well as in America. By the time she retired to marry in 1890, at age thirty, she was regarded as America's finest classical actress.

Between 1886 and 1899 the Irish-born Ada Rehan captivated American and English play-goers with a series of heroines she performed with Augustin Daly's company. She played Mistress Ford, Rosalind, the Princess of France, Helena and many more; her greatest triumph came as Katharina in *Taming of the Shrew*. Her acting, wrote Winter, was characterised by 'buoyant glee, which rippled over a depth of warm, sensuous feeling', but she could also be 'stately, forcible, satirical, violent, arch, flippant, and demure'.[15] Rehan's success is almost inseparable from that of Daly, America's first great *régisseur*, whose opulent revivals in the eighties and nineties were among the most fashionable and glamorous theatrical events presented at the height of the Gilded Age. Between 1886 and 1899 he produced or revived at least one of the comedies or romances per season, and he brought his company to London a number of times. His productions, as was the fashion of the time, were pictorially spectacular, and his ensemble acted in a style characterised as 'quiet, elegant, languid'.[16]

The eighties also saw the rise to prominence of the dynamic and versatile tragedian Richard Mansfield, who between 1889 and 1906 performed Richard III, Shylock, Henry V and Brutus. Mansfield was gifted with mimetic powers and a 'deep and thrilling' voice of exceptional range; contemporary critics often said that his acting failed to reach 'the loftier heights of tragic emotion', yet they also acknowledged that he possessed an 'electric quality' that aroused excitement and enthusiasm.

This same period saw a number of distinguished foreign visitors. A rapidly expanding network of rail transportation made it possible for both domestic and foreign stars to tour from the older eastern metropolitan centres to the cities of the heartland and the west. Henry Irving toured North America eight times between 1883 and 1903 with his Lyceum company and scenery; Ellen Terry was his leading lady on every tour but the last. Lillie Langtry came with Rosalind in her repertory; Sarah Bernhardt would offer American play-goers her Hamlet. The Italian tragedian Tomasso Salvini toured America five times and acted Othello, Lear and Macbeth; he played Othello and the Ghost to Edwin Booth's Iago and Hamlet during the 1885/6 season. His countryman Ernesto Rossi came many times as well, as did the

German Shakespeareans Ludwig Barnay and Daniel Bandmann. With few exceptions, the stars from non-English speaking countries performed in their native tongues with American supporting casts. Yiddish theatres in New York offered successful adaptations with stars such as Boris Thomashefsky and Jacob Adler. The African-American tragedians Benjamin J. Ford and J. A. Arneaux performed in a number of major cities. It was an era in which foreign and domestic stars who featured Shakespeare at the heart of their repertories were welcomed; even 'lesser' tragedians such as Frederick Warde and Walker Whiteside could tour the land with a Shakespearean repertory and draw audiences.

By the end of the nineteenth century, however, the American Shakespeare tradition, then more than a century old, had fallen into sharp decline, due in part to a cultural shift and modification that radically altered the way in which Shakespeare's plays were perceived by the public. As Lawrence W. Levine demonstrates, Shakespeare, during the first two-thirds of the nineteenth century, had been perceived in America as a popular playwright whose works appealed to all classes of society.[17] Typically the plays were presented with contemporary songs between the acts and comic afterpieces, thus attracting popular as well as 'cultivated' audiences. The heroic style of Shakespearean acting that flourished through mid-century and beyond was in many ways similar to the style of popular melodrama, and thus attracted a broad spectrum of play-goers. The touring star system, which enabled celebrated actors to travel from one local stock company to the next, was facilitated by the existence of a well-known repertory, at the heart of which lay bravura Shakespeare. New York alone saw ten *Hamlets* during the 1857/8 season; it was common for even the smaller cities to witness half a dozen *Lears* and *Othellos* each year.

However, by the end of the civil war a number of tendencies had emerged that led ultimately to a new attitude towards Shakespeare. The advent of more rigid class distinctions and the gradual elimination of the comic afterpieces and popular songs resulted in a growing disparity between 'refined' and 'popular' entertainment. During the eighties and nineties, Americans were reminded time and again that a level of education and cultivation were required to appreciate the plays, an emphasis that soon came to affect their widespread popularity. Audiences, comprised increasingly of the burgeoning middle class, demanded less 'challenging' fare. The advent of the Theatrical Trust, which controlled booking and production for several decades, resulted in a repertory consisting primarily of modern 'entertainments'; by the turn of the century, the prevailing wisdom among most American managers was that Shakespeare had become the province of a 'refined minority' of play-goers and thus held limited appeal to the ticket-buying public.

Although Shakespeare remained a presence in the American theatre, the first decade of the twentieth century, especially, saw a further loss of vitality. Foreign stars such as Johnston Forbes-Robertson continued to tour the land, but many native actors with leanings towards the classics – James O'Neill or Otis Skinner, for example – were discouraged from carrying on the tradition of Edwin Booth and the tragedians of the recent past by the commercial realities of their era. Nonetheless, a small commercial niche still existed for 'culture' and 'tradition', and during this period there emerged a new generation of performers who earned a measure of success by staging and playing Shakespeare in the time-honoured style of their predecessors.

Between 1904 and 1924, E. H. Sothern and Julia Marlowe toured North America regularly with a Shakespearean repertory. The Sothern–Marlowe team earned respect for their competent interpretations, but even the most favourable critics often conceded that they possessed limited skills. They were praised in their early years for their grace and charm, especially in the comedies; however, the passing of time saw a diminishing tolerance for their neo-Victorian performance style.

Similarly dedicated to Shakespeare during the century's first two decades was the Scottish-born actor Robert Bruce Mantell. A robust, muscular figure with a powerful voice, he brought a modified version of the Edwin Forrest–John McCullough acting style into the twentieth century, which greeted his 'old school' methods with surprising enthusiasm. For thirty years he toured the country, bringing Shakespeare to innumerable small cities and towns. Mantell earned respect for his competent craftsmanship; by the late teens, however, his skills had eroded and he was regarded as increasingly old-fashioned by sophisticated audiences and critics. His last Broadway appearance came in 1919; thereafter he kept to the provinces.

During the early 1910s America witnessed the cautious début of innovative British and continental production methods, led by John Corbin's 1910 'Elizabethan' production of *The Winter's Tale* in New York and Margaret Anglin's 1913/14 season of Shakespearean repertory, which featured 'simplified' scenery designed by Livingston Platt. Caution was thrown to the winds, however, when Harley Granville Barker came to New York to revive his production of *A Midsummer Night's Dream* as part of his 1915 repertory season. Barker's staging was praised by the *Times* for its vitality, and for exposing New York audiences for the first time to 'an unreserved application of some of the new art of the theatre to a Shakespearean text' (17 February 1915). The tercentenary of Shakespeare's death brought a flurry of productions, led by Herbert Tree's appearances in *Henry VIII*, *The Merchant of Venice* and *The Merry Wives of Windsor*; the highlight of the festivities, to many critics, was a John Corbin-Louis Calvert production of *The Tempest*, which featured minimal scenery and an uncut text.

In 1916, Walter Hampden, who had served an apprenticeship with Frank Benson's company in England, established his American credentials as a Shakespearean with a highly regarded Caliban in the Corbin–Calvert *Tempest*; two years later he won further acclaim with special Broadway matinée performances as Hamlet and Macbeth. Between 1923 and 1930 he managed his own Broadway theatre, where he presented a number of Shakespeare revivals. Although he was admired throughout his career, many observers felt that he lacked spontaneity and often made Shakespeare 'sound not like poetry, but like verse'.[18] Nonetheless, he was a capable actor-manager whose dedication to poetic drama during the twenties and thirties was almost unique among American performers.

Canada between 1860 and 1920 saw the coming of professional Shakespeare to the western and central regions; local stock companies continued to feature Shakespeare prominently, with or without visiting stars. In 1864, Charles Kean and Ellen Tree played an engagement in Victoria, British Columbia, at the time a city with a population of between 5,000 and 6,000. The rapid expansion of the railways during the post-Confederation era made Canadian cities increasingly accessible to touring American and foreign stars, who often made the journey from Seattle to Victoria and Vancouver, Minneapolis to Winnipeg, and Buffalo to Toronto and Montreal. Throughout the 1870s 'name' tragedians such as Fechter, McCullough and Salvini performed with local companies, as did leading actresses including Adelaide Neilson. From the mid-1880s onwards combination companies featuring entire troupes and their scenery criss-crossed the land. Henry Irving and Ellen Terry came in 1884 on the first of six visits to Canada; they played smaller cities including London and Hamilton, Ontario, along with larger metropolitan venues.

During the late nineteenth century Canada produced two actresses who earned substantial reputations as Shakespearean interpreters: Margaret Anglin, the daughter of the Speaker of the Canadian Parliament, and Julia Arthur. However, both made their careers primarily in the United States. (Canada could also claim two of the first leading ladies of sound-era Hollywood Shakespeare – Mary Pickford, Katharina in the 1929 *Shrew*, and Norma Shearer, Juliet in the 1936 MGM film.) Other performers, such as John Nickinson's daughter, Charlotte Morrison and Albert Tavernier, spent much of their careers in Canada and became local and nationwide favourites. After 1900 Canada saw visits by Forbes-Robertson, Ben Greet and the Stratford-upon-Avon company. During the post-1920 era Maurice Evans, Donald Wolfit and the Old Vic Company offered Shakespeare productions.

The plays continued to be produced regularly by local companies; in 1949, the English actor-manager Earle Grey founded a Shakespeare festival in Toronto that offered productions for a decade. Throughout the first half of the twentieth century, however, major Shakespeare in Canada would remain largely an extension of the American touring circuit.

Shakespearean upheaval and transition: 1920–1945

Few Shakespeare productions in the annals of the American stage have been greeted with the critical acclaim bestowed upon the 1920 John Barrymore–Arthur Hopkins–Robert Edmond Jones *Richard III*. Hopkins and Jones, influenced by Craig, Appia and recent continental practice, and Barrymore, guided by a gifted vocal coach with little tolerance for the 'tragic elevation' that had typified many performances of the Victorian and Edwardian eras, deliberately sought to dream up a production 'more vivid, newer, more audacious, with more imaginative resources' than any which had come before. Jones designed a mood-evoking unit set of the Tower of London, with other locales suggested by easily moved set pieces; his subtle lighting effects facilitated 'cinematic' scene changes, as opposed to the lengthy intervals necessary with productions in the Irving–Tree tradition. Hopkins's austere staging, which dispensed with traditional crowds of supernumeraries, similarly helped to create an atmosphere of foreboding. *Variety* called the production 'a revolution' that 'brings one era in the legitimate [theatre] to a close and begins another'. Barrymore's 'intellectual, stealthy, crafty and subtly malevolent' portrayal – 'the most inspired performance which this generation has seen', according to Heywood Broun of the *Tribune* – was greeted by the critical fraternity as both an 'amazing triumph' and a theatrical changing of the guard.[19]

In 1922, Barrymore, Hopkins and Jones reunited to produce *Hamlet* (fig. 32). Jones's set, inspired by the work of Craig and Leopold Jessner, featured a massive flight of stairs centre stage, beyond which rose a towering Gothic arch. The production featured revolutionary Freudian interpretations of the Queen's Closet scene and Ophelia's mad scene; the Ghost was represented by a shaft of wavering greenish light projected onto a cyclorama beyond the arch. Barrymore's portrayal, 'alive with virility and genius', according to *Theatre Magazine*, was colloquial and restrained, yet forceful and startlingly clear. He brought glamour, athleticism, striking good looks and a profound spirituality to the role, along with speech and movement that were far more natural than those of his immediate predecessors. His performance and the Hopkins–Jones production were greeted as theatrical landmarks; the revival ran for 101 performances, one more than

32 John Barrymore as Hamlet in the 1922 New York production.

Edwin Booth's record. In 1925 Barrymore produced, directed and starred in *Hamlet* at the Haymarket in London, where he repeated his American success. The young John Gielgud and Laurence Olivier saw and later praised Barrymore's portrayal, and Olivier admitted, 'I admired Barrymore and used much of his Hamlet in mine'. Although Barrymore later contemplated a number of Shakespeare stage projects, his post-1925 career was devoted almost exclusively to motion pictures.[20]

Two other Hopkins–Jones Shakespeare productions during the 1920s proved less successful. In February 1921, Hopkins and Jones presented *Macbeth*, starring Lionel Barrymore, John's brother. Alexander Woollcott reflected the critical consensus when he wrote that Barrymore, 'while often good ... never once brushed greatness' (*Times*, 18 February 1921), and audiences and critics were generally shocked at Jones's expressionistic settings, which included three giant silver masks above the heath and disturbingly slanted and distorted arches. The Hopkins–Jones–Ethel Barrymore *Romeo and Juliet* that opened in December 1922 was also a critical failure.

The generation of American stars that emerged during the twenties and thirties did not ignore Shakespeare entirely, but their efforts tended to be sporadic. Alfred Lunt and Lynn Fontanne (whose performances in *Taming of the Shrew* inspired the Cole Porter musical *Kiss Me, Kate*), Katherine Cornell, Helen Hayes and the actress-manager Eva Le Gallienne performed Shakespeare occasionally and at times with great success. Their repertories, however, were comprised almost exclusively of modern plays; audiences of the depression era generally wanted lighter fare. Many of the noteworthy portrayals of this era would come not from American actors but rather from visitors from abroad.

In 1931 the Canadian-born, English-trained actor Raymond Massey played Hamlet on Broadway; building on the 'psychological' example of the Barrymore revival, he recited the Ghost's lines while a dimly lit figure stood mutely by, as if the apparition's presence had emerged from his own subconscious. Norman Bel Geddes's arrangement of stairs, levels, and platforms, influenced by Robert Edmond Jones, was praised for its 'brooding symbolism'. Jones's influence was also evident in the Jo Mielziner setting for John Gielgud's 1936 *Hamlet* in New York, which featured a comparable arrangement of stairs and platforms. The revival, directed by Guthrie McClintic, featured Lillian Gish as Ophelia and Judith Anderson as Gertrude. Gielgud was greeted as the finest interpreter of the role since Barrymore, and the production ran for a record 132 performances. A month after Gielgud opened in *Hamlet*, Leslie Howard opened on Broadway in a rival production. It failed in New York, though it toured successfully. Laurence Olivier made his Broadway Shakespeare début in 1940 as Romeo in a production that augured success; he had triumphed in Hollywood as a romantic leading man, and his soon-to-be wife and co-star, Vivien Leigh, had recently starred in *Gone With the Wind*. The production was a critical disaster, however, and closed after four weeks.

Paradoxically, the English actor who exemplified Shakespearean acting to American audiences of the era was not Gielgud or Olivier, but someone who came to stay. On 10 May 1937, James Agate, on a visit to New York, noted in his diary his surprise that American audiences rated Maurice Evans more highly than Gielgud.[21] Posterity has treated Evans less kindly, but to playgoers of the late thirties and forties he was without question America's leading interpreter of the Bard. Evans first rose to prominence as a Shakespearean at the Old Vic during the 1934/5 season, when he played Richard II, Benedick, Petruchio, Iago and an uncut Hamlet. The following season he was engaged by Guthrie McClintic to play Romeo in America to Katherine Cornell's Juliet; Ralph Richardson made his American Shakespearean début with the company as Mercutio.

In 1937, Evans, with the aid of a wealthy backer, produced *Richard II* on Broadway with Margaret Webster as director (fig. 33). It was the first

33 Maurice Evans as Richard II in the 1937 production.

production of the play to be seen at a major New York venue since Edwin Booth's revival during the 1870s. Evans's portrayal took Broadway by storm; the production ran for 133 performances and toured the country. During the 1938/9 season Evans presented the first uncut *Hamlet* to be seen on Broadway, in which he was again directed by Margaret Webster; the play began at 6.30 and ran for four and a half hours, with a short interval for dinner. In subsequent seasons, he played Falstaff in *I Henry IV*, a cockney Malvolio to Helen Hayes's Viola, and the Thane opposite Judith Anderson's Lady Macbeth. In 1941 Evans became a United States citizen; after America entered the Second World War he enlisted in the army, where he presented *Macbeth* and an abridged *Hamlet* for servicemen in the South Pacific. In 1945 he presented his 'G. I. Hamlet' on Broadway. Thereafter, he devoted his career largely to Shaw, commercial Broadway drama, films and television; in the 1950s he appeared in a number of televised Shakespeare plays.

During the same era that Evans was establishing his reputation on Broadway, the American actor-director Orson Welles enjoyed a similarly meteoric rise to prominence. In 1932, at age sixteen, he played the Ghost and Fortinbras to Micheál MacLiammoir's Hamlet at the Gate Theatre, Dublin;

at eighteen, he was Mercutio on tour with Katherine Cornell's company; at twenty, Tybalt and Chorus on Broadway with Cornell. Soon afterwards, John Houseman offered the twenty-year-old Welles a job as director of the Negro People's Theatre unit of the Federal Theatre Project, where in 1936 he staged a provocative all-black 'Voodoo' *Macbeth* set in early nineteenth-century Haiti. The production, which took place at the Lafayette Theatre in Harlem, was greeted by mixed reviews; nonetheless, it ran for twelve weeks and toured successfully. The following year, under the auspices of the Mercury Theatre, which he co-founded, Welles directed a modern-dress *Julius Caesar* set in Mussolini's Italy, in which he played Brutus. This production was far more successful with the critics. John Mason Brown wrote that 'Of all the many new plays and productions the season has so far revealed, this . . . is by all odds the most exciting, the most imaginative, the most topical, the most awesome, and the most absorbing. The touch of genius is upon it' (*Post*, 12 November 1937).

Indeed, the consensus was that the touch of genius was upon Welles; yet the four Shakespeare plays he subsequently acted on stage yielded mixed results. In 1939, Welles presented *Five Kings*, adapted from *Richard II*, *1 and 2 Henry IV*, *Henry V*, all three parts of *Henry VI* and *Richard III*; Welles played Falstaff with Robert Speaight linking the scenes as Chorus. After a chilly reception in Boston, Washington and Philadelphia it closed on the road. Twelve years later, at Laurence Olivier's invitation, he acted in and directed *Othello* in London to generally good reviews; only Kenneth Tynan weighed in with a largely negative notice. In 1956 he played a six-week engagement as King Lear at City Center in New York, a production that was indifferently received; and in 1960 he appeared in Belfast and Dublin as Falstaff in *Chimes at Midnight* (which he later adapted as a film), based on *1 and 2 Henry IV* and *Henry V*. Welles also made films of *Macbeth* and *Othello*. Although his career was marred by indirection, and he succumbed to the temptation of films that affected the post-Barrymore generation, Welles contributed a provocative body of work to the Shakespearean stage.

The most significant Shakespeare production to appear in America during the years of the Second World War was Paul Robeson's *Othello* (fig. 34). After establishing himself during the late 1920s as a gifted stage and concert performer, Robeson, the son of a former slave, attempted his first Othello at the Savoy Theatre in London in May 1930 with a stellar supporting cast that featured Peggy Ashcroft as Desdemona, Sybil Thorndike as Emilia, and Ralph Richardson as Roderigo. Robeson's portrayal was greeted by mainly favourable reviews, although James Agate was among the dissenters. In 1943, Robeson opened as Othello on Broadway under the auspices of the Theatre Guild. The husband and wife team of José Ferrer and Uta Hagen played Iago

34 Paul Robeson as Othello in the 1943 production.

and Desdemona; Margaret Webster directed and played Emilia. The production was greeted as a theatrical landmark, and the reviews in the New York dailies were generally ecstatic. 'Margaret Webster's production of *Othello*, with Paul Robeson making the Moor the great and terrible figure of tragedy which he has so rarely been on the stage, is in every sense a memorable offering', wrote Howard Barnes of the *Herald Tribune* (20 October 1943). A 17-year-old African-American actor, Earle Hyman, saw the production ten times and recalled years later that 'There was this tremendous excitement – the first African-American onstage to be playing this role. It was incredible for all of us, white and black. Certainly to all of the blacks, he *represented* us. It was a moment of great pride.'[22]

During the 1944/5 season the production toured the nation; overall, it was seen by more than half a million people. In 1959, after a decade in which his career was curtailed when his social activism and leftist political sympathies led to ostracism in America and the revocation of his passport, Robeson reprised his Moor at Stratford-upon-Avon in a production directed by Tony Richardson. In the English-speaking Shakespeare theatre, particularly in America, his Othello was an important harbinger of the multicultural revolution to come.

The modern era: 1945 to the present

The most important phenomena of post-Second World War Shakespeare theatre in North America were the rapid growth of regional Shakespeare festivals and the advent of multicultural casting. At the beginning of the twenty-first century more than a hundred festivals in the United States and Canada were offering Shakespeare on a regular basis. Two of the earliest and most successful festivals, the Oregon Shakespeare Festival in Ashland, Oregon, and the Old Globe in San Diego, California, trace their origins to 1935, although neither festival became fully professional until the 1950s. Both festivals feature main stages modelled after Elizabethan theatres; in these and in many other regional North American Shakespeare festivals, William Poel's vision of a return to the staging methods of Shakespeare's day found regular practical applications (see also chapter 5 above).

By the mid-fifties, major professional Shakespeare festivals had emerged that attracted top-flight stars. The American Shakespeare Theatre Festival in Stratford, Connecticut, began producing summer Shakespeare in 1955 and offered productions regularly until 1979 and sporadically thereafter until 1982, when financial difficulties forced the company's operations to cease. During its peak years the company attracted major actors such as Katharine Hepburn, Christopher Plummer, Morris Carnovsky, Earle Hyman and Jessica Tandy. More successful still was the Stratford, Ontario Shakespeare Festival, which began in 1953 when Tyrone Guthrie directed Alec Guinness in *Richard III* and *All's Well That Ends Well* in a temporary tent theatre. Subsequently the festival became one of Canada's major cultural institutions. A noteworthy production during the early years was Michael Langham's acclaimed *Henry V*, with French-Canadian actors playing the French. The festival often attracted major stars such as Zoe Caldwell, Christopher Plummer (fig. 35), Brian Bedford and Maggie Smith; a number of important Canadian actors including William Hutt spent much of their careers there.

The most significant Shakespeare producing organisation to emerge in New York during the post-war era was the New York Shakespeare Festival (NYSF). Founded on the Lower East Side in 1954 by Joseph Papp, the organisation's aim was to establish a summer Shakespeare festival that would bring popularly conceived productions to a broad, multicultural audience. The massive post-war migration of blacks and Hispanics to American cities, particularly New York, had changed the demographic composition of American society; Papp was determined to bring Shakespeare to 'dispossessed' audiences. For several years the festival offered admission-free outdoor productions in different locations and finally found a permanent summer home in

35 Joy Lafleur, Douglas Campbell and Christopher Plummer
in the Stratford, Ontario production of *Hamlet*, 1957.

Central Park. After 1961 plays were performed during the summer in the
Delacorte Theatre, and after 1967 year-round at the Public Theatre in the
East Village.

Within a decade of its creation the NYSF had established itself as one of
North America's most influential production organisations, offering vital and
at times irreverent productions that often featured a blend of Shakespeare
and sociocultural awareness. The festival offered opportunities for black,
Hispanic and Asian actors to perform Shakespeare in unprecedented numbers, both in lead and supporting roles. James Earl Jones, Earle Hyman
(fig. 36), Raul Julia, Randal Duk Kim and André Braugher were but a few of
the minority actors who performed there with distinction. In 1987 the NYSF
began an ambitious 'Shakespeare Marathon', which offered all of the Bard's
plays over the next six years. Since its inception, the overall quality of the festival's productions has tended to be erratic; plays have often been marred by
inconsistent performances and directorial inventiveness gone awry. However,
the 'anything goes' atmosphere also produced a number of strikingly original productions and portrayals, and gifted American actors such as George
C. Scott, Meryl Streep, Stacy Keach and Kevin Kline have been given the

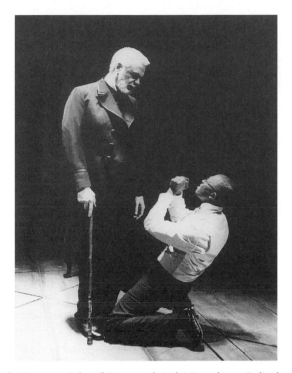

36 Earle Hyman as John of Gaunt and André Braugher as Bolingbroke in
the New York Shakespeare Festival production of *Richard II*, 1994.

opportunity to demonstrate their skill in leading roles. The NYSF has provided American directors and actors with a venue to experiment freely with
new interpretations in a non-commercial atmosphere; its productions have
brought Shakespeare to hundreds of thousands of New Yorkers who might
otherwise have not experienced the plays.

The era following the Second World War was also characterised by the
continuing flow of eminent performers and noteworthy productions from
abroad. During the 1945/6 season Laurence Olivier and Ralph Richardson
came to America with the Old Vic company, which offered a repertory that
included *1 and 2 Henry IV*; Olivier played Hotspur and Shallow, while
Richardson reprised his acclaimed Falstaff. John Gielgud returned in his
one-man Shakespearean *tour de force*, *The Ages of Man*, in 1957. During
the 1959/60 season Gielgud appeared on Broadway and on national tour
as Benedick, and in 1964 he directed Richard Burton's 'rehearsal clothes'
Hamlet, which opened in Toronto before moving to Broadway. Peter Brook's
visit in 1970 with his experimental 'white box' production of *A Midsummer
Night's Dream* was as well received as Barker's provocative revival more
than half a century earlier. Tours by the Royal Shakespeare Company and

the Royal National Theatre – frequent visitors to American shores – as well as Kenneth Branagh's Renaissance Theatre Company and numerous non-English language productions, such as Ingmar Bergman's *Hamlet* and Ariane Mnouchkine's *Richard II,* exposed North American audiences to the latest British and continental trends in production.

Throughout the post-war era North America has witnessed performances by native actors that might compare favourably with nearly any given in that time by visiting English luminaries: George C. Scott's Richard III, Meryl Streep's Katharina and Isabella, Stacy Keach's Hamlet, André Braugher's Henry V, to name but a few. Such performances, however, have been sporadic. Like others of their generations, and indeed, of the generations since Barrymore, these leading actors have realised that film and television can provide a steady livelihood for even the most artistically minded performers in an era when Broadway and the commercial theatre have become increasingly the province of musicals, comedies, light dramas and foreign imports. As a result, many gifted contemporary performers have spent much of their careers away from the stage.

In the early years of the post-war era, too, many American actors 'unfitted' themselves for Shakespeare due to the widespread influence of the Actors Studio, which stressed 'Method' emotion and psychological realism – techniques ideally suited to modern naturalistic plays and film acting but in many ways antithetical to Shakespeare performance. Studio members such as Marlon Brando became paradigms for a generation of performers in much the same way as Forrest and Booth had been a century earlier.

By the late sixties the Method's influence had begun to wane, and the last quarter of the twentieth century saw an increased emphasis on classical technique in North American training programmes. Although North American performers during the latter part of the century found a lack of consistent opportunity to act Shakespeare on Broadway or at commercial venues, where an actor might receive national and international attention, this same period saw an extraordinary increase in the number of productions on a regional level; actors in unprecedented numbers were given a chance to appear in Shakespeare in non-profit regional and festival theatres.

North America during the second half of the twentieth century did not produce an actor whose skill and cultural impact might be said to rival that of Booth or Barrymore; however, the Canadian actor Christopher Plummer, who performed Shakespeare with distinction at all three Stratfords, on Broadway, and in a televised *Hamlet,* earned a reputation as a gifted interpreter whose abilities compare favourably with those of his eminent British contemporaries. Brian Bedford, like Maurice Evans an English actor who made his career almost exclusively in North America, acted Shakespeare

regularly and with distinction at Stratford, Ontario, at the Shakespeare Theatre in Washington, DC, and occasionally in New York. The African-American actor Earle Hyman played leading Shakespeare roles from the early 1950s onwards, in New York, in regional theatre, and in Scandinavia, earning a reputation as one of the most accomplished American classical actors of his generation.

In a sense, Shakespeare in North America has come full circle in its two-and-a-half-century history; the flourishing regional festivals are in many ways analogous to the local stock companies that prospered in the early days of American independence and beyond. The playwright whose works ruled the North American stage, with occasional lulls, for two and a half centuries, today reaches a greater number of play-goers than ever before.

NOTES

1 My intention in this chapter is to survey the major performers, productions and developments in the English-language Shakespeare theatre in the United States and Canada during its first two and a half centuries; I have deliberately excluded non-English-language performance with the exception of a few visiting and native stars who made their mark.

2 Holcroft to Cooper, 26 August 1796, quoted in William Dunlap, *History of the American Theatre*, 2 vols. (1833; reprinted New York: Burt Franklin, 1963), I, 349.

3 'Stagestruck': Hugh F. Rankin, *The Theatre in Colonial America* (Chapel Hill: University of North Carolina Press, 1960), 42; 'sett': New York *Mercury*, 2 July 1753; 'idle': Dunlap, *History of the American Theatre*, I, 31.

4 Alexander Graydon, *Memoirs of a Life, Passed Chiefly in Pennsylvania* (Harrisburgh, PA: John Wyrth, 1811), 76–8.

5 Rankin, *Theatre in Colonial America*, 191.

6 'Handsome' and 'full': James H. Hackett, *Notes and Comments Upon Certain Plays and Actors of Shakespeare* (New York: Carleton, 1868), 118–19; Noah M. Ludlow, *Dramatic Life As I Found It* (1880; reprinted New York: Benjamin Blom, 1966), 234.

7 *Virginia Gazette*, 12 June 1752.

8 John Bernard, *Retrospections of America, 1797–1811* (1887; reprinted New York: Benjamin Blom, 1969), 353. Yashdip S. Bains, *English Canadian Theatre, 1765–1826* (New York: Peter Lang, 1998), 199–200.

9 William R. Alger, *Life of Edwin Forrest*, 2 vols. (Philadelphia: Lippincott, 1877), I, 142. See also chapter 3 above.

10 Ludlow, *Dramatic Life*, 724; 'fire': Whitman quoted in David S. Reynolds, *Walt Whitman's America* (New York: Vintage Books, 1996), 159.

11 Richard Moody, *Edwin Forrest: First Star of the American Stage* (New York: Knopf, 1960), 398.

12 *The Times*, 3 January 1846; William Winter, *The Wallet of Time*, 2 vols. (New York: Moffat, Yard, 1913), I, 176.

13 New York *Tribune*, 26 October 1875.

14 Winter, *Wallet of Time*, I, 557.

15 ibid., II, 138.

16 Marvin Felheim, *The Theatre of Augustin Daly* (Cambridge, MA: Harvard University Press, 1956), 16.

17 Lawrence W. Levine, *Highbrow/Lowbrow* (Cambridge, MA: Harvard University Press, 1988).

18 Brooks Atkinson, *Broadway*, revised edn (New York: Macmillan, 1974), 385.

19 'More vivid': Robert Edmond Jones, unpublished notes, Wesleyan University; *Variety*, 12 March 1920; 'intellectual, stealthy' and 'amazing': New York *Evening World*, 8 March 1920; 'inspired': New York *Tribune*, 8 March 1920.

20 *Theatre Magazine* (January 1923), 21; Laurence Olivier, *On Acting* (New York: Simon & Schuster, 1986), 98.

21 Herbert Van Thal (ed.), *James Agate: an Anthology* (New York: Hill & Wang, 1961), 152.

22 Earle Hyman interview with the author, 9 April 1999.

14

JOHN GILLIES, RYUTA MINAMI,
RURU LI, POONAM TRIVEDI

Shakespeare on the stages of Asia

While the man in the street is unperturbed at the thought of Shakespeare being performed some 400 years after his death, he is astonished to hear that Shakespeare is performed in Asia (never mind 400 years after his death). Commonality of language, culture, history, country and 'race' conspire to naturalise Shakespeare's otherwise highly 'unnatural' cultural longevity. By the same token, the sheer discontinuity and remoteness represented by 'Asia' exposes not just the longevity of Shakespeare but the workings of cultural value itself. It seems not just strange for Shakespeare to be performed in Asia, but somehow unfit. 'Part of an Englishman's constitution' (as Jane Austen put it), is Shakespeare therefore part of an Asian constitution too?

For a somewhat different reason, the notion of an 'Asian Shakespeare' may well seem odd to a Japanese, Chinese or Indian. In terms of what culture in the geographic domain of Asia does 'Asia' make sense? No one particular culture, of course. As Edward Said has suggested, 'Asia' is a geographic fiction rather than a life world. The difficulty is not got round by substituting the grouping of 'India', 'China' and 'Japan'. The very bracketing of these countries bespeaks an implicitly Orientalist standpoint. Nor is a counter-paradigm – such as the post-colonial – much better. While post-colonialism suits and is to some extent tailored to the Indian experience, it cannot simply be stretched to fit the Japanese or Chinese experience. Like Orientalism and Asianism, post-colonialism is a perspective rather than a historical experience. It cannot without severe loss of cogency be applied to historical experiences and discourses remote from those within which it has taken shape.

How, then, do we even begin to consider 'Shakespeare on the stages of Asia'? The positive point to be emphasised in this collection of negatives is that no single paradigm of cultural production can be invoked independently of the very different performance practices to be considered. Shakespeare's assimilation into India is not a pattern for his assimilation into China and Japan. Nor is Shakespeare's assimilation into China a variant of his assimilation into Japan. While in some ways alike, these histories do not really fit together. They do not share the same discursive space, the same analytic imperatives, the same values or voice. In each case, the story is significantly different. We begin, then, with three stories and inevitably find ourselves selecting exemplary productions from each country. The productions will not so much be exemplary of given countries as exemplary of their resistance to translation into some wider domain of cultural Asianism.

Japan

In James Brandon's influential account, there are three Shakespeares in Japan: one localised, one canonical and one intercultural and postmodern.[1] As the third of these Shakespeares dates from the 1970s, and is essentially a more self-conscious and multicultural version of the first, this leaves only two. Paradoxically, Shakespeare's first steps on Japanese soil were as a local, in the sense of being a cultural hybrid. Shakespeare was indigenised not just in terms of theatre genre, which was mostly *Kabuki* at the earliest stage, the popular indigenous theatre, involving speech, song and dance, but also in terms of source and cultural motive. The source of these early localisations was the pioneering translations and adaptations of Lamb's *Tales From Shakespeare* in the Meiji period (1868–1912), when Japan opened its doors to the West and modernity. The cultural motive emerges clearly from one of the most impressive early examples. *Sakuradoki Zeni no yononoka* (Life is as fragile as a cherry blossom in a world of money) was an 1885 *Kabuki* adaptation of *The Merchant of Venice*.[2] What was adapted here was less Shakespeare in the sense of an acknowledged cultural authority, than an apparently generic western narrative of coping with a money economy (as suggested by the fact that another source was Edward Bulwer-Lytton's play *Money*). In terms of cultural production, *Zeni* can be seen as an attempt to fashion a positive image of adaptation to western monetary values, one that meant retaining a traditionalised (if highly artificial) image of itself. Accordingly, the usury of the Shylock-figure (Gohei) is rejected as being un-Japanese, while the enterprise of the Bassanio-figure (Shôtarô) is applauded. (For all his apparent reading of the self-improvement classic, *Self-Help*, 1859, by Samuel Smiles,[3] Shôtarô shows an old-fashioned sense of piety belonging more to the pre-western Edo period than the contemporary Meiji period.) The sheer unselfconsciousness of this adaptation emerges in what must have seemed a self-evident improvement to the casket scene, where the winning casket is not lead but iron (a more useful metal).

For all the inventiveness of this particular *Kabuki* adaptation, *Kabuki* finally proved an unreceptive host. While Shakespeare's text could be adapted or translated, his world was simply too foreign to the traditional dramatic 'worlds' of *Kabuki* to offer purchase to local performance conventions or initiative.[4] Accordingly Shakespeare was next acted in a non-traditional performance mode – that of *Shimpa* or 'new school theatre', staging contemporary events and western plays in adaptation. In 1903, *Hamlet* and *Othello* were performed under Otojiro Kawakami,[5] an actor-impresario recently returned from a tour of America and Europe. *Othello* in particular was a highly inventive localisation (Shakespeare's Moor being translated into a sun-tanned native of a rural Japanese province, and his Cyprus being transposed to Taiwan – then a Japanese colony). *Shimpa* proved a viable approach until the 1920s, when it was displaced by the first wave of 'canonical' Shakespeare.

Unlike localised Shakespeare, canonical Shakespeare was always (until relatively recently) foreign. At its root was the profoundly different cultural act of translation. Where adaptation meant a blithe disregard for accuracy and an indifference to the text as a source of independent cultural authority, translation meant a concern for accuracy and a deference to the authority of the text. Canonical Shakespeare was at once too foreign for the indigenous performance genres, and too closed to local initiative (or creative misprision) for *Shimpa*. Essentially it could only be done justice by a generically foreign performance idiom, an echo of the nineteenth-century performances staged by visiting western troupes at the Gaiety Theatre for the benefit of the western residents of Yokohama. One of a privileged minority of local intellectual visitors to the Gaiety in the 1890s was the scholar and theatre amateur, Shoyo Tsubouchi, whose translation of the Shakespeare canon was popularly available by the 1930s (it should be noted that the first Chinese and Korean translations – the work of resident students – were from Tsubouchi rather than from English). Partly influenced by the Shakespeare he had seen at the Gaiety, Tsubouchi staged *Hamlet* in 1911. Not only was this one of the first local performances of a translated text, but it was the first to employ actresses for the female roles.[6] While translation-based performances gradually came to supplant adaptation-based performances in the 1920s, they also led to a decline in stagings as such. By the 1930s Shakespeare was read rather than acted.

Shakespeare's next incarnation on the Japanese stage was in the form of *Shingeki*, or 'new drama', which was modern European realism transplanted to Japan. This differed from *Shimpa* in its more educated grasp of the text, its appreciation of western naturalism, and its dedication to the modernising ethic of writers such as Ibsen and Chekhov. For these reasons, *Shingeki* Shakespeare was an anomaly, the intellectual and political dynamism of *Shingeki* being replaced by a deadening equation of naturalism with textual authority. Tsubouchi's Shakespeare productions can be regarded as a blend of *Shingeki* and *Kabuki*. They suggest the former in their faithfulness and use of western costuming and stage design, and the latter in their vocal delivery (the style and phraseology of the translations was based on *Kabuki*). Interrupted by the war, this genre reached its apogee in Tsuneari Fukuda's production of *Hamlet* in 1955, a dutiful replication of a canonically English (and notionally authentic) production witnessed in London in 1953. Translations of Shakespeare continued (Fukuda's among them), but Tsubouchi's translation generally held the stage until the appearance of a new translation by Yushi Odashima in the 1970s. Odashima succeeded not by being more faithful than Tsubouchi, but by being less faithful. Specifically, his translation was colloquial and hospitable to the idioms of the contemporary young theatre movement. It worked not by giving greater access to Shakespeare's meaning, but by freeing the contemporary Japanese voice and personality. Accordingly, Odashima's translation was acted as much as it was read. In the 1970s, Norio Deguchi staged the entire canon according to Odashima in a small basement venue in downtown Tokyo called the *Jean Jean*. The stagings however were not canonical but as indigenous as the indigenous theatre genres themselves. Shakespeare had become a native again. But this was only because urban Japanese audiences were effectively cosmopolitan.[7]

Since the 1970s, and particularly since the opening of the Tokyo Globe in 1988, Japan has become a fixture on the international touring theatre circuit. Shakespeare is seen performed by an indefinite number of leading international companies. In addition to Deguchi, moreover, Shakespeare was performed by a new cadre of directors from the postmodernist *Shogekijo Undo* (or 'Little Theatre') movement. In the productions of Yukio Ninagawa and Tadashi Suzuki, Shakespeare came to seem ever more indigenous, though somewhat less cosmopolitan. In both cases Shakespeare is performed in conspicuously indigenous performance styles: not *Kabuki* or *Noh* as such, but a disconcerting pastiche of those styles. In perhaps the most famous of these, the 1980 *Macbeth* of Yukio Ninagawa, 'traditional' (medieval) Japan was evoked through costume, setting and the generally *Kabuki*-like deportment of the actors (only one of whom – a 'witch' – had been *Kabuki* trained; fig. 37). Implicitly criticising this approach, Suzuki aspires towards what he calls a 'solid' indigenous performance style – a style based on his own actor-training method, itself based on *Kabuki* and *Noh*.[8]

Neither kind of indigeneity has found favour with Deguchi, however (for whom they are artificial and backward looking), nor with the much younger director, Hideki Noda, who prefers a less portentously Japanesque and markedly more lively performance language. A writer as well as a performer, Noda stages both adaptations and translations. An example of the former is his *Sandaime Richâdo* (1990; fig. 38), an extremely free-wheeling adaptation of *Richard III* partially inspired by Josephine Tey's *The Daughter*

37 *Macbeth*, directed by Yukio Ninagawa, Nissei Theatre, Japan, 1980. The witches are played in *Kabuki* style.

of Time. Here Shakespeare is put on trial for having turned Richard into a villain. An example of the latter is Noda's 1992 production of *A Midsummer Night's Dream* (fig. 39). Here Theseus's court became a restaurant, the lovers were cooks (fighting with kitchen knives) and love itself a taste for the local cuisine ('Beautiful Soboro, you're as beautiful and transparent as *shirataki*. My bosom is pierced through like *yakitori*').[9] In a 1992 production of the same play, Deguchi too found a way of being truly local without being Japanesque.[10] Set in a school, Shakespeare's play is framed within an autobiographical dream play in which Deguchi represents himself as director encountering himself as a schoolchild. As the director falls asleep (apparently in a fit of despair) a small winged figure dressed as a schoolboy of the immediate post-war years appears to him, takes his hand and leads him into the world of the play – which is also the world of his own past, his own unconscious, his own dreaming. The director becomes Theseus and then Oberon. The schoolchild becomes Puck. More than private symbolism is on offer. The local past is thickly rather than thinly evoked. It is available to the audience as well as the director. And it is wittily grafted to a deep reading of the play. Thus Bottom – originally recognisable as a penniless returned soldier-cum-black-marketeer – becomes upwardly mobile as his 'play is preferred', and is last seen in the uniform of an American NCO.

38 The trial scene from *Sandaime Richâdo*, directed by Hideki Noda, 1990.

39 Hermia and Lysander, *A Midsummer Night's Dream*, directed by Hideki Noda, Nissei Theatre, 1992.

Contemporary Japanese Shakespeare is so various as to be hard to charac-terise in anything other than negative terms. The unselfconscious localism of the Meiji adaptations is no longer possible, nor the unreflective imitativeness of *Shingeki*. The last two decades have seen an outpouring of eclectically in-digenised Shakespeares in both translation and adaptation, featuring actors from *Kabuki*, *Noh* and *Kyogen*. Unlike the Meiji localisations, these tend to be reflective, sometimes even self-ironising (such as Yasunari Takahashi's *The Braggart Samurai*, a *Kyogen* version of *The Merry Wives of Windsor*). *Shingeki* too has become culturally self-reflective. In 1991 the *Seinen-za* com-pany staged the script of Kawakami's 1903 *Othello*, and in a specially written induction depicted *Shingeki* actors actively preferring the adaptation to the translation. Irony also marks the plays of Hisashi Inoue, whose *Shakespeare in the Twelfth Year of the Tempô era* contains the following lines:

> Had it not been for Shakespeare,
> The *Shingeki* world, which has produced few original plays,
> Would be quite at a loss.
>
> Shakespeare is a rice chest, a source of income.
> As long as he is with us, we will never starve.
> Shakespeare is a rice granary, a substantial food source.[11]

In a sense, Shakespeare has fed not just *Shingeki* but the avant-garde 'Little Theatre' movement as well. The most enduring influence on contemporary production is probably the one-time 'Little Theatre' director, Yukio Nina-gawa. With his 1998 *Romeo and Juliet*, Ninagawa launched his Sainokuni Shakespeare Series, a project to stage the complete canon in thirteen years. Ten productions have appeared so far.

Finally we should note a trend towards inter-Asian Shakespeare. This is best exemplified by the 1997 *King Lear* by the Singaporean director Ong Ken Sen (in the adaptation of the Japanese playwright Rio Kishida) and the adaptation *Desdemona* (2000) by Rio Kishida. In these productions actors from at least six different Asian traditional performing genres are brought together to play opposite each other in their traditional idioms. Thus in the former, Lear is played by a *Noh* master in *Noh* against a Goneril played by a *Dan* master in *Jingju* ('Peking Opera'). Impressive though they are, it is hard to account for the effect of these performances. In one sense they speak to pan-Asian concerns (the *Lear* being concerned with the loss of parental and patriarchal authority in Asian Pacific countries). In another, they create a sense of shared performance heritage – shared in the sense of being non-western and pre-modern. They speak to no constituency (Ong's boast is that no audience member anywhere could possibly be in the position of cultural 'insider' in such a performance). They stylise, but in a troublingly fragmented and alienated way. They are, so to speak, 'transindigenous' – a manifest and deliberate contradiction in terms.

China

In some ways Shakespeare's introduction to China is a carbon copy of his introduction to Japan. As in Japan, *The Merchant of Venice* was an early favourite, being adapted in 1913 and performed in Shanghai under the title, *The Contract of Flesh*.[12] Here, too, the source was a local translation/adaptation of Lamb's *Tales From Shakespeare*. On such grounds, James Brandon draws a close analogy between the Chinese and Japanese experiences of Shakespeare.[13] However, in view of the gulf separating the political fortunes of these two countries over much of the subsequent century, it may be wise not to push the analogy too far. While it is true that there is a similar tension in China between indigenous theatres and introduced western texts (such as Shakespeare), the meaning of that tension is very different in each case. To begin with, the drive towards modernisation and westernisation in China (the force behind the introduction of western texts and dramatic forms) is vastly complicated by the victory of communism and the establishment in 1949 of the People's Republic of China (one of the most profoundly transformative events in China's 5,000-year history). Much of Shakespeare's history in China is in fact the history of his assimilation within the People's Republic.

Notwithstanding, the two major performative modes in which Shakespeare appears in China – *Huaju* (or 'spoken drama' on the modern western model) and *Xiqu* (a generic term for all 300 varieties of indigenous theatre) – predate the People's Republic. Not unlike *Shingeki* in Japan, *Huaju* (the introduced western theatre genre) tended to be associated with political and social modernisation. Again as in Japan, western theatre was adopted in the first place out of a perception that indigenous theatre genres had been all but overwhelmed – or at best marginalised – by the tidal wave of modernisation (in China's case exacerbated by political disintegration, invasion and revolution). To begin with, therefore, the contrast between modern and traditional modes was even starker in China. Unlike *Kabuki,* which had energetically generated new repertoires and kept abreast of social development up to about the 1920s, *Xiqu* seemed irremediably tied to the past by a static and antiquated repertoire reflective of traditional court institutions and culture.[14]

Here, however, is where the two experiences of Shakespeare begin to diverge. In neither theatrical form – *Huaju* nor *Xiqu* – is Shakespeare registered as an object of cultural 'anxiety of influence'. Unlike in Japan, where

Shakespeare had – so to speak – stolen into the *Shingeki* repertoire as a sheep in wolf's clothing (to remain bleating long after the wolf had lost his teeth), in China, Shakespeare exerted a quickening influence on the most important and progressive dramatist-intellectuals of the early to mid-century. Both Tian Han (1898–1968) and Cao Yu (1910–96) allowed that Shakespeare had helped them create a truly modern drama.[15] Neither conforms to the over-dutiful textualism of Tsubouchi. Neither made a translation of the entire canon. In addition to translating some fourteen plays from Japanese and English originals, Tian Han wrote some sixty *Huaju* plays, some twenty *Xiqu* scripts and some 800 poems (including the text of the national anthem). Scholarship and theatrical vitality were also combined in Cao Yu, perhaps the most significant Chinese playwright of the twentieth century (*The Thunderstorm* is a modern classic and is translated into English). In 1942 Cao produced what is still regarded as the most elegant Chinese translation of a Shakespeare play (*Romeo and Juliet*), and carried the quickening influence of the translation into his next Chinese play *The Family*.

In addition, there is a venerable association between Shakespeare and progressive Chinese patriotism. In 1916 a loose adaptation or mixture of *Hamlet* and *Macbeth* was staged by Gu Wuwei under the title of *The Usurper of State Power* as a veiled attack on the recent attempt by Yuan Shikai to overthrow the republic and install himself as emperor. Gu was imprisoned and saved from death only with Yuan's fall from power. In 1942 *Hamlet* was staged by Jiao Juyin in a Confucian temple in Sichuan province to which the government had retreated from the advancing Japanese. Jiao saw in Hamlet 'a mirror and a lesson for us Chinese'. In one pregnant moment, Hamlet walked slowly away into the depths of the temple after passing up the opportunity of killing a praying Claudius. Nicety and delay in the face of outrage was shown to be fatal. The war brought about another mythic connection between Shakespeare and Chinese patriotism. The first translation of the canon (albeit not quite in its entirety) took place under Japanese bombing. Working at nights and in conditions of extreme difficulty and eventually of peril, Zhu Shenghao translated some two-thirds of Shakespeare's plays between 1935 to 1944 in a heroic assertion of Chinese cultural pride.

Zhu's translation provided the scripts for most subsequent *Huaju* productions. Yet notwithstanding the heroic context from which it sprang, *Huaju* Shakespeare has had quite a different political character. Though to some extent moulded by the aesthetic and political modernism of 'spoken drama', *Huaju* Shakespeare is silently at odds with its notional genre due to the very revolution to which *Huaju* owed its success and influence within modern China. With the advent of the People's Republic in 1949, all artistic and dramatic activity became guided by the aesthetic protocols established by Mao at the Yan'an forum on Literature and Art a few years earlier.[16] Among much else, these dictated that all artistic activity should be relevant to the masses. Shakespeare qualified both by association with *Huaju* and by virtue of the enthusiasm he had once inspired in Marx and Engels, for whom he was paradigmatic of an art that was historically engaged without being one-dimensionally programmed. (In a particularly influential passage, Marx criticised a revolutionary play text for turning historical characters into mouthpieces of the author's revolutionary agenda, rather than – like Shakespeare – allowing them to speak for themselves.[17]) Paradoxically however, Shakespeare's very passport into the People's Republic would allow him to become slyly, persistently and deliberately 'irrelevant' in a way that is quite unlike anything in the post-Kottian West (with its 'relevance-at-all-costs'). In short, *Huaju* Shakespeare has long been valued as a haven of aesthetic freedom in an over-politicised aesthetic landscape.

Xu Xiaozhong's 1980 production of *Macbeth* at the Central Academy of Drama in Beijing is a good example. Only a few years removed from the Cultural Revolution (during which Shakespeare had been proscribed along with all other western drama and literature), this production needed to be unpolitical in the way that Jan Kott needed to be political. Safety was a virtue in the way that danger is often (though emptily) said to be in the West. To this end, Xu warily cited Engels's warnings against turning characters into mouthpieces. Setting and costumes must have seemed safely remote from contemporary Chinese experience and concerns. The set was cardboard-medieval, and the costumes doublet-and-hose (set off with blond wigs and prosthetic noses) – all a legacy of Xu's training under Russian teachers in the 1950s. Beneath this plodding imitativeness however – beneath the studied irrelevance – lurked some interesting correspondences. Xu's Macbeth was a hero who had blundered off course, a giant stumbling through a sea of blood. The resemblance to Mao must have been even more provoking, given that the ostensible source was Marx's description of Louis Napoleon.[18] Xu did not have to work to emphasise the moral (it was there for the taking). He worked in order to adorn the tale, to deepen his understanding of the text – and thereby (and secondarily) his understanding of the moment.

A mere decade after this (1980) – but in another political and stylistic world – Lin Zhaohua staged *Hamlet* in Beijing. Shocked by the collapse of the student protest at Tianamen Square earlier in the year, Lin might easily have opted for 'relevance'. Instead, like Xu, he used the situation to covertly explore the text (rather than vice versa). Lin's Hamlet was not the Renaissance giant – the proto-revolutionary culture hero – of Engels's imagination, but a more ordinary figure tortured by relativism and loss of meaning

40 *Huaju Hamlet*, directed by Lin Zhaohua, Beijing, 1990. The final transformation, the stabbing of Claudius. Hamlet and Claudius rush to meet over the metal bar. They are locked in hatred, then Claudius falls to the ground. But the actor who joins the corpses is the person who has been playing Hamlet only a moment ago. The body on the ground is Gertrude.

('Socialism with Chinese characteristics' was no compensation for the Cultural Revolution[19]). Disconcertingly, the actors playing Hamlet, Claudius and Polonius all exchanged roles at various moments of the production, while predominantly remaining identified with a single character. What this meant was that the Claudius actor (Ni Dahong) spoke Hamlet's 'O that this too too solid flesh' soliloquy, finally going on to die as Hamlet just after stabbing the Hamlet actor (at this point Claudius) at the culmination of the duel. What was the point of this device? The answer to this question is interestingly relative. Admiring the pared down modernism of the design (not unreminiscent of his own style), the prominent Japanese Shakespeare director, Deguchi, saw only a gimmick. What Deguchi failed to appreciate however, was the intimately Chinese resonance of the production, the depth at which it answered its contemporary moment. For Lin, Hamlet was unredeemed, his existential malaise untransfigured by tragedy. Hamlet's existential agonies were thus also Claudius's. Each character was equally agonised and equally unsanctified. Ni Dahong played Hamlet within the same emotional range and moral spectrum that he played Claudius. The difference between Lin's Shakespeare and the relevant (or Kottian) brand expected by Deguchi is that relevance is more private and indirect in Lin's case. Rather than a public statement, it is effectively indistinguishable from a politically un-entailed exploration of the text.

Indigenous (or *Xiqu*) performances of Shakespeare are no less paradigm-bending than the *Huaju* tradition. Instead of the quasi-post-colonial angst that Brandon finds between the Shakespearean text and the indigenous Asian performance genre (best exemplified by *Kabuki*), there is evidence of just the opposite in the case of indigenous Chinese adaptations of Shakespeare. To grasp this, it is necessary to understand something of the position of *Xiqu* in contemporary Chinese culture. Earlier in the century *Xiqu* was scorned by progressive intellectuals such as Lu Xun for its cultural and political backwardness (Lu Xun was infuriated that condemned men would go to their deaths with snatches of *Xiqu* arias on their lips). Paradoxically, however, *Xiqu* was promoted and protected by the state at the institution of the People's Republic (rescuing ancient forms such as *Kunju* from extinction). Not all intellectuals shared Lu Xun's scorn for *Xiqu*. Recognising its cultural inveteracy, many tried to resuscitate *Xiqu* by controlled injections of Shakespeare. In 1947 (five years after his *Hamlet*) Jiao Juyin staged a Peking Opera (*Jingju*) version of *Romeo and Juliet* under the title of *The Moulding of Love*. Bringing Shakespeare to *Jingju* (rather than *Jingju* to Shakespeare), Jiao aerated the *Jingju* conventions by adapting them to the unusual material. At the same time, the unusual material was not allowed to smother *Jingju* resource and inventiveness for the reason that it was adapted rather than translated. Thus, the Capulet ball was the pretext for a martial arts display, yet not such as to have been entirely familiar to the *Jingju* actors, who were obliged to wield real swords – the added weight of which forced changes to conventional movement and gesture. In a sense what Jiao had done was merely to return *Jingju* to an earlier and more culturally healthy phase in which (like other *Xiqu* genres) it flourished by borrowing freely from other genres.

A more spectacular recent example of this kind of Shakespearean fertilization of *Xiqu* is the *Kunju Macbeth* of Huang Zuolin, performed at the inaugural Chinese Shakespeare festival of 1986. While (again) the Shakespearean material was adapted rather than translated, there was a genuine and extraordinarily rich sense of cultural dialogue. Huang approached both Shakespeare and *Kunju* from the position of a Brecht scholar. Each alike was distanced and – appropriate perhaps to a Sinified tragedy and a tragedised *Kunju* – touched by the uncanny. *Kunju* was crossed not just with Shakespeare but with a multitude of other indigenous genres. Thus the witches were played by generic martial clown figures (two of whom squat grotesquely in the *Kunju* convention of *aizi bu*). Exemplifying the teasing equivocation of Shakespeare's witches, they wear grotesque masks borrowed from the genre of *Chuanju* on the backs of their heads – for which there is no precedent in *Chuanju*.

41 *Much Ado About Nothing*, directed by Jiang Weiguo. The merry war between Bicui (Beatrice) and Bai Lidi (Benedick) is presented in *Duichang* style, a duet in the form of question and answer or statement and comment.

The same festival witnessed an adaptation of *Much Ado About Nothing* to another of the 300 extant traditional performance genres in China, *Huangmeixi*, or 'the theatre of yellow plums' native to southern Anhui and Hubei.[20] Having emerged more recently than *Kunju* (c. 1820), it is also far more 'common', having arisen from local tea-picking ballads and evolved via popular song and variety show. Accordingly, the director, Jiang Weiguo, felt that it was suited to comedy rather than tragedy. Here, Shakespeare's story was translated to an unspecified time in a remote border region of ancient China, where the majority *Han* people were imagined living cheek-by-jowl with minority peoples of un-Chinese habits. The context made the female insubordination of Shakespeare's Beatrice (Bicui) comprehensible in Chinese terms (Bicui's 'wildness' was wittily betokened by a feathered headdress suggestive of bordering tribes). Surprisingly, perhaps, in view of its humble origins, *Huangmeixi* gleefully accommodated the formal exchanges of wit between Beatrice and Benedick. Thus, employing the native convention of the *Duichang* (a two-person aria with alternating lines allowing metrical tit-for-tat exchanges), Bai Lidi (Benedick) boastfully asserts that the youthful Lou Di'ao (Claudio) is a mere 'one inch whiter' than he. Bicui retorts by likening Bai to 'donkey droppings dusted with white powder'.

The stylistic depth and inventiveness of these productions contrast interestingly with the postmodern indigeneity of Suzuki and Ninagawa. What separates the *Kunju Macbeth* and the *Huangmeixi Much Ado About Nothing* from their postmodern equivalents in Japan is that the former are exercises in style while the latter are exercises in stylisation. *Xiqu,* in other words, is a living and breathing stylistic world (where style is ultimately a means of emotional expression that the actor inhabits from within), whereas the productions of Ninagawa and Suzuki are reconstituted by *auteur* directors from closed stylistic worlds (*Noh*, *Kabuki*), which they visit rather than inhabit. The effect of this stylistic reconstitution is thus 'stylisation' – a style effect has been deliberately lifted and alienated from the stylistic world that had once given it meaning. Ninagawa and Suzuki are perhaps aware of this, which may be why their styles are so haunting, uncanny, and (in Suzuki's case) absurdist. One reason that *Xiqu* styles are not entirely offered up on the altar of director's theatre in China is that *Xiqu* productions of Shakespeare are always directed in tandem with a *Huaju* director (or directors) in collaboration with a *Xiqu* director (or directors). While it is true that the upper hand and controlling vision belong to the *Huaju* director, and that the results of such collaborations are not uniformly happy, it is also true that the *Xiqu* performance idiom tends not to be overpowered by an imposed directorial vision.[21]

India

While the histories of Shakespeare in China and Japan are different, they can be seen to share a family resemblance – at least when compared to the history of Shakespeare in India. India differs from both in having experienced the full brunt of western colonial power. If the former two experiences are quasi-colonial (adoption of western modes is driven at least partly by the desire to pre-empt full colonial subjection), the latter is properly colonial. Thus Shakespeare is sponsored into India by the full colonial apparatus: specifically as a mainstay of the entertainment programme for English residents of Bombay and Calcutta from about 1775. Colonialism accounts for the earliness of this date relative to China and Japan (though he would eventually serve a modernising function, Shakespeare does not enter India as a modernist). Colonialism also accounts for the comprehensiveness of Shakespeare's Indian presence from the first. This Shakespeare does not arrive clinging to the driftwood of Lamb's *Tales*, but comfortably accommodated within a modern English-style theatre sponsored by David Garrick. With this as a model, an indigenous proscenium theatre – Prasanna Kumar Tagore's Hindu Theatre – opened in Calcutta in 1831 with scenes from *Julius Caesar* and a Sanskrit play (*Uttarramcharitam*) in English translation. The Hindu Theatre was one of several new theatres financed by Indians in Calcutta and Bombay during the 1830s.

Subsequently, Shakespeare served the colonial apparatus in a more overt capacity. In 1835 English became the language of administration and government-funded education. Shakespeare's plays became the centre of a curriculum designed to produce 'a class of persons Indian in blood and colour, but English in taste, in opinion, in morals and in intellect'.[22] Indians would speak English with proper enunciation. Elocution and declamation contests were held annually, with the highest accolades reserved for the recitation of Shakespeare (scenes and whole plays had been performed from about 1824). School performances constitute an important part of the early performance tradition. While as 'pedagogical' as the mid-century Japanese *Shingeki* or the Chinese *Huaju*, the Indian schools tradition did not extend to 'doublet and hose' costuming or the mimicry of blond wigs and whitened faces.

While entirely distinct as social phenomena, the Indian schools tradition and the expatriate English performance tradition inadvertently merged in a single remarkable production. In 1848, Barry Lewis staged *Othello* at the Sans Souci Theatre in Calcutta, starring Mrs Anderson (the 'Mrs Siddons of Bengal') in the role of Desdemona and Baishnav Charan Auddy in the role of Othello. A decade before the Mutiny of 1857, the pairing of white English woman and dark Indian man was at once shocking and complex – paradigmatic of the cultural ambiguity of Shakespeare's presence in India. While effectively an English social event – even the doormen and ushers (not to mention the audience) were white – the ramifications appear to have been as wide as the response was divided. A letter in the *Calcutta Star* announced how the 'début of a real unpainted nigger Othello' had set 'the whole world of Calcutta agog'.[23] The performance was anticipated with a mixture of complacency and apprehension. A notice in the *Bengal Harkaru and India Gazette* (1 August 1848) doubted 'whether anyone able to play the moor without paint possessed enough of physical energy'. Praising 'the young Bengali . . . for his devotion to Shakespeare in the school and in the closet', the writer judiciously opined that 'it will be something entirely new to see him endeavouring to embody the glorious creations of that mighty intellect' (127). Anxieties of a more frankly racial (and perhaps military) order led to the fiasco of the opening night, when half the cast (army men) were 'prohibited . . . by the peremptory order of the Brigadier of Dum Dum' from leaving barracks.[24] The show opened to a full house the following week. The conflicting nature of the response to 'this Hindoo Othello' was registered by the publication of two reviews in the *Bengal Harkaru and India Gazette* (19 August 1848), one by their 'own critic' and another by an 'anonymous critic'. The first account is relatively approving, both of the venture itself and of the lead actor: 'his delivery was somewhat cramped, but under all circumstances his pronunciation of English was for a native remarkably good. Othello's self command before the Venetian senate was well upheld, and . . . the feelings of the audience were fairly enlisted on his side' (193–4). The second review was sneeringly hostile: 'nature never designed the ambitious youth for an actor . . . his figure is inelegant, his manner undignified, his gait awkward and ungainly . . . he did not deliver a single sentence with any degree of feeling and was totally wanting in energy'. The two critics also offered differing assessments of the audience's reaction. While the *Gazette's* critic heard 'thunders of applause', the anonymous critic heard 'a cry, an out-cry rather, for Othello . . . of course in mockery'. This was dismissed by the former as 'the gross misbehaviour of a number of Calcutta gents, genus snob, who amused themselves between the pieces by setting up the hideous howl of the jackal'.

Whatever is made of this production (was it boldly subversive or pathetically collaborationist?), the two English-language traditions (Anglo and Indian) did not intermingle again until about the time of the 'Shakespeare Wallah', Geoffrey Kendal. About a century before that, however, the Indian schools tradition led in the direction of new and alternative modes of writing and staging in native languages. Plays modelled on the five-act Shakespearean structure, with soliloquies, were written, especially in Bengali and Marathi, the languages of the two main areas of colonial dominance. One of the earliest examples is Madhusudan Datta's play *Shormishtha* (1858), based on *As You Like It*. College graduates raised on Shakespeare went on to join the burgeoning public theatre movements of Calcutta and Bombay. These included Jehangir Khambatta, Edulji Khori and C. S. Nazir, pioneers of the Parsi theatre – the first modern theatre of India (1860–1920). All were graduates of the dramatic society of Elphinstone College in Bombay. There was a sense that English-language Shakespeare, though performed by Indians, was not yet Indian and that it would not be so until it was transmitted into the local tongues. Translations begin to appear in print and on the stage from the 1850s. Dutiful translations had little impact on the popular stage, however. Of greater popularity were adaptations. These were of two types: first an experimental and unfettered form of localising adaptation, and second a form of deliberate indigenisation.

In the first of these, Shakespeare was transposed wholesale into Indian milieux. In general, early adaptations not only changed names and places but rearranged plots, rewrote characters and were liberally embellished with Indian songs and dances. Playwrights of the Parsi theatre plundered the canon, translating, adapting and collating to satisfy commercial theatre's demand for new material. Parsi touring companies then disseminated this Indianised Shakespeare throughout the subcontinent. Nearly half the canon was adapted and performed in the characteristically hybrid and extravagant Parsi style, mostly without acknowledgement or 'anxiety of influence'. Though entirely driven by commercial interests and in effective collaboration with the colonial order, Parsi theatre was profanely subversive of the élitist English-language Shakespeare prescribed by the colonial regime – one reason, perhaps, for its popularity among ordinary people. Shakespeare's colonial underpinnings were all too visible in such productions. An 1882 Hindi translation of *The Comedy of Errors* by Munshi Ratan Chand inserts 'Hindustan' into the niche occupied by England in the satirical hierarchy of countries discovered by Dromio of Syracuse in the globe-like kitchen wench by whom he has been accosted.[25] India thus stands 'in her face, for just as Hindustan is the best of all countries, so was her face the best part of her person'. In this sexual cartography, England takes the place of The Netherlands – the last and lowest in Shakespeare's list of countries: 'this was such a tiny country that exceedingly hard as I looked, I could find it nowhere. It must be hidden among those parts of the body I didn't look at.' Though hand-in-glove with the colonial order, Shakespeare could also lend himself to subversive uses. Overt political lampoon was banned. However, politically suggestive uses of past history – a highly developed Shakespearean skill – were less detectable, and accordingly feasible (though for these very reasons, difficult to demonstrate).

No account of Shakespearean adaptations would be complete without mention of the cinema. The development of Bombay cinema in the 1930s and the consequent decline of the Parsi theatre that fed it, led to a further dissemination of Shakespeare within popular culture. Early Indian films reveal unexpected traces of Shakespearean conventions, such as heroines in male disguise. Snatches of Shakespearean dialogue, images, scenes and scenic sequences are also found, filtered through the redactions of Parsi theatre. A long view reveals a kind of trickle-down effect: from the initiation of the élite via the educational system and the printed page, to redactions into more popular theatrical forms, finally including cinema.

In the second of the two adaptive modes, Shakespeare is indigenised and traditionalised. Unlike the broad localisation of Parsi theatre – a kind of creative assimilation of foreign cultural streams – this was an appropriation into specific native performance genres. The earliest known example is the adaptation of *As You Like It* to the genre of *Yakashagana* in 1860. In 1878 *The Tempest* was adapted as a Marathi *Sangeet Natak*, as later were *Romeo and Juliet* and *A Midsummer Night's Dream*. Musical Marathi versions of *Cymbeline* and *The Winter's Tale* were staged with some success in 1880 and 1906 respectively. In 1906 *A Midsummer Night's Dream* was adapted as a Sanskrit play in Malayalam, with generic music and dance. The play also incorporated generic conventions such as the *nandi* (prayer-prologue) and *sutradhar* (chorus).

Adaptation 'in Indian style and conventions' (as playbills commonly proclaimed) was inevitable if a western dramatist like Shakespeare was to be performed in traditional regional genres. The cultural distance was strangely inviting. In their present form, regional and folk theatres can be traced back to *circa* 1500. At some stage before that date (though this is open to dispute) they probably derived from the ancient Sanskrit drama that flourished chiefly from 200 BC to 700 AD. Sanskrit drama was courtly and poetic. It aimed to evoke the essence of feelings or states of being (*rasas*) through a combination of music, dance and words. The principle of development was not action or *agon*, but contrast and elaboration. Conclusions were neither tragic nor comic, but reunifying and harmonising. The folk and regional offshoots of the ancient courtly drama incorporate many of its core aspects. They are thus non-illusionistic, symbolic, presentational, iterative, accretive and celebratory (what was celebrated was a unified view of the universe). For its part, folk theatre contributed new elements: informality, improvisation, a sense of community participation, also popular festivity. For all its adaptiveness, the encounter of such a theatre and drama with the opposing western logic represented by Shakespeare was inherently disruptive. How, then, did traditional Indian theatre manage to incorporate Shakespeare? Why did it not – as the Japanese *Kabuki* eventually did – refuse incorporation? The answer appears to be that Shakespeare breathed much needed new life. As with traditional Chinese theatre (*Xiqu*), many traditional Indian forms had become moribund by the end of the eighteenth century. New hybrids of western illusionism and Indian presentationalism – also Shakespearean material and modified Indian conventions – became popular. Though some folk traditions declined, others revived, including the classical Sanskrit drama. The translators and performers of Shakespeare were also translating and performing Kalidasa, dubbed 'the Shakespeare of India' by Sir William Jones in the preface to his 1789 translation of the classic sanskrit drama *Shakuntalam*.[26]

A more self-conscious and thoroughgoing kind of indigenisation has emerged since independence in 1947. Typically in such productions, Shakespeare is systematically adapted to various indigenous genres, which are in turn modified in various ways for the purpose of accommodating Shakespeare. B. V. Karanth's *Barnam Vana* (1979) was the first full-scale adaptation of a Shakespeare play (*Macbeth*) into *Yakshagana*, (a traditional genre of the south-western state of Karnataka). The adaptation here worked both ways. *Yakshagana* was evident in the rhythmic and gliding entrances and exits of the actors, in the acrobatic leaps and pirouettes during the battle

a.

b.

42 *Barnam Vana*, the 1979 production of *Macbeth*, in Hindi, in *Yakshagana* (South Indian folk theatre) style. Directed by B. V. Karanth for the National School of Drama, New Delhi. (a) The witches: 'When shall we three meet again?'; (b) the banquet scene. Macbeth and Lady Macbeth with Banquo's ghost: 'Avaunt! and quit my sight!'

scenes, and (particularly) in the projection of shadow effects on a hand-held curtain. *Macbeth* also left its mark on *Yakshagana*. Gone was the elaborate (*Kathakali*-like) headgear of the actors, symbolic colour coding and improvisatory give-and-take between lead-character and audience. Habib Tanveer's *Kaam Dev ka Apna Basant Ritu ka Sapna* (Love God's own Springtime Dream) of 1996, adapted *A Midsummer Night's Dream* into *Nacha*, a form evolved by Tanveer himself from an eclectic mix of several north Indian traditions and characterised by episodic plot structure, absence of illusion, audience address and chorus-like use of song and dance. Unlike *Barnam Varna*, the adaptation here was essentially in the direction of the host form. Tanveer omitted the lovers and anything else with no resonance in *Nacha*. His focus was on the mechanicals, the fairy quarrel (about the Indian boy), the love potion and Bottom's bestial metamorphosis. Tanveer's mechanicals – who were in fact from various rural and tribal regions – did not have to play 'down' or to play stereotype, but could draw on their own regional accents and gestures, and a rich folk-based slapstick. More recently a number of Shakespeare plays have been adapted into *Kathakali*, the ritual dance-drama of the state of Kerala. These include a *Lear* (1989), controversially conceived and directed by westerners,[27] Sadanam Balakrishnan's *Kathakali Othello* (1996) and Sadanam HariKumar's *Charudatham* (2001), an adaptation of *Julius Caesar*. In the latter production a new role type had to be invented to accommodate the morally ambiguous figure of Cassius, a role for which no plausible equivalent existed in *Kathakali*. In 1997, Lokendra Arambam adapted *Macbeth* as *Stage of Blood*. In this case the host form was no single native genre but an eclectic blend of martial art, dance and acrobatics generic to the north-eastern state of Manipur. In addition to fusing eastern and western performance codes, some of these productions attempt a more ambitious rapprochement of philosophical perspective. Thus, Arambam's *Stage of Blood* invoked *Meitei* tribal beliefs to stage *Macbeth* as a parable of disharmony between human and environmental forces. In this production the stage – representing the human domain – literally floated on a lake of water under the bare sky – water and sky providing a cosmic reflection on the vanity of human discord (fig. 43). In *Barnam Vana*, Shakespeare's 'Birnam Wood' became a 'forest' (*vana*), in the sense of the *maya-jaal* of Vedantic philosophy – a 'labyrinthine jungle of ambition which ensnares'. Actualised on stage in terms of a dappled lighting effect, the forest was represented as preventing Macbeth from expressing his *dharma* or inner essence of 'human kindness'. Some recent indigenisations have taken an overtly post-colonial turn. In Roysten Abel's *Othello: a Play in Black and White*, a group of actors is discovered rehearsing a *Kathakali* version of *Othello* for 'export' (the director is represented as an Italian). The rehearsal is less cosmetic than it

a.

b.

43 *Stage of Blood*, the 1979 production of *Macbeth*, directed by Lokendra Arambam, at
Ningthem Pukri Reservoir, Imphal, India (also staged at Waterman's Art Centre,
Brentford, UK). (a) Macbeth at Dunsinane; (b) Birnam Wood advances.

seems, however, as the Shakespearean themes are doubled in the dynamics of the group. Thus, a seasoned old-hand is passed over for the title role by a young upstart from the north-east who is befriended by a well-regarded young actress who (in her turn) is burdened by a jealous lover (Roderigo, but also Cassio). Iago's seduction of Othello is played out in terms of a Guru–disciple relationship, but also in terms of a politics of centre-and-periphery. Othello is represented as coming from the north-east, a grouping of seven self-consciously 'peripheral' Indian states, all of which have dissented from the Union at various times since its foundation in 1947. In addition to their relative underprivilege, these states see themselves (and are seen) in terms of traditional and folk values as against the metropolitanised values of Delhi, the capital. The play thus addressed the thorny issue of identity in modern India. What is 'Indian'? The metropolitan or the regional, the modern or the traditional? The marked success of this production – particularly with young people – was due to the deft (and novel) interpolation of felt geographic and cultural tensions into Shakespeare's text.

Conclusion

What if anything is the common denominator between these three performance histories of Shakespeare in different national contexts? Does a common cultural history of the kind envisaged by James Brandon underwrite their evident diversity? To some extent perhaps. The broad outline described by Brandon – a struggle between western/canonic and indigenous orientations, between translation and adaptation, between cultural mimesis and cultural dialogue – remains discernible. More problematic however is the implicit teleology of Brandon's thesis: the suggestion (however guarded) that these tensions can be mapped as a common cultural evolution whereby the 'Asian' encounter with Shakespeare evolves from an unselfconsciously localising phase, to a slavishly canonical phase, to an intercultural and dialogical phase. Time and again our 'histories' suggest otherwise. Thus, whereas we suggest a Brandon-like tension between translation and adaptation in all three countries, we do not suggest that the meaning of this tension is similar in all cases. *Xiqu* performances of Shakespeare work from adaptations rather than translations, but for reasons of practical necessity rather than an urge to assert local values over canonic values. Discerning common patterns in three such different histories requires perhaps too great a level of abstraction. 'Perspective' in the end is linked to experience. Anxiety of influence has to be felt in order to be real. In the end perhaps, Japan, China and India are as sharply divided by their political histories over the last century, as they are united by a notional Asianism.

NOTES

1 James R. Brandon, 'Some Shakespeare(s) in Some Asia(s)', *Asian Studies Review* 20: 3(April 1997), 1–26. Brandon finds these three categories useful to account for Asian Shakespeare generally. While we would agree, we would disagree with any suggestion of the one-size-fits-all nature. We find them particularly pertinent however in the case of Japan.

2 See Yoshihara Yukari, 'Japan as "Half-Civilized": an Early Japanese Adaptation of Shakespeare's *The Merchant of Venice* and Japan's Construction of its National Image in the Late Nineteenth Century' in Minami Ryuta, Ian Carruthers and John Gillies, (eds.), *Performing Shakespeare in Japan* (Cambridge: Cambridge University Press, 2001), 21–32.

3 The full title is *Self-Help: With Illustrations of Conduct and Perseverance* (London, 1859). The most influential Japanese translation of *Self-Help* was by Nakamura Masanao. It was titled *Saigoku risshi hen* (1871, Tales of Successful Men). See Yoshihara, 'Japan as "Half-Civilized"', 23.

4 See James R. Brandon, 'Shakespeare in Kabuki', in Minami *et al.* (eds.), *Performing Shakespeare in Japan*, 33–53.

5 Where the conventional Japanese usage is surname first, we follow the English usage of surname last.

6 In 1906, Tsubouchi's *Bungei Kyōkai* (Literary Society) staged the trial scene of *The Merchant of Venice* with actors only. An abridged version of *Hamlet* was staged in 1906, with Gertrude played by an actor and Ophelia by an actress (the names were not Japanised). Both productions can be regarded as prologues to the *Hamlet* of 1911.

7 Audiences were not monolithic. While Deguchi's audience tended to be in their twenties or early thirties, an older and more conservative generation of theatre-goers were simultaneously attending *Shingeki*-style productions. It is important to remember that Deguchi's audience was urban rather than rural, a distinction to be understood as much in temporal (modern vs. past) as in geographic terms. See Joseph J. Tobin (ed.), *Re-Made in Japan: Everyday Life and Consumer Taste in a Changing Society* (New Haven: Yale University Press, 1992), 16.

8 See 'Interview with Suzuki Tadashi' in Minami *et al.* (eds.), *Performing Shakespeare in Japan*, 196–208.

9 See Ryuta Minami, 'Shakespeare Reinvented on the Contemporary Japanese Stage' in Minami *et al.* (eds.), *Performing Shakespeare in Japan*, 148–53.

10 See John Gillies, 'Afterword', in Minami *et al.* (eds.), *Performing Shakespeare in Japan*, 244–5.

11 Hisashi Inoue, *Tempô Jûninen no Shakespeare* (Shakespeare in the Twelfth Year of the Tempô era) in *Complete Plays of Inoue Hishashi*, 5 vols. (Tokyo: Shinchôsha, 1984), II, 9. The play was first performed in January 1974 with Norio Deguchi as director.

12 The Chinese title is *Rouquan*.

13 See Brandon, 'Some Shakespeare(s) in Some Asia(s)'.

14 The impression was not entirely fair. Mei Lanfang, the most celebrated master of the *Dan* (female) role in the modern era staged modernised costume plays early in the century. Some were new plays altogether and others revisions of the

traditional repertoire. In the Cultural Revolution too, *Xiqu* was approved by Jiang Qing as the vehicle of a revolutionary drama.

15 We have followed the Chinese usage of surname first for the reason that this is how eminent Chinese names are known in the West.

16 'Talks at the Yan'an Forum', in *Selected Works of Mao Tse-Tung* (Peking: Foreign Language Press, 1967), III.

17 In a letter of 19 April 1859 Marx criticised Ferdinand Lassalle's *Franz von Sickingen* – about a sixteenth-century uprising of knights against their feudal masters – for turning characters into proleptic mouthpieces of his modern revolutionary agenda: 'You would then have Shakespearized more; at present, there is too much Schillerism, which means making individuals into mere mouth-pieces of the spirit of the times, and this is your main fault.' (Lee Baxandall and Stefan Morawski (eds.), *Karl Marx/Friedrich Engels on Literature and Art: a Selection of Writings* (New York: International General, 1974), 107.)

18 The image of a literally blundering Macbeth came, Xu has said, from this passage in Marx: 'He (Louis Napoleon) may recoil before the storm he has raised, and again receive the benedictions of the Pope and the caresses of the British Queen; but neither will be more than lip-service. They know him now, what the people knew him long since – a reckless gambler, a desperate adventurer, who would as soon dice with royal bones as any other if the game promised to leave him a winner. They know him as one who, having, like Macbeth, waded to a crown through human gore, finds it easier to go forward than to return to peace and innocence.' (*Karl Marx/Friedrich Engels, Collected Works*, 47 vols. (London: Lawrence & Wishart, 1980), XVI, 273.)

19 As a result of the Soviet influence of the 1950s, Chinese attitudes to Shakespeare in general and heroes such as Hamlet in particular have been influenced by Engels's praise of the Renaissance imagination and Renaissance achievement: 'It was the greatest progressive revolution that mankind has so far experienced, a time which called for giants and produced giants – giants in power of thought, passion and character, in universality and learning.' (Friedrich Engels, *Dialectics of Nature*, ed. Clemens Dutt (New York: International Publishers, 1960), 2–3.)

20 The source for much of the following is Ruru Li and John Gillies, *Performing Shakespeare in China, 1980–1990: a Multimedia History* (unpublished).

21 An exception to the rule is a 1986 production of *Twelfth Night* directed in tandem by Hu Weimin (*Huaju*) and Sun Hongjiang (*Yueju*). In this case the *Huaju* director's vision did overpower that of the *Yueju* director, resulting in a production in which much of the conventional integrity of *Yueju* was sacrificed in the interests of what was felt to be a 'proper' (doublet-and-hose) performance style for Shakespeare.

22 'Indian Education: Minute of 2nd Feb. 1835' in G. M. Young (ed.), *Macaulay: Prose and Poetry* (London: Rupert Hart-Davis, 1967), 729.

23 Kironmoy Raha, *Bengali Theatre* (New Delhi: National Book Trust, 1980), 10.

24 *Bengal Harkaru and India Gazette*, 12 August 1848, 193–4.

25 For the original passage, see 3.2.115–52, in Stanley Wells and Gary Taylor (eds.), *William Shakespeare: the Complete Works* (Oxford: Clarendon Press, 1987).

26 Satya S. Pachori (ed.), *Sir William Jones: a Reader* (Oxford and New Delhi: Oxford University Press, 1993), 90–1.
27 See Philip B. Zarilli, 'For Whom is the King a King? Issues of Intercultural Production, Perception, and Reception in a *Kathakali King Lear*' in Janelle G. Reinelt and Joseph R. Roach (eds.), *Critical Theory and Performance* (Ann Arbor: University of Michigan Press, 1992), 16–40.

15

MARTIN BANHAM, ROSHNI MOONEERAM,
JANE PLASTOW

Shakespeare and Africa

Shakespeare's work reached Africa no later than it reached the most distant parts of his own country. In 1607 there are reports of performances of *Hamlet* and *Richard II* by British sailors off the coast of Sierra Leone. This hardly raised the floodgates of performance, but in 1800 the African Theatre – an amateur theatre set up in Cape Town, South Africa, by the soldiers of the British garrison[1] – opened with a performance of *I Henry IV*, and since then the amateur entertainments of colonial officers, the educational priorities of missionary and colonial government schools, plus tours of professional actors from Britain to South Africa from the early nineteenth century and throughout Africa from the mid-twentieth century onwards, ensured that the plays of Shakespeare – played in English (and in the nineteenth century often adapted, in the tradition of the times, to make them more acceptable to contemporary tastes) – had a significant presence. But Shakespeare – perhaps more pertinently for our interests in this chapter – has also been performed and explored through the medium of translation and adaptation in a range of African languages and performance cultures. *Macbeth*, *The Merchant of Venice*, *The Tempest* and *Julius Caesar* have all been translated into Kiswahili[2] – a language spoken extensively throughout East Africa – perhaps most interestingly by the distinguished statesman Julius Nyerere, who was the first president of independent Tanzania. Nyerere, a Shakespeare enthusiast, seems to have undertaken his translations in the 1960s, initially as a celebration of the richness and beauty of the Kiswahili language, showing – with a clear ideological purpose – that the major indigenous language of the new nations of East Africa was every bit as sophisticated as the language of the world's greatest poet. The university travelling theatres in Nigeria and Uganda in the 1950s and 1960s, student companies touring their own countries, often brought 'pidgin' – a lingua franca built from elements of colonial and indigenous languages – to their adaptations of Shakespeare, in order to make their performances both accessible and popular. In Francophone Africa there have been French language versions, for instance *Macbeth* at

Sonar Senghor's Théâtre Daniel Sorano in Dakar (*c.* 1965), the Congolese Sony Labou Tansi's *Romeo and Juliet* (1990) and in Côte d'Ivoire an adaptation of *Macbeth* (*Macbet*) by Marie-José Hourantier performed, in 1993, by the Bin Kadi-So group.[3] In Egypt *Othello* was translated and performed early on in the twentieth century as '*Utayl* by Khali l Mutran, and there are versions and translations of *King Lear* in Arabic from 1927 to 1970.[4] In the 1930s there were translations of *The Comedy of Errors* and *Julius Caesar* into the South African language Setswana by Solomon Tashekisho Plaatje and *King Lear* (*Koning Lear*) into Afrikaans by Uys Krige in 1971. This list is far from exhaustive but serves to show that Shakespeare's plays have excited audiences and intrigued artists in Africa as elsewhere throughout the world. In order to illustrate this in more detail, and to give some indication not only of the translation of the *language* of Shakespeare but also the translation of the *performance* of Shakespeare into other cultural forms, we will now look in more detail at a range of specific productions and adaptations from different parts of Africa.

We started off in Sierra Leone, the territory on the west coast of Africa initially colonised by Britain in the eighteenth century and selected as a place to resettle liberated slaves who had been taken from various parts of the region. This resettlement of people from different areas, combining with the indigenous people, had important linguistic repercussions. Freetown, the capital, became a cosmopolitan centre, dominated by the resettled slaves and their descendants. It is not surprising that they created a common language, which by the end of the nineteenth century had become the sophisticated Krio. Krio, like pidgins, drew upon imported and indigenous languages, with a strong influence from English. The Krio speaking people of Freetown were educated and interested in western culture and it is not surprising that Shakespeare was well known to them and that a specific Krio theatre should eventually emerge. It was with Thomas Decker's 1964 translation of *Julius Caesar* that the beginning of Krio theatre was defined, followed by his version of *As You Like It*, called, in Krio, *Udat Di Kiap Fit* (literally, Who the Cap Fits).[5] Decker's purpose in translating Shakespeare parallels that of Nyerere. He wrote about his *Julius Caesar*:

> my aim was twofold, first to make propaganda for the Krio language by proving that the most serious things could be written in it and secondly, to make it possible for people who had not had the opportunity of reading Shakespeare at school [to] taste of the excellence of this great writer by seeing one of his most popular plays staged in their own language.

As the distinguished Sierra Leonian Shakespeare scholar Eldred Durosimi Jones has pointed out, Decker 'realised' the sense of the text and made it work in a context that his audience would appreciate. For instance, in *As You Like It* the line 'What prodigal portion have I spent, that I should come to such penury' (1.1) becomes, in *Udat Di Kiap Fit*, 'Wetin a du fo kam ton di prodigal son ?', playing on his audience's assumed knowledge of the biblical story. And 'I pray thee Rosalind, sweet my coz, be merry' translates as 'Dy ya cozin Rozalin lus bodi'. 'Lus bodi' means 'loosen body' – that is, relax baby!

Sierra Leonian audiences, like audiences throughout Africa, enormously appreciate the clever and witty use of language; storytelling, complex riddles and proverbs are forms of entertainment common to many cultures and languages and illustrate a delight in the spoken word and the 'sounds' of theatre. Audiences will applaud and respond vocally to verbal performance as much as to action. For the English speaker Krio, though operating as a language in its own right, is far from inaccessible and often exciting to hear in performance. So when we listen to Brutus at Caesar's funeral, we find the echoes of Shakespeare's text in Decker's words on stage:

Padi dem, khontri, una ohl wey day
Na Rom. Meyk una ohl kak una yeys.
A kam ber Siza, a non kam preyz am.

[My friends, countrymen, you who are of
Rome. Listen to me.
I come to bury Caesar, I don't come to praise him.]

Throughout Africa, dance, music and spectacle are also integral parts of indigenous performance, ranging from masquerades to community festivals, from 'traditional' to modern theatre. Perhaps, outside the continent, one of the best-known examples of an African Shakespeare production is the South African version of *Macbeth* called *Umabatha*, created by the Zulu playwright and actor Welcome Msomi. Created and first performed in South Africa in 1970, the production drew international attention when it was performed at the 1972 World Theatre Season in London, going on to play worldwide throughout the 1970s. 'What inspired me to choose *Macbeth*', Msomi wrote in 1995, 'is that the intrigue, plots and counterplots of the Scottish clans were almost a carbon copy of the drama that took place with the early nations of Africa.'[6] The transposition of the play into a Zulu world was effected through adopting not only the Zulu language but also the means of Zulu performance – choral dancing, songs, percussive music. Its impact in the 1970s was remarkable – 'the show that hit London theatre-goers like an assegai between the eyes', as one newspaper put it. The production, however, had its critics, some seeing its elaborate display of dancing, costuming and display, and the depiction of a confident black African nation, as a distraction from the realities of apartheid and as commercial exploitation of a section of South African society oppressed at home. Nevertheless, South Africa's iconic post-apartheid leader, President Nelson Mandela, encouraged Msomi to revive the production in 1995, again touring internationally. Reviews variously describe the show's style. The New York *Times* (23 July 1997) observed that it was 'punctuated with stately processions of an earthy but uncanny beauty and invigorating tribal dances'. The London *Times* (6 August 1997) saw it set in a land 'of dancing sorceresses with beaded hair and leopard-skin robes'. The London *Independent* (8 August 1997) made a point that is pertinent to many of the other examples of Shakespeare adaptations in Africa: 'In some ways *Umabatha* is more "authentic" than any modern *Macbeth* – Msomi and his athletic, dynamic cast manage to suggest vividly a warrior society in which fighting prowess is not simply an admirable but incidental attribute, it is central to man's identity.'

Decker's *Julius Caesar* and *Udat Di Kiap Fit*, and Msomi's *Umabatha* illustrate the way in which specific indigenous performance elements – verbal, visual and aural – have been used to rework Shakespeare in African terms. Three specific productions – from Ethiopia, Nigeria and Mauritius set within their national cultural and ideological traditions, will illustrate these qualities in more detail.

Ethiopia: Tsegaye Gebre-Medhin's *Othello*

Tsegaye Gebre-Medhin (b. 1936) is Ethiopia's most famous, and probably its most prolific playwright. He is well known for his translations of Molière and is probably the only Ethiopian to have translated Shakespeare into a local language. Western-influenced theatre in Ethiopia dates back to *circa* 1916. It is significant that, rather than European theatrical notions being imported by missionaries or colonialists, in independent Ethiopia ideas were brought back by Ethiopians who had travelled in Europe, and who wanted to make a theatre in their own language – the ruling class language of Amharic. They mediated the forms they adopted from the West through their own cultural traditions, most specifically the iconography of the enormously influential Ethiopian Orthodox Church. Consequently, and uniquely in Africa, a vigorous, increasingly state-supported, modern theatre tradition arose in the Ethiopian capital of Addis Ababa, strongly patronised by the Christian ruling classes.

Until the 1960s drama, all of which had to be submitted for imperial censorship, was largely a vehicle of praise for the nation, the church and above all the glory of the supposed direct descendant of King Solomon, the Emperor Haile Selassie I. Tsegaye Gebre-Medhin was the man who above all others broke this tradition, bringing in a new theatre in support of ordinary people and introducing a host of ideas about staging and content. He had begun writing plays as a student, and in 1958 was greatly helped by winning a scholarship that allowed him to spend a year in England and France (studying and working at the Theatre Royal in Windsor and the Comédie Française in Paris). When he returned to Ethiopia in 1959 as director of Addis Ababa's premier theatre – the Haile Selassie I Theatre – Tsegaye started to produce a steady stream of plays championing the common man and subtly questioning both church and state. These enormously increased the popularity and relevance of Ethiopian theatre. Among the original scripts were a considerable number of Shakespeare translations. In the 1960s and 1970s, Tsegaye translated and adapted in various formats *Othello*, *A Midsummer Night's Dream*, *Macbeth*, *King Lear* and *Hamlet*. These were all produced at the 2,000-seat Haile Selassie I Theatre. They were immensely popular with Ethiopian audiences accustomed to large-scale tragedies focusing on the doings of kings and warriors, used to verse presentations and quite happy to sit through performances lasting several hours. As has already been noted in passing in relation to *Umabatha*, Shakespeare's world of princes, kings, warriors, fate, allegory and magic is much less difficult to accept at face value for many African societies than it is today for super-sceptical rationalist Europeans.

The following description of Tsegaye's *Othello* refers specifically to the revival that ran for three years, performed twice a week, at the municipal City Hall Theatre in Addis Ababa in the mid-1980s. Since Tsegaye translated all the four major Shakespeare tragedies, not a great deal needs to be made of his choice of *Othello*. However, the reception of the play would undoubtedly be influenced by Ethiopian race perceptions. Highland Christian Ethiopians, with their Semitic roots, ancient Christian heritage, and relatively light complexions, have traditionally seen themselves as superior to the surrounding lowland, often Muslim or animist, black Africans, who they have fought, often conquered and traditionally enslaved over thousands of years. The presentation of Othello as a hero obviously questions such race perceptions, and Tsegaye, who is of mixed ethnic origin (and who makes a point of not being an upper-class Amhara, like most Ethiopian playwrights), may have felt particularly drawn to this work. It has notable parallels with his most famous play, *Tewodros*, about the eponymous Ethiopian hero who combatted class snobbery and religious intolerance to become Ethiopian Emperor in the nineteenth century. What would perhaps be most notable to an outsider watching Tsegaye's *Othello* would be the dark colours and the static, almost monolithic nature of the performance. In Ethiopian drama words have always been the central element. Hence a playwright who can produce majestic verse and purple passages will be greatly honoured. Until the 1980s actors were untrained and seen merely as tools; the playwright either directed his own script or worked very closely with a trusted director. Tsegaye's *Othello* therefore emphasises the grand speeches, and an Ethiopian audience would expect them to be delivered in what would appear to western ears to be a florid and declamatory style. In accordance with Amharic social mores the leading characters tend not to move much and to occupy large chairs and raised platforms. This is part of the iconography of the Ethiopian stage. Comedians tend to rush around frantically and are often deformed; tragic actors sit or stand and declaim. The dark, rich colours of the stage, set and costumes are also part of a recognised symbolism, which draws heavily on the dark, richly painted interiors of Ethiopian churches. *Othello* was presented in dark shades, except when the slapstick comedians were on stage (difficult to locate in the original, but an intrinsic part of much African entertainment!), when the entire tone changed to frenetic, banana-skin humour. The three-year run of Tsegaye's *Othello* indicates its popularity with Ethiopian audiences. However, many of the *petit bourgeoisie* who commonly attend the contemporary theatre take a rather literalist line in interpreting what they see. The actor who played Iago throughout the run of the play became a figure of such universal opprobrium that he attracted insults and threats of violence, and was forced to take care when going out alone at night.[7]

Mauritius: Dev Virahsawmy's *Zeneral Makbef*[8]

Dev Virahsawmy (b. 1942) is a major figure of theatre in Mauritius, having written over twenty plays. He writes exclusively in Mauritian Creole. This is the mother tongue, and the most used language, of an overwhelming majority of the population, despite the presence of English and French as the official and semi-official languages, respectively. Creole is the national language *de facto* amongst the various ethnic groups of Mauritius and has become the natural language of Mauritian theatre. Virahsawmy is concerned, however, about the dangers of 'ghettoising' the language by restricting it exclusively to local issues and prefers to initiate a dialogue between Creole and other languages, between the imaginative and symbolic space of Mauritius and other cultures. It is within this context of bringing together local and international literary and cultural trends that he situates his copious rewriting/translation of Shakespeare. Virahsawmy has translated *Julius Caesar* as *Zil Sezar* (1987), *Much Ado About Nothing* as *Enn ta Senn dan Vid* (1995), *Macbeth* as *Trazedji Makbess* (1997) and rewritten *The Tempest* into a highly subversive and dynamic version entitled *Toufann* (1991).[9] After Virahsawmy's first play in Creole, *Li* (1972), *Zeneral Makbef* marks a turning point not only in the playwright's career but also within Mauritian theatre as a whole. The play, his first experiment with Shakespeare,[10] is deeply satirical as well as political. Its wide success – produced by Quisnarajoo Ramana, director of the Mauritius Drama League initially in 1982 and many times subsequently at the prestigious venues Plaza and Théâtre de Port-Louis – relied on Virahsawmy's literary connivance both with Shakespeare and a local audience, bringing to Shakespeare's text post-colonial cultural references and performance modes that were alien to it. Writing at a time of political uncertainty in Mauritius (and many other nations in post-independence Africa), Virahsawmy exploits social structures and historical realities that successfully connect with the audience's experience and cause them to engage with the play.

Makbef, who makes himself emperor of a republic, with a lust for power matched only by an unnaturally intense sexual appetite for both men and women, is a satirical comment on African leaders such as Bokassa and Idi Amin Dada. 'Mak' in Creole is the abbreviation for 'makro', meaning 'pimp'. At one point Makbef, being too busy indulging in sexual exploits, asks his servant to sleep with his wife. 'Bef' not only means 'bull' but also suggests intellectual lethargy. The connotations of his name already highlight the treacherous gap between his status as political leader and his private characteristics. Other characters within the play have names with local roots and meaning. Sergeants Sitronel, Yapana and Kâpes, who restore power to the people after a coup, bear the names of local medicinal plants, pointing out that the remedy for political problems is present locally and not in magical solutions proposed by imperialist superpowers. The play warns against two types of oppression faced by newly independent countries; becoming victims of their own leaders, or puppets in the hands of alien powers. Instead of the invasion of Scotland by Norway, the fictional Third World country of the play runs the risk of being invaded by two rival, and somewhat transparent, superpowers, the Rouspoutchik and Yankidola.

The most ridiculous, tangible and visual symbol of Makbef's new regime is his introduction of alien ritual greetings, requiring a close physical embrace, to the embarrassment of the young men of whom this response to the sexually predatory leader is demanded. The play focuses on the satirical portrait of a new leader who sells out to imperialist powers in his attempt to consolidate his own position. To mask this, Makbef has to take measures to ensure the loyalty of the local people. He decides on the organisation of various *jalsa* (parties), focusing specially on free football matches, events seen as prime entertainment in Mauritius. The satirical action brings the audience into direct involvement with the play. The actor Gaston Valaydon, who played the role of Makbef in all three productions, attributes the dynamism of the

a.

b.

44 *Zeneral Makbef* by Dev Virahsawmy, 1982, at Plaza, Mauritius. (a) The excessive decoration of Zeneral Makbef's military medals, along with Ledi Makbef's rich gold dress, deliberately clash with the bare stage design, symbolising the 'clean slate' appearance of a newly independent Third World country. (b) The end of the play. The people replace Makbef by Mazor Kaskotur, who is escorted through the audience and on to the stage to the sound of the *jal*. The audience reconciles two contrasting images: the defeat of a sick Makbef on stage and the glory of an emerging new leader next to them.

play to its immense cultural and political relevance to its audiences, and also to the interaction between actors and audience created by the incorporation of well-known songs in Creole, accompanied by sitar and guitar. At the ceremony marking Makbef's rise to power, cheering crowds and the members of the Revolutionary Council who assisted his coup welcome the new regime by beating the *dolok* (drum) and *jal* (little cymbals) while Makbef and Lady Makbef appear on a balcony dancing a tango. As the saying goes, and this scene makes graphic, it takes two to tango, and Lady Makbef's collaboration in her husband's rise to power is wittily symbolised. The action of the crowd satirises supporters who attend political meetings in Mauritius at the beat of the *dolok* and *sega* (national dance) and whose eagerness for blind sensations and *jalsa* obliterates the serious implications of choosing a political leader. The tango, on the other hand, symbolises the opportunism and western aspirations of the *nouveau riche* couple, distanced from the crowd by their position on the balcony and their intense self-centredness. This coronation scene gives a powerful visual and aural image of the total alienation between two worlds; the people and the leader oblivious of each other yet intimately bound to and dependent on each other.

The Mauritius Drama League's repeated and highly successful performances of *Zeneral Makbef* illustrate the abundant potential of the stage to achieve different meanings or readings according to the context in which a play is staged. For Mauritian theatre the mixture of politics, folklore and humour, via Shakespeare, pointed a new direction forward. *Zeneral Makbef* showed that theatre, whilst being provocative and relevant to local issues, need not rely only on local sources. A young theatre of protest was enhanced by the stature of Shakespeare, with deeply political issues tackled with humour and music.

Nigeria: Wale Ogunyemi's *A'are Akogun*

Wale Ogunyemi (1939–2001) was one of Nigeria's longest-established playwrights, his plays ranging from popular domestic comedies to reworkings of the myth and history of the Yoruba people of western Nigeria. *A'are Akogun*, staged in Ibadan, Nigeria in 1968, is a strikingly compact version of *Macbeth*,[11] which depicts the 'Macbeths' (A'are Akogun, the leader of the army, and his wife Olawumi) entirely bewitched and manipulated by the wizard and creature of many disguises, Osowole (Hecate?) and the three witches.The play, which lasts for an energetic hour, uses both English and Yoruba languages, switching between them in a manner which in the words of one contemporary critic gives the action 'feverish intensity'.[12] Rich areas of action are depicted in scenes of ritual, mime and rhythmic dialogue, with the constant presence of the rich and evocative sounds of Yoruba drumming. Basic parallels exist with Shakespeare's story. A'are Akogun is praised by the old king (the *Oba*, played in the original production by Ogunyemi himself) for his valour in battle and elevated to the rank of *A'are-Ona Kakanfo*, Chief Warrior. The *Oba*'s son Daodu (Malcolm) and a fellow-warrior Jagun (Banquo) witness A'are Akogun's elevation with some concern. No sooner has A'are Akogun acquired his new rank than, working through the vehicle of his wife, Olawumi, whom they take over in a ritual of possession, the witches plant the seed of ambition, driving A'are Akogun to murder the *Oba*. The text here, in a manner typical of Yoruba storytelling, utilises both proverbial riddles and a powerful repetitive choric chant. As in the single sequence shown below, a series of proverbs are followed by the witches urging 'Kill him!'

> OLAWUMI: *Ijó omodé bá dári kànrókò*
> *Nírókò ó kòó.*
> The day a child strays into the forest
> Is the day he meets with the tree elf.
> ÀWON ÁJÈ: *Paá!*
> (WITCHES) Kill him

This rises to a violent climax that sends A'are Akogun on his murderous mission. Much of the action of the play is in mime and movement, driven at all times by the sound of chants and drumming. It is interesting to see how closely the action follows that of *Macbeth*, though entirely recreated in Yoruba performance idiom. One can reconstruct the stage action from the text's stage directions. A'are Akogun is so affected by the compelling chanting that he finds himself forced to climb the steps towards the *Oba*. He attempts to pull back with superhuman effort, but greater magical powers pull him upward. Osowole the wizard, unmasked and therefore invisible, closes in on him, pointing a dagger at A'are Akogun's throat. As he backs away from the disembodied dagger he falls and is forced to grab it. The wizard disappears, leaving A'are Akogun with the dagger in his hand. The chanting increases in a frenzy as the helpless A'are Akogun rushes into the *Oba*'s bedchamber. An absolute silence falls on the stage; A'are Akogun comes 'chuckling madly to himself' from the room, the dagger still in his hand.

> OLAWUMI: You must return the dagger to the bedchamber.
> Give it to me.

Olawumi takes the dagger and enters the bedchamber. From here the action moves swiftly, with A'are Akogun taking the throne, the *Oba*'s son Daodu fleeing and being hunted by the 'murderer' Osowole. At this point Ogunyemi

45 The original production of *A'are Akogun*, a version of *Macbeth* by Wale Ogunyemi, performed in 1968 at the Arts Theatre, University of Ibadan, Nigeria. The first photo shows Ogunyemi himself as *Oba* (Duncan).

ingeniously and wittily offers a second parallel to a famous scene from *Macbeth* – the Porter's scene. The three witches settle down to a game of *ayo*. This is a game played – under a range of different names – throughout Africa, but enthusiastically by the Yoruba, in which hard seeds (or small stones) are distributed around receptacles in a wooden board, with the intent of 'capturing' the opponent's seeds. The game is played rapidly and the sound of the seeds being dropped into the holes on the board echoes, in this instance, the 'knocking' on the door of Macbeth's castle. The following quotation, reproducing just the English text, shows how the spirit of the Shakespeare text is basically retained, though placed firmly into a Yoruba context:

WITCH 1: *knock, knock.* Wait!
WITCH 2: *knock, knock, knock.* Speak on.
    The mounds on your chest.
    Are things of inheritance. *Laugh*
WITCH 1: *knock, knock.*
    Tell me, has anyone seen a bird fly
    And he crashes into a tree?
WITCH 2: *knock, knock, knock.*
    A bird never flies and crashes into a tree, never!
WITCH 1: *knock, knock.*
    That never happens where we are – in hell,
    But it happens daily in the world.
    When a drunkard drinks his senses with wine
    His path becomes darkened
    He dies
    Not knowing when he runs into his doom.
WITCH 1: *knock, knock, knock.*
    When a drunkard is drunk
    He has an urge for sex
    He runs madly after women
    And when the woman finally submits
    He is too tired and breathes heavily like *agalinti* [a lizard]
    . . .
    Where we are is hell.

Olawumi, 'holding her bloody right hand before her', comes across the witches at their game, but the witches place an invisible barrier around themselves as they discard her now as useless. A'are Akogun, his wife mad and destroyed, appeals to the gods to deliver him from his fate, taking courage in Osowole the wizard's prediction that he can only be killed 'during the total intervention of the moon between earth and sun'. This eclipse inevitably comes about as, in an ending sequence of mime and dumb show, Daodu and Jagun reappear (no murdered ghost of Banquo in this version) and cut A'are Akogun down. As he falls, the play closes with the unmasked Osowole entering with the witches, who carry the body of Olawumi. A'are Akogun *'raises himself on one elbow and points back helplessly to them whom he is seeing for the first time as if to ask why they have done this to him. They are still. The drums and lights fade as the assembly cowers back from Osowole, the witches, and their burden.'*

Ogunyemi's version of *Macbeth* offers a confident translation of the play into Yoruba idiom and traditional performance forms. It puts at the heart of the action the power of the supernatural in a cultural context where such forces retain a relevance in society's consciousness and myths. In this version Macbeth inevitably has less freewill than in Shakespeare's play. The dramatic structure is tight and fast-moving, layering language, music and movement in a manner typical of Yoruba popular theatre. The engagement with Shakespeare's text is one that celebrates it but moves beyond translation into cultural recreation.

Macbeth, that most atmospheric of Shakespeare's tragedies, has been a popular play for performance, translation or adaptation throughout Africa. As well as those discussed above there are two others of particular interest. The Ghanaian playwright Joe de Graft (1924–78) created a very broad – but entirely recognisable – version of the play entitled *Mambo, or Let's Play Games, My Husband* (1978).[13] This has a contemporary setting, with the ambition to inherit the chairmanship of Ghana's most powerful commercial firm, the Brempong Corporation, at the heart of the action. A fascinating device is de Graft's amalgamation of the Lady Macbeth figure and the witches into a composite character, Mrs Mambo 1, 2 and 3. As with Ogunyemi, the witches are seen to be at the heart of the destruction of the hero, but entirely inhabit the person of his wife. At times the three will speak together; on other occasions they will speak sequentially as if they are one person. Placing the play in modern times allows de Graft to comment on modern politics. In *A'are Akogun*, as with *Zeneral Makbef*, there are direct or indirect political points to be made. Virahsawmy's, as has been shown, are explicit; Ogunyemi's, implicit. *Mambo* ends with a peroration from the leader of the workers of the Brempong Corporation, remonstrating with those who see the death of the avaricious Mambo as a chance for their own advancement. In a style reminiscent of agitprop the Workers' Leader admonishes them:

> It is bigger than Mambo,
> Bigger than Kwakye,
> Bigger than the governing body
> Bigger than all its employees put together.
> The Brempong Corporation is a multi-million complex

That sustains vital areas of the economy of this nation
And every citizen has an interest in it –
Its sound and efficient operations
Its sane and honest management.
We would all do well to think about that
While we think about better pay for ourselves.

De Graft's message, if idealistic, is clear; modern Ghana must resist the destructive qualities of greed and exploitation. The future will be built on unselfishness and unity of purpose. *Mambo* also reflects de Graft's considerable sense of stagecraft. The play opens with a mystical prologue – very much in the style of the traditional opening 'glee' of popular West African theatre. A blind itinerant musician comes on to the dimly lit stage from the auditorium, setting the mood and the scene through proverb and oblique description; by contrast, when the lights come fully up, the scene is an airport arrivals lounge, into which Mambo emerges from his travels. The downfall of Mambo, at the end of the play, is effected by his confession to his mistress being broadcast through the auditorium via microphones and loudspeakers that have been set up previously by 'technicians' working amongst the audience.

Another and more recent version of *Macbeth* is *Makbutu*, created by Chuck Mike and the Nigerian Performance Studio Workshop (PSW), staged in Lagos in 2000. PSW is a company better known for its creation of theatre for development, and *Makbutu* works within this focus. Using pan-African performance idioms, with strong elements of music and dance, *Makbutu* shows the overthrow of an elected democratic leader by an ambitious (and eponymous) army general, somewhere in Africa. General Makbutu is himself finally overthrown by a popular uprising. Parallels with the contemporary situation in Nigeria are clear, with the message that if democracy is to survive, the people must be vigilant.

Julius Caesar ranks with *Macbeth* in terms of popularity in Africa – to audiences and theatre-makers. *Macbeth*, as the examples discussed above show, attracts not only because of its universal theme of the cancer of ambition, but also because its cast of kings and warriors, its setting in ancient kingdoms, and its mystical and magical theatricality carry echoes of the great sagas of African lore and history. For instance, the mighty but ambiguous figure of Chaka, the Zulu king and warrior of the nineteenth century, who has been celebrated in storytelling and in the work of such leading African writers as Léopold Sédar Senghor[14] and Wole Soyinka, in many ways inhabits the same awe-inspiring world as Macbeth. *Julius Caesar*, with its political intrigues and its sense of the danger in which the common man is put by the ambitions of power-seekers, is another play that speaks to the experiences of modern Africa. *Hamlet* – its introspection perhaps creating only impatience – is a tragedy rarely to be seen after its brief sighting off the coast of Sierra Leone, and *King Lear* appears to be limited to the versions noted above. Comedies, too, are relatively rare, though Virahsawmy and Decker have worked effectively with them, and there have been productions of *The Taming of the Shrew, The Comedy of Errors* and *A Midsummer Night's Dream* – the first, in a version entitled *A Taming of the Shrew*, being one of the great successes of the University of Ibadan Travelling Theatre when it was staged in the early 1960s. Over the years Shakespeare has intrigued and challenged African audiences, playwrights and actors. His work has been translated, closely or broadly adapted, or drawn upon in the creation of new work that relies upon its audience's awareness of and affection for Shakespeare. In Thomas Decker's rendering, Shakespeare indeed 'tinap ober we leck giant' – 'bestrides the narrow world like a Colossus'.

NOTES

1 See Jane Wilkinson, 'The Sayings of Tsikinya-Chaka: Shakespeare in South Africa', *AFRICA: Rivista trimestrale di studi e documentazione dell'Istituto italiano per l'Africa e l'Oriente* 2 (June 1999), 193–230 for a full and authoritative description of Shakespeare performances, adaptations and translations in South Africa, to which we are greatly indebted. Wilkinson's comments on the Shakespearean theatre and apartheid are particularly fascinating. We are also grateful to Jane Wilkinson for sharing with us her research on Shakespeare translations in Arabic from North Africa.

2 See Alamin M. Mazrui, 'Shakespeare in Africa: Between English and Swahili Literature', *Research in African Literatures* 27:1 (spring 1996). This is an important and informative source article. This volume of *RAL* also contains three other pertinent essays under the general heading of 'Shakespeare in Africa', by Lemuel Johnson, Lupenga Mphande and S. Ekema Agbaw.

3 See Marie-José Hourantier, 'Gestural Interpretation of the Occult in the Bin Kadi-So Adaptation of *Macbeth*' in *Research in African Literatures* 30:4 (winter 1999), 135–43. This is richly illustrated.

4 An important source of reference for North Africa is Kole Omotoso, 'Arabic Drama in North Africa' in Oyin Ogunba and Abiola Irele (eds.), *Theatre in Africa* (Ibadan: Ibadan University Press, 1978).

5 More detail on Decker's work can be found in Martin Banham and Eldred Jones, ' "tinap ober we like giant": African Celebrations of Shakespeare' in Shirley Chew and Alistair Stead (eds.), *Translating Life* (Liverpool: Liverpool University Press, 1999), 121–36.

6 Welcome Msomi, programme note for a performance of *Umabatha* at the Civic Theatre, Johannesburg, 1995.

7 There are many instances of such danger for the actor. In a Nigerian production of *The Merchant of Venice* in the University of Ibadan's Arts Theatre in the early 1960s, Shylock had to be placed well up-stage, so that he would not be attacked by the audience.

8 Dev Virahsawmy, *Zeneral Makbef* (Rose Hill: Bukié Banané, 1981).

9 *Toufann* has been translated into English and was staged in London by Michael and Nisha Walling in 1999.

10 Not to be confused with the 1997 *Trazedji Makbess*, which is a line-by-line verse translation of *Macbeth*.

11 Ogunyemi worked, together with Dexter Lyndersay, with students of the University of Ibadan to adapt the play. The University has a long tradition – dating back to the Unibadan Travelling Theatre established in the late 1950s – of translating Shakespeare into Nigerian terms. *A 'are Akogun* is published in *Nigeria Magazine* (Lagos: Federal Government of Nigeria Publication, April 1969), 100, 404–14. Lyndersay also staged a version of *Macbeth* at the University of Calabar some years later.

12 Chris Dunton, *Wale Ogunyemi*, in *DNB*, CLVII, 251–61.

13 De Graft had previously, in 1964, created a version of *Hamlet*, entitled *Hamile*, which had its setting in northern Ghana. A film was made of this, which is reputedly held in the Ghana Government Film Unit archives.

14 See also Wilhelm Hortmann's comments on Senghor and others in chapter 12 of this volume.

FURTHER READING

The reading list is organised according to chapter titles. Books listed immediately below are relevant to more than one chapter of this book.

Avery, Emmett L., Charles Beecher and others (eds.), *The London Stage: a Calendar of Plays, Entertainments and Afterpieces, 1660–1800*, 11 vols. (Carbondale: Southern Illinois University Press, 1960–5)

Barton, John, *Playing Shakespeare* (London: Methuen, 1984)

Bate, Jonathan, *Shakespearean Constitutions: Politics, Theatre, Criticism, 1730–1830* (Oxford: Oxford University Press, 1989)

Bate, Jonathan and Russell Jackson (eds.), *Shakespeare: an Illustrated Stage History* (Oxford: Oxford University Press, 1996)

Brockbank, Philip (ed.), *Players of Shakespeare I* (Cambridge: Cambridge University Press, 1985)

Brown, John Russell, *New Sites for Shakespeare: Theatre, the Audience and Asia* (London and New York: Routledge, 1999)

Highfill, Philip H. and others, *A Biographical Dictionary of Actors, Actresses, Musicians, Dancers, Managers, and Other Stage Personnel in London, 1660–1800*, 16 vols. (Carbondale: Southern Illinois University Press, 1973–93)

Holland, Peter, *English Shakespeares: Shakespeare on the English Stage in the 1990s* (Cambridge: Cambridge University Press, 1997)

Hortmann, Wilhelm, *Shakespeare on the German Stage: the Twentieth Century. With a Section on Shakespeare on Stage in the German Democratic Republic* by Maik Hamburger (Cambridge: Cambridge University Press, 1998)

Hughes, Alan, *Henry Irving, Shakespearean* (Cambridge: Cambridge University Press, 1981)

Jackson, Russell and Robert Smallwood (eds.), *Players of Shakespeare 2, 3* (Cambridge: Cambridge University Press, 1988, 1993)

Kennedy, Dennis, *Looking at Shakespeare: a Visual History of Twentieth-Century Performance* (Cambridge: Cambridge University Press, 1993; 2nd edn, 2001)

Kennedy, Dennis (ed.), *Foreign Shakespeare: Contemporary Performance* (Cambridge: Cambridge University Press, 1993)

Loomba, Ania and Martin Orkin (eds.), *Post-Colonial Shakespeares* (London: Routledge, 1998)

Odell, George C. D., *Shakespeare from Betterton to Irving*, 2 vols. (New York: Scribner, 1920)

Pavis, Patrice (ed.), *The Intercultural Performance Reader* (London: Routledge, 1996)

Sasayama, Takahashi, J. R. Mulryne and Margaret Shewring (eds.), *Shakespeare and the Japanese Stage* (Cambridge: Cambridge University Press, 1998)

Shattuck, Charles H., *Shakespeare on the American Stage*, 2 vols. (Washington: Folger Shakespeare Library, 1976, 1987)

    The Shakespeare Promptbooks: a Descriptive Catalogue (Urbana: University of Illinois Press, 1965)

Smallwood, Robert (ed.), *Players of Shakespeare* 4 (Cambridge: Cambridge University Press, 1998)

Speaight, Robert, *Shakespeare on the Stage* (London: Collins, 1973)

Sprague, Arthur Colby, *Shakespeare's Histories: Plays for the Stage* (London: Society for Theatre Research, 1964)

Stříbrný, Zdeněk, *Shakespeare and Eastern Europe* (Oxford: Oxford University Press, 2000)

Styan, J. L., *The Shakespearean Revolution: Criticism and Performance in the Twentieth Century* (Cambridge: Cambridge University Press, 1977)

Trewin, J. C., *Shakespeare's Plays on the English Stage, 1900–1964* (London: Barrie & Rockliff, 1964)

Weimann, Robert, *Shakespeare and the Popular Tradition in the Theater* (Baltimore: Johns Hopkins University Press, 1978)

Wells, Stanley (ed.), *Shakespeare in the Theatre: an Anthology of Criticism* (Oxford: Oxford University Press, 1997)

Wiles, David, *Shakespeare's Clown: Actor and Text in the Elizabethan Playhouse* (Cambridge: Cambridge University Press, 1987)

Williams, Simon, *Shakespeare on the German Stage* (Cambridge: Cambridge University Press, 1990)

Shakespeare plays on Renaissance stages

Astington, John H., *English Court Theatre, 1558–1642* (Cambridge: Cambridge University Press, 1999)

Bawcutt, N. W. (ed.), *The Control and Censorship of Caroline Drama: the Records of Sir Henry Herbert, Master of the Revels 1623–73* (Oxford: Oxford University Press, 1996)

Bradley, David, *From Text to Performance in the Elizabethan Theatre: Preparing the Play for the Stage* (Cambridge: Cambridge University Press, 1992)

Cox, John D. and David Scott Kastan (eds.), *A New History of Early English Drama* (Oxford: Basil Blackwell, 1997)

Dessen, Alan C. and Leslie Thomson, *A Dictionary of Stage Directions in English Drama, 1580–1642* (Cambridge: Cambridge University Press, 1999)

Foakes, R. A., *Illustrations of the English Stage 1580–1642* (Aldershot, UK: Scolar Press, 1985)

Gurr, Andrew, *Playgoing in Shakespeare's London* (Cambridge: Cambridge University Press, 1987)

    The Shakespearean Playing Companies (Oxford: Oxford University Press, 1996)

Hunter, G. K., 'Flatcaps and Bluecoats: Visual Signals on the Elizabethan Stage' in *Essays and Studies* (1980), 16–47

Jones, Ann Rosalind and Peter Stallybrass, *Renaissance Clothing and the Materials of Memory* (Cambridge: Cambridge University Press, 2001)

Jowett, John and Gary Taylor, *Shakespeare Reshaped, 1606–1623* (Oxford: Oxford University Press, 1993)

King, T. J., *Casting Shakespeare's Plays: London Actors and Their Roles, 1590–1642* (Cambridge: Cambridge University Press, 1992)

  Shakespearean Staging, 1599–1642 (Cambridge, MA: Harvard University Press, 1971)

Knutson, Roslyn Lander, *The Repertory of Shakespeare's Company, 1594–1613* (Fayetteville: University of Arkansas Press, 1991)

MacIntyre, Jean, *Costumes and Scripts in the Elizabethan Theatre* (Edmonton: University of Alberta Press, 1992)

McMillin, Scott, *The Elizabethan Theatre and the 'Book of Sir Thomas More'* (Ithaca: Cornell University Press, 1987)

Middleton, Thomas, *Collected Works*, general editor Gary Taylor (Oxford: Oxford University Press, forthcoming)

Orgel, Stephen, *Impersonations: the Performance of Gender in Shakespeare's England* (Cambridge: Cambridge University Press, 1996)

Orrell, John, *The Human Stage: English Theatre Design, 1567–1640* (Cambridge: Cambridge University Press, 1988)

Smith, Bruce, *The Acoustic World of Early Modern England: Attending to the O-Factor* (Chicago: University of Chicago Press, 1999)

Taylor, Gary, 'Feeling Bodies' in *Shakespeare in the Twentieth Century: Proceedings of the Sixth World Shakespeare Congress*, ed. Jonathan Bate *et al.* (Newark: University of Delaware Press and London: Associated University Presses, 1998), 258–79

  '*Hamlet* in Africa, 1607' in *Travel Knowledge*, ed. Ivo Kamps and Jyotsna Singh (Basingstoke: Palgrave, 2000), 211–48

Wells, Stanley and Gary Taylor, with John Jowett and William Montgomery, *William Shakespeare: a Textual Companion* (Oxford: Oxford University Press, 1987)

Improving Shakespeare: from the Restoration to Garrick

Clark, Sandra (ed.), *Shakespeare Made Fit: Restoration Adaptations of Shakespeare* (London: Everyman, 1997)

Dobson, Michael, *The Making of the National Poet: Shakespeare, Adaptation and Authorship, 1660–1769* (Oxford: Clarendon Press, 1992)

Marsden, Jean I. (ed.), *The Appropriation of Shakespeare: Post-Renaissance Reconstructions of the Works and the Myth* (Hemel Hempstead, UK: Harvester Wheatsheaf, 1991)

  The Re-Imagined Text: *Shakespeare, Adaptation and Eighteenth-Century Literary Theory* (Lexington: University Press of Kentucky, 1995)

Sorelius, Gunnar, '*The Giant Race Before the Flood': Pre-Restoration Drama on the Stage and in the Criticism of the Restoration* (Uppsala: Almquist & Wiksells, 1966)

Spencer, Christopher (ed.), *Five Restoration Adaptations of Shakespeare* (Urbana: University of Illinois Press, 1965)

Taylor, Gary, *Reinventing Shakespeare: a Cultural History from the Restoration to the Present* (London: Weidenfeld & Nicolson, 1989)

Wilkes, Thomas, *A General History of the Stage* (1759)

Romantic Shakespeare

Bate, Jonathan (ed.), *The Romantics on Shakespeare* (Harmondsworth: Penguin, 1992)

Carlson, Julie, *In the Theatre of Romanticism: Coleridge, Nationalism, Women* (Cambridge: Cambridge University Press, 1994)

Donohue, Joseph, *Theatre in the Age of Kean* (Oxford: Basil Blackwell, 1975)

[Gifford, William], 'Hazlitt's *Characters of Shakespeare's Plays*', *Quarterly Review* 18 (1817–18), 458–66

Hazlitt, William, *A View of the English Stage* (1818), in *The Complete Works of William Hazlitt*, 21 vols. (London: Dent & Co., 1930–34), volume v

Hillebrand, Harold, *Edmund Kean* (New York: Columbia University Press, 1933)

Kelly, Linda, *The Kemble Era: John Philip Kemble, Sarah Siddons and the London Stage* (London: Bodley Head, 1980)

[Kemble, John Philip] *John Philip Kemble Promptbooks*, ed. C. H. Shattuck, 11 vols. (Charlottesville: University Press of Virginia for Folger Shakespeare Library, 1974)

Manvell, Roger, *Sarah Siddons: Portrait of an Actress* (London: Heinemann, 1970)

Moody, Jane, *Illegitimate Theatre in London, 1770–1840* (Cambridge: Cambridge University Press, 2000)

Rostron, David, 'Contemporary Political Comment in Four of J. P. Kemble's Shakespearean Productions', *Theatre Research* 12 (1972), 113–19

Wells, Stanley, 'Shakespeare in Leigh Hunt's Theatre Criticism', *Essays and Studies* (1980), 118–38

Pictorial Shakespeare

Booth, Michael, *Victorian Spectacular Theatre* (London: Routledge & Kegan Paul, 1981)

'Shakespeare as Spectacle and History', *Theatre Research International* 1:2 (1976), 99–113

Foulkes, Richard (ed.), *Shakespeare and the Victorian Stage* (Cambridge: Cambridge University Press, 1986)

Jackson, Russell (ed.), *Victorian Theatre* (London: A. & C. Black, 1989)

Mazer, Cary, *Shakespeare Refashioned: Elizabethan Plays on Edwardian Stages* (Ann Arbor: UMI Research Press, 1981)

Meisel, Martin, *Realizations: Narrative, Pictorial, and Theatrical Arts in Nineteenth-Century England* (Princeton: Princeton University Press, 1983)

Paulson, Ronald, *Book and Painting: Shakespeare, Milton, and the Bible* (Knoxville: University of Tennessee Press, 1982)

Rees, Terence, *Theatre Lighting in the Age of Gas* (London: Society for Theatre Research, 1978)

Schoch, Richard, *Shakespeare's Victorian Stage: Performing History in the Theatre of Charles Kean* (Cambridge: Cambridge University Press, 1998)

Reconstructive Shakespeare: reproducing Elizabethan and Jacobean stages

Adams, John C., *The Globe Playhouse: its Design and Equipment* (Cambridge, MA: Harvard University Press, 1942; 2nd edn, London: Constable, 1961)
Atkins, Robert, *An Unfinished Autobiography*, ed. George Rowell (London: Society for Theatre Research, 1984)
Bowmer, Angus, *As I Remember, Adam: an Autobiography of a Festival* (Ashland: Oregon Shakespeare Festival, 1975)
Day, Barry, *This Wooden 'O': Shakespeare's Globe Reborn* (London: Oberon Books, 1996)
Egan, Gabriel, 'Reconstructions of the Globe: a Retrospective', *Shakespeare Survey* 52 (1999), 1–16
Engle, Ron, Felicia Hardison Londré, and Daniel J. Watermeier (eds.), *Shakespeare Companies and Festivals: an International Guide* (Westport, CT: Greenwood Press, 1995)
Gurr, Andrew, J. R. Mulryne and Margaret Shewring (eds.), *The Design of the Globe* (London: International Shakespeare Globe Centre, 1993)
Gurr, Andrew with John Orrell, *Rebuilding Shakespeare's Globe* (London: Weidenfeld & Nicolson, 1989)
Guthrie, Tyrone, *A Life in the Theatre* (New York: McGraw-Hill, 1959)
Hildy, Franklin J., *Shakespeare at the Maddermarket: Nugent Monck and the Norwich Players* (Ann Arbor: UMI Research Press, 1986)
Hodges, C. Walter, *The Globe Restored: a Study of the Elizabethan Theatre* (London: Benn, 1953; 2nd edn, Oxford: Oxford University Press, 1968)
Mazer, Cary, *Shakespeare Refashioned: Elizabethan Plays on Edwardian Stages* (Ann Arbor: UMI Research Press, 1981)
Mulryne, J. R. and Margaret Shewring (eds.), *Shakespeare's Globe Rebuilt* (Cambridge: Cambridge University Press, 1997)
O'Connor, Marion, *William Poel and the Elizabethan Stage Society* (Cambridge: Chadwyck-Healey, 1987)
Payne, Ben Iden, *A Life in a Wooden O* (New Haven: Yale University Press, 1977)
Poel, William, *Monthly Letters*, ed. A. M. T. (London: Werner Laurie, 1929)
    Shakespeare in the Theatre (London: Sidgwick & Jackson, 1913)
Speaight, Robert, *William Poel and the Elizabethan Revival* (London: Barrie & Rockliff, 1953)

Twentieth-century performance: the Stratford and London Companies

Beauman, Sally, *The Royal Shakespeare Company: a History of Ten Decades* (Oxford: Oxford University Press, 1982)
Berry, Ralph, *On Directing Shakespeare: Interviews with Contemporary Directors*, 2nd edn (London: Hamish Hamilton, 1989)
Brown, John Russell, *Shakespeare's Plays in Performance* (London: Edward Arnold, 1966)
Crosse, Gordon, *Shakespearean Playgoing, 1890–1952* (London: Mowbray, 1953)
David, Richard, *Shakespeare in the Theatre* (Cambridge: Cambridge University Press, 1978)

Miller, Jonathan, *Subsequent Performances* (London: Faber, 1986)

Rowell, George, *The Old Vic Theatre: a History* (Cambridge: Cambridge University Press, 1993)

Trewin, J. C., *Shakespeare on the English Stage, 1900–1964* (London: Barrie & Rockliff, 1964)

Warren, Roger, *Staging Shakespeare's Late Plays* (Oxford: Oxford University Press, 1990)

Wells, Stanley, *Royal Shakespeare: Four Major Productions at Stratford-upon-Avon* (Manchester: Manchester University Press, 1977)

The tragic actor and Shakespeare

Bartholomeusz, Dennis, *Macbeth and the Players* (Cambridge: Cambridge University Press, 1969)

Carlson, Marvin, *The Italian Shakespeareans* (Washington: Folger Books, 1985)

Cole, Toby and Helen Krich Chinoy (eds.), *Actors on Acting* (New York: Crown, 1970)

Donohue, Joseph W., *Dramatic Character in the English Romantic Age* (Princeton: Princeton University Press, 1970)

Joseph, Bertram, *The Tragic Actor* (London: Routledge & Kegan Paul, 1959)

Roach, Joseph, *The Player's Passion* (Ann Arbor: University of Michigan Press, 1993)

Rosenberg, Marvin, *The Masks of Macbeth* (Berkeley: University of California Press, 1978)

The comic actor and Shakespeare

Lewes, G. H., *On Actors and the Art of Acting* (London: Smith, Elder & Co., 1875)

Soule, Lesley, *Actor as Anti-Character: Dionysus, the Devil, and the Boy Rosalind* (Westport, CT and London: Greenwood Press, 2000)

Stern, Tiffany, *Rehearsal from Shakespeare to Sheridan* (Oxford: Clarendon Press, 2000)

Thomson, Peter, *On Actors and Acting* (Exeter: University of Exeter Press, 2000)

West, Shearer, *The Image of the Actor* (London: Pinter, 1991)

Women and Shakespearean performance

Dusinberre, Juliet, 'Squeaking Cleopatras: Gender and Performance in *Antony and Cleopatra*' in James C. Bulman (ed.), *Shakespeare, Theory, and Performance* (London: Routledge, 1996), 46–67

Gay, Penny, *As She Likes It: Shakespeare's Unruly Women* (London: Routledge, 1994)

Howe, Elizabeth, *The First English Actresses: Women and Drama, 1660–1700* (Cambridge: Cambridge University Press, 1992)

Jamieson, Michael, 'Shakespeare's Celibate Stage' in G. E. Bentley (ed.), *The Seventeenth-Century Stage: a Collection of Critical Essays* (Chicago: University of Chicago Press, 1968), 70–93

Mullin, Donald (ed.), *Victorian Actors and Actresses in Review* (Westport, CT: Greenwood Press, 1983)

Rutter, Carol, *Clamorous Voices: Shakespeare's Women Today* (London: Women's Press, 1988)

Salgādo, Gāmini, *Eyewitnesses of Shakespeare* (London: Sussex University Press, 1975)

Shapiro, Michael, *Gender in Play on the Shakespearean Stage* (Ann Arbor: University of Michigan Press, 1994)

International Shakespeare

Bharucha, Rustom, *Theatre and the World: Essays on Performance and Politics of Culture* (New Delhi: Manohar, 1990)

Brook, Peter, *The Shifting Point, 1946–1987* (New York: Harper & Row, 1987)

Budick, Sanford, and Wolfgang Iser (eds.), *The Translatability of Cultures: Figurations of the Space Between* (Stanford: Stanford University Press, 1996)

Cartelli, Thomas, *Repositioning Shakespeare: National Formations, Postcolonial Appropriations* (London: Routledge, 1999)

Joughin, John J. (ed.), *Shakespeare and National Culture* (Manchester: Manchester University Press, 1997)

Kennedy, Dennis, 'Shakespeare and the Global Spectator', *Shakespeare-Jahrbuch* 131 (1995), 50–64

McLuskie, Kate, '*Macbeth/Umabatha*: Global Shakespeare in a Post-Colonial Market', *Shakespeare Survey* 52 (1999), 154–65

Novy, Marianne (ed.), *Cross-Cultural Performances: Differences in Women's Re-Visions of Shakespeare* (Urbana: University of Illinois Press, 1993)

Pavis, Patrice, *Theatre at the Crossroads of Culture* (London: Routledge, 1992)

Touring Shakespeare

Bogdanov, Michael and Michael Pennington, *The English Stage Company: the Story of 'The Wars of the Roses' 1986–1989* (London: Nick Hern Books, 1990)

Brennecke, Ernest, *Shakespeare in Germany 1590–1700* (Chicago: University of Chicago Press, 1964)

Faust, Richard and Charles Kadushin, *Shakespeare in the Neighborhood: Audience Reaction to 'A Midsummer-Night's Dream' as Produced by Joseph Papp for the Delacorte Mobile Theater, A Report* (New York: Twentieth Century Fund, 1965)

Harwood, Ronald, *Sir Donald Wolfit* CBE (London: Secker & Warburg, 1971)

Hatton, Joseph, *Henry Irving's Impressions of America*, 2 vols. (London, 1884)

Hodgdon, Barbara, 'Looking for Mr Shakespeare After "The Revolution": Robert Lepage's Intercultural *Dream* Machine' in James C. Bulman (ed.), *Shakespeare, Theory, and Performance* (London: Routledge, 1966), 68–91

Holloway, David, *Playing the Empire* (London: Harrap, 1979)

Howarth, W. D., *Sublime and Grotesque: a Study of French Romantic Drama* (London: Harrap, 1975)

Kobayashi, Kaori, 'Shakespeare Wallah: George C. Miln's Shakespearean Productions in India', *Australasian Drama Studies* 33 (1998), 117–27

'Touring in Asia: the Miln Company's Shakespearean Productions in Japan' in Edward J. Esche (ed.), *Shakespeare and his Contemporaries in Performance* (Aldershot: Ashgate, 2000), 53–72

Lewes, George Henry, *On Actors and the Art of Acting* (London, 1875)
Raby, Peter, *'Fair Ophelia': a Life of Harriet Smithson Berlioz* (Cambridge: Cambridge University Press, 1982)
Reade, Simon, *Cheek by Jowl: Ten Years of Celebration* (Bath: Absolute Classics, 1991)
Trewin, J. C., *Benson and the Bensonians* (London: Barrie & Rockliff, 1960)

Shakespeare on the political stage in the twentieth century

Dollimore, Jonathan and Alan Sinfield (eds.), *Political Shakespeare: New Essays in Cultural Materialism* (Manchester: Manchester University Press, 1985)
Drakakis, John (ed.), *Alternative Shakespeares* (London: Methuen, 1985)
Greenblatt, Stephen, *Renaissance Self-Fashioning: From More to Shakespeare* (Chicago: University of Chicago Press, 1980)
Hawkes, Terence (ed.), *Alternative Shakespeares,* vol. II (London and New York: Routledge, 1996)
Kott, Jan, *Shakespeare Our Contemporary* (London: Methuen, 1965)
Kujawińska-Courtney, Krystyna, 'Der polnische Prinz: Rezeption und Appropriation des *Hamlet* in Polen' in *Shakespeare-Jahrbuch* (1995), 82–92

Shakespeare in North America

Benson, Eugene and L. W. Conolly (eds.), *The Oxford Companion to Canadian Theatre* (Oxford: Oxford University Press, 1989)
Dunn, Esther Cloudman, *Shakespeare in America* (New York: Macmillan, 1939)
Engle, Ron, Felicia Hardison Londré and Daniel J. Watermeier (eds.), *Shakespeare Companies and Festivals: an International Guide* (Westport, CT: Greenwood Press, 1995)
Hill, Errol G., *Shakespeare in Sable* (Amherst: University of Massachusetts Press, 1984)
Levine, Lawrence W., *Highbrow/Lowbrow* (Cambridge, MA: Harvard University Press, 1988)
Odell, G. C. D., *Annals of the New York Stage,* 15 vols. (New York: Columbia University Press, 1927–1949)
Wilmeth, Don B. and Christopher Bigsby (eds.), *The Cambridge History of American Theatre,* 3 vols. (Cambridge: Cambridge University Press, 1998–2000)
Wilson, Garff B., *A History of American Acting* (Bloomington: Indiana University Press, 1966)

Shakespeare on the stages of Asia

Brandon, James R., 'Some Shakespeare(s) in Some Asia(s)', *Asian Studies Review* 20: 3 (1997), 1–26
Fischer-Lichte, Erika, Josephine Riley and Michael Gissenwehrer (eds.), *The Dramatic Touch of Difference* (Tübingen: Gunter Narr Verlag, 1990)

Japan

Minami, Ryuta, Ian Carruthers and John Gillies (eds.), *Performing Shakespeare in Japan* (Cambridge: Cambridge University Press, 2001)

Minoru, Fujita and Leonard Pronko (eds.), *Shakespeare East and West* (Richmond, UK: Japan Library, 1996)

Senda, Akihiko, *The Voyage of Japanese Theatre*, trans. Thomas Rimer (Hawai'i: University of Hawai'i Press, 1997)

Ueno, Yoshiko (ed.), *Hamlet and Japan* (New York: AMS Press, 1995)

China

He, Qi-xin, 'China's Shakespeare', *Shakespeare Quarterly* 37 (1986), 149–59

Li, Ruru, 'The Bard in the Middle Kingdom', *Asian Theatre Journal* 12: 1 (1995), 50–84

'Macbeth Becomes Ma Pei: an Odyssey from Scotland to China', *Theatre Research International* 20: 1(1995), 42–53

'Shakespeare on the Chinese Stage in the 1990s', *Shakespeare Quarterly* 50: 3 (1999), 355–67

Stanley, Audrey, 'The 1994 Shanghai International Shakespeare Festival', *Shakespeare Quarterly* 47 (1996), 72–80

Zhang, Xiaoyang, *Shakespeare in China: a Comparative Study of Two Traditions and Cultures* (Newark: University of Delaware Press and London: Associated Universities Press, 1996)

India

Indian Literature, Special Issue on Shakespeare in Indian Languages (New Delhi: Sahitya Academy, 1964)

Loomba, Ania, *Gender, Race, Renaissance Drama* (Oxford: Oxford University Press, 1992)

Mukherjee, S. K., *The Story of Calcutta Theatres: 1753–1980* (Calcutta: K. P. Bagchi, 1982)

Paul, Sunita (ed.), *A Tribute to Shakespeare* (New Delhi: Theatre and Television Associates, 1989)

Shankar, D. A. (ed.), *Shakespeare in Indian Languages* (New Delhi: Sahitya Academy, 1964)

Singh, Jyotsna, 'Different Shakespeares: the Bard in Colonial/Postcolonial India', *Theatre Journal,* 4 (1989), 445–58

Trivedi, Poonam, 'Interculturalism or Indigenisation: Modes of Exchange, Shakespeare East and West' in Edward J. Esche (ed.), *Shakespeare and his Contemporaries in Performance* (Aldershot, UK: Ashgate, 2000), 73–88

Viswanathan, Gauri, *Masks of Conquest: Literary Study and British Rule in India* (New York: Columbia University Press, 1989)

Yajnik, R. K., *The Indian Theatre* (London: Allen & Unwin, 1933)

Shakespeare and Africa

Banham, Martin (ed.), *The Cambridge Guide to Theatre* (Cambridge: Cambridge University Press, 1995)

Banham, Martin, Errol Hill and George Woodyard (eds.), *The Cambridge Guide to African and Caribbean Theatre* (Cambridge: Cambridge University Press, 1994)

Clark, J. P., *The Example of Shakespeare* (London: Longman, 1970)

Johnson, Lemuel A., *Shakespeare in Africa (and Other Venues): Import and Appropriation of Culture* (Trenton, NJ and Asmara: Africa World Press, 1998)

Plastow, Jane, *African Theatre and Politics* (Amsterdam: Rodopi, 1996)

Soyinka, Wole, *Art, Dialogue and Outrage* (London: Methuen, 1993) – of particular relevance is the essay 'Shakespeare and the Living Dramatist'

Wilkinson, Jane, *Remembering 'The Tempest'* (Rome: Bulzoni Editore, 1999)

INDEX

Page numbers for illustrations are in italics

Abbott, William, 204
Abel, Royston, 278–80
Ackland, Joss, 106
Actors from the London Stage, 197–8, 199, 200
Adams, John Cranford, 80–1, 87
Adams Memorial Shakespeare Theatre, 90
Addison, Joseph, 30
Adelphi Theatre, 38, 39
Adler, Jacob, 244
Admiral's Men, The, 2
Agate, James, 249, 251
Agbaw, S. Ekema, 298 n.2
Ainley, Henry, 149
Akimov, Nikolai, 224
Aldridge, Ira, 239
Aldwych Theatre, 104
Alger, William, R., 257 n.9
Allen, Edward, 234
Alleyn, Edward, 2, 4, 12, 144
Alma-Tadema, Lawrence, 59, 63
American Company, The, 231, 232
American Shakespeare Theatre Festival, 253
Andersen, Hans Christian, 68
Anderson, Judith, 249, 250
Anderson, Mary, 243
Anderson, Mrs, 273
Andrews, Harry, 103
Anglin, Margaret, 245, 246
Appia, Adolphe, 72, 247
Arambam, Lokendra, 278, 279
Archer, William, 95
Armin, Robert, 5, 143, 144
Arneaux, J. A., 244

Artaud, Antonin, 130–1, 174, 179
Arthur, Julia, 246
Arts Theatre, London, 104
Arts Theatre, University of Ibadan, Nigeria, 294, 298 n.7
Ashcroft, Dame Peggy, 102, 103, 114, 167–9, 251
Assembly Hall, Edinburgh, 112
Assmann, Aleida, 189
Atkins, Robert, 81, 86, 102
Atkinson, Brooks, 258 n.18
Attenborough, Michael, 115
Auddy, Baishnav Charan, 273
Auerbach, Nina, 166
Axelrad, A. José, 191 n.16
Ayliff, H. K., 102

Bacon, Francis, 15
Bains, Yashdip, S., 234, 257 n.8
Baker, George Pierce, 80
Bakhtin, Mikhail, 220
Balakrishnan, Sadanam, 278
Balustrade Theatre, Prague, 225
Bancroft, Marie, 62
Bancroft, Sir Squire, 62
Bandmann, Daniel, 244
Banham, Martin, 228 n.13, 229 n.15
Bannister, Charles, 140
Barba, Eugenio, 179, 182
Barber, Samuel, 135
Barbican Theatre, 115, 116
Barnay, Ludwig, 244
Barnes, Howard, 252
Barnes, Thomas, 41, 56
Barrett, Lawrence, 242
Barry, Elizabeth, 158

Barrymore, Ethel, 248
Barrymore, John, 247–8, 248, 256
Barrymore, Lionel, 248
Bartholomeusz, Dennis, 136 n.14
Barton, John, 105, 110, 115, 120, 173 n.22,
    217
Bate, Jonathan, 56 n.8, 57 n.25, 57 n.41
Baylis, Lilian, 99, 100
Beauman, Sally, 96 n.11, 109, 116 n.2,
    117 n.4, 117 n.11, 117 n.15
Beaumarchais, Pierre-Augustin, 146
Beckett, Samuel,
    Endgame, 219
    Waiting for Godot, 104
Bedford, Brian, 253, 256–7
Beier, Karin, 182–3
Bell, G. J., 57 n.18
Bensley, Thomas, 42
Benson, Constance, 206
Benson, Sir Frank, 98, 115, 205–6, 246
Benthall, Michael, 103, 106, 112
Bentley, John, 234
Berardinis, Leo de, 177
Berger, Harry, 175
Bergman, Ingmar, 256
Berlin National Theatre, 126
Berliner Ensemble, 104, 115, 216
Bernard, John, 234, 257 n.8
Bernhardt, Sarah, 164, 243
Berry, Cicely, 110
Berry, Ralph, 117 n.6
Bertrand, Joachimus, 231
Bestrafte Brudermord, Der, 176, 197
Betterton, Mary, 158
Betterton, Thomas, 29, 30
Bharucha, Rustom, 179, 181, 229 n.15
Billington, Michael, 168, 169
Bin Kadi-So, 285
Birmingham Repertory Theatre, 102, 106,
    115
Blackfriars, 2, 143
Bloom, Claire, 106
Bloom, Harold, 228 n.2
Boaden, James, 48, 56 n.11, 57 n.35, 57 n.39
Bogdanov, Michael, 114, 168, 206
Bond, Edward, 219
Booth, Edwin, 201, 234, 236, 240–2, 241,
    243, 245, 248, 250, 256
Booth, John Wilkes, 236
Booth, Junius Brutus, 39, 235, 236, 236–7,
    240
Booth, Junius II, 236
Booth, Michael, 166, 167, 173 n.14

Boswell, James, 33
Bowdler, Henrietta, 57 n.28
Bowdler, Thomas, 57 n.28
Bowmer, Angus, 87
Boyd, Michael, 116
Boydell, John, 59
Bracegirdle, Anne, 158
Branagh, Kenneth, 106, 256
Brando, Marlon, 256
Brandon, James, 260, 266, 270, 280, 281 n.4
Brassington, W. S., 96 n.12
Braugher, André, 254, 255, 256
Brecht, Bertolt, 130, 185, 213, 216–17
Bridges-Adams, William, 100, 101, 109
Brink, André, 227
Bristol Old Vic, 106
Britten, Benjamin (Baron), 35
Britton, Jasper, 91, 138
Brook, Peter, 103, 111, 112, 114, 117 n.8,
    145, 175, 177, 179, 181, 182, 189,
    192 n.34, 219, 226–27, 255
Broun, Heywood, 247
Brown, Ford Madox, 59, 63
Brown, Frederick, 240
Brown, John Mason, 251
Brown, John Russell, 182, 211 nn.34–5,
    229 n.15
Browne, Robert, 196, 197
Bulwer-Lytton, Edward, 260
Burbage, Richard 4–5, 10, 11, 16, 144
Burian, Jarka, 228 n.11
Burrell, John, 105
Burton, Richard, 103, 106, 255
Burton, William E., 240
Bury, John, 115

Caldwell, Zoë, 253
Calvert, Louis, 246
Cambridge Experimental Theatre, 198
Campbell, Thomas, 43, 56 n.10, 57 n.12,
    57 n.22, 173 n.13
Cao, Yu, 267
Capon, William, 47
Carey, Denis, 106
Carnegie Institute of Technology, Pittsburgh,
    80
Carnovsky, Morris, 253
Cartelli, Thomas, 193 n.50
Cathcart, James, 200
Césaire, Aimé, 227
Chamberlain's Men, The (Lord), 2, 3, 13,
    93, 116, 138, 139, 140, 141–42, 143
Chambers, Sir E. K., 191 n.14

Chand, Munshi, Ratan, 275
Charles II, King, 21, 27, 28
Cheek by Jowl, 106, 154 n.13, 207
Cheer, Margaret, 232
Chekhov, Anton, 261
Chesterfield, Lord, 123
Chestnut Street Theare, Philadelphia, 232, 233
Chichester Festival Theatre, 112
Chimes at Midnight, 251
Churchill, Diana, 105
Cibber, Colley, 29, 161
    Richard III, 29–30, 33, 39, 231
Cibber, Theophilus, 27, 31
Cliff, Michelle, 229 n.14
Coburg Theatre, 38, 39, 40
Cochrane, Claire, 117 n.7
Cole, John, 75
Coleman, John, 173 n.16
Coleridge, Samuel Taylor, 56, 69
Colman, George, 33
Comédie Française, 177
Congreve, William, 158
Conway, John Ashby, 80, 87
Cook, Douglas N., 97 n.22
Cook, Dutton, 166
Cooke, George Frederick, 42, 54, 146, 235, 236
Cooper, Thomas Abthorpe, 230, 232–4, 233, 235, 240
Copeau, Jacques, 144–45
Corbin, John, 245, 246
Corbould, E. H., 60
Cornell, Katherine, 249, 251
Cotton, William, 57 n.34
Covent Garden Theatre, 32, 33, 38, 39, 42, 47, 48, 50, 61, 67, 76, 127, 204, 232
Cox, John F., 154 n.16
Craig, Edward Gordon, 72, 73, 77, 99, 247
Crosby Hall, 84
Crowley, John, 106
Crowne, John,
    Henry the Sixth, the first part, 27–8
    Misery of Civil War, The, 27–8
Cushman, Charlotte, 162, 163, 164, 239
Cushman, Susan, 162, 163
Czech National Theatre, Prague, 224

Daly, Augustin, 243
Damas, Léon, 227
Daniels, Ron, 113
Datta, Madhusudan, 274

Davenant, Sir William, 22, 24, 25–6
    Law Against Lovers, The, 25–6
    Macbeth, 23, 24, 25, 26, 122, 157
    Tempest, The, 26, 47, 157–8
Davenport, E. L., 239
Davies, Thomas, 172 n.12
Davis, Judy, 171
Davis, Natalie, 188
Day, Barry, 97 n.23
Decker, Thomas, 285–6, 287, 298
De Grazia, Margreta, 190 n.8
Deguchi, Norio, 262, 263, 269, 281 n.11
Dekker, Thomas, 2, 10
Delacorte Theatre, New York, 254
Delacroix, Eugène, 204
Dench, Dame Judi, 106, 107, 132, 153, 169, 170
Dent, Alan, 168
Deutsches Theater, Berlin, 221
Devine, George, 103
De Witt, Johannes, 80
Dexter, John, 108
Dmitriev, Y., 192 n.46
Dobson, Michael, 36 n.20, 190 n.8
Doggett, Thomas, 146
Dollimore, Jonathan, 228 n.1
Donohue, Joseph, 124
Doran, Gregory, 111, 114
Dostoevsky, Fyodor, 223
Douce, Francis, 41
Douglass, David, 231–2
Downes, John, 24
Drakakis, John, 228 n.1
Drescher, Piet, 221
Dresen, Adolf, 219
Drury Lane Theatre, 32, 38, 39, 40, 41–2, 43, 47, 50–1, 61, 67, 124, 126, 146, 153, 204, 205, 232
Dryden, John, 85, 161
    All for Love, or, The World Well Lost, 26, 157–8, 168
    Tempest, The, 22–3, 24, 26, 47, 157–8, 159
    Troilus and Cressida, 26
Ducis, Jean-François, 204, 205
Duke's Company, The, 22, 24
Dumas, Alexandre, 204, 205
Dunlap, William, 231, 257 n.3
Dunphy, Charles, 60
Dunton, Chris, 299 n.12
Durosimi, Eldred, 285–6
Dürrenmatt, Friedrich, 217

Dusinberre, Juliet, 172 n.2
Dyer, Chris, 81

Edward III, 3, 98
Edwards, Christopher, 207
Edwards, Gale, 168
Egan, Gabriel, 97 n.23
Eliot, T. S., 120
Elizabeth I, Queen, 175
Elizabethan Stage Society, 81, 96 n.9
Elliston, Robert, 38–9
Engels, Friedrich, 268
English Comedians, The, 196–7, 200
English Shakespeare Company, The, 106,
    114–15, 206–7
English Touring Theatre, The, 209 n.3
Essex, Earl of, 175, 213
Etherege, Sir George, 158
Evans, Dame Edith, 100, 102, 105–6, 114
Evans, Maurice, 246, 249–50, 250
Everyman, 92
Ewbank, Inga-Stina, 117 n.8
Eyre, Richard, 108, 113, 114

Fairfield, Robert, 88
Falstaff, 232, 239, 251   *see also The*
    Merry Wives of Windsor
Farquhar, George, 158
Faucit, Helena, 147, 152, 161–2, 163
Fauré, Gabriel, 135
Faust, Richard, 210 n.11
Fechter, Charles, 62, 208, 242, 246
Fehling, Jürgen, 214
Felheim, Marvin, 258 n.16
Fennell, James, 232
Ferrer, José, 251
Findlater, Richard, 131, 136 n.20
Finlay, John, 45
Fischer-Lichte, Erika, 229 n.15
Fleck, Ferdinand, 126
Fletcher, John, 21
    Cardenio, 3, 18, 19
    Henry VIII, 3, 18, 19
    Tamer Tamed, The, 19
    Two Noble Kinsmen, The, 3, 18, 19
Flower, Sir Archibald, 99, 100
Flower, Charles, 205
Flower, Sir Fordham, 103
Fontanne, Lynn, 249
Forbes-Robertson, Johnston, 67,
    245, 246
Ford, Benjamin J., 244

Forman, Simon, 18
Forrest, Edwin, 202, 234, 237–9, 238, 240,
    242, 245, 256
Forster, John, 202
Fortune Theatre, 78–80, 81–2, 82–3, 84, 87,
    89, 90
Frederick the Great, 184
Freiligrath, Ferdinand, 184
Fujita, Minoru, 181
Fukuda, Tsuneari, 262
Fulda, Ludwig, 183
Furnivall, F. J., 96 n.4

Gaiety Theatre, London, 149
Gaiety Theatre, Yokohama, 202, 261
Gallienne, Eva Le, 249
Garrick, David, 27, 31–4, 35 nn.11–12, 40,
    54, 59, 124–5, *125*, 126, 131, 140, 146,
    152–3, 158–9, 162, 231, 272
    Catharine and Petruchio, 32, 234
    Florizel and Perdita, 32
Gate Theatre, Dublin, 250
Gautier, Théophile, 173 n.15, 204
Geddes, Norman Bel, 249
Genest, John, 57 n.27
George III, King, 38, 43
Gielgud, Sir John, 102, 103, 105–6, 110,
    111, 167, 168, 248, 249, 255
Giffard, Henry, 234, 235
Gifford, William, 49, 56 n.1
Gildon, Charles, 29
Gish, Lillian, 249
Globe of the Great Southwest, The, 90
Globe Theatre, London, 1, 2, 15, 69, 81,
    89–90, 92, 95, 143, 155, 178
Glossop, William, 39
Godard, Colette, 174
Godfrey, Derek, 153
Godwin, William, 232
Goebbels, Joseph, 214
Goethe, Johann Wolfgang von, 183–4
Golub, Spencer, 228 n.10
Gomme, Allan, 96 n.4
Gould, Robert, 22
Graft, Joe de, 296–7
Granville Barker, Harley, 78, 95, 96 n.13,
    99, 100, 105, 109, 111, 119, 144–5,
    145–6, 149, 245, 255
Graydon, Alexander, 231–2
Gray's Inn Hall, 83
Green, John, 197
Greenaway, Peter, 35

Greenblatt, Stephen, 228 n.1
Greene, Robert, 3, 18
Greet, Ben, 80, 100, 246
Grey, Earle, 247
Gross, Edgar, 136 n.13
Gu, Wuwei, 267
Guglia, Eugen, 136 n.16
Guinness, Sir Alec, 102, 105, 253
Gurr, Andrew, 97 n.23
Guthrie, Sir Tyrone, 87, 102, 103, 104, 106,
    111–12, 114, 253
Guthrie Theatre, Minneapolis, 112

Hackett, James H., 239, 240, 257 n.6
Hagen, Ute, 251–2
Haile Selassie I Theatre, Addis Ababa, 288
Hall, Edward, 116
Hall, Sir Peter, 103–4, 105, 107, 108, 110,
    113, 115, 217
Hallam, Lewis, 230, 231
Hallam, Lewis Jr., 231, 232, 234
Hallam, Nancy, 232
Hallam, William, 230, 231
Halpern, Richard, 189
Hamburger, Maik, 228 n.4, 228 n.6
Hampden, Walter, 246
Hands, Terry, 108, 115
Harikumar, Sadanam, 278
Harington, Sir John, 14
Harper, Jack, 150
Harris, Arthur, 96 n.9
Harris, Robert, 103
Hartung, Gustav, 215
Harvard University, 80
Harwood, Ronald, 205, 211 n.30
Hauptmann, Gerhart, 183
Hay, Richard, 87
Hayes, Helen, 249, 250
Haymarket, The, 38, 76, 77, 93, 105, 204,
    248
Hazlitt, William, 37, 40, 41, 49, 50, 51,
    52–3, 54, 56, 57 n.17, 126, 127, 159
Helgerson, Richard, 190 n.8
Helpmann, Sir Robert, 106, 112
Henry, John, 232
Henslowe, Philip, 2, 11, 13
Hepburn, Katharine, 253
Herder, Johann Gottfried, 184
Her/His Majesty's Theatre, 80, 82, 93, 98,
    137, 150
Heyme, Hansgünter, 185, 220
Heywood, Thomas, 18
    Apology for Actors, An, 16

Hildy, Franklin J., 95 n.2, 96 n.15, 97 n.18
Hitler, Adolf, 214, 215
Hodgdon, Barbara, 211 nn.36–8
Hodges, C. Walter, 86, 87
Hodgkinson, John, 232
Hofmannsthal, Hugo von, 189
Hofstra, 80–1, 82
Hoftheater, Munich, 78
Holcroft, Thomas, 230, 232, 233
Holderness, Graham, 210 n.8
Hollmann, Hans, 220
Holloway, Baliol, 101
Holloway, David, 210 n.25
Holloway, W. J., 203
Hopkins, Sir Anthony, 169
Hopkins, Arthur, 247, 248
Hoppe, Marianne, 171
Hordern, Sir Michael, 106
Horniman, Annie, 83
Hortmann, Wilhelm, 183, 192 n.31,
    nn. 42–3, 299 n.14
Hourantier, Marie-José, 285
Houseman, John, 251
Howard, Alan, 115
Howard, Jean, 172 n.4
Howard, Leslie, 249
Hu, Weimin, 282 n.21
Huang, Zuolin, 270
Hugo, Victor, 204
Hunt, Hugh, 106
Hunt, Leigh, 37, 41, 42, 50, 136 n.12
Hunter, Kathryn, 171
Hutt, William, 253
Hyman, Earle, 252, 253, 254, 255, 257
Hytner, Nicholas, 108

Ibsen, Henrik, 129, 261
    Hedda Gabler, 10
Imperial Theatre, 73
Inchbald, Elizabeth, 44
Inoue, Hisashi, 265
Ionesco, Eugène, Macbett, 219
Irving, Sir Henry, 59, 62–3, 63, 64, 66, 67,
    68, 69, 72, 74, 129–30, 145, 147, 148,
    149, 153, 165, 166, 200–1, 203, 205,
    235, 242, 243, 246

Jackson, Sir Barry, 102–3, 110, 111
Jackson, Russell, 117 n.8
Jacquot, Jean, 191 n.17
James, Henry, 166
Janauschek, Fanny, 242
Jefford, Barbara, 106

Jerrold, Douglas, 67
Jessner, Leopold, 184–5, 213, 214, 215, 247
Jeyifo, Biodun, 229 n.15
Jiang, Weiguo, 271
Jiao, Juyin, 267, 270
Johnson, Lemuel, 298 n.2
Johnson, Samuel, 29, 76
Jones, Eldred, 298
Jones, Ernest, 102, 104
Jones, Inigo, 14
Jones, James Earl, 254
Jones, Robert Edmond, 247, 248, 249, 258 n.19
Jones, Sir William, 276
Jonson, Ben, 3, 4, 14, 18, 21, 22, 23, 76, 139, 193 n.62
    Alchemist, The, 5, 83
    Every Man in His Humour, 140
    Hymenaei, 12
    Masque of Blackness, The, 11
    Volpone, 4, 5, 141
Jordan, Dorothy, 144, 159–61
Jordan, Thomas, 35 n.7
Joseph, Bertram, 93
Julia, Raul, 254

Kadushin, Charles, 210 n.11
Kani, John, 216
Karanth, B. V., 276, 277
Kawakami, Otojiro, 261, 265
Kazinczy, Ferenc, 186
Keach, Stacy, 254, 256
Kean, Charles, 59, 60, 61–2, 64, 65, 67, 68, 69, 70, 71, 74, 74 n.6, 162–3, 200, 201, 202–3, 239–40, 246
Kean, Edmund, 37, 43, 50–6, 52, 53, 55, 121, 126–7, 146–7, 149, 234, 235–6, 237, 240
Kean, Thomas, 231
Keats, John, 54
Kemble, Charles, 76, 203, 204, 205, 237, 240
Kemble, Fanny, 159, 237, 240
Kemble, John Philip, 38, 40–50, 46, 52, 56, 124–6, 127, 131, 144, 232, 233, 235, 240
Kemble, Stephen, 150
Kemp, Will, 5, 138, 141–3, 150
Kendal, Geoffrey, 274
Kennedy, Dennis, 62–3, 67, 72, 116 n.1, 117 n.14, 175, 182, 189, 191 n.26, 193 n.50
Khambatta, Jehangir, 274

Khori, Edulji, 274
Killigrew, Thomas, 21, 172 n.8
Kim, Randal Duk, 254
King, T. J., 172 n.3
King's Company, The, 21–2
King's Men, The, 2, 3, 4, 5, 6, 7, 10, 11, 13, 15, 17, 18, 19, 139
Kirkman, Francis, 19
Kirov, Sergei, 186
Kishi, Tetsuo, 180
Kishida, Rio, 265
Kline, Kevin, 254
Knack to Know a Knave, A, 142
Knight, Charles, 59
Knight, G. Wilson, 119, 120
Knowles, James Sheridan, 119, 162
Kobayashi, Kaori, 210 n.23
Kolin, Philip C., 228 n.3
Komisarjevsky, Theodore, 101, 111, 224
Kortner, Fritz, 214, 215
Kott, Jan, 115, 217, 219, 268
Kozintsev, Grigori, 186, 224
Krauss, Werner, 214
Krejča, Otomar, 225
Krige, Uys, 227, 285
Kujawínska-Courtney, Krystyna, 228 nn.7–8
Kustow, Michael, 208–9
Kyd, Thomas, Spanish Tragedy, The, 17, 18

Lacy, John, 35 n.9
Lafayette Theatre, Harlem, New York, 251
Lal, L., 188
Lamb, Charles, 37, 40, 47, 54, 118, 260, 266, 272
Lamming, George, 227
Lang, Alexander, 221
Langbaine, Gerard, 22
Langham, Michael, 253
Langtry, Lillie, 243
Lansdowne, Lord, 146
Lassalle, Ferdinand, 282 n.17
Laughton, Charles, 102
Laurence, Margaret, 227
Laurent, Emile, 204
Laurier, Angela, 208
Leday, Annette, 178
Leicester, Earl of, 12
Leigh, Vivien, 103, 106, 249
Lepage, Robert, 207–8
Lermontov, Mikhail, 223
Lester, Adrian, 154 n.13
Levenson, Jill L., 96 n.8
Levin, Bernard, 152

Levine, Lawrence W., 244
Lewes, George Henry, 57 n.37, 127,
    146–7, 208
Lewis, Barry, 273
Lin, Zhaohua, 268–9, 269
Lincoln's Inn Fields Theatre, 25, 29
Liston, John, 142
Locke, John, 124
Lo Liyong, Taban, 227
Londré, Felicia Hardison, 97 n.19
Loomba, Ania, 178, 187–8, 191 n.18
Lowe, Robert, 173 n.16
Lowin, John, 5
Lu, Xun, 270
Ludlow, Noah, 233, 237
Luhrmann, Baz, 35
Lunt, Alfred, 249
Lutyens, Edwin, 89
Lyceum Theatre, 62, 63, 66, 145, 147, 149,
    165, 200, 205, 235, 243
Lyly, John, 7
Lyndersay, Dexter, 299 n.11
Lyubimov, Yuri, 186, 224

Macaulay, Alastair, 209
Machiavelli, Niccolò, 212
Macklin, Charles, 50–1, 121, 146
MacLiammóir, Micheál, 250
Macready, William Charles, 43–4, 59, 60,
    61, 64, 65, 67, 68, 71, 74, 127–8, 128,
    147, 161, 202, 237, 238, 239, 240
Maddermarket Theatre, Norwich, 78,
    84–6, 85
Maley, Willy, 191 n.13
Malone, Edmond, 41, 76, 80
Mandela, Nelson, 188–9, 287
Mansfield, Richard, 147, 243
Mantell, Robert Bruce, 245
Manzoni, Alessandro, 177
Mao, Zedong, 268
Market Theatre, Johannesburg, 114, 216
Marlowe, Christopher,
    Doctor Faustus, 18, 84
    Jew of Malta, The, 2, 11
Marlowe, Julia, 245
Marowitz, Charles, 219
Marston, John, 2
    Malcontent, The, 4
Marston, Westland, 173 n.16
Marx, Karl, 268
Massey, Raymond, 249
Massinger, Philip, A New Way to Pay Old
    Debts, 146

Matkowsky, Adalbert, 130
Matthews, Brander, 136 n.10
Mazrui, Alamin M., 298 n.2
McCarthy, Lillah, 84
McClintic, Guthrie, 249
McCowen, Alec, 106
McCullough, John, 242, 245, 246
McDonald, Jan, 96 n.3
McKellen, Sir Ian, 114, 131, 132–4, 133,
    169
McLuskie, Kate, 188, 189, 193 n.50,
    193 n.60
McRuvie, David, 178
Mei, Lanfang, 281–2 n.14
Meisel, Martin, 67
Melmoth, Charlotte, 232
Mendes, Sam, 112, 113
Mermaid Theatre, 83, 93
Merry, Ann Brunton, 232, 233, 235
Middle Temple Hall, 83–4
Middleton, Thomas, 2, 4
    Chaste Maid in Cheapside, A, 11
    Game at Chess, A, 11, 13, 17
    Macbeth, 8, 18
    Measure for Measure, 18
    Revenger's Tragedy, The, 4
    Roaring Girl, The, 10
    Timon of Athens, 3
    Trick to Catch the Old One, A, 19
    Your Five Gallants, 13
Mielziner, Jo, 249
Mike, Chuck, 297
Miles, Bernard, 83, 93
Miller, Jonathan, 112
Miln, George Crichton, 202–3
Milner, Henry, 40
Milton, John, Samson Agonistes, 92
Mitterwurzer, Friedrich, 129–30
Mnouchkine, Ariane, 174–5, 177, 181,
    190 n.7, 256
Mochalov, Pavel, 186
Modjeska, Helena, 242
Moiseiwitsch, Tanya, 88, 103, 112
Molière, 141
    Tartuffe, 149
Monaco, Marion, 210 n.27
Monck, Nugent, 84, 103
Moncrieff, William, 39
Moody, Richard, 257 n.11
Moore, William, 234
Morgan, MacNamara, Florizel and Perdita,
    32
Morison, Fynes, 196–7, 209 n.4

Morley, Henry, 65
Morley, John, 161
Morrison, Charlotte, 246
Morton, Thomas, 38
Motley, 111
Mphande, Lupenga, 298 n.2
Msomi, Welcome, 286–87
Mucedorus, 18
Müller, Heiner, 185, 192 n.43, 221, 222
   Hamletmaschine, 221
Mullin, Donald, 162, 166
Mulryne, J. R., 97 n.23
Munden, Joseph, 144
Murcell, George, 86
Murdoch, James E., 239
Murphy, Arthur, 34
Murphy, Sarah, 227
Murray, Walter, 231
Mutran, Khali l, 285

Napier, John, 81
Napoleon, Louis, 268
Nashe, Thomas, 3, 15
National Theatre   *see* Royal National
   Theatre
Nazir, C. S., 274
Neilson, Adelaide, 242, 246
Neilson, Julia, 98
Nelson, Richard, 210 n.22
Neville, John, 106
New Place, Stratford-upon-Avon, 12
New Shakespeare Company, 84
New Theatre, 102, 105, 110
New York Shakespeare Festival, 253–5,
   255
Ni, Dahong, 269
Nickinson, John, 240
Nicoll, Allardyce, 81
Nightingale, Benedict, 173 n.28
Ninagawa, Yukio, 134, 179–80, 181, 207,
   208, 262, 263, 265, 271–2
Noble, Adrian, 108, 115, 170
Noda, Hideki, 262–3, 264
Northern Broadsides, 207
Norwich Players, 84, 86
Noverre, Jean-George, 124
Nunn, Trevor, 108, 112, 113, 114
Nyerere, Julius, 284, 285

Odashima, Yushi, 262
Odell, George C. D., 36 n.27, 95 n.1, 172 n.9
Office of the Revels, 13
Ogunyemi, Wale, 292–6, 294

Old Vic, 81, 99, 100, 101–2, 104–7, 109,
   111, 112, 113, 115, 150, *151*, 169, 201,
   206, 246, 249, 255
Olivier, Laurence (Baron), 35, 102, 103, 104,
   105, 106, 108, 110, 131–2, *132*, 135,
   147, 149, 168, 201, 248, 249, 251, 255
Omotoso, Kole, 298 n.4
O'Neill, James, 245
Ong, Ken Sen, 265
Oregon Shakespeare Festival, 87, *88*, 89,
   121, 253
Orgel, Stephen, 74, 156
Orrell, John, 97 n.23
Osborne, John, *Look Back in Anger, 104*
Other Place, The, 113, 132, *133*, 195
O'Toole, Peter, 108
Otway, 33
   History and Fall of Caius Marius, The,
    26–7, 28, 34, 36 n.14
Overbury, Sir Thomas, 16

Palitzsch, Peter, 217, *218*
Papp, Joseph, 199, 200, 219, 253
Park Theatre, New York, *233*, 235, 237
Pasco, Richard, 145
Pasternak, Boris, 224
Paul, Noel, 84
Paul's Boys, 7
Pavis, Patrice, 179, 180, 190 n.1, 190 n.3,
   191 n.21, 229 n.15
Payne, Ben Iden, 80, 81, 87, 89, 101
Peacham, Henry, *14*
Peele, George, *Titus Andronicus*, 3, 14
Pennington, Michael, 114, 206
Pepys, Samuel, 21, 35 n.10
Performance Studio Workshop, 297
Peter, John, 173 n.29
Peymann, Claus, 220
Phelps, Samuel, 59, 61, 64, 65–7, 74, 149
Pickford, Mary, 246
Pickup, Ronald, 154 n.13
Pimlott, Steven, 115
Piscator, Erwin, 213, 214
Pit, The, 116
Plaatje, Solomon Tashekisho, 285
Planché, J. R., 76, 77
Plantagenets, The, 115
Platt, Livingston, 245
Platter, Thomas, 13
Playfair, Nigel, 100
Plummer, Christopher, 253, 254, 256
Poel, William, 72, 77–80, *79*, 81–4, 89,
   92–3, 94, 95, 99, 100, 114, 253

Pope, Alexander, 30
Porter, Cole, *Kiss Me Kate*, 35, 249
Porter, Henry, *The Two Angry Women of Abington*, 2
Pralipe, 186
Prasanna Kumar Tagore's Hindu Theatre, Calcutta, 272
Pratt, Samuel Jackson, 32
Price, Addison B., 240
Prigmore, William H., 234
Princess's Theatre, 61–2, *70*, 74 nn.9–10, 75 n.29, 162
Pringle, Marian J., 117 n.5
Pritchard, Hannah, 43, 124, 152, 153, 158–9
Public Theatre, New York, 254
Purdom, C. B., 84
Pushkin, Alexander Sergeyevich, 223

Quayle, Sir Anthony, 103–4, 115
Queen Mary and Westfield College, University of London, 81
Queen's Men, The, 5
Queen's Theatre, 102, 106
Quin, James, 150, 231

Raby, Peter, 204, 210 n.26
Raha, Kironmoy, 282 n.23
Raleigh, Sir Walter, 12
Ramana, Quisnarajoo, 290
Rankin, Hugh F., 232, 257 n.3
Ravenscroft, Edward, *Titus Andronicus*, 27
Raymond, James Grant, 51
Reade, Simon, 211 n.33
Redgrave, Sir Michael, 102, 103, 105, 137
Redgrave, Vanessa, 137, 138, 152, 171–2
Rehan, Ada, 153, 164, 243
Reinhardt, Max, 99, 184–5
Renaissance Theatre Company, 106, 256
Reynolds, Sir Joshua, 43, 159
Richardson, Sir Ralph, 102, 103, 104, 105, 150, *151*, 249, *251*, 255
Richardson, Samuel, *Clarissa*, 30
Richardson, Tony, 252
Ristori, Adelaide, 164, 242
Robeson, Paul, 251–2, *252*
Robey, George, 150
Robson, Dame Flora, 102
Rogers, Paul, 106
Rose Theatre, 88–9, 95
Rossi, Ernesto, 243
Rowe, Eleanor, 192 n.45
Rowe, Nicholas, 30, 41, 59
Rowell, George, 117 n.2

Royal Gaiety Theatre, Manchester, 83
Royal Lyceum, Toronto, 240
Royal National Theatre, 95, 100, 106, 107–9, 112, 113, 114, 154 n.13, 169, 170, 206, 207, 256
Royal Shakespeare Company, 98, 100, 104, 106, 107, 108–9, 110, 111–12, 113, 114, 115–16, 153, 170, 194, 195–6, 197, 199, 205, 206, 255–6
Royal Shakespeare Theatre, 104, *171*
Royalty Theatre, 78, 79, 81, 82
Rutter, Carol, 173 n.27
Rylance, Mark, 90, 94
Rylands, George, 105

Sadler's Wells, 61
Said, Edward, 175, 259
Saint-Denis, Michel, 104
St George's Church, Tufnell Park, 86
St George's Hall, 77
St James's Theatre, 106
St Paul's Cathedral, 7
Salgādo, Gāmini, 20 n.1
Salmon, Eric, 154 n.5
Salvini, Tommaso, 130, 208, 243, 246
Sampson, Anthony, 193 n.56
San Diego National Shakespeare Festival, 89, 253
Sans Souci Theatre, Calcutta, 273
Sargent, John Singer, 59, 166
Savits, Jocza, 78
Savoy Theatre, 78, 99, 111, 144, 149, 251
Scala Theatre, 105
Schanzer, Ernest, 20 n.2
Schauspielhaus, Zurich, 215
Schechner, Richard, 179
Schiller, Friedrich, 119, 183–4
    Macbeth, 126
Schlegel, A. W., 183–4, 223
Schorm, Evald, 225
Schroth, Christoph, 221
Scofield, Paul, 103, 112
Scott, Clement, 165–6
Scott, George C., 254, 256
Scott, Sir Walter, 43
Seale, Douglas, 106, 115
Selbourne, David, 117 n.15
Senghor, Léopold Sédar, 227, 297
Sewell, Rufus, 106
Shadwell, Thomas,
    Tempest, The, 26, 33
    Timon of Athens, 25, 28, 36 n.14

Shakespeare, William,
All's Well That Ends Well, 8, 112, 114,
143, 159, 168, 253
Antony and Cleopatra, 4, 5, 7, 9, 11, 24,
26, 94, 102, 106, 114, 119, 143, 144,
152, 155, 156, 157, 167, 168, 169, 170,
173 n.29, 237
As You Like It, 1, 7, 8, 10, 12, 42, 100,
102, 114, 143, 144, 145, 150, 151–52,
155, 156, 158, 159, 161, 162, 163,
164–6, 167, 169, 170–1, 171, 172, 213,
239, 242, 243, 274, 275, 285–6
Cardenio, 3, 19
Comedy of Errors, The, 9, 83, 84, 113,
114, 169, 275, 285, 298
Coriolanus, 5, 7, 28, 37, 38, 41, 43, 44–5,
46, 49, 56, 60, 61, 62, 63, 104, 112, 114,
122, 159, 165, 169, 177, 216–17, 233,
237, 238, 240, 242
Cymbeline, 6, 8, 10, 102, 113, 144, 159,
165–6, 167, 169, 176, 232, 242, 275
Hamlet, 2, 4, 6, 9, 10, 13, 15, 16, 18, 19,
22–3, 32, 33, 35, 40, 41, 44, 54, 59, 62,
77, 94, 102, 105, 108, 112, 114, 119,
122, 123, 138, 139, 156, 158, 159, 164,
165, 166, 169, 171, 176, 180, 184,
185–6, 188, 192 n.34, 197, 198, 200,
201, 202, 203, 204–5, 208, 213, 214,
219, 221, 222, 223, 224, 225, 231, 232,
233, 234, 235, 237, 238, 239, 240, 241,
241–2, 243, 244, 246, 247–8, 248, 249,
250, 254, 255, 256, 261, 262, 267,
268–9, 269, 281 n.6, 284, 288, 298
Henry IV, 16, 19, 103, 105, 115, 140, 142,
143, 150, 151, 232, 234, 251, 255
1 Henry IV, 6, 8, 18, 21, 235, 250, 284
2 Henry IV, 7, 9
Henry V, 1, 3, 4, 7, 38, 42, 45, 61, 65, 69,
70, 71, 103, 105, 115, 116, 169, 206–7,
243, 251, 253, 256
Henry VI, 5, 27, 99, 106, 115, 116,
173 n.22, 209 n.2, 217, 251
1 Henry VI, 3, 15
3 Henry VI, 7
Henry VIII, or, All is True, 3, 8, 9, 26, 42,
61, 62, 64, 65, 68, 69, 74 n.9, 105–6,
111, 159, 165, 235, 238, 245
Julius Caesar, 6, 7, 9, 13, 14, 22, 94, 109,
143, 176, 193 n.56, 203, 237, 241, 242,
243, 251, 272, 278, 284, 285, 286, 289,
297–8
King John, 7, 9, 42–3, 60, 61, 76, 159,
162, 210 n.19, 217, 232, 235, 237, 239

King Lear, 1, 5, 6, 8, 16, 17, 19, 24, 28–9,
30, 32, 33, 34, 38, 40, 59, 62, 63, 78, 94,
105, 113, 114, 117 n.8, 119, 122, 143,
157, 158, 161, 165, 167, 169, 171, 176,
178, 201, 219, 232, 234, 235, 237, 239,
241, 242, 243, 244, 251, 265, 278, 285,
288, 298
Lover's Complaint, 1
Love's Labour's Lost, 1, 3, 5, 7, 10, 11,
103, 105, 112, 114, 140, 142, 162, 243
Macbeth, 7, 8, 9, 18, 22, 23, 25, 26, 33,
38–9, 43, 47, 59, 61, 62, 64, 67, 84, 93,
102, 104, 106, 109, 113, 114, 119, 121,
122–35, 125, 128, 132, 133, 139, 155,
157, 158–9, 160, 161, 162, 163–4, 165,
166–7, 169, 176, 180, 188, 198, 201,
207, 208, 219, 224, 232, 233, 234, 235,
237, 238, 239, 242, 243, 246, 248, 250,
251, 262, 263, 267, 268, 270, 272,
276–8, 277, 279, 284–5, 286–7, 288,
289–97, 291, 294
Measure for Measure, 4, 7, 18, 25, 37, 43,
44, 47–9, 78, 79, 80, 81, 83, 100, 114,
142, 150–1, 155, 169, 213, 215, 219, 256
Merchant of Venice, The, 2, 8, 10, 11, 12,
37, 40, 41, 50–1, 52, 62, 75 n.29, 87,
111, 112, 113, 114, 121, 126, 139, 140,
141, 142, 143, 145, 146–9, 148, 150,
165, 166, 167, 168, 169, 197, 201, 203,
213, 230, 231, 232, 234, 235, 239, 240,
241, 243, 245, 260, 266, 281 n.6, 284,
298 n.7
Merry Wives of Windsor, The, 2, 7, 21, 24,
141, 162, 169, 176, 235, 240, 243, 245,
265
Midsummer Night's Dream, A, 5, 6, 8, 17,
19–20, 35, 40, 62, 64, 65, 71, 96 n.7,
98, 99, 111, 114, 139, 142, 143, 145,
155, 156, 162, 169, 182–3, 197, 199,
207–8, 221, 240, 243, 245, 255, 263,
264, 275–6, 278, 288, 298
Much Ado About Nothing, 9, 25, 59, 62,
66, 67, 72, 73, 102, 142, 152–3, 158,
159, 163, 165, 165, 166, 167, 169, 201,
240, 241, 249, 255, 271–2, 271, 289
Othello, 1, 4, 5, 9–10, 11, 15, 16, 21, 25,
39, 41, 43, 47, 50, 53, 53–4, 94, 104,
108, 112, 113, 114, 119, 122, 123, 126,
139, 143, 146, 156, 157, 158, 159, 162,
165, 166, 167, 178, 203, 208, 216, 220,
231, 232, 233, 234, 235, 237, 239, 240,
241, 242, 243, 244, 249, 251–2, 252,
261, 265, 273–4, 278–80, 285, 288–9

Shakespeare, William, (cont.)
  Pericles, 3, 8, 9, 18, 102
  Phoenix and Turtle, The, 3
  Richard II, 1, 9, 18, 22, 61, 75 n.13, 98,
    102, 103, 105, 113, 114, 115, 137, 171,
    174–5, 191 n.14, 213, 249–50, 250, 251,
    255, 256, 284
  Richard III, 4, 7, 8, 9, 15–16, 18, 24,
    29–30, 31, 32, 33, 39, 42, 47, 50, 53,
    54–6, 55, 105, 114, 115, 121, 126, 127,
    139, 146, 147, 149, 173 n.22, 201,
    209 n.2, 214, 215, 217, 220–1, 231,
    232, 233, 234, 235, 236, 237, 239, 240,
    243, 247, 251, 253, 256, 262
  Romeo and Juliet, 3, 9, 18, 26–7, 32,
    33, 34, 35, 47, 62–3, 63, 102, 107,
    110, 114, 119, 122, 142, 143, 155,
    159, 162, 163, 165, 167, 169,
    176, 186–7, 198, 199, 203, 225, 231,
    232, 233, 234, 237, 239, 240, 242,
    243, 246, 248, 249, 251, 265, 267,
    270, 275, 285
  Taming of the Shrew, The, 8, 10, 32,
    35 n.9, 76, 77, 93, 102, 114, 152, 164,
    167, 168, 241, 243, 246, 249, 256, 298
  Tempest, The, 24, 26, 33, 42, 44, 47, 59,
    64–5, 67, 68, 91, 113, 114, 137–8, 139,
    140, 158, 159, 171–2, 175, 180, 181,
    187, 195–96, 197, 205, 213, 226–7,
    234, 240, 246, 275, 284, 289
  Timon of Athens, 3, 25, 28, 36 n.14, 94,
    113, 114
  Titus Andronicus, 3, 5, 7, 9, 11, 12, 14, 17,
    27, 103, 113, 114, 176, 177, 197, 239
  Troilus and Cressida, 8, 24, 26, 100, 112,
    114, 143, 212, 216
  Twelfth Night, 8, 10, 83–4, 87, 89, 94,
    96 n.7, 99, 114, 139, 143–4, 145,
    149–50, 155–6, 158, 159, 162, 163, 164,
    165, 167, 169, 239, 242, 250, 282 n.21
  Two Gentlemen of Verona, The, 8, 9, 59,
    80, 82, 93, 106, 114, 142, 143, 164
  Two Noble Kinsmen, The, 3, 7
  Venus and Adonis, 1
  Winter's Tale, The, 6, 7–8, 9, 24, 31, 32,
    47, 62, 96 n.7, 99, 109, 113, 143, 159,
    169, 240, 243, 245, 275
Shakespeare Ladies Club, 31
Shakespeare Memorial Theatre, 81, 96 n.12,
  98, 99, 103, 104, 112, 113, 224
Shakespeare Theatre, Washington, DC, 257
Shakespeare Wallah, 188
Shapiro, Michael, 172 nn.3–4, 172 nn.6–7

Shattuck, Charles H., 210 n.17, 210 n.21
Shaw, Fiona, 114, 137, 170, 171, 171
Shaw, George Bernard, 68, 153
Shaw, Glen Byam, 103–4
Shearer, Norma, 246
Shenandoah Shakespeare Express, 198–9
Sher, Sir Antony, 131, 134, 135, 147, 149
Sheridan, Richard Brinsley, 40, 42, 44, 204
Shewring, Margaret, 97 n.23
Siddons, Sarah, 40–1, 42–3, 45, 48, 56 n.10,
  119, 125–6, 144, 159, 160, 161, 164, 232
Sinden, Sir Donald, 103, 153
Sinfield, Alan, 228 n.1
Singh, Jyotsna, 187–8
Sir John Oldcastle, 17
Skinner, Otis, 245
Smiles, Samuel, 260
Smith, Dame Maggie, 106, 152, 253
Smithson, Harriet, 204, 205, 210 n.26
Snodgrass, Wanda, 97 n.21
Sothern, E. H., 245
Soule, Lesley, 151–2
Southerne, Thomas, 41
Southwark Globe (Shakespeare's Globe),
  90–2, 91, 94, 112–13, 137, 138, 171,
  178, 193 n.55
Soyinka, Wole, 297
Speaight, Robert, 201–2, 251
Spencer, Charles, 208
Spencer, John, 197
Sprague, A. C., 36 n.17
Spriggs, Elizabeth, 153
Sreedharan, Iyyamkode, 178
Staatstheater, Berlin, 214, 215
Stalin, Joseph, 213, 224
Stanfield, Clarkson, 59, 65, 71
Stanford University, 80
Stanislavsky, Konstantin, 130, 145, 168
Stein, Peter, 185, 220
Stein, Philipp, 136 n.19
Stendhal, 204
Stern, Tiffany, 153 n.1
Stevens, Thomas Wood, 80, 89
Stevenson, Juliet, 170–1, 171
Stevenson, Robert Louis, 130
Stopes, C. C., 20 n.6
Stoppard, Sir Tom, 219
Strand Theatre, 39, 105
Strange's Men, The (Lord), 142
Stratford Festival Theatre, Ontario, 87–8,
  112, 184, 257
Stratford, Ontario Shakespeare Festival, 87,
  112, 121, 253

Streep, Meryl, 254, 256
Strehler, Giorgio, 177, 217
Stříbrný, Zdenek, 192 n.44, 192 nn.46–7,
    193 n.49, 225, 228 n.9
Sturua, Robert, 192 n.34
Styan, J. L., 96 n.5, 116 n.1, 117 n.7,
    117 n.11
Sumarokov, Alexander, 185–6
Sun, Hongjiang, 282 n.21
Supple, Tim, 112
Surrey Theatre, 38–9
Suzman, Janet, 216
Suzuki, Tadashi, 262, 271–2
Svoboda, Josef, 225
Swan Theatre, London, 80
Swan Theatre, Stratford-upon-Avon, 88,
    113, 115, 116

Tabori, George, 220
Taganka Theatre, Moscow, 224
Takahashi, Yasunari, 265
Talma, François-Joseph, 118
Tandy, Jessica, 253
Tansi, Sony Labou, 285
Tanveer, Habib, 278
Tarlton, Richard, 76, 141, 142, 150
Tate, Nahum, 161
    Ingratitude of a Common-Wealth, The, 28
    King Lear, 28–9, 30, 33, 34, 122, 157
Tavernier, Albert, 246
Taylor, Paul, 209
Tearle, Godfrey, 103
Telbin, William, 67
Terry, Dame Ellen, 59, 130, 136 n.17, 147,
    149, 153, 164–7, 165, 243, 246
Tey, Josephine, 262–3
Thacker, David, 112
Théâtre du Soleil, 174
Theatre Royal, Halifax, Nova Scotia, 234
Theatre Royal, Montreal, 240
Theatres Regulation Act (1843), 38, 61
Theobald, Lewis, 30
Thomas, Audrey, 227
Thomashefsky, Boris, 244
Thompson, Emma, 171
Thorndike, Dame Sybil, 100, 104, 251
Tian, Han, 267
Tieck, Ludwig, 126, 183–4, 223
Tokyo Globe, 181, 195, 262
Tolstoy, Count Leo Nikolayevich, 223
Tree, Ellen, 163–4, 246
Tree, Sir Herbert Beerbohm, 59, 69, 71, 74,
    98, 137–8, 202, 245

Trewin, J. C., 117 n.2, 117 n.10, 117 n.14,
    150, 168, 211 n.30
Tsegaye, Gebre-Medhin, 287–9
Tsubouchi, Shoyo, 261, 262, 267
Tsukayama, Masane, 134–5
Turgenev, Ivan, 223
Turner, J. M. W., 65
Tynan, Kenneth, 117 n.12, 131, 150, 251

Ungerer, Gustav, 20 n.3
United Company, The, 29
University College, London, 93
University of Ibadan Travelling Theatre, 298
University of Illinois (Champaign-Urbana),
    80–1
University of Washington, 80
Upton, Robert, 231
Usher, Noble Luke, 234

Vakhtangov Theatre, Moscow, 224
Valaydon, Gaston, 290–2
Verdi, Giuseppe, 177
Vestris, Eliza, 162
Victoria, Queen, 59–60
Vieux Colombier Company, 144
Vigny, Alfred de, 204
Vinohrady Theatre, Prague, 225
Virahsawmy, Dev, 289–92, 291, 298
Voltaire, 177, 184, 192 n.40
Vysotsky, Vladimir, 224

Wajda, Andrzej, 223
Walker, Roy, 96 n.14
Waller, David, 145
Walling, Michael, 299 n.9
Walling, Nisha, 299 n.9
Walter, Harriet, 134
Warde, Frederick, 244
Warner, Deborah, 113, 114
Warner, Marina, 229 n.14
Wars of the Roses, The, 115, 167, 217
Watermeier, Daniel J., 97 nn.19–20
Webster, Benjamin, 76, 77
Webster, Margaret, 249–50, 252
Weimann, Robert, 220–1
Wekwerth, Manfred, 221
Welles, Orson, 250–1
Wells, Stanley, 56 n.9, 57 nn.15–16, 57 n.38
Westmacott, Charles, 39
Wheale, Nigel, 210 n.8
White, Martin, 97 n.18
Whiteside, Walker, 244
Whitlock, Elizabeth Kemble, 232

Whitman, Walt, 237
Wignell, Thomas, 232
Wiles, David, 142
Wilkes, Thomas, 30
Wilkins, George, *Pericles*, 3, 18
Wilkinson, Jane, 298 n.1
Wilkinson, Norman, 96 n.7, 149
Wilkshire, Frances, 192 n.40
Williams, David, 190 n.2, 190 n.5, 190 n.7
Williams, Gary Jay, 20 n.10
Williams, Harcourt, 102, 109, 117 n.11
Williams, Simon, 184, 191 n.15, 192 n.38,
    209 nn.5–6
Williamson, Nicol, 149–50
Wilson, Josephine, 83
Winkler, Angela, 171
Winter, William, 173 n.21, 239, 241,
    242, 243

Winter Garden Theatre, New York, 241
Wolfit, Sir Donald, 84, 104–5, 106,
    205, 206, 246
Woollcott, Alexander, 248
Worcester's Men, 17
Wycherley, William, 36 n.24

Xu, Xiaozhong, 268

Young, Charles, 45
Young Vic, 116
Yuan, Shikai, 267
Yukari, Yoshihara, 281 nn.2–3

Zadek, Peter, 171, 185, 220
Zarilli, Phillip, 191 n.19, 191 n.21, 283 n.27
Zeffirelli, Franco, 107
Zhu, Shenghao, 267